MEDIA PARENTING

MEDIA PARENTING

Theory and Research on Parent, Child, and Media Interactions

Eric E. Rasmussen
Texas Tech University, USA

BLOOMSBURY ACADEMIC
NEW YORK • LONDON • OXFORD • NEW DELHI • SYDNEY

BLOOMSBURY ACADEMIC
Bloomsbury Publishing Inc
1359 Broadway, New York, NY 10018, USA
50 Bedford Square, London, WC1B 3DP, UK
29 Earlsfort Terrace, Dublin 2, Ireland

BLOOMSBURY, BLOOMSBURY ACADEMIC and the Diana logo are trademarks of
Bloomsbury Publishing Plc

First published in the United States of America 2026

Copyright © Bloomsbury Publishing Inc, 2026

Cover design: Chloe Batch
Cover image © iStock / Prostock-Studio

All rights reserved. No part of this publication may be reproduced or transmitted in any form or by any means, electronic or mechanical, including photocopying, recording, or any information storage or retrieval system, without prior permission in writing from the publishers.

Bloomsbury Publishing Inc does not have any control over, or responsibility for, any third-party websites referred to or in this book. All internet addresses given in this book were correct at the time of going to press. The author and publisher regret any inconvenience caused if addresses have changed or sites have ceased to exist, but can accept no responsibility for any such changes.

A catalog record for this book is available from the Library of Congress.

ISBN: HB: 979-8-8818-0054-3
PB: 979-8-2163-7956-0
ePDF: 979-8-8818-6043-1
eBook: 979-8-8818-0056-7

Typeset by Deanta Global Publishing Services, Chennai, India
Printed and bound in the United States of America

To find out more about our authors and books visit www.bloomsbury.com and sign up for our newsletters.

CONTENTS

Chapter 1
THE NATURE OF CHILDREN 1

Chapter 2
MEDIA AND THE HOME ENVIRONMENT 15

Chapter 3
EFFECTS OF CHILDREN'S MEDIA USE 29

Chapter 4
ROOTS AND EVOLUTION OF MEDIA PARENTING 43

Chapter 5
PREDICTORS FOR APPROACHES TO MEDIA PARENTING 57

Chapter 6
CHILDREN'S MEDIA USE AND MEDIA PARENTING 75

Chapter 7
PHYSICAL HEALTH AND MEDIA PARENTING 89

Chapter 8
SOCIO-EMOTIONAL WELL-BEING AND MEDIA PARENTING ... 103

Chapter 9
MENTAL HEALTH AND MEDIA PARENTING 117

Chapter 10
COGNITIVE DEVELOPMENT, ACADEMIC PERFORMANCE, AND
MEDIA PARENTING 127

Chapter 11
MEDIA PARENTING METHODS AND MEASURES 139

Chapter 12
PRESCRIPTIVE MODELS OF MEDIA PARENTING 153

Conclusion
A ROADMAP FOR FUTURE RESEARCH 165

Notes 169
Bibliography 227
Index 278
About the Author 283

Chapter 1

THE NATURE OF CHILDREN

A book about media parenting might rightfully begin with a consideration of "children," the primary object of media parenting. Children constitute a central figure of international conventions, judicial decisions, legislation at the highest levels of civilized governments, war and conflict, educational systems, families, community resources, and global economics. A global consensus of policymakers agreed that "the child, by reason of his physical and mental immaturity, needs special safeguards and care."[1] Indeed, children dwell in "a very unique time in the human cycle that deserves our special attention as well as the best of our resources and human investment."[2]

Simply defined, every human being under 18 years of age is a child.[3] For some, humans are considered children only between the period of infancy and puberty.[4] While definitions and descriptors vary, each refers to relatively young humans who are in some ways dependent on their older counterparts for safety and survival, all while exercising a form of agency to various extents in different contexts.[5] But beyond age-related definitions, the way policymakers, researchers, and parents uniquely conceptualize children has considerable implications for children's well-being, and the differences in those conceptualizations are enormously meaningful. From policymaking organizations, we learn that among the nearly 8 billion humans currently living on the planet, about 2.5 billion are under age 18—nearly one-third of the world's population.[6] Broadly speaking, policymaking organizations at the macro level, such as WHO and UNICEF, consider children in the aggregate, as members of a demographic or psychographic group. Children are not considered individually beyond the stories these organizations tell to exemplify the impact made by organizational efforts. Children are separated into distinct groups based on descriptors such as age, ethnicity, socioeconomic status, country of origin, and gender. The U.S. Federal Interagency Forum on Child and Family Statistics, a network of twenty-three U.S. federal government agencies that in some way advocate for the well-being of children and their families, explained the value of aggregating children in these ways: "Understanding the changing demographic characteristics of America's children is critical for shaping social programs and policies. The number of children determines the demand for schools, health care, and other social services that are essential for meeting the daily needs of families."⁷ A national foundation dedicated to reducing the need for placing children in foster care likewise claims that demographic data helps "systems better understand any disparate outcomes from their programs, and then use what they have learned to better serve the needs of children and families."⁸

Such large-scale groupings or indicators of child characteristics provide invaluable data for global and national organizations that design programs and policies. For them, children constitute objective, apolitical data, and each child is regarded as a number to be included as part of larger numbers. In this type of data, children are assumed to be neutral actors in a larger story of concerned adults solving problems created by other adults. Children are assumed to be powerless, speechless, and nameless. For these macro-oriented organizations, the hopes, feelings, attitudes, dreams, and agency of individual children need not be considered, because adults assume that these higher level elements of self-actualization pursuit cannot be performed unless programs and policies solve other problems first. The loss of children's individuality is by no means the intent of policymakers, but it is a natural byproduct of the scope of both the problems and their policy-driven, programmatic solutions. Less important is who an individual child is, and more important is what children suffer, both individually and collectively, simply because they are human.

The work of researchers informs the work of policymakers, but researchers' concept of children is somewhat different. For the purposes of researchers who study interactions between children, media, and parents, defining a human child causes few problems beyond the need to clarify populations of interest and establish ethical research protocols. But defining what it means to be "human" has caused centuries-long debates that, even today (and perhaps especially today), have weighty implications for our understanding of past research and the future direction of the field of children and media itself.

Albert Bandura, perhaps the most-cited scholar by children and media researchers, argued that one's beliefs about what people are is important to what one believes people can become. He said, "What theorists believe people to be determines which aspects of human functioning they explore most thoroughly and which they leave unexamined. Conceptions of human nature thus focus inquiry on selected processes and are in turn strengthened by findings of paradigms embodying the particular view . . . Conceptions of human nature can influence what people become."⁹ Therefore, at the risk of resurrecting the historical dispute about what it means to be human, as well as the debate about the locus of human consciousness between "hard-core religious fundamentalists on one side and the equally hard-core scientific fundamentalists on the other,"¹⁰ this book begins by prying up a nail in the coffin of long-held assumptions that communication researchers decided long ago to bury.

Communication researchers seek to understand the processes through which one human mind affects another,¹¹ or how humans interact with their interpersonal and mediated environments. Since the advent of electronic-based mass communication technologies in the early twentieth century, communication researchers, which include hardcore positivists, rhetoricians, and everyone in between, have worked alongside governments, policymakers, and parents to explore the influence of media exposure on children. Now, well into the twenty-first century, the field of communication research is in the process of a fundamental paradigm shift,[12] a shift with assumptions about the meaning of being human that inherently restrict the ability of communication researchers to more completely understand the interpersonal and media-related interactions that both reveal and contribute to children's (and adults') humanness.

This paradigm shift, with its associated assumptions, can be seen in the widespread change in focus from media effects to understanding communication processes.[13] If it does not yet, this zealous focus on communication processes will soon constitute what Lang argued to be "a scientific achievement of such extreme excellence, that it attracts followers who then adopt its fundamental assumptions, methods, and questions."[14] A focus on communication processes requires that communication scientists view communication as it travels through psychological processes,[15] a view that has encouraged research from a new generation of scholars and has further opened our understanding of the cognitive processes at work during communication.

Lang, citing Kuhn's[16] reasoning, further argued that for a paradigm to prove profitable, it must provide "an understanding of the fundamental nature of the thing which he or she is studying."[17] And one fundamental assumption about humans upon which this rising paradigm rests is that of the *embodied mind*.[18] The embodied mind refers to the idea that our "minds necessarily include our brains but also are necessarily not restricted to our brains. This entails that minds are irreducible to our brains, not because they are in any way immaterial properties or facts, but instead because they are necessarily and wholly spatially spread throughout our living organismic bodies and belong to their complete neurobiological constitution."[19] Under the embodied mind perspective, "humans are defined as evolved, embedded, embodied brains,"[20] and human behavior is determined by the integration of personal and social factors without the possibility of a "disembodied duality."[21]

One method of inquiry among communication researchers that rests squarely on the shoulders of the embodied mind philosophy involves the collection of psychophysiological data. In fact, "the first and foremost central assumption of psychophysiology is the concept of the embodied mind,"[22] and its corollary that there is "no place for Cartesian dualism" in communication research.[23] It follows, then, that any insight gained from research that does not allow for the possibility of human dualism—the idea that the mind and the body are separate entities and that the mind can live without the human body—cannot provide an understanding of the human condition outside the confines of the embodied mind framework.

In other words, the dominant paradigm of communication research—the attempt to understand the psychological processes at play when humans encounter messages—is limited to viewing those experiences as embodied. That is, if there are human experiences that are not embodied, they cannot be understood nor explained by an embodied mind perspective. While the knowledge and understanding achieved by research working under an embodied mind assumption cannot be overstated, research and data in other areas suggest that our understanding of the human condition and human communication may be incomplete because this paradigm's primary assumption about what humans are does not allow for the possibility that human agency might rest in a place outside the boundaries of dominant, contemporary, scientific thinking.

An embodied mind approach to the study of human communication provides us with insights about humans' interactions with their environments. It can help us understand how humans make choices. It can help us understand the antecedents and outcomes of motivation and emotions. But, by its very nature, an embodied mind approach cannot provide us with knowledge about the condition of being human. Tim Ingold, a professor in the Department of Anthropology at University of Aberdeen, wrote, "The concept of human has a particular history in western discourses that has been decisively inflected by the rise of modern science. What science did was to split the human into two: on the one side lie human beings; on the other lies the condition of being human."[24] He continued, "human beings ... are individuals of a species. They are imagined, for the most part, as objects of empirical inquiry, pre-programmed with traits that are supposed to have been bestowed upon them by either genetic inheritance or social learning, or by some combination of the two."

This distinction between "human being" and "being human" has potentially enormous implications for the study of human communication, and specifically for the study of interactions between parents, children, and media. Adherence to the dominant, scientific assumptions about human beings "systematically disenfranchise[s] those humans—laypersons, children, 'folk'—deemed to be of lesser humanity."[25] While scientists may speak of the ability to exercise agency as one of many factors that make us human, the dominant scientific view of humans is that we are objects to be acted upon, instead of people with the potential to develop our humanness. This argument is not a condemnation of the embodied mind perspective and all that the approach has done to increase our understanding of what it means to be a human being, but it is a suggestion that communication scientists should take another hard look at the "fundamental nature of the thing" we are studying.[26]

"Mind embodied," in contrast to the embodied mind, refers to the idea that the human mind, while it works in conjunction with the brain and the body, may also function independently of biology, and may even continue to exist once the body ceases to live.[27] Regardless of what cultures call the mind (e.g., the soul, the conscience, etc.), such a disembodied, dualistic concept of human nature exists in major world religions and languages,[28] and is even thought to be innate, or common sense, among human infants.[29]

In contrast to the embodied mind and its conclusion that our behaviors are ultimately determined by the interaction of an undefined self, biology, and the environment, mind embodied suggests that there is at least a part of the mind, whether encapsulated in the workings of the brain and body or not, that functions at a level of independence from the brain and body, that is not necessarily a function of "biological energy" and "blood, oxygen, chemicals, enzymes, neurotransmitters, electricity"[30] and other systems encapsulated in the embodied mind. The difference between "mind embodied" and "embodied mind" is subtle, to be sure, but words matter when it comes to communication research.[31] The transposition of "embodied" and "mind" has consequences for where one thinks the human mind can and cannot go, and ultimately the very idea of what it means to be human. Mind embodied suggests that the mind can go places that the body cannot, and therefore, has experiences that the body and brain might not be able to make clear. Mind embodied suggests that human experiences exist that occur outside the confines of the embodied mind. Mind embodied also suggests that humans are more than byproducts of evolutionary processes and social learning, and that there is something innate within us at birth that yearns to become more than just a human being. The mind embodied perspective also suggests that human agency is different from the process of enacting that agency. Instead of automatically assuming that "thoughts are higher brain processes rather than psychic entities that exist separately from brain activities,"[32] mind embodied assumes that the mind has agency independent of biological and psychological processes, and that it works in conjunction with those processes to enact that agency. In other words, the self, or mind, of a person is born with agency that is not limited by the human body. The enactment of that agency might be constrained by the body's inherent limitations, but the agency itself, and thus the mind, are completely free in their own sphere. Agency is thus independent, and though enacted within the constraints of mortality, is nonetheless independent.

Allowing for the possibilities espoused by those on both sides of the dualism debate could help us piece together some of the "puzzles" that "the best science we can produce" is currently "failing to solve."[33] In 2009, Bryant and Zillmann lamented that "many of the most important media effects questions remain unanswered, at least to the satisfaction of many communication scholars."[34] In order to answer those questions, they argued, "the fundamental discussion of the nature of media effects must be renegotiated."[35] Perhaps even more so must the nature of the primary participants of media effects research—humans—be renegotiated.

If humans can be considered minds embodied with independent agency, then the stakes of communication research are far higher than currently conceived. It is not the development of attitudes and behaviors, motivation or efficacy, or the role of emotion that becomes preeminent in the study of media effects and processes. The development of the mind and its use of independent agency becomes the overriding focus of communication researchers. The development of the mind becomes both the antecedent and outcome, the mediator and the moderator, of interest in all communication research. In essence, the process of becoming more human today than we were yesterday, rather than the attributes and processes of human beings' interactions with our environments, outweighs all other considerations.

Such an argument is at once philosophical and practical, as efforts to understand human communication constitute an endeavor to understand much more, including our hopes, fears, and connections with each other and with our environments. A pursuit into such areas of ignorance is the way knowledge is created and leads to "the discovery that there is a world far larger than the one that is known, one that (whether we know it or not) shapes all our knowns."[36] Therefore, if we truly want to move the disciplines of human communication research forward, we must first deal with phenomena about which we know very little due to a limited allowance of our paradigms for such discovery, without diminishing or devaluing in any way the knowledge gained about human communication processes and effects provided by researchers through the years.

Other fields of scientific inquiry already allow for conceptions of human nature that, at the very least, lean toward a mind embodied perspective. Some neuroscientists have determined that not all human cognitions and behaviors are a result of observable physical processes, lending empirical support for an alternative way of conceptualizing the connection between the mind and the brain.[37] For example, scholars in other areas of brain science, such as neuroimaging, increasingly admit that traditional methods of learning about human cognitions and emotions do not and cannot capture the entire human experience—in fact, conscious effort can have a measurable effect even if its source may be unmeasurable with current tools. Said another way, humans have the capacity to override the chemical, mechanical processes of the embodied mind. As Bandura himself argued, "the capacity to exercise control over one's own thought processes, motivation, and action is a distinctively human characteristic" and that "any account of the determinants of human action must, therefore, include self-generated influences as a contributing factor."[38] Rather than allow for the possibility of dualistic humanity, however, Bandura argued that such self-generated human agency "does not imply psychophysical dualism"[39] and that human agency that allows humans to intentionally, through a process of self-influence, alter one's cognitions is "a product of reciprocal interplay of intrapersonal, behavioral, and environmental determinants."[40] He also argued that the idea of a mind independent of the brain is a "throwback to medieval theology"[41] that needs to experience a "dignified burial"[42] in order for social scientists to be able to tackle the challenge of understanding the human condition. The same logic could be used, however, to argue that such self-generated human agency does not rule out the possibility of psychophysical dualism to which billions of people worldwide currently, not just medievally, subscribe.

Beauregard calls for consideration of a Psychoneural Translation Hypothesis (PTH) to describe the relationship between mind and brain. At its most basic level, PTH suggests that the mind and the brain are two distinct, irreducible entities that work together to dictate human behavior: "The tendency of modern neuroscience and biological psychiatry toward neurobiological reductionism, i.e., the reduction of persons to their brains (a form of 'neural anthropomorphism'), is ill-advised and socially hazardous."[43] Indeed, Beauregard's review of neuroimaging research concluded that mentalistic variables such as "consciousness, metacognition, volition, beliefs, hopes"[44] are not reducible to biological processes of the brain. Beauregard concluded that these mentalistic variables, combined with their neurophysiological counterparts, are both needed to understand human behavior. Other areas of science are likewise making room for approaches to science from both sides of the mind-brain "problem" aisle. For example, the field of psychology struggles precisely with allowing for the possibilities associated with both perspectives of the mind–brain dichotomy:

> Psychology may more or less accept the Kantian idea that the knowledge stored in a human brain contributes to thoughts, feelings, memories, and perceptions in a top-down fashion, but at the same time we accept without question that emotions, thoughts, memories, the self, and the other psychological categories in folk psychology reflect the basic building blocks of the mind.[45]

While a scientific approach under monistic (as opposed to dualistic) assumptions allows for the study and better understanding of cognitive processes that help define the human experience, it, in effect, secularizes and dehumanizes humanity, and in the process, fails to capture parts of the human experience that make us human. As Rabbi Jonathan Sacks argued, "What the secularists forgot is that Homo sapiens is the meaning-seeking animal. If there is one thing the great institutions of the modern world do not do, it is provide meaning. Science tells us how but not why," and

> cannot answer the three questions every reflective individual will ask at some time in his or her life: Who am I? Why am I here? How then shall I live? These are questions to which the answer is prescriptive not descriptive, substantive not procedural. The result is that the twenty-first century has left us with a maximum of choice and a minimum of meaning.[46]

Thus, by absolving science of the responsibility of considering all the possible ways that the human experience may be constructed, it is possible that communication researchers are missing out on a clear opportunity to grapple with *who we are* as humans—and who our children are—and our role in providing evidence-based prescriptions for how one *should* live in order to maximize well-being. An approach to communication research that allows for the possibility of the mind embodied may also allow us to go beyond our fanatical focus on predicting human behaviors and communication processes to understanding *who we are* as humans and how that understanding relates to our own and others' well-being.

The dominant embodied mind approach, then, lets us explore *what* humans are, but the mind embodied approach allows us to explore *who* humans are. If we are interested in what media messages do to the human brain and what effects those messages have on human behavior, the embodied mind approach is sufficient. But questions of *who* must be asked using complementary perspectives in order to more fully understand how *who* people are influences human communication and behavior, and how human communication itself influences *who* people are. The inclusion of a mind embodied approach may help us to rehumanize and de-secularize our scientific efforts, and in the process, gain a better understanding of the human experience and increase the prescriptive reach of our research.

When we talk of the *who* of human beings, and especially of children, we are talking about many things, including the self and identity. The dominant view of the self is that "whether we believe it is material or not, we believe there is a 'part' of ourselves that is who we are and we tend to think of it as a stable core, relatively untouched or stable at the deepest level."[47] Regardless of whether or not humans are dual beings, if a proportion of both the lay, non-scientific population of the world,[48] as well as a sizable proportion of scientists,[49] believe in concepts such as the mind's or soul's ability to survive after death, it is incumbent upon scientists, and especially communication researchers, to both discover and communicate knowledge in a way that takes into account the mind embodied worldview of the audience. To not do so is a disservice to the societies and communities we serve. O'Connor and Joffe concluded that "ideas that reach the public sphere do not encounter passive receptacles of information, but active audiences who approach it through the lens of pre-existing worldviews, assumptions and agendas."[50] And the most important of those active audiences, at least in terms of media parenting, are parents themselves. But communication researchers and parents do not always see eye to eye, including when it comes to what comes to mind when they think of a human child. For starters, those outside the circle of communication researchers tend to criticize the academy, and in particular, Western-oriented universities, for their entrenchment of secularism as the standard for the pursuit of knowledge:

> There exists an international subculture composed of people with Western-type higher education, especially in the humanities and social sciences, that is indeed secularized. This subculture is the principal "carrier" of progressive,

Enlightened beliefs and values. While its members are relatively thin on the ground, they are very influential, as they control the institutions that provide the "official" definitions of reality, notably the educational system, the media of mass communication, and the higher reaches of the legal system. They are remarkably similar all over the world today.... What we have here is a globalized *elite* culture.[51]

Most parents, on the other hand, find themselves outside the circle of elites. Parents are considered laypeople, everyday folk, whose thoughts and opinions are valued by researchers mainly in terms of their ability to describe what is happening, and not for their thoughts and opinions about what truth or reality is, let alone what they believe about the nature of human children:

> Scientists, along with their philosophical cheerleaders, are reluctant to admit that people with experience in other walks of life are equally capable of deep and disciplined thought, or that they might have valuable insights to offer. The default assumption is rather that, in their comparative ignorance, the public has nothing to contribute to the conversation ... the study of human nature, they insist, belongs to science, and science alone.[52]

Mind embodied, on the other hand, places greater intrinsic value on the perspective of parents because they are in a position relative to their children that no one else is, and thus see children differently than how anyone else sees them. To parents, children are everything, not just something. And it is the job of parents to help children develop their use of agency in a way that maximizes their well-being and their potential for being human. The job of science should be to meet parents where they are and to help parents in these efforts. While scientists often give lip service to "theology, philosophy, jurisprudence, the arts, literature"[53] as conceptual approaches to discovering meaning, it seems that researchers rarely put that acknowledgment into practice by allowing approaches to the discovery of meaning that are different from those to which a majority of those in our comfortable scientific circles adhere. A mind embodied approach discourages any elitism and secular objectivity that may be engendered by thinking that it is through the scientific process alone that meaning can be found. It invites parents into the glow of the campfire and incorporates their views of children into its assumptions, methods, theorizing, and hypothesizing.

How parents conceive of children appears to be substantially different from the ways in which policymakers and researchers conceive of children. "It has been established that parents hold a variety of views about children and parenting and that these views are not always in agreement with formal psychology."[54] In social scientific terms, parents' beliefs about their children are the basis of parenting decisions and behaviors. Miller asked,

"Do parents' beliefs affect how they treat their children? The answer is yes—not always, often not strongly, not necessarily as a sole cause of parental behavior, but as one cause . . . parents' beliefs and behaviors are one contributor to how children develop, and there is arguably no more important question to which psychology speaks."[55]

Thus, parenting beliefs about the nature of children implicitly and fundamentally influence parenting behaviors. Much of the research linking parenting beliefs with subsequent parenting behaviors involves parents' beliefs about children's autonomy, abilities, skills, or developmental trajectories of children—the 5,000-foot view of children. Little, if any, research takes a step back to view parents' beliefs about the nature of children's humanness—a 30,000-foot view of children—and its role in parenting behaviors. And it is this 30,000-foot view of human nature that may have a "dominant influence" compared to the 5,000-foot view, which "is like a shallow consciousness, clear and easy to extract, but it is not really a strong dominant factor" in parents' behavior.[56]

In other words, parents have an implicit belief about who children are, where they come from, and their potential as human beings. These beliefs are most often referred to by researchers, perhaps condescendingly, as folk psychology.[57] "Folk," in this sense, are viewed as everyday people, and not as experts whose views have any scientific validity. The theories of everyday people about why people behave the way they do are called folk theories. Concerning folk psychology, the American Psychological Association's Dictionary of Psychology explains, "There are those who view it as illusory or mythological and hold its tenets unworthy of scientific consideration."[58] But if parenting beliefs, and parents' beliefs about human nature in particular, predict parenting behavior, it does not make any difference one way or another whether or not those beliefs are considered mythological or illusory by researchers (presumably the "those" mentioned by the APA dictionary), if those beliefs are considered to be truthful, genuine, or innate by parents themselves. Either way they guide parenting behavior, and to neglect those beliefs is to neglect a powerful motivation and explanatory mechanism for the ways in which parents engage in parenting generally, and media parenting specifically.

Parents' folk beliefs about the nature of human children are different from those of policymakers and researchers. First, many parents believe that children are inherently good. Lin argued that parents have theories about the original state of virtue and about the plasticity of virtue—this refers to parents' beliefs about whether children are born good or evil, and whether children's virtue is fixed or able to be developed.[59] Lin argued that these basic views of human nature constitute one factor that affects the attributions people make about others' behavior, as well as the parenting methods parents choose for raising their children. Lin's study of more than two thousand Taiwanese parents found that nearly three-quarters of parents believe that human nature is inherently good. What's more, Lin's study found that the more people agree that children are inherently good, the more likely they are to also believe that virtue can be taught. Said differently, a belief that children come into the world with an innate goodness is related to the motivation to engage in parenting behaviors intended to augment that goodness.

Many parents also view their child "as having an autonomous mind," as "an intentional person with a mind of their own."[60] This view motivates parents to treat their child as an individual with unique thoughts and feelings. While individual differences in levels of parental mind-mindedness exist, all parents, especially mothers, "will perceive their infant to be an intentional agent"[61] to some extent and at least some of the time. The belief in children's inherent agency is also a belief that children are beings now, and not just that they are becoming human beings. This is different from the belief that children can learn, grow, improve, and develop additional traits of humanity. A belief in children's agency assumes that what children think and feel is valuable and valid, important and worthy of others' attention. It assumes that children are not simply blank slates upon which adults write a formula for living, but that children's agency interacts with the lessons learned from the shared experiences of others. It does not mean that children should necessarily be given Golding-esque free rein to create and run their own society. But it does mean that adults, and especially parents, have a responsibility to teach children to use their agency in productive and meaningful ways:

> All children, by virtue of their immaturity, have similar needs and limitations. Infants are dependent on others for their physical care: for food, shelter, hygiene and safety. An abandoned infant cannot survive for very long. Children also need emotional attachment and, as with their physical care, how and who forms emotional bonds with the young child can be subject to a great deal of variation but the forming of strong emotional attachments to close caregivers is apparently a universal feature of human society. . . . Children may not be born as blank slates, but teaching young humans the whole range of cultural practices from how to eat their food to living ethically or morally is a shared concern of all human societies.[62]

Next, many people (including, presumably, parents) in many cultures in many regions of the world hold beliefs consistent with intuitive dualism,[63,64] the innate belief that the mind is separate from the human body and that it continues to exist after death. Thus, we can assume that many parents believe that their children are made up of two distinct entities: the mind and the body. That belief assumes that the mind and the body can each develop and grow. And since many parents believe in the plasticity of virtue, as noted above, parents must then believe that the mind, or the core of one's personhood, can likewise be taught to become subjectively better than it is now, often in preparation for the mind's life after mortality. If this is a common belief of parents, then parents inherently have beliefs about what their child can become, both in this life and in an extra-mortal life of the mind. If the human mind can develop—and parents believe that it can—and if parents' beliefs affect their parenting behaviors, then the argument of Stone and Church in 1973 becomes all the more relevant for a discussion of media parenting: "Perhaps the most important single principle of human development is the self-fulfilling prophecy which says simply that our children become what we expect them to become."[65] If parents believe that children become something after this life because their mind is not limited to the material body, it follows that their parenting behaviors will reflect what they want the child to eventually become.

Becoming a person of character and someone who possesses positive virtues may be at the top of the list of these parental desires for their children's becoming. About 94 percent of American parents, for example, agree that it is extremely important or very important that their children develop the qualities of honesty and ethics.[66] Similarly, 88 percent of these parents hope their children grow up to be hardworking, 81 percent as someone who helps others in need, and 81 percent as someone who is accepting of people who are different from them. Perhaps more importantly, however, is the characterization of these hopes as they relate to parents' ultimate hopes for their children's futures. That is, some parents see children as "being," while others see children as "projects."[67] Hallden explained that "child as being" refers to children and their development as directed by an inner drive, with parents' desires for their children culminating in the development of the child's unique individuality. "Child as project" refers to children and their development as a snapshot in a development process, and that children are expected to be shaped by parents in a way that will allow them to advance to the next stage of development. Most parents in Hallden's study subscribe to the "child as being" worldview. When parents see their child as being, they are motivated to help their child learn the difference between right and wrong, so the child grows into a moral human being. They see their child, in the future, as a being that is independent and self-reliant and that uses common sense. They see their child as a being with innate potential who is free to choose. "Child as project" speaks more to the way parents perceive their own responsibilities to nurture and protect, and less to the child's innate individuality and potential. "Child as being" suggests that "what there is to develop in the child was there from the beginning,"[68] and that the child's potential will emerge given the right environment and enough time.

This is not the first time someone has philosophized about what childhood is and is not. Nor am I the first to seemingly contradict myself by claiming that children are beings who are in the process of becoming. The discourse surrounding the being versus becoming dichotomy is solved, though, when we consider that part of children's being is their place in the process of becoming. The now affects the future, and what children choose to be today has implications for the kind of child they will be tomorrow and the kind of adult they will someday be.

To move the field of children and media, and more specifically, the discipline of media parenting, forward, we as researchers can do more to meet children and parents where they are. We can do that by putting ourselves in the shoes of parents, the humans who quite literally meet children where they are day to day, hour by hour. We may not meet every child in the school pickup line or at the dinner table, but we can conceptualize them in ways more closely aligned with the ways parents conceptualize them. As humans with independent minds. As humans born into the world with agency, and who want to use that agency. As people living in the here and now with the potential for both humanity and to develop the human characteristics of kindness and love, concern and empathy, morality and care.[69] And perhaps most importantly, if parents see children as minds embodied, as souls who will live on after the body dies, then meeting parents and children where they are means that we likewise consider the possibility that the media's effect on children is on more than children's attitudes, beliefs, behaviors, and physiology. The media's effect, then, becomes an effect on children's souls. Children may be much more than we give them credit for, and it seems parents already know that. And to best serve families we must, at least to some extent, lay aside our scientific assumptions and give due consideration to folk theories about the nature of children. If we do, we give ourselves the opportunity to learn things about parents, children, and media that our current approaches cannot. And if we fail to do so, we run the risk of missing out on what could be phenomena of most lasting import for children.

Chapter 2

MEDIA AND THE HOME ENVIRONMENT

Jennifer Keishin Armstrong, the author of several best-selling books about pop culture, gender, and media, once said that "the history of the sitcom is the history of America."¹ If this is true, then it is also true that we get our ideas about what the typical American and Western home and family look like from television sitcoms. From *I Love Lucy*, we learned that the typical life of a Western middle-class married couple was centered around a living room, and that humor is an excellent way to deal with life's stressors. The show also introduced us to the pedestal upon which the TV is placed in Western culture—in one episode, Lucy Ricardo and her husband Ricky buy a TV set for their friends, the Mertz's. Ricky breaks the new TV set, motivating Fred Mertz to break the Ricardo's TV set, sending both couples to court. Implicit in the sketch is the lesson that TV in the home is worth fighting for, that television was and is "a standard and often idealized domestic object—something that often signified family togetherness and the bounty of postwar consumer pleasures."² From *Married . . . with Children*, we learned that family time is successful even when filled with raunch, insults, bickering, and of course, watching TV. *The Cosby Show* broke stereotypes about race, gender roles, and class as it taught viewers about representation and the value of education, while portraying the upward social mobility of an African American family, in part evidenced by their ownership of a large TV set placed in a position of honor in their living room. As Spigel argued, the TV set (and now newer devices) on American family sitcoms was not necessarily "the main object on display; rather, it is a setting in which some other action or object takes center stage."³ The TV on set is evidence of the "changing practices of everyday life in the new TV home, practices like homemaking, childcare, socializing, and interior design."⁴

To understand the ways in which a child develops, we must first understand the environments in which that development occurs. The primary environment for child development is the home, and thousands of characteristics of the home play at least some small role in altering the trajectory of a child's development. The place of media in the home is an increasingly significant characteristic of the home. Today, "the media are an integral part of the way the everyday is conducted,"⁵ and media "decisions are constantly crossed through and influenced by nonmedia conditions and decisions."[6] Therefore, to set the stage for our discussion of media parenting, it is worthwhile to explore the types of home environments that are most conducive to helping children thrive.

The Place of the Home

Children come into the world with certain attributes and characteristics that affect their ability to meaningfully navigate life—we call this "nature." We use the term "nurture" to describe other influences on children's development. Nurture refers to everything and everyone in a child's environment from which/whom children learn. Children learn to use their agency largely through their interactions with their environments and the people therein. And among the many aspects of a child's environment, the home environment is the most important and influential teacher. The home, as we know, does not function in a vacuum. It is one of many systems with the potential to influence children, but it is the closest system to the child. Bronfenbrenner's ecological systems theory[7] is perhaps the most widely employed explanatory model of the different systems affecting child development, and the home is primary among the many systems in a child's ecology. For the first few years of a child's life, the primary actors in the home microsystem are the children's parents, and it is not possible to overstate the influence that parents have in all aspects of a child's development. Parents' actions play a major role in children's well-being. They are the primary determinants of whether a child is protected from all types of physical harm—they decide on the type, location, size, and standards of safety and comfort of a child's home. They set rules about, and an example for, how to interact with others, the practice of discipline, school attendance, eating habits, hygiene practices, and health care. Parents provide lessons on religion and culture. Indeed, "the family environment into which a child is born will exert the most powerful and long-lasting influence over his or her development and future life chances."[8]

Decades of research has identified a multitude of home and family conditions that seem most conducive to children's well-being. Our understanding of home environments most conducive to childhood well-being comes from an amalgamation of thousands of studies exploring only a limited number of the nearly countless aspects of the home environment, and an equally sizable number of child outcomes. To collate this research into succinct, conclusive statements does not do justice to the ways in which these aspects of the home environment interact to produce the precise form of "nurture" required for the well-being of each unique child. Nor can one chapter in a single book effectively summarize all the research about these related topics. That said, we can make general statements from examples of research about some things that have been found to influence children's well-being in many locations, among people with diverse racial and ethnic backgrounds, for people from varied income groups, and from families with different structures. Also to be noted is the Western, globally northern-centric focus of much of the literature.

Home Environment Effects

As one aspect of children's well-being, physical health is strongly tied to characteristics of the home environment. For example, the nature of the structure of a child's home relates to children's health habits. In a study involving 235 English parent–child dyads (children were ages 9–12), living in a detached house was associated with increased time children spent sitting at home, compared to attached housing; on the other hand, living in a home with an open floor plan in the main living area, a relatively larger house, and access to musical instruments in the home was related to less sitting and higher levels of physical activity.[9] In addition, children from households without the use of a car, with a single mother, lower levels of mother's education, lower family income, and no home ownership were more likely to have relatively higher levels of physical activity.[10]

Children's overweight and obesity are closely related to their physical activity, and the home environment plays a dominant role in the prevalence of each. A systematic review of thirty-two studies found that higher levels of home organization, indicated by family routines and limit setting, were related to lower child weight across several child age groups.[11] Another review found that parents' food intake, the provision and availability of different types of foods in the home, parents' encouragement or discouragement of consuming various foods, parent–child relationships, and parenting styles were each associated with both the types of foods children consumed and children's weight.[12] A longitudinal study of Chilean youth at ages 5, 10, 15, and 21 years found that family stress, the absence of a father in the home, mother's depression, frequent child containment in a playpen, and a dirty home environment were related over time to body mass index at age 21.[13] The home environment can even affect children's susceptibility to various illnesses and injury.

Generally speaking, then, children cannot be physically well if their physical environment is unwell. But physical health is only one aspect of a child's well-being. Well-being also includes social, mental, cognitive, and other forms of health. Some home environments are more conducive than others to children's health in many of these areas. For example, it is well established that children are more likely to experience mental health distress if their parents have a diagnosed mental health disorder.[14] The home environment can make the relationship between parents' and children's mental health distress more or less likely. For example, a Dutch study involving 522 7-year-olds found that children's home environment, operationalized by 59 binary items related to a variety of topics (such as emotional climate, learning materials, family companionship, and physical environment), mediated the relationship between parents' mental illness and child psychopathology.[15]

On the other hand, aspects of the home environment can protect against children's mental health problems and promote socio-emotional and academic development. For example, the predictability of family routines served as a protective factor against negative child mental health among U.S. preschoolers during the Covid-19 pandemic.[16] Children's self-esteem was likely to be higher in homes where parental warmth, parental monitoring, economic security, and presence of the father were relatively high.[17] Living with two parents was also related to higher executive function for children, as was family companionship and parental responsivity.[18] A low level of household chaos, characterized by low levels of background stimulation, high levels of family routines, presence of predictability and structure in daily activities, and a slower pace of family life, was associated with higher levels of children's social-emotional functioning, cognitive development, academic achievement, and physical health and healthy behaviors.[19] Educational development is also facilitated by quality parent–child interactions, children's access to learning materials in the home, and children's participation in learning activities at home.[20]

Home Media Environment

As children grow, they increasingly interact with people and messages not curated by their parents that can likewise influence their well-being. Children's relationship with media is an increasingly influential part of their lives. The home environment does not function in isolation and interacts with other systems. Bronfenbrenner's model states that the microsystem of the home is nested within a mesosystem, exosystem, and macrosystem. Depending on who is asked or how it is conceptualized, mass media fits within either the child's mesosystem or exosystem. Regardless of where it fits in the model, mass media interacts with the child's home microsystem—in fact, the interactions and interrelationships between the child, the home/family, and mass media have important ramifications for child development and well-being.

In what may become one of the great understatements in twenty-first-century media scholarship, Dr. Amy Jordan said, "Television and other media have become intricately woven into the fabric of the daily lives of families." She continued, "The family system provides a rich context for understanding how children develop notions about how to use media and what to think about the world of ideas delivered electronically to the home."[21] The home media environment is a broad construct that consists of the media available in the home, the personal media ownership of children and youth, the household's media orientation,[22] and the time spent with media in the home. It includes the number and placement of devices, the timing of media use, attitudes toward media, and media use norms of every person (individually and collectively) in the home. It also includes parent–child interactions and rules about media use, as well as every other person, activity, or factor related to both the content and context of media use within the home.

Parents' Media Use

Many characteristics of the home media environment play a role in children's media use and in the effects of media on children, but parents' media use constitutes perhaps the single most influential predictor of children's media use both in and out of the home. In U.S. samples, parents' screen time and media use were significantly associated with children's time spent using television and other media.[23,24] In fact, parents' television use was a stronger predictor of children's time using television than factors such as children's access to television in the home and bedroom.[25] This pattern of results has been found in samples worldwide. For example, a Portuguese study involving parents of more than seventeen thousand children ages 3–10 found that parents' TV viewing time, especially that of mothers, was strongly associated with children's TV viewing time.[26] A two-year longitudinal study of Canadian families found that parents' screen time was positively associated with preschoolers' screen time.[27] In Denmark, a survey of more than five thousand parent–child dyads found that children of parents in the highest quartile of screen use had between 2.1 and 2.5 greater odds of screen use before bedtime.[28] And in Australia, parents' time spent on social media was related to an increase in adolescents' subsequent time spent on social media.[29] Some research has even gone so far as to conclude that parental smartphone addiction is positively associated with adolescent smartphone addiction.[30]

In addition to time spent with media or screens, the type of content to which parents are regularly exposed, or the media activities in which they regularly engage, likewise relate to the types of content viewed and media activities engaged in by their children. For example, the frequency of parent–adolescent dyads' engagement in each of seven online activities was significantly associated.[31] In addition, a longitudinal study of 519 parents and young children found that parents' exposure to both antisocial/aggressive and prosocial media content was positively associated with children's subsequent exposure to corresponding types of content.[32] The frequency with which parents read the newspaper was associated with watching the news on television and reading a newspaper or news magazine among young adult children several years later,[33] and the relationship between parents' news consumption via television, computer, and mobile phone was associated with adolescents' news use on each of the respective devices.[34]

Parents' Attitudes About Media

Parents' attitudes are also strongly predictive of both the time children spend with media and the media content to which children are exposed. For example, parents' positive attitudes about technology were positively associated with the time children ages 3–5 spent with a tablet and/or smartphone.[35] Among parents of children ages 6 months to 5 years, parents' positive attitudes about media were positively related to children's exposure to both educational and non-educational media, as well as to time spent watching TV; on the other hand, parents' concern, or negative attitudes, about media use were related to less TV use but not to reductions in exposure to specific types of content.[36] A study involving parents of children ages 4 to 6 found that parents' positive attitudes about media were related to higher amounts of daytime media use for children, while negative attitudes were not related to children's media use.[37] Parents' positive attitudes about screen media were related to more viewing of educational content for children ages 4 to 8,[38] but among parents of infants aged 6–18 months, parents' attitudes about media were associated with the content, but not the amount, of their children's television exposure.[39] Parents' positive beliefs about the value of media were positively associated with parents' provision of digital devices to their young adolescent children (average age 13).[40] A nationally representative sample of U.S. parents of 8- to 18-year-olds found that parents' attitudes toward media were generally positive and related to children's media use, that parents were more likely to be concerned about children's use of the Internet than they were about adolescents' use of the Internet, and that the role of parents' attitudes about media became non-significant when parents' own media use was added to the analysis.[41]

Devices in the Home

Another aspect of the home media environment that plays a role in children's media use includes the number of devices, their placement, and access to media devices in the home. Most U.S. 8- to 18-year-olds live in a home with multiple media devices,[42] and the prevalence and placement of devices in the home have implications for children's media use. For example, some estimates suggest that children ages 3–5 with their own mobile device used it for nearly two hours each day.[43] Smartphone ownership among high school juniors and seniors in Taiwan was related to excessive smartphone use.[44] Similarly, the presence of a television in children's bedrooms was positively associated with children's average daily television viewing.[45] The number of television sets in the home was also associated with screentime.[46] Scholars argued that "getting a smartphone is now a rite of passage for most children and adolescents in the United States,"[47] so it should come as no surprise that media use among children of all ages has likewise grown[48] to "almost constant" levels.[49]

Heterogeneity in the Home Media Environment

Just as families are not homogeneous, neither is the home media environment. The home media environment looks drastically different, and has differing influences on children's screen time, depending on family characteristics, child attributes, and socio-demographics. Note again, however, that much of the easily accessible data about these contributing factors is found in research with the United States and other Western samples.

Age

First, the home media environment changes based on the ages of children in the home, changes that often manifest themselves in different media use patterns in the home. A nationally representative survey of 8- to 18-year-olds in the United States showed that teens (ages 13–18) consistently used screen media substantially more than tweens (ages 8–12). In 2021, for example, teens spent an average of eight hours and thirty-nine minutes daily with screen media, compared to five hours and thirty-three minutes for tweens.[50] Children ages 5–8 used screens more than children younger than age 5.[51] Beyond simple time spent with screens/media, the media activities of youth differ by age. For example, U.S. tweens watched TV more than teenagers, while teenagers used social media and watched online videos more than tweens.[52] Older teens (ages 15–17) were more likely than younger teens to be online constantly.[53] Children ages 5–8 spent more time playing video games and engaging in other digital activities, such as video chatting, educational/homework, and virtual reality than children ages 0–4.[54] In the United Kingdom, children ages 4–11 watched more broadcast television than adolescents ages 12–15.[55] When they went online, U.S. children ages 3–11 primarily watched videos or communicated with others via messages or voice/video calls; adolescents ages 12–17, however, went online to use social media nearly as much as watching videos and communicating with others.

Gender

The home media environment, and thus children's media use, changes based on children's gender. Among both tweens and teens, boys tended to use about 1 hour and 15 minutes more screen media daily than girls.[56] Likewise, among children ages 0–8, boys spent more time than girls with screens.[57] For various media activities, research found no significant differences between tween and teenage boys and girls who said they watched TV every day, but did find significant differences for other media activities—more boys played video games every day than girls, boys used YouTube more than girls, and girls used social media and read for pleasure daily more than boys.[58] Teen girls were also more likely than boys to say they almost constantly use TikTok.⁵⁹ Among children ages 0–8, boys watched more TV and played video games more than girls.⁶⁰ In the United Kingdom, as in the United States, girls ages 3–17 were more likely than boys to use social media and to actively comment, share, or post on social media; UK boys, though, were more likely than girls to play video games during late adolescence, but prior to age 16, there were no gender differences in likelihood of playing video games.⁶¹

Race/Ethnicity

Children's screentime also varies by race/ethnicity. Both Black and Hispanic/Latinx tweens and teens spent more time than White youth with screens each day; these differences existed despite a gap in access to home computers.⁶² Asian children ages 9–10 in the United States were exposed to less screen time daily than White children, and among kids ages 10–14, Native American, Black, and Hispanic/Latinx youth had higher problematic screen use scores than non-Hispanic/Latinx White youth.⁶³ In terms of media activities, more Black youth said they watch TV every day and play video games on a console, computer, or portable player every day than both White and Hispanic/Latinx youth; in addition, more Hispanic/Latinx youth watched online videos every day than White youth, fewer White youth said they use Instagram than both Black and Hispanic/Latinx youth, and among youth who use social media, Black youth spent more time on social media than White youth.⁶⁴ Black and Hispanic/Latinx teens were more likely than White teens to say they are online almost constantly, and more Black and Hispanic/Latinx teens also reported being constantly on YouTube, Instagram, and TikTok than White teens.⁶⁵

Family Income

Family income also makes a difference in children's screentime. Among tweens and teens, youth from families with relatively higher income ($100,000+) spent less time with screen media than youth from families with either middle ($35,000–$99,999) or lower income (less than $35,000); not surprisingly, about 94 percent of higher-income youth had access to a laptop or desktop computer at home, compared to 89 percent of middle-income youth and 67 percent of lower-income youth.⁶⁶ In terms of media activities, the same report found that more lower- and middle-income youth watched TV and played video games on a console, computer, or portable player every day than higher-income youth, and more lower-income youth watched online videos every day than middle- and higher-income youth. On the other hand, more higher- and middle-income youth used social media every day than lower-income youth, and more higher-income youth also read for pleasure every day than lower-income youth. Income gaps also existed for usage of specific social media sites—lower-income teens were more likely to use Facebook and TikTok than higher-income teens, while higher-income teens were more likely to use BeReal.[67]

Parent Education

With relative consistency in studies around the world, parents' education is related to children's screen time. Specifically, the higher the parents' level of education, the less screen time. This was found among children ages 2–3 in Singapore,[68] among children under age 8 in English language studies,[69] among both English- and Persian language samples of children ages 0–19,[70] young adolescents in Norway,[71] children ages 0–5 in Canada,[72] female adolescents in Finland,[73] and U.S. children ages 0–8,[74] 1–3,[75] and 6 months to 5 years.[76] Parents' education was also inversely related to the presence of a TV in a child's bedroom and eating meals in front of the TV among children ages 0–18 from developed countries.[77]

Siblings

Like parents, siblings also play a role in children's media use. Perhaps the most telling research related to the influence of siblings on children's media time was conducted by Davies and Gentile.[78] The study involved two sets of data—a nationally representative random sample of U.S. parents of children ages 2–17 and a national convenience sample of American families. Results of the study showed that families with preschoolers used media in healthy ways more often than families with school-age children and adolescents. The study also found that families with siblings reported healthier media use than families with just one child, across all three age groups. These findings are consistent with earlier research that found that boys without any siblings spent more time daily watching TV.[79] On the other hand, a study involving Australian families found that adolescents with siblings watched relatively more TV.[80] Yet another Australian study, however, found that toddlers with fewer than three siblings were more likely to engage in more than two hours of screen time daily.[81] In Canada, children ages 3–5 with one sibling watched significantly less TV/video and reported less overall screen time than children with no siblings.[82] In China, passive screen time was higher for children without siblings than it was for those with siblings.[83] Other research has found that children's electronic media use (TV, electronic games, and computer) tended to mirror that of siblings,[84] especially older siblings. Having an older sibling increased both the range and number of online activities in which younger siblings engaged.[85] In a study involving families in eight European countries, children's screen time patterns tended to mimic those of siblings when children were younger than age seven, but resembled those of peers more than those of siblings among children ages 11 and older.[86] And younger siblings in France tended to use media for longer durations than firstborn children, and younger siblings were also more likely to own their own device than firstborn children.[87]

Parents' Marital Status

Children of all ages in single-parent homes are consistently shown to use screens more than children from two-parent homes. For example, children ages 6–11 in Denmark living in a single-parent home were more likely to use screen media for more than four hours per day than children living in a home with more than one adult.[88] Among youth ages 11–16 in Norway, living with a single parent and living with a "reconstituted" family (stepparents) were both related to more hours of total screentime,[89] though no such significant differences were found in a similar study in Canada.[90] U.S. children ages 10–14 whose parents were unmarried or unpartnered had higher levels of problematic social media use.[91] Girls from single-parent families watched more TV per day than girls from two-parent families.[92] Evidence also suggests that children ages 6 months to 5 years from single-parent households consumed more of both educational and non-educational media content than children from two-parent households.[93]

Geography

Where families live also seems to make a difference in children's screen time. Data from the WHO European Childhood Obesity Surveillance Initiative, a twenty-five-country study involving more than 150,000 girls and boys ages 6–9 in Europe, found substantial differences in children's screen time based on geography.[94] The report found wide variance in the percentage of children who reported less than two hours per day of screen time. In Italy, for example, 32.3 percent of children engaged in screen time for less than two hours, but in Spain approximately 80 percent of children engaged in less than two hours of screen time daily. About 50 percent or fewer of the children in six countries engaged in less than two hours of screen time daily, including children in Italy, San Marino, Turkmenistan, Romania, Croatia, and Montenegro. Countries with the highest percentage of children (more than 66.6 percent) who engaged in two hours or less of screen time daily included Spain, Portugal, Kazakhstan, Russia, France, and Tajikistan. Other research found similar cross-country disparities in screen time, though once again, children in Spain spent the least amount of time using screens.[95] Canadian children ages 2–5 spent an average of 159 minutes with screens daily, compared to 110 minutes for their South Korean counterparts.[96] Children ages 8–17 in the United Kingdom spent more time with devices than those in the United States, though U.S. children spent more time watching TV and playing video games than those in the United Kingdom.[97] A sixteen-country study involving more than nineteen thousand children around 12 years old showed that geography played a distinct role in the percentage of children who watched TV or spent time on a computer every day.[98] For example, only

19 percent of children in Ethiopia watched TV every day compared to 88 percent of children in Estonia. Similarly, only 3 percent of children in Ethiopia spent time on the computer daily, compared to 76 percent in Estonia. Among children ages 2–3 in East Asia, Malay and Indian children spent more time viewing screens than children in China.[99] And nine-year-old children in Brazil spent more time with screens than their Portuguese counterparts.[100]

Family Connection, Bonding, and Communication

Beyond the noted socio-demographic variables with the potential to affect children's screen time, the culture, norms, and practices of families can also alter the home media environment, and ultimately, children's media habits. For example, the strength or quality of the relationship that children have with parents can have a substantial impact on media use. A 2019 study of nearly ten thousand adolescents ages 11–20 in Canada found a significant association between negative mother–daughter, father–daughter, and father–son relationships and heavy social media use among youth.[101] Other self-report data of adolescents ages 12–16 and their parents in Israel found a positive association between conflict within the family and adolescents' problematic Internet use, and negative associations between both expressiveness and cohesion in the family and problematic Internet use.[102] Similarly, analysis of a sample of 453 U.S. adolescents (mean age of 14) and their parents found significant positive associations between several types of joint parent–child media use (texting/calling on cell phones, watching TV/movies, and playing video games) and parent–child connection.[103] While the authors suggested that media use predicted parent–child connection, they conceded that the cross-sectional nature of the data leaves open "the possibility that families who are already connected are simply using more media together," and that "it is likely that the relationship between family media use and family connection is a bidirectional one."[104] In another study, family conflict at Time 1 was related to time spent watching TV at Time 2 (5 years later) among U.S. children ages 0–8.[105] Feeling alienated or disconnected from both their father and mother was related to excessive Internet use among children ages 7–17 in Finland.[106] And among German youth ages 8–14, secure parent–child attachment was related to lower levels of youths' problematic mobile phone involvement.[107]

Context

The above factors, and many more, contribute to children's media use, but it is important to be cautious about assuming both a linear relationship between the correlates noted above and the independence of their role in children's media use. Each correlate heretofore discussed, with perhaps the exception of geography, seems to fall squarely into what Bronfenbrenner would call the child's microsystem. Not discussed are the unique impacts of variables from the mesosystem, exosystem, and macrosystem within which the child's home environment is nested. Nor have the within- and cross-system interactions between variables been considered. While such a discussion is necessary to go beyond the "single minded focus on the internal dynamics of the household to the exclusion of any concern with the mechanism of the family's wider social engagement,"[108] it is beyond the scope of the current discussion. However, in the absence of a detailed exploration of the myriad complex forces operating on children, and within which children's media choices are made, a brief conversation about these wider interactions is warranted, even though it may be unsatisfactorily brief.

First, children and families do not simply stay in their homes their entire lives without connection to the outside world. Children go to daycare and school, participate in sports teams and in the orchestra, are involved with church youth groups, play at friends' houses, and participate in hundreds of other activities and interactions with people. Each of these activities, in turn, influences children's interactions with each of the other activities. National and international policy about the availability of certain social media platforms or about the types of content that are suitable for children influences the activities of every child and family. And amid it all, families develop their own unique culture around media use. This "technological culture refers to the set of values and activities that define a family's systematic relationship to the technologies within its own domestic environment and to those technologies which in one way or another impinge on that environment . . . The family's technological culture requires that the family's relationship to technology be itself understood within the context of the family's place in the wider culture."[109]

Furthermore, a family's technological culture is nested in a wider culture with assumptions about childhood socialization and parenting. Dr. Lara Perez-Felkner argued that since the early 2000s, children have occupied a unique stage in human development in which they should be protected and in which their agency should be recognized and fostered.[110] Across cultures, the role of parents is one of both protector and provider of life's necessities, as well as of teacher and nurturer.[111] Parents are expected to try to develop a warm, loving relationship with their children, in addition to providing physical care, cognitive stimulation, warmth, control, and monitoring.[112] Parents' choices relating to each of these parenting behaviors affect, and are affected by, the norms of the culture in which they live. They also affect, and are affected by, the technological culture that either intentionally develops or unintentionally emerges in individual families. Thus, children's media use, in terms of both time and content, is both affected by and affects their family's technological culture.

Whether by their parents, siblings, some aspect of culture, or the media itself, children's use of media is in large part socialized by the environments in which they grow. The home media environment is primary among children's socialization agents, but it functions interconnectedly with all aspects of larger societal systems and organizations to define the constraints within which children learn to use their agency to make media choices. Disentangling the multitude of forces that help determine children's media habits may be nigh impossible, but the accumulated research about the place of media in the lives of children is conclusive that children's media use choices are a "product of complicated family constraints and possibilities, and long-term socialization processes. Children learn from their parents, older siblings, friends, and other significant people in their lives a variety of media use habits and appropriate gendered and age-related behaviors, all of which become part of their independent media repertoire."[113]

Chapter 3

EFFECTS OF CHILDREN'S MEDIA USE

With a clearer understanding of the significance of the home media environment and media use in the lives of children, it is logical to next explore the outcomes of children's media use. As we will see, children are affected by media, making media parenting a significant and important aspect of parenting children today. The purpose of this discussion is not to comprehensively review all the research related to ways that children are affected by media. Instead, this chapter will make clear the need for the substantive consideration of media parenting that will follow.

There is no longer any worthwhile debate about whether media use affects children. It unequivocally does. To deny the media's effect on children, or on anyone of any age for that matter, is like denying that reading can lead to knowledge or that sunlight is related to photosynthesis. As food and water are to the body, information is to the mind. Media content is simply encoded information, and that information changes the mind. From a systems perspective, media content is an input that changes the system's homeostasis, the system's status quo. From an embodied mind perspective, the process of encoding information into some form in the brain causes electrical impulses, the firing of neurons, or any number of chemical or electrical processes. And from a mind embodied perspective, every bit of information absorbed by the mind has the potential to change who we and our children are.

Decades of research makes it clear that media influences children's attitudes, behaviors, beliefs, knowledge, and perceptions in a host of life domains. Levels of wellness in one domain are related to levels of wellness in other domains, and media use outcomes are part of an interconnected network of forces that determine an individual's collective well-being. It should also be acknowledged that much of the research related to the media's effect on children relates to the risks of children's media use and less to the potential benefits of media exposure.

To begin, children's developmental health can be considered via four broad domains: physical health, socio-emotional well-being, mental health, and cognitive development/academic performance. These domains do not always go by these names in the literature, nor are they inclusive of all variables that contribute to children's well-being, but most outcomes of children's media use can find a fitting home in at least one of the four. In exploring media effects in each of these domains, researchers often focus on children in one developmental group for one set of related outcomes, though some research is broader in scope and encompasses additional domains. For example, Canadian researchers explored the "developmental vulnerability" of children around age 5 and found that more than one hour of time spent daily using an electronic device by themselves was related to developmental vulnerability (the lowest 10th percentile) in the domains of physical, social, emotional, and cognitive developmental health.[1] Another systematic review of research involving more than thirty-eight thousand children ages 2–6 from eleven countries concluded that screen time is related to poorer health in the physical, social-emotional, and cognitive domains.[2] A systematic review of reviews involving children and adolescents reported strong associations between screen time and poorer physical and mental health.[3]

Determining the media's effect on children's well-being is much more nuanced than an exploration of the relationship between screen time and overall health in one or more developmental domains. For example, in their narrative review of studies involving children and youth ages 0–19, Cullen and colleagues found that screen time is related to problems with physical health, such as dry eye disease among both children and adolescents; short-sightedness, especially among children and adolescents using screens up close; hearing loss among both children and adolescents who use earbuds and headphones; and obesity, back/neck pain, and sleep disturbance among children and adolescents.[4] In the cognitive domain, the study found a relationship between screen time and impaired executive control and attention in children under 6 years old, language delays among infants and toddlers, and increased language skills among young children who watched educational screen content. Similarly, the study found that educational viewing was related to increased cognitive performance, while a positive association between screen time and mental health problems was found to be most likely among females.

We can come to two primary conclusions from this brief overview of research reviews about the effect of media use on children. First, children are affected by media. And second, screen time has some effect on some indicators of well-being for some children under some conditions. The use of the ambiguous word "some" is used intentionally to indicate the nuance involved in children's media effects. The rest of the chapter will address both general and nuanced findings about the ways in which media use affects children's well-being in the four primary developmental domains.

Physical Health

Many measures exist to quantify physical health, but body composition is the most common indicator of physical health in research involving children; thus, much of the research related to media and children's physical health concerns children's weight, diet, and exercise.

Weight/Diet/Fitness

Several systematic reviews and meta-analyses have found a significant association between children's screen time and overweight/obesity among children of all ages. For example, a meta-analysis found that children ages 0–7 who used screens for one or more hours per day were significantly more likely to be overweight/obese than those who used screens for less than one hour; similarly, children who used screens for two or more hours per day were more likely to be overweight/obese than those who used screens for less than two hours per day.[5] A meta-analysis among mainly Chinese children and adolescents (ages 6–18) found that using screens for two hours per day was associated with significantly higher risks of overweight/obesity.[6] A main assumption of this type of research is that as screen time increases, physical activity decreases, and the study found evidence to support this assumption— screen time use in excess of two hours per day was associated with a 20 percent increase in poor physical fitness. Yet, another systematic review and meta-analysis of studies involving children and adolescents ages 0–18 likewise found a consistent association between screen time and obesity.[7] Other research suggests that adolescents ages 10–19 from twenty countries at the highest levels of screen time were 1.27 times more likely to develop overweight/obesity than those at the lowest levels of screen time, especially when considering only TV viewing compared to other types of screen use.[8]

Other research suggests media content also affects children's diet. For example, a meta-analysis found that exposure to marketing that promotes fatty, salty, and/or sugary foods and beverages was associated with the amount of food children and adolescents (ages 0–19) eat, the choice of and preference for marketed food, and requests for purchase of the advertised food.[9] Source of screen time also seems to make a difference, with one systematic review concluding that TV viewing was more likely to result in significant changes in weight among children and adolescents compared to computer use and playing video games, possibly because TV contains more food advertising than other mediums.[10] Exposure to food advertising via social media influencers was also related to an increase in unhealthy beverage consumption,[11] and heavy social media use among adolescents in 7th–12th grades was related to higher body mass index (BMI) scores.[12] The relationship between unhealthy food advertising and unhealthy food intake and preferences for those ages 0–18 was more likely among ethnic minority children and low SES children.[13]

Media can also be used to reduce the risk of overweight/obesity and to encourage physical activity. For example, a systematic review found that the use of smartphone interventions was significantly associated with an increase in physical activity among children and adolescents.[14] Technology-based interventions have also been shown to relate to more physical activity and fruit and vegetable consumption.[15] Improving healthy eating and activity habits appears to be a more common outcome of media-based overweight/obesity interventions than decreasing unhealthy behaviors among adolescents.[16] Text- and web-assisted interventions can be effective at encouraging adolescents' participation in exercise programs.[17] Digital interventions aimed at improving diet quality and increasing physical activity appear to be most successful when they incorporate education, goal setting, self-monitoring, and parental involvement.[18] Finally, another systematic review found that digital interventions employing wristbands, smartphones (calling and texting), and computers can be successful at reducing BMI among children and adolescents.[19]

Sleep

Screen time can affect both sleep duration and sleep quality for children at all age levels. For infants and toddlers, higher levels of daily screen time were associated with shorter sleep duration, waking up more often at night, and taking longer to fall asleep.[20] Among preschoolers, daily screen time was associated with having a later bedtime and lower sleep quality. Children ages 0–7 with excessive screen time were twice as likely to experience shorter sleep duration.[21] Some estimates suggest that each additional hour of using a portable electronic device was associated with a six to eleven minute reduction in average daily sleep duration among preschoolers.[22] One systematic analysis found an association between electronic media use and both delayed bedtime and poor sleep quality among children ages 6–12, between screen time and problems falling asleep for adolescents ages 13–15, and between social media use and poor sleep quality for adolescents ages 13–15.[23] Research among youth ages 13–15 shows that heavy Internet users were five times more likely than light Internet users to have shorter sleep duration on school nights.[24] Those who spent high levels of time gaming and watching TV were two to three times more likely to sleep less than seven hours every school night than light gamers and TV watchers. And it is not just time spent on social media that relates to poor sleep quality, as research suggests that different social media activities can affect sleep outcomes. For example, a study involving more than four hundred adolescents ages 12–18 found that adolescents who preferred using Snapchat went to bed later than those who preferred Instagram.[25] The study also found that viewing posts about sports, friends, and family actually resulted in better sleep quality, while using social media excessively or at night resulted in poorer sleep outcomes, suggesting that both social media content and the timing of social media use are important factors in the relationship between screen time and sleep outcomes.

Screen devices can also be used to help improve sleep outcomes. For example, Canadian adolescents and young adults ages 15–24 who used a sleep app called DOZE for four weeks reported better sleep efficiency, total amount of time sleeping, and fewer troubles falling asleep.[26] Use of another app, Sleep Ninja, for six weeks predicted improvements in insomnia and sleep quality among Australian adolescents ages 12–16.[27] And in Japan, parent–child use of Nenne Navi, a sleep hygiene app, combined with watching an educational health video about sleep health, resulted in improved sleep habits for young children.[28]

Sexual Health

An abundance of research shows that adolescents' screen use relates to their sexual health behaviors and cognitions. A Dutch study involving adolescents ages 12–14 found that boys who watched two or more hours per day of TV, and girls who used the computer for two or more hours daily, were significantly more likely to have engaged in sex at an earlier age.[29] Among southern U.S. adolescents, the likelihood of ever having had sex was higher for those at high levels of TV use and recreational computer use, especially among those who use screens for six or more hours daily.[30] The same study found that using screen media for three or more hours daily was related to the likelihood of ever having had sex, having sex before age 11, and having three or more sexual partners. In addition, sending more than one hundred text messages per day was related to greater involvement with risky sex among Latino adolescents in the United States.[31] Greater exposure to sexual media content was positively associated with initiation of intercourse one to two years later, and even with subsequent pregnancy.[32] Some evidence suggests that social media use was more likely to relate to early sexual activity for girls than for boys.[33] In Taiwan, 7th and 8th grade students' exposure to sexually explicit media was related to early sexual activity, unsafe sex, and multiple sexual partners in young adulthood.[34] Upon first viewing pornography, 11- to 16-year-olds in the United Kingdom experienced curiosity, sexual arousal, shock, and confusion, and these decreased upon repeated viewing, suggesting a catharsis effect.[35] Older boys reported a desire to act out the behaviors they see in pornography; overall 44 percent of boys and 29 percent of girls said that exposure to pornography gave them ideas about sexual behaviors they wanted to try out.

Like with other outcomes already noted, media can be used positively to educate about and encourage healthy sex-related cognitions and engagement in healthy sexual behaviors. For example, in 2019–2020 nearly eight hundred 9th and 10th graders from seventeen different high schools across the United States participated in a study testing the efficacy of an Internet-based sexual health program.[36] The study found that students in the treatment group had improved sexual health knowledge and more accurate beliefs about the frequency of risky teen sex. The treatment also helped increase girls' sexual health communication with parents and reduce boys' acceptance of dating violence. In another study, the sexual health attitudes and knowledge of minority adolescents were supported by using a video game structured around the theme of the social nature of decision making, with a focus on sexual health and risk.[37] Similarly, participation in a series of Internet-based lessons about sexual health resulted in increased self-efficacy related to negotiating with others to protect their personal rules related to sexual health, increased knowledge about what constitutes a healthy relationship, more reasons for not having sex, greater self-efficacy for using condoms, and greater intentions to abstain from sex until marriage.[38] Beyond the role of interventions, less exposure to sexually explicit media content among Belgian teens ages 15–18 was related to a decreased notion of women as sex objects, which in turn related to less resistance toward the MeToo movement of the late 2010s.[39]

Substance Use

For some children and adolescents, media use is related to substance use. A meta-analysis of studies involving more than sixty-seven thousand adolescents ages 12–18 in sixteen countries found a significant association between social media use and adolescents' use of a variety of substances.[40] Exposure to alcohol marketing/advertising was likewise related to youths' initiation of alcohol use and binge/hazardous drinking.[41] Likewise, increased exposure to medical marijuana advertising was related to middle schoolers' marijuana use and intentions to use.[42] In addition, exposure to tobacco content on social media was related to greater odds of lifetime tobacco use, past thirty-day tobacco use, and susceptibility to tobacco use.[43]

Because of the strength of the associations between exposure to substances in the media and substance use, much effort over several decades has been made to use media to discourage children and adolescents from engaging in substance use. Adolescents' exposure to smoking cessation interventions on social media was effective at increasing rates of tobacco abstinence in the past seven days.[44] Use of social media, texting, and mobile phone apps for alcohol use interventions was also effective at encouraging reduced alcohol consumption among adolescents and young adults.[45] And among Nigerian youth, a social-media based intervention was effective at reducing drug abuse propensity both immediately following the intervention and two years later.[46]

Disordered Eating and Body Image

Media use in its various forms is related both correlationally and causally to body image-related cognitions and behaviors. For example, a five-year longitudinal study involving more than 2,500 middle-school and high-school students in the United States found that increased reading of dieting/weight loss magazine articles was related to both unhealthy and extreme weight control behaviors among girls.[47] Reading girl-oriented magazines and listening to the radio were related to an increase in the incidence of eating disorders among Spanish females ages 12–21.[48] Adolescent boys' exposure to media messages about becoming both more muscular and thin predicted their compulsive exercise, and messages about being thin predicted adolescent girls' compulsive exercise.[49] Research has shown that use of appearance-focused social media platforms (Snapchat and Instagram) was related to lower body satisfaction among Australian adolescents through thin-ideal internalizations and comparisons.[50] A study of nearly two thousand adolescents in Austria, Belgium, Spain, and South Korea found that greater use of Instagram and exposure to pornography were both related to self-objectification, which in turn was related to less positive body image,[51] though effects differed by gender and nationality. In Belgium, the more that children ages 8–11 wanted their body to look like those of people in media, felt that media made them want to diet, or thought that physical shape indicates attractiveness, the higher their levels of restraint and concern about weight, eating, and shape were at one-year follow-up.[52] Some research even found that every one-hour increase in daily screen time was related to 1.11 higher odds of binge-eating disorder one year later among children ages 9–10.[53]

Socio-Emotional Well-Being

In 2018, researchers published a meta-analysis of seventy-two studies related to the influence of prosocial media exposure on several socio-emotional competencies among people of all ages.[54] Results showed that prosocial media exposure was related to increases in helping behaviors and prosocial thinking in both children and adolescents. For example, de Leeuw and van der Laan[55] conducted an experiment in which some children ages 7–11 were assigned to watch a video clip portraying helping behaviors from the Disney movie *Cars*, while others watched a clip from *Cars* that did not portray helping behaviors. Those who watched the clip with the helping behaviors were more likely to help others with a puzzle task. Similarly, in what researchers called a randomized controlled trial, researchers worked with parents of children ages 3–5 to substitute prosocial and educational content for violent and non-age-appropriate content.[56] Results showed that children in the intervention group scored significantly higher six months later on a battery of tests designed to measure socio-emotional competence compared to those in a control group. In addition, a meta-analysis of both cross-sectional and experimental research involving more than ten thousand children in fifteen countries found that children who watched *Sesame Street* exhibited higher levels of prosocial reasoning, more favorable attitudes toward members of out-groups, and higher levels of empathy for people with stigmatized identities.[57] A more recent study found that playing an app focused on social skills helped children ages 2–6 use emotional regulation strategies more frequently.[58]

Time spent with media is also related to both positive and negative interpersonal relationship outcomes. For example, a systematic review of forty-nine studies involving children, adolescents, and emerging adults found that social media use introduced challenges related to alienation from peers, family, and school; relational aggression; parent–child relationship quality; and feelings of isolation from others.[59] On the other hand, the study also found that social media use was related to having a sense of belonging, social capital, and both frequency and degree of offline social interactions. Social media use among 10- to 18-year-olds was related over time to more time spent with friends offline.[60] As with other media effects, time is once again not the only media use variable that makes a difference—the ways in which time is spent with media are also important. For example, a study involving more than forty-six thousand Chinese children in grades 4–8 found that using smartphones for playing games, watching video clips, and reading novels were each negatively correlated with the quality of interpersonal relationships between children and their parents, peers, and teachers.[61] On the other hand, the study found that using smartphones for making calls, listening to music, browsing the news, taking online courses, using search engines, using dictionaries, using cameras, using fitness apps, and obtaining life information were each related positively to the quality of interpersonal relationships. Interestingly, results also showed no significant association between using smartphones for social media-related applications and the quality of interpersonal relationships. Relatedly, a study that employed semi-structured interviews with twelve Norwegian high-school students found that online relationships were considered affiliative, while offline relationships were more amenable to attachment.[62]

Mental Health

In the midst of the Covid-19 pandemic in the United States, three organizations (American Academy of Pediatrics, American Academy of Child and Adolescent Psychiatry, and Children's Hospital Association) jointly declared a U.S. national state of emergency in children's mental health.[63] Then, in 2023, U.S. Surgeon General Vivek Murthy issued an advisory in which he said, "The current body of evidence indicates that while social media may have benefits for some children and adolescents, there are ample indicators that social media can also have a profound risk of harm to the mental health and well-being of children and adolescents."[64]

Evidence to support these two assertions—one, that the mental health of children and youth has deteriorated, and two, that the media has played a role in that decline—is abundant. The mental health crisis appears to have been worsening for decades, though changes to both the prevalence of mental illness among children and youth and to the media landscape since the early 2010s suggest that some sort of connection indeed exists between media use and mental health. For example, in 2010 approximately 3.9 out of every 100,000 youth in the United States died by suicide; by 2020, that number had risen to 6.3—a 62 percent increase.[65] A meta-analysis of research involving approximately eighty thousand youth worldwide found that 20 percent of youth experienced anxiety symptoms during the Covid-19 pandemic.[66] A thirty-seven-country study involving more than one million 15- and 16-year-olds found that rates of loneliness increased in thirty-six of the thirty-seven countries and that almost twice as many youth had elevated levels of loneliness in 2018 than in 2012.[67] And rates of depression among adolescents ages 12–17 increased from 8.1 percent in 2009 to 15.8 percent in 2019, before the start of the pandemic.[68]

A parallel increase in the media use of children and adolescents was observed during roughly the same timeframe. In 2012, for example, 41 percent of U.S. teens ages 13–17 had their own smartphone, compared to 89 percent in 2018.[69] Among 8- to 12-year-olds, time spent using entertainment screen media increased from four hours twenty-six minutes daily in 2015 to five hours 33 minutes in 2021; teens' entertainment screen use increased from six hours forty minutes to eight hours thirty-nine minutes during the same span.[70] Use of Instagram and Snapchat among U.S. teens ages 13–17 increased by 10 percent and 18 percent, respectively, from 2014/15 to 2022.[71]

It would be easy to jump to the conclusion that increases in media ownership and use among children and youth are *the* cause of the rise in rates of mental health problems. But as with all other media use outcomes, many interrelated factors are part of the recipe for mental health problems. In an April 2024 address at the Stanford Cyber Policy Center, media researcher Dr. Patti Valkenburg said that two of the many reasons for an increase in cases of mental illness among youth include "concept creep," or the trend of more and milder mental issues progressively considered mental health problems, as well as the unintended normalization of mental health issues by mental health awareness initiatives in the last decade.[72] "The decline in mental health has accelerated in the last decade," she said. "The decline in mental health did not suddenly start in the early 2010s . . . but the evidence does suggest that due to a sizeable expansion of causes of explanation it did accelerate in the past decade." Evidence suggests that media use is among those causes.

Before the pandemic, researchers reviewed the scholarly literature about children's media use, anxiety, and depression.[73] In their review, the authors explored research dating back to the 1930s showing that media use is related to fear, social comparison, and dissatisfaction with self. As early as 2012, they noted, research began to show an association between social networking and depression among high school students.[74] In terms of causality, they cited research by Nesi and Prinstein showing that social media use for social comparison and feedback-seeking was associated with depressive symptoms over time.[75] They then summarized research showing that the use of digital media is related to problems with emotion regulation: "Adolescents may seek digital distraction from emerging anxiety or distress emotions, creating a reinforced behavioral avoidance of emotional experiences,"[76] and that those who suffer from social anxiety who choose "to substitute digital media for interpersonal communication to avoid feared situations may become cyclically reinforced over time, making the person even more avoidant and worsening the symptoms and severity of social anxiety disorder."[77] This argument was substantiated in cross-sectional research among emerging adults showing that those who had difficulties with emotion regulation also felt greater stress, which contributed to mental health problems, which, in turn, related to greater use of social media.[78] In addition, the study provided evidence for the cyclical reinforcement of impaired emotion regulation as social media use was also found to precipitate difficulties with emotion regulation, which in turn related to stress and mental health problems. Among 12- to 15-year-olds in the United States, the use of mobile phones and TV viewing were associated with higher levels of depression one year later.[79] A meta-analysis likewise found that screen time was significantly associated with both depression and anxiety among children ages 12 and younger.[80] And in the aforementioned thirty-seven-country study of adolescent loneliness, researchers found that even when accounting for unemployment, income inequality, fertility rates, and GDP, both smartphone access and Internet use were significant predictors of adolescents' loneliness.[81]

In terms of media content, a 2023 review of research related to social media use and depression and anxiety among those ages 12–26 concluded that social media activities such as multitasking, appearance-based activities, passive media use, excessive social media use, cyberbullying, and sexting were related to poorer mental health outcomes.[82] Adolescents who brought internalizing symptoms to their media experiences were also more likely to report that they compare themselves negatively to others while on social media.[83]

On the other hand, the ways in which media is used can make a difference in the valence or nature of mental health outcomes. For example, a study of adults in the United Kingdom, Norway, the United States, and Australia found that using social media for entertainment was related to poorer mental health, but using it for personal contact or for maintaining relationships was associated with better mental health.[84] A systematic review and meta-analysis of research involving youth ages 10–24 found that one-to-one communication, self-disclosure to online friends, and exposure to positive or funny online experiences helped reduce feelings of loneliness and stress.[85] In addition, adolescents often use social media and the Internet to find information about mental health and to build communities of like-minded individuals for support,[86] to give and receive support from others who are likewise struggling with mental health problems,[87] and to proactively cope with feelings of anxiety.[88]

Cognitive Development/Academic Performance

As one indicator of (or proxy for) cognitive development, academic performance is of interest to parents, teachers, and policymakers, and media use is related to children's performance on several important measures. A meta-analysis of sixty-three studies involving more than eleven thousand children ages 0–6 found an overall positive association between screen media exposure and vocabulary learning.[89] Another meta-analysis and systematic review involving forty-two studies with nearly nineteen thousand participants found a negative association between time spent with screens and child language skills; however, the same study found that time spent with "quality" screen content, such as educational content, was positively associated with the language skills of children ages 0–12.[90]

Subject-specific media use also helps children learn both generally and in specific subject areas. One study defined academic performance as students' average grade for eleven subjects.[91] The study, which included youth ages 5–17 in Australia, found an association between meeting screen guidelines (spending less than two hours daily with a variety of screen media) and academic performance. Another study found that using the child-friendly computer coding application *ScratchJr* was related to significant improvements in certain computational thinking and coding skills among children ages 4–6.[92] Use of math and reading apps was related to short- and long-term improvements in certain math and reading competencies.[93] And children's use of transmedia materials related to popular children's programming helped improve children's math knowledge and math vocabulary.[94]

Differences in Susceptibility to Media Effects

Because no two children are alike, no two children are affected by media exposure in exactly the same ways. All we can do as media scholars is generalize about the impact of media on broad categories of children. Restricted in this way, research will never be completely generalizable or prescriptively accurate, but we can claim, to a certain extent, that some childhood characteristics make some children more susceptible to some media effects.

Valkenburg and Peters' Differential Susceptibility to Media Effects Model (DSMM)[95] may be the most widely cited framework for understanding why children respond to media exposure in different ways. The authors argued that individual differences in responses to media exposure are due to differences in the dispositional, developmental, and social characteristics individuals bring to the media experience. While we may never be able to determine the discrete role of media in certain behaviors of a child, we can, with certainty, claim that children are affected by the time they spend with media. And those effects are at least in part determined by what children bring to the viewing experience and, in part by the nature and characteristics of the media content.

Piotrowski and Valkenburg (2015) concluded:

> If we, as scholars, agree that the media's influence on youth is not monolithic, then our empirical approaches should reflect this. By ignoring conditional media effects, not only are we disregarding key theoretical propositions that

are central to many media effects theories but we are also putting ourselves at increased risk for drawing invalid conclusions about the magnitude of media effects . . . It is imperative for our hypotheses to reflect a priori *for whom* media effects should occur.[96]

Media Effects Processes

Understanding, to the extent we can, *that* children are affected by media use is not the same as understanding *how* media use affects children. Media scholars must understand the processes through which media effects operate if we want to make a meaningful contribution to the well-being of children. Thus, a discussion about media effects is incomplete without consideration of the processes through which media generates those effects. The most prominent media effects theories employed by communication researchers since the 1950s, in alphabetical order, include agenda setting, cultivation, diffusion of innovations, dual processing theories (e.g., ELM), entertainment theories (e.g., transportation), framing, information processing theories (e.g., LC4MP), knowledge gap, Laswell's communication model, linear theory, McLuhan's medium theory, medium dependency, mood management/hostile media effect, priming, reasoned action, selective exposure, social learning and social cognitive theories, third-person effect, and uses and gratifications.[97,98,99,100,101] Other prominent, relevant mass and interpersonal communication theories include communication privacy management, uncertainty reduction, protection motivation, identity management, health disclosure decision-making model, expectancy violations, health belief model, theory of planned behavior, models of entertainment-education, and others.

When it comes to children, theories from other disciplines are likewise employed, and necessary, to better understand media effects. For example, children at different stages of development both choose and react to media in different ways, necessitating that research be grounded in theories of human development. A classic theory, or model, that has ties to many other theories or models in human development is Piaget's theory of human development.[102] Other relevant theories include those related to theory of mind, memory development, language development, moral reasoning and moral development, executive function, the work and theorizing of Vygotsky, and theories of biological development.

Because media use must be seen in the social context in which it occurs, theories, models, and constructs of social cognition and social psychology are likewise important for our understanding of children's media choices and effects. Such theories, models, and constructs include, but are not limited to, social identity, social learning, social exchange, schema, self-determination, social comparison, culture, race and ethnicity, religion, parents, peers, brain development and neuroscience, evolutionary developmental psychology, socialization, social facilitation, attachment, human and environmental ecology, physical environments, gender, educational settings, siblings, social penetration, play, cooperation, mental states, modeling, imitation, and many more.

There is still much that we do not know about how media affects children. The consistent introduction of new technologies, including autonomous agents, leaves the field playing a constant game of catch-up. It seems that media is not only a large part of children's lives, but it is becoming increasingly so. That does not mean that children are left alone to navigate environments that are becoming ever more mediated, but it does mean that parents must continue to adapt their parenting strategies to meet the unique challenges and opportunities children encounter. Media parenting has always been essential to helping children acquire the benefits and avoid the risks associated with media use. And if something essential can become even more so, then media parenting is a good candidate to write a new definition of "essential" in the lives of the next generation.

Chapter 4

ROOTS AND EVOLUTION OF MEDIA PARENTING

Children learn lessons about life and about how to behave from the interactions they have with people, groups, and institutions in society—socialization agents. Seen within the lens of Bronfenbrenner's ecological systems theory,[1] socialization agents may have differing levels of influence throughout the span of childhood and include agents at all levels of children's ecology. But the socialization agents of highest import appear to include children's families, peers, teachers, religious communities, ethnicity, political climate,[2,3] and increasingly, media. And among these, perhaps the most influential are parents and media.[4] The interplay between parents, children, and media becomes a relationship of supreme importance in children's socialization. In their efforts to help their children become, to facilitate the development of their character, and help them be contributing members of society, parents must account for media influences in their socialization efforts.

Until now, the relationship between parents, children, and media has been known by scholars as "parental mediation." Parental mediation refers to parents' efforts to guide children toward getting the most out of potentially beneficial media content, as well as safeguarding them against the potential risks resulting from exposure to less beneficial media content. Parental mediation is a "socialization practice"[5] that includes all the strategies parents adopt to "regulate, discuss and monitor children's media use."[6] We are now in the sixth decade of employing the words "parental mediation" to refer to parent–child media-related interactions. But in this chapter I will argue that the label "parental mediation" is no longer sufficient to describe the parent–child–media relationship. Some may wonder if the label we give to this relationship matters as long as we continue to provide research that gives parents tools. I will argue, however, just as Lang and Ewoldsen argued, that "words are powerful and that the words we choose to describe what we do influence both what we choose to do and how we are perceived."[7] Our choice of words to describe the parent–child–media relationship has implications for the types of questions we ask, the ways we design studies, and the conclusions we draw from our research. A new label for this research sub-discipline may help to better align our questions, methods, and conclusions with contemporary ways of thinking about both parenting and the agentic, mind embodied nature of children themselves.

To understand how we arrived at the point of considering a change in words used to describe this area of study, it is beneficial to look at the beginnings of "parental mediation." The term "mediation" hearkens back to its introduction and use by Vygotsky,[8,9] whose ideas originated in the first half of the twentieth century and gradually made their way from Russian psychology into Western ideas of child development. Karpov explained:

> According to Vygotsky, mediation is the process of equipping children with mental tools, the instruments they will need for mediating their mental processes. Mediation begins with an adult's involving children in the course of shared activity, with the goal of solving a problem . . . Gradually, the adult passes greater and greater responsibility to the child. The adult also facilitates the child's internalization of the newly acquired tool. As a result, the child's activity, which began as a shared child–adult activity that was mediated by an external tool turn into the child's independent activity that is now mediated by the child's internalized representation of the mental tool. When that occurs, the process of Vygotskian mediation is successful and completed.[10]

Within this view, the parent is seen as a wiser, more knowledgeable adult who facilitates children's learning through guided experiences in which children take on more and more of the responsibility of learning, until they have internalized and mastered the concept for themselves. Much of Vygotsky's discussion about mediation focused on children's learning of self-regulation, arguing that parents must first tell a child what is and is not acceptable behavior, which leads to a child telling themselves what is and is not acceptable behavior, and ultimately to the child internalizing the behavior without the need of any sort of verbal or non-verbal reminder. Parents do not determine a child's behavior, but supply the child with tools so the lesson becomes their own. In other words, parents can influence the mind and behavior of children by giving them a framework within which to make decisions.

The term "parental mediation" was used prior to 1960, but in the context of parenting and child rearing more generally[11] and in a time when television was just entering the American mainstream. It is not exactly clear when the term "parental mediation" was first introduced into research related to the relationship between parents, children, and media, but by the late 1970s and early 1980s researchers began using the term with regularity. Through the 1980s and 1990s, parental mediation research focused mostly on children's experiences with television content. Then, in the mid-2000s, researchers began consistently exploring parental mediation in the context of children's video game and Internet use. Today, children use an astonishingly wide array of media for an equally astonishing number of purposes, and parental mediation researchers are doing their best to keep up with current trends and understand the ways that parents and children interact with these media and each other.

What has not changed across these decades of research is the term "parental mediation." For a number of reasons, however, "parental mediation" no longer makes sense as the primary umbrella term used to describe this specific type of parenting. First, "parental mediation" is not exclusive to the media context. Mediation, according to its Vygotskian origins, refers to adults teaching children, and can presumably include adults such as other family members, religious leaders, coaches, and others. Speaking strictly semantically, "mediation," then, refers to any adult-driven effort to teach a child to adopt a lesson, skill, characteristic, or quality as their own, regardless of context. In the family context, some might even argue that "mediation" is simply another word for parenting, making "parental mediation" a redundant form of "parental parenting." In Vygotskian parlance, "parental mediation" could refer to a parent's attempts to help a child to choose not to throw toys at their siblings, to eat their vegetables at dinner, or to ride a bike without training wheels. But somewhere along the way communication scholars claimed "parental mediation" as their own, leaving parenting scholars to find other labels for the daily mediation of children's non-media behaviors. It is true that parental mediation in the context of children's media use includes a nice play on words, but this play on words has the effect of excluding all non-media parental mediation from its connotation, something that I am not sure Vygotsky had in mind.

Next, "parental mediation" connotes parents serving an intermediary role, suggesting that their role is to stand between children and media. While this certainly was not the meaning originally ascribed to "mediation," today's connotation of the word outside the realms of academia implies that the way parents help guide children's media use is by serving as a barrier between media and children. In this sense, the sole role of a parent is to protect children from media, an idea that does not coincide with Vygotsky's conceptualization of mediation nor with the reality of today's media environment. This type of protection mediation is akin to removing the TV from the house, or the parent being the only person able to use the TV remote. It is prevention of media effects through prevention of exposure. This may have been possible in the 1980s and 1990s when TV was the main source of media exposure for children, but it is not possible now given the saturation of devices in the lives of children. Even for children without a TV in the house, with Internet access only on a shared computer in a public area of the house, or without a smartphone, as soon as they leave the house they become susceptible to media exposure. The exposure parents try to prevent may occur on friends' devices, in the classroom, in the check-out aisle at the grocery store, on billboards, listening to the radio, or even indirectly through conversations with peers. Complete prevention today is not only not possible, but research shows that it may not even be advisable, especially for older children and adolescents.

Third, "parental mediation" implies conflict resolution. A mediator is somebody that helps two parties come to an amicable, or if not amicable, acceptable agreement. This type of mediation is intended to resolve conflicts between two parties. In the case of parents, children, and media, a parent mediator would expect to resolve conflicts between children and the media they consume, but in actuality, the parent is really trying to resolve conflicts between media content and their own values and expectations for their child. And in attempting to resolve the conflict between media content and parents' values, parents can actually create unintended conflict between the parent and child.[12]

Lastly, "parental mediation" connotes both theoretical and statistical mediation. For example, a researcher might suggest that time spent with social media leads to mental health problems because it first leads to loneliness—loneliness, in this case, mediates the relationship between time spent with social media and mental health problems. Statistical procedures are now easily conducted with typical software packages to determine if the relationship between an independent variable and a dependent variable is due to the relationship of each with an intervening variable. "Parental mediation" implies that a parent's effort to engage with children about media is something that happens after media exposure but before an effect. In some cases, this is a completely plausible process for media effects, but it does not account for parent–child media-related interactions that happen before or during media exposure. It allows only for these interactions to occur after the child's media activity, and research shows that the timing of such a parental intervention makes a difference in the outcomes of media exposure.[13] It also precludes the possibility of parent–child media-related interactions serving as a moderator, or variable upon which associations are conditioned, in a media effects process.

Media Parenting

To resolve the difficulties created by the label "parental mediation," I propose the use of a logical and theoretically sound alternative: "media parenting." "Media parenting" as an umbrella term has numerous benefits, as well as advantages over "parental mediation."

First, media parenting encourages researchers to more fully embed our focus on media effects and media effects processes within the parenting scholarship. A cursory online search reveals research related to food parenting, sport parenting, spiritual parenting, academic parenting, emotion parenting, cultural parenting, and financial parenting. Vygotskian mediation can presumably occur in each of these parenting contexts, as well as in the media context. Media parenting as a research discipline has grown to the extent that it is worthy of its own context. As such, scholars in tangential disciplines may find it easier to find media parenting than parental mediation for the simple reason that the name itself has a parallel structure to parenting in other contexts.

Next, media parenting adjusts the connotation of parenting serving a primarily protective role to serving a supportive and responsive role in the process of children's socialization, a shift that more fully aligns the field with the original meaning of mediation and with current knowledge about what constitutes effective parenting. Mediation constitutes just one form of, or strategy for, parenting. Scholars agree, however, that "there appears to be no universal 'right way' to parent, and contexts of many sorts matter to the expression and consequences of parenting,"[14] and that "parents possess a keen desire to improve the lives and well-being of their children, and happily a remarkable bank of credible scientific information is accruing about parenting and its effects on children to guide them."[15] This body of work includes research about the characteristics of parenting that have consistently been shown to be effective at propagating positive outcomes for children. Media parenting, rather than parental mediation, is better equipped to accommodate the variety of parenting practices that constitute effective parenting. It allows parents to be considered in one or more of the developmentally appropriate positions throughout childhood as guides, modelers, monitors, gatekeepers, protectors, and providers. In other words, media parenting more effectively facilitates the incorporation of child-centered parenting strategies into efforts to understand effective parenting in the media context.

Whereas parental mediation implies an intentional effort to influence children's media exposure or the effects of media on children, media parenting suggests that all media-related parenting behaviors, whether intentional or not, explicit or implicit, constitute a parent's influence on children. For example, an unintentional media parenting behavior that is not nicely encapsulated by parental mediation, but which can be considered media parenting, is parents' own media use. Parents' media use is perhaps the strongest predictor of children's media use.[16,17] If all parents' media use occurred because of an intentional effort to guide children's media use and affect media use outcomes, then parents' media use might rightly be described as parental mediation. But not all parents' media use is intended to influence children's relationship with media. Phubbing, for instance, refers to ignoring someone in favor of giving one's attention to a digital device. Parental phubbing, then, refers to a parent using a digital device, such as a smartphone, during interactions with their child.[18] We cannot reasonably assume that phubbing constitutes a parent's intentional effort to parent. It is, however, a manifestation of unintentional, ineffective parenting that is related to higher levels of both children's media use and children's problematic media use.[19,20] Similarly, research related to parent–child "coviewing" is beset with problems related to the intentionality of a parent's participation in a media activity together with a child. Parents understand that to accomplish some household tasks it is sometimes helpful to turn the TV on to direct a child's attention away from the parent. If the parent's task takes place in the same room as the child's TV watching, this technically constitutes coviewing. Such coviewing effects have been explained as implicit approval of the media content,[21] even if the parent does not participate in the activity jointly with the child. Media parenting, and not parental mediation, better accounts for the unintentionality of such parenting practices.

Finally, media parenting implies a relationship between parent and child, while parental mediation implies parents' one-way parenting. In other words, media parenting more fully aligns media parenting research with research in the fields of child development and child psychology related to best practices in parenting and the establishment of successful parent–child relationships. A parent–child relationship suggests give and take and a parent's regard for the child's skills, emotions, and development. Media parenting better allows for additional consideration of sensitive parenting, autonomy-supportive parenting, cooperation in making media decisions, and other applications of the characteristics of authoritative parenting. Whether it occurs through mediation as originally defined, or through other strategies, "parenting is the process of supporting and promoting a child's physical, emotional, mental, and social development."[22] This is accomplished through "quality of instructions, animation, cognitive stimulation, physical care, parent-child synchrony, sensitivity, and positive responsiveness."[23] Media parenting encourages much more research related to the role of these types of parenting strategies and characteristics in the context of children and media. This research, in turn, may be based on different research questions and be explored through different methodologies that are more securely connected to the theorizing and findings from parenting research in other contexts.

Media Parenting Model

With the term media parenting and its ties to parenting research now established, we can create a model of media parenting behaviors that encapsulates previous media parenting research related to both TV and newer digital media while allowing space for future media and types of children's media use. The Media Parenting Model (MPM, Figure 4.1) incorporates media parenting behaviors previously identified under the parental mediation umbrella—"active mediation," "restrictive mediation," and "coviewing"—but uses different labels to more directly connect media parenting concepts to ongoing parenting research in multiple disciplines. It also adds additional categories of media parenting to better capture the range of media parenting behaviors in which parents engage. Proposing the MPM is, in part, a response to scholars' conclusions that there is no consensus about a typology of media parenting in the digital age,[24] and in part a response to the maturation of the state of media parenting research. In the MPM, media parenting can take the form of (1) parental media modeling, (2) parental media monitoring, (3) parental media control, (4) parent–child media conversations, and (5) joint media engagement.

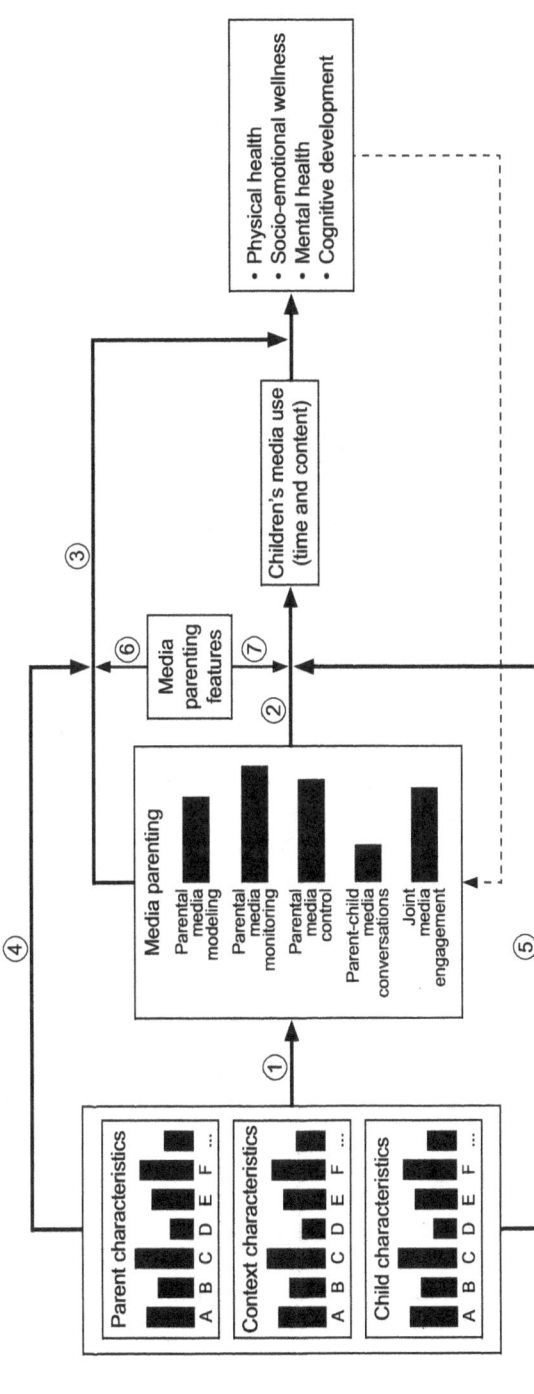

Figure 4.1 Media Parenting Model.

Parental Media Modeling

Parental media modeling refers to parents' own media use behaviors. To understand the role of parents' own media use behaviors in children's media use behaviors it is helpful to understand parenting within the framework of social learning. One of the primary ways children learn is through observation. Explained by Bandura[25] and others since, social learning theory suggests that people model the behavior of important others in their life. But social learning among children is more than simple imitation of their parents. As agentic beings, children consider information and beliefs related to the behavior, the modeler, and themselves. They are active participants in the behavior decision-making process and make inferences about behaviors and about other people by active observation.[26] They tend to model the behaviors of those they consider to be teachers, those they perceive to be competent, similar others, and those with perceived high status.[27] For children, the strongest and most influential models are often their parents or other primary caregivers.

Parent modeling has an impact on many child behaviors. A simplistic example suggests that children can learn to avoid touching a hot stove by touching a hot stove, or they can observe what happens when somebody else touches a hot stove. Similarly, they can learn language by imitating the sounds of parents and others, and they can learn how to interact with others by observing how their parents interact with others. And a growing body of evidence shows that parents' media use is related to children's media use. For example, one study showed that parent media use and attitudes were strongly associated with the media use of children and adolescents[28]—the addition of parent media use nearly doubled the variance in children's media use explained by a regression model that included child age, child gender, parent age, parent gender, parent education, income, race/ethnicity, attitudes about media, rules for children's media use, and enforcement of those rules. The authors concluded, "Even among older children and adolescents who presumably have more independence and choice with their own media use, parental media use time is still the strongest predictor of youth media use time."[29] In some research, parents' media use is considered to be a construct separate from media parenting behaviors generally, but the MPM considers parental media modeling to be a type of media parenting, whether parents' engage in media use with or without the intent to influence children's media use.

Parental Media Monitoring

Parental monitoring has been explored, explicated, and reinterpreted in a number of ways over many years. In the 1990s, parental monitoring was defined as "a set of correlated parenting behaviors involving attention to and tracking of the child's whereabouts, activities, and adaptations."[30] By 2010, parental monitoring was conceptualized as knowledge, solicitation, and control, which refer, respectively, to parents' knowledge of children's activities, asking for information from children, and setting rules about children's information disclosure.[31] Under these and similar conceptualizations, parental monitoring has been found to relate to numerous outcomes, such as better academic performance, better mental health, lower levels of sexual activity, and less delinquency.[32] Parenting monitoring was also associated with less adolescent sexual risk behavior,[33] prevention or delay of substance use,[34] lower levels of youth aggression,[35] and less antisocial behavior.[36]

It is difficult to determine the effect of parental *media* monitoring on children's media use and media use outcomes because of the collectively haphazard nature of the conceptualization of parental monitoring of media. For example, most parental media monitoring research equates the construct to other media parenting behaviors—parental monitoring of media has been characterized as only restrictive mediation,[37] as a combination of "active" and "restrictive mediation,"[38] and as a combination of the three main types of "parental mediation."[39] Another study operationalized parental media monitoring via five measures, including frequency of personally monitoring children's access to social media, solicitation, communication about appropriate and inappropriate online behavior, intrusive monitoring, and rule-setting about social media use.[40] Thus, the disparate and inaccurate nature of the conceptualization and operationalization of parental monitoring in the context of children's media use makes it impossible to paint of picture of the role of parental monitoring in the mediated lives of children.

Due to the various ways parental monitoring is conceptualized in multiple disciplines, scholars are considering its reconceptualization in the child development and psychology literature. Most recently, parental monitoring has been defined as "all behaviors performed by caregivers with the goal of acquiring information about the youth's activities and life."[41] It is conceptualized as a distinct behavior performed at a given point in time, and is different than a dyadic, over time process that includes elements such as knowledge and control. Thus, consistent with this latest reconceptualization, the MPM defines parental media monitoring as parents' non-dyadic behaviors intended to acquire information about children's media use activities, cognitions, and emotions. Congruent with the differing ways of acquiring information identified by the noted parental monitoring reconceptualization, parental media monitoring is limited to the behaviors meant to acquire information. Thus, parental media monitoring can include (1) asking children directly for media-related information; (2) establishing rules for children's disclosure of media-related information; (3) using technology or other methods to track, monitor, and measure media-related information, whether done surreptitiously or with the child's knowledge; (4) observing children; and (5) asking others to engage in information gathering of children's media-related information.

Parental Media Control

In general parenting literature, parental control refers to a parent's attempt to manage children's behavior "by creating a regulating structure through such actions as supervision, setting limits, and establishing and enforcing household rules,"[42] or as "rules, regulations, and restrictions that parents have for their children."[43] Parental control has been shown to both help and hinder youth. For example, a study involving Swedish youth ages 12–17 found that restrictions were associated with increased norm breaking and depression symptoms for youth who feel over-controlled, while overall, parental control was associated with decreases in norm breaking,[44] likely because parents engage in several types of control: behavioral, psychological, and physical. Behavioral control refers to parental attempts to control children's behavior through the setting of expectations, rules, and guidelines; psychological control involves parents' manipulation of the parent–child relationship to induce shame in order to elicit a desired behavior; and physical control is defined as parents' physical punishment or threats of physical punishment, restriction, or redirection.[45] Among young children, rules can be helpful at reducing externalizing behaviors,[46] but too much control, especially as children progress through childhood and into adolescence, provides "few opportunities for children to self-regulate, and results in an inability to rely on themselves for emotional and behavioral regulation due to an intensive and restrictive approach to discipline,"[47] which is antithetical to Vygotsky's concept of mediation. Behavioral control can concurrently help improve academic achievement and induce children's anxiety, though parental control looks and functions differently in different cultures.[48] Psychological control has been shown to relate to adolescents' anxiety.[49] Even among emerging adults, parental psychological control is related to anxiety, depressive symptoms, and antisocial personality problems.[50] A meta-analysis confirmed that a relationship exists between parental psychological control and youths' problem behaviors.[51] Some research even shows that parental control may be associated with behavioral compliance, but not with children's inhibition and emotion regulation.[52]

In the context of media parenting, "parental media control" refers to parents' attempt to manage children's media use, cognitions, and emotions through the development, implementation, and enforcement of rules related to children's media use. Parental media control, heretofore known primarily as "restrictive mediation," is intended to protect children from undesirable media content and its potentially undesirable effects, and research shows that the effects of parental media control mirror those of parenting control generally. For example, young children tend to respond more positively to parental media control than older children—parental media control was related to reduced aggression among elementary school children,[53] lower levels of problematic video game use among children ages 3–9,[54] and higher levels of emotion regulation and lower levels of impulsivity among pre-adolescents and adolescents.[55] Parental media control can also reduce time spent with media among elementary school children.[56] However, parental media control often backfires among adolescents, and was related to adolescents' less positive attitudes toward parents, more positive attitudes toward restricted content, and increased viewing of restricted content.[57]

Parental media control may also include "parental induction," which refers to the "communication of expectations or rules for conduct" for children's media use.[58] Features of parental induction may include direct communication of rules to children, parents' explicit justification for media rules, sanctioning (or consequences) for rule violation, and managing compliance with parents' media rules.[59] It may also include parent–child negotiation of rules for children's media use. Parental induction is a construct that bridges the media parenting behaviors of conversation, monitoring, and control, and future research may provide insights allowing for a clearer categorization of parental induction within the MPM.

Parent–Child Media Conversations

"Parent–child media conversations" refers to the substance of media-related communication or discussion, whether the conversations occur before, during, or after individual or joint media use. Generally referred to as "active mediation" until now, "parent–child media conversations" refers to both one-way and two-way, verbal and non-verbal parent–child media-related expressions of feelings, thoughts, values, and needs.[60] Parent–child media conversations can be intentionally designed to affect children's media use and cognitions, or can include other comments without such a purpose but which may have unintentional effects on children's media use and cognitions.

Research under the label of "active mediation" has identified several types of parent–child media conversations, such as factual and evaluative statements about media content,[61] discussions about benefits and risks of media use,[62] and conversations related to "the meaning of the content and its influence."[63] While parental media monitoring refers to the behaviors parents employ to acquire information about children's media use and cognitions, including the asking of questions, parent–child media conversations can include children's disclosure of that information to parents. And since disclosure comprises part of parent–child media conversations, so too must a consideration of aspects of communication that either facilitate disclosure or that act as a barrier to disclosure. For example, research in health information disclosure suggests that individuals consider many things when deciding whether or not to disclose information to another person, such as their own knowledge or perceptions about a topic, perceptions of aspects of the potential recipient of the disclosure, and perceptions of both their ability to disclose the information and of the expected outcomes of the disclosure.[64] In the context of parent–child media conversations, children's disclosure of their media activities and of their attitudes or feelings about media content may depend on their perceptions of their own media literacy, perceptions of the appropriateness of their media activities or cognitions, a consideration of the expected response of their parents to the disclosure, and perceptions of their ability to make the disclosure and of the disclosure's ability to have positive outcomes. Similarly, while parental media monitoring constitutes parents' attempts to learn information that children may be hiding about their media use, parent–child media conversations should consider adolescents' media-related secret keeping efforts. In this way, media parenting may be seen as a dynamic, ever-evolving process that includes multiple media parenting behaviors performed simultaneously, in response to children's actions, in preparation for children's expected actions, and over time.

Joint Media Engagement

Joint engagement is "the ability the coordinate attention toward a social partner and an object of mutual interest."[65] Joint engagement is related to joint attention. Joint attention is the process of coordinating engagement with someone else, while joint engagement results when the attention has become shared either passively or in coordination with another person.[66] Bakeman and Adamson[67] distinguished between two types of joint engagement: passive joint engagement and coordinated joint engagement. Passive joint engagement, also referred to as supported joint engagement, refers to someone, such as a parent, attending to the same object as their child while the child's attention is fixed on the object. Coordinated joint engagement refers to both parent and child focusing on the same object while switching their focus between the object and each other. Research shows that joint engagement is related to a host of positive outcomes for children, such as children's early word learning[68] and language development,[69] theory of mind,[70] improvement in conduct problems,[71] social competence,[72] and relational quality.[73]

By definition, parent–child joint engagement can occur in any number of settings and contexts, including when using media. The joint participation in a media activity between parent and child uses the term "joint media engagement" in the MPM, and is conceptualized by others as "the new coviewing,"[74] since joint media engagement "extends the notion of coviewing to a wide range of modern media."[75] Joint media engagement refers to "viewing, playing, searching, reading, contributing, and creating" together with media.[76] Joint media engagement can facilitate quality interactions that involve conversations, such as asking questions and labeling objects,[77] but it does not encapsulate the feelings, thoughts, values, and needs that are explicitly communicated during the joint media engagement experience. Certainly, both joint media engagement and parent–child media conversations can happen concurrently, but the MPM considers them separate and distinct constructs. In addition, joint media engagement does not include any parent–child media conversations that occur outside of joint media engagement experiences. Joint media engagement can be either intentional or unintentional, "spontaneous and designed."[78]

A review of research related to joint media engagement found that joint media engagement can occur with or without parent–child media conversations and that joint media engagement is associated with decreased parent language quantity and quality compared to joint engagement in other activities, such as book reading and playing with toys.[79] Results also suggest that parents do not devote as much attention or interest during digital media activities as they do when participating in non-media activities with their child. Joint media engagement also appears to elicit less warmth from both parents and children during device use than it does during toy play or book reading.

Child-Centered Media Parenting

Every parent knows that no two children are alike. As a result, parenting strategies that prove effective for one child may not be similarly effective for their sibling. In other words, each individual, as an agentic being, has the capacity to surprise even their parents by the way they exercise their agency when responding to parenting efforts. If the essence of media parenting is to influence children[80] then it must also be targeted, for homogenous persuasion will likely fail to sufficiently capture the attention and alter the behavior of a heterogenous audience. Media parenting should thus be person-centered, specific, and tailored to the developmental stage and needs of each child.

But in our efforts to understand and enact media parenting, let us remember that childhood agency as a construct is not binary, as cultures that tend to the individualistic might suggest. It should not be understood that a child either has or does not have agency. Each has agency, but children's ability to choose their behavior and their belief in their ability to make effective choices must be considered within the contexts of culture, family history, geography, political climate, macro- and micro-level societal norms and expectations, structural influences, religion, financial circumstances, race, and many more. In short, children's agency is exercised within the ecology, and the levels of the ecology, within which they live. Abebe put it this way:

> Rather than striving to give children more autonomy from adults, there is a need to create an environment within which children can participate— exercise agency—together with and alongside adults. Instead of focusing on the actor per se, it is useful to explore the actions and interactions of children within social contexts. This approach intersects with the recent resurgence in childhood studies to "bring back" other generations—adults—into the debates on child agency. We need to take a *relational* approach to children's agency, recognizing the respective roles and positions of children and adults as well as how they are connected.[81]

Indeed, as Abebe argues, children's ability to enact agency resides on a continuum, and as such, may ebb and flow as children's activities change, where they are, and the people they are with,[82] including, and perhaps especially, the family. In other words, media parenting efforts both impact and are impacted by the child. What might work today with a child may not work the same way tomorrow. What rules are acceptable in Texas may not ever cross the minds of parents or children in Nigeria. Children are somewhat unpredictable. We may generalize. We may categorize. And we may prescribe media parenting behaviors we believe are most appropriate. But as scientists we can never expect to know as much about a child as the child's parents, and we can never truly fully predict children's responses to media parenting efforts. The best we can do is approximate, and as the following chapters will show, our best scientific efforts have given us a wealth of knowledge with which to understand the dynamic interactions between parents, children, and media.

Chapter 5

PREDICTORS FOR APPROACHES TO MEDIA PARENTING

Media parenting is an important aspect of overall parenting strategy, and accumulated research provides compelling evidence that researchers and policymakers have an obligation to persuade parents to engage in media parenting practices that have been shown to be the most effective. To fulfill that part of our stewardship, it is helpful to first understand which parents engage in which media parenting behaviors, to what extent they engage in those behaviors, and why some parents are more intentional than others in the implementation of media parenting. Predictors of media parenting can be grouped into three primary, interrelated categories: parent characteristics, context characteristics, and child characteristics. These categories are reminiscent of Belsky's process model of the determinants of parenting, which includes contributions from parents, context, and children. Belsky argued, "(1) parenting is multiply determined; (2) with respect to their influence on parenting, characteristics of the parent, of the child, and of the social context are not equally influential in supporting or undermining growth-promoting parenting; and (3) developmental history and personality shape parenting indirectly, by first influencing the broader context in which parent-child relations exist."[1] In other words, parenting is predicted by a combination of one or more characteristics of parents, context, and children. In terms of media parenting, we should expect characteristics from all three domains to work together in an interactive process to determine the types and extent of media parenting strategies in which parents choose to engage.

But first, one caveat. Most of the data we have about media parenting has come to us through cross-sectional research by way of surveys and focus groups. This means that correlational research that conceptualizes one or more forms of media parenting as a predictor must also allow for the possibility that media parenting is also an outcome. This chapter, however, discusses predictors of media parenting as they are conceptualized in the research, and the word "predictor" is used even if it may not necessarily occur before the enactment of media parenting in order to stay true to the theoretical pathways hypothesized by much of the correlational research.

Parent Characteristics

Two general types of parent characteristics have been shown to predict media parenting with some level of consistency: parent cognitions and parent socio-demographics. "Parent cognitions" refers to parents' thoughts and thought processes, and "parent socio-demographics" refers to both the social and demographic attributes of parents.

Attitudes About Media

Primary among parent characteristics that affect media parenting behaviors are parents' attitudes toward media. For example, results of one study showed that parents' concern about children's exposure to relational aggression in the media was positively associated with their engagement in both parent–child media conversations and parental media control.[2] Relatedly, perceptions of media risk were related to parental media control among U.S. children of various ages.[3] Similar results were found among a sample of German-speaking Swiss parents of children ages 3–14.[4] The latter study found that parents' concerns about the possible negative effect of exposure to violent and sexual content were associated with their engagement in parent–child media conversations, and that parents' attitudes about the possible positive effect of educational television on children's development was associated with higher levels of joint media engagement. From a survey of parents of children ages 10–17 in Ireland we likewise learn that parents' worries about online risks and their negative attitudes toward digital technology were associated with engagement in parental media control and parent–child media conversations.[5] Similar results were found in a sample of Belgian parents' of children ages 3 to 9—parental media control was more likely among parents with negative attitudes about digital gaming.[6] In Korea, parents' perceptions of the negative influence of the Internet were related to their engagement in parental media control,[7] and scholars argued that negative attitudes about media are a manifestation of parents' "protective instincts,"[8] causing them to set rules and talk with their children about media content. On the other hand, joint media engagement was more likely when parents expected positive socio-emotional effects of media use, possibly as a manifestation of their interest in the media content and their willingness to share in the media experience with their child.[9]

Media Literacy

Parents' media literacy is next among cognitive factors that predict media parenting behaviors. Media literacy refers to the ability to decode, evaluate, and analyze media content.[10,11] It can also include media skills, such as knowing how to use digital devices and how to produce media content. One study surveyed 177 U.S. parents of children ages 4–11 and found that parents' ability to think critically about media was positively associated with their engagement in both parent–child media conversations and parental media control.[12] Interestingly, the study found that parents' attitudes about media parenting mediated the association between parents' critical thinking about media and their engagement in media parenting. In other words, parents who think about and question media content likewise had positive attitudes about talking with their children about those same thoughts and questions and about setting rules for children's media use. Those attitudes, then, related to their associated behaviors, similar to the connection between attitudes and behaviors in many other contexts. In another study, parents' digital skills were described as the ability to use digital media to achieve positive results for one's well-being,[13] and results showed that digital skills of parents of children younger than age 10 predicted parental media control, results which at first appear inconsistent with other research showing that digital skills of parents of children ages 6–14 were related to less use of parental media control.[14] In the latter research, parents' digital skills were, however, related to more engagement in "enabling mediation," a construct that included what the authors termed active mediation, technical controls, and parental monitoring. In other words, some aspects of parental media control were included in the conceptualization of enabling mediation, which is in part consistent with the results of the former study. Computer/Internet skills of Dutch parents of children ages 2–12 have also been shown to predict their engagement in parental media monitoring.[15] In a sample of highly educated Pakistani parents or caregivers of teens ages 13–19, "good" digital skills were related to parent–child media conversations, parental media control, and parental media monitoring.[16] Internet skills of Czech parents of youth ages 5–17 were likewise related to "active mediation," operationalized as a combination of both parent–child media conversations and joint media engagement, and with parental media monitoring.[17] The Internet skills of six hundred Korean parents of children ages 10–15 were also related to parental media control,[18] while parents in Singapore and Australia with high levels of digital literacy were more likely to engage in parent–child media conversations than in parental media control.[19]

Parenting Efficacy

Parents' beliefs in their own parenting ability likewise play in role in their media parenting. For example, a cross-national study involving parents in Singapore and Australia found that parents who felt confident in their parenting abilities were more likely to engage in parental media monitoring, parental media control, and parent–child media conversations.[20] Similar results were found among U.S. parents of children ages 10–17.[21] Dutch-speaking Belgian parents of adolescents with higher levels of confidence in their ability to help their children navigate advertising and media-related data collection practices were more likely to engage in parental media control and parent–child media conversations.[22] Similarly, Internet-specific parental self-efficacy was related to both parent–child media conversations and parental media control among a national sample of U.S. parents.[23] Digital parenting readiness, of which parents' confidence in their own digital parenting ability comprised part (digital parenting efficacy), was related to parent–child media conversations, parental media control, and parental media monitoring among U.S. parents of 10- to 17-year-olds.[24]

In addition to parenting or media parenting efficacy, it appears that parents' response efficacy, or their belief in media parenting's ability to have beneficial outcomes, may also help determine engagement in media parenting behaviors. Focus groups and interviews involving parents of youth ages 10–17 in three U.S. states found that some parents believed that "mediation practices were not actually effective for protecting adolescents from risks associated with digital media use, or that the payoff from monitoring or limiting media use wouldn't be worth the time and effort."[25] Parents also said that some media parenting, such as monitoring children's smartphone use, is not worth the time, energy, and money because children can communicate online in ways that are not discoverable by parents.

Values

Parents' values drive their engagement in media parenting. Researchers in the Netherlands interviewed twenty-four parents of children ages 6–7 and found that the value of maintaining balance between digital media use and other activities was mentioned most frequently as a motivation for media parenting.[26] In a separate study, parents who valued adolescents' autonomy to make their own media decisions said adolescents "did not need the guardrails around decision making that were enforced through parental monitoring or limits."[27]

If the aforementioned parent characteristics can be described as cognitions, the next category of parental characteristics that have been shown to predict media parenting involves parents' socio-demographics. In the literature, many of these individual attributes are related to media parenting behaviors, though research suggests that socio-demographics may sometimes serve as proxy for other related factors. For example, Taraban and Shaw argued that some parenting traits, such as personality, psychopathology, and behaviors learned from their own parents may keep people in low-income situations. They concluded, "Thus, when considering direct associations between SES and parenting, or the moderating role of SES on associations between contextual predictors and parenting, it is important to keep in mind that SES itself is very unlikely to be a mechanism, and that it represents a broad and varied influence."[28] Nevertheless, in the relative absence of research related to other, more proximal mechanisms, socio-demographic characteristics are now discussed.

Parent Gender

One parent demographic attribute of significance to media parenting is the gender of the parent—that is, whether the media parent is the mother or father. For example, in two-parent households in the Czech Republic, mothers were more likely to engage in both parent–child media conversations and parental media monitoring, suggesting that mothers are more actively involved in media parenting than fathers.[29] In addition, Israeli fathers of youth ages 10–14 were more likely to engage in lower quality communication about pornography with their kids, and thus, engaged in less frequent parent–child media conversations, than did mothers.[30] A U.S. study found that mothers were more likely than fathers to have discussions with children about what they see on television, using apps on a tablet or smartphone, using a computer, playing video games, and using social media.[31] Similar results were found for Dutch parents and their media parenting of children's Internet use[32] and television viewing.[33] Fathers in Hungary were also less likely to engage in parental media control than mothers.[34]

Education and Income

Worldwide, more educated and higher-income parents are more likely to engage in higher amounts and a greater variety of media parenting strategies than their lower SES counterparts. In their review, Koch and colleagues argued that parents with higher socioeconomic status "have the skills and resources necessary" for media parenting, and that "they are often more knowledgeable regarding digital devices, and are likely to invest their resources and knowledge into their children."[35] This was true among parents of children ages 3–6 in China[36] and among parents of youth ages 13–18 in Nigeria.[37] Parents' education level also influences the type of media parenting in which they engage. Parents of children ages 2–12 in the Netherlands with lower levels of education were more likely to engage in parental media control.[38] Similarly, a study involving parents in seven European countries found that less educated parents were more likely to engage in parental media control, and that more educated parents were more likely to engage in both parent–child media conversations and more nuanced, or varied, media parenting activities.[39] In Hungary, relatively more educated parents were more likely to engage in what authors called "balancing mediation," which is a combination of parental media control and parental media monitoring, and in "permissive" media parenting, which refers to a hands-off media parenting style.[40] Lower-income and lower educated parents were found to have lower levels of media proficiency, which reduced the ease with which they engaged in several types of media parenting behaviors.[41] Parents with higher income and higher education were more likely to provide "tech guidance" to children, operationalized as parents ever having helped their child learn how a computer or mobile device works, fix things that go wrong with a computer or mobile device, find information online, translate online content into another language, and download media content.[42]

Race/Ethnicity

Parents' racial/ethnic background seems to make a difference for media parenting. A 2016 study found that Black and Hispanic parents were significantly more likely than White parents to engage in parent–child media conversations about the media content of five different media platforms with their children.[43] The report also found that Hispanic parents were more likely than both Black and White parents to check the content of children's devices and social media accounts, to keep all devices out of children's bedrooms at night, to be copied on their child's texts and emails, and to turn off the home Internet at a certain time each night. Also, Black and Hispanic parents were more likely than White parents to use a third-party app or tool to manage children's device use.

Unfortunately, race/ethnicity is most often employed as a covariate, as a moderator, or as an afterthought in media parenting research, and few studies have explicitly assessed the role of race/ethnicity in media parenting practices. One exceptional study involving low-income families found several race/ethnicity-related differences in media parenting;[44] results showed that African American parents were the least likely (compared to Non-Hispanic White, English-speaking Hispanic, and Spanish-speaking Hispanic) to teach their children how to use digital devices, Spanish-speaking Hispanic parents were least likely to help their children find information online, and Non-Hispanic White parents were the most likely to guide their children's technology use. Another study found that White parents were more likely than Hispanic parents to engage in joint media engagement with books and video games, but less likely than Hispanic parents to jointly engage with tablets.[45] In addition, other research found that Latino and African American parents were the most likely to allow their children unlimited media use.[46] Finally, Black parents were more likely than White parents to recall having conversations with their children about race after seeing the movie *Black Panther*.[47]

Religion/Religiosity

In a study involving Slovakian parents and adolescents, results showed that religiousness was positively associated with parent–child media conversations and parental media control, and was negatively associated with joint media engagement.[48] Maternal religiosity has also been shown to relate positively to parent–child media conversations and parental media control among U.S. parents.[49,50] Religiosity was also related to lower levels of allowing a child to make their own media choices.[51] Among three of the largest Christian groups in the United States, both Catholics and Protestants were more likely than Latter-Day Saints to practice joint media engagement.[52] Protestants in the study were also more likely than both Catholics and the non-religiously affiliated to engage in parental media control, and Catholics were more likely than Latter-day Saints to engage in parent–child media conversations.

Political Orientation

Though research is limited, parents' political characteristics appear to affect their media parenting. For example, Nathanson and Eveland conducted a study of U.S. parents' media parenting during the 2016 presidential election between Hillary Clinton and Donald Trump.[53] In the study, parents' interest in the campaign and the strength of their partisanship were both related to joint media engagement. Parents' interest in the campaign was also related to more parent–child media conversations. Another study of U.S. parents found that liberal parents were more likely to engage in parent–child media conversations about a film trailer featuring a transgender adolescent,[54] and conservative parents were more likely to disapprove of children's exposure to the movie trailer than liberal parents.

Context Characteristics

In addition to characteristics of the parent, characteristics of the environmental context in which parenting occurs are consistently related to media parenting behaviors. These contexts include macro categories such as culture and geography, and more meso or micro categories such as family structure and parenting style.

Cultural Norms

Many ways exist to conceptualize culture and norms and their impact on parenting. In the context of media parenting, geography is often employed as an implicit proxy for culture, but research has explored a few variables more directly related to culture that impact media parenting. For example, a survey involving parents from both India and the United States found that cultural dimensions of individualism-collectivism and self-construal influenced media parenting indirectly through family communication styles.[55] Specifically, individualism and independent self-construal both indirectly predicted parent–child media conversations, and collectivism and interdependent self-construal both predicted parental media control. A survey of Islamic Middle Eastern parents found that parents who preferred to speak in their native, non-English language were less likely to engage in parent–child media conversations and more likely to engage in parental media control, but parents who identified as more North American were more likely to engage in parent–child media conversations.[56] Another study involving families in twenty-five European countries found that uncertainty avoidance was negatively related to parent–child media conversations and that collectivism was negatively associated with parent–child media conversations, joint media engagement, and parental media monitoring.[57]

As an implicit proxy for culture, geography plays a unique role in predicting media parenting. For example, much of the media parenting research has been conducted in either the United States or in the Netherlands, and as authors of one study argued, "Research clearly demonstrates that parenting styles (e.g., authoritative, authoritarian) differ between cultures, suggesting that parental mediation might differ between cultures as well."[58] The study, a comparison of media parenting between parents of youth ages 10–18 in the United States and the Netherlands, found that American parents engaged in more parent–child media conversations and parental media control than Dutch parents, though no cross-country differences existed for joint media engagement. A cross-country comparison of parents in Australia and Singapore found that Australian parents engaged in significantly more parent–child media conversations, parental media control, and parental media monitoring, even after controlling for parent and child demographic characteristics.[59] In Europe, different childrearing cultures are thought to exist in different countries, and one study found that parents in countries with a collectivistic childrearing orientation engaged in parental media control more than parents from countries with an individualistic childrearing orientation, while the opposite was found for engagement in joint media engagement.[60] Similarly, the study found that parents in non-English-speaking countries tended to more often limit the time children spend with media than parents in English-speaking countries. Another study involving children ages 11–16 in twelve European countries found that parent–child media conversations increased in all countries between 2010 and 2018, while parental media control decreased in most of the countries in the same timeframe,[61] though differences in the employment of each media parenting strategy still existed on a region-to-region and country-to-country basis.

Family Structure

Family structure/composition seems to make a distinct difference in the media parenting that occurs in the home. For example, parental media control was employed more often in larger families in the Netherlands,[62] a composite of participation in four types of media parenting was less common among Israeli mothers with more children,[63] and parent–child media conversations were more common and parental media control less common among Nigerian parents who were married.[64] Those in two-parent families in the United States also tended to engage in parent–child media conversations more often than those in single-parent families.[65] Married parents have also been shown to engage in parental media control more often than divorced or single parents,[66] as have parents from households with relatively more people.[67]

Parenting Styles and Family Interaction Styles

Parents' behavior in other contexts also transfers to the media context. For example, parents who are highly accessible to their children and who are highly engaged in their children's lives were more likely to engage in parent–child media conversations,[68] parental media control,[69] and joint media engagement[70] than less involved parents.[71] Parents with a responsive parenting style were also more likely to engage in parent–child media conversations.[72] Parents with a more authoritative parenting style were also more likely to engage in proactive forms of media parenting,[73] including proactively setting rules and having conversations with children.[74]

Related to parenting style are the ways in which families communicate with each other, often referred to as family interaction patterns or family communication patterns. Family interaction patterns have been shown to affect parent–child media conversations, parental media control, and joint media engagement.[75] Families who interact openly, who place importance on shared activities, and who are highly communicative were all characterized by higher levels of several types of media parenting.[76,77] In addition, families with a concept-orientation communication pattern were more likely to engage in parent–child media conversations, while a socio-orientation was associated with joint media engagement.[78] Socio-oriented families were also more likely to engage in parental media control, especially parents who felt that children's media exposure was a high risk activity.[79]

Home Media Environment

The availability of media and the ways in which media are used in the home tend to likewise be highly predictive of subsequent media parenting. For example, parents whose children have access to a home computer were more likely to engage in parental media control than parents of children without access to a home computer.[80] Parents who allow a child (ages 2–11) to have a TV in their bedroom were more likely to allow unlimited media use.[81] Having cable television in the home was related to more parental media control.[82] And having screen media in the child's bedroom was related to less parental media monitoring.[83]

Perhaps more important than the accessibility or availability of media in the home are the ways in which family members use the media. For example, parents who themselves watch relatively high levels of television each week were more likely to engage in joint media engagement with their children.[84] Interestingly, parents who play video games more often were actually more likely to engage in parental media control, joint media engagement, and parent–child media conversations involving video games.[85] Other research found that parents were more likely to engage in parental media control and less likely to engage in joint media engagement and parent–child media conversations when their own media use was relatively low.[86] Parents' time spent with books, television, video games, computers, and tablets was related to joint media engagement with each respective media, though their time spent with smartphones was not related to joint media engagement with a smartphone.[87]

Child Characteristics

The third category of predictors of media parenting relates to attributes of children. Parents and children affect each other in transactional, reciprocal ways, including in the context of media parenting.

Age

Parents' media parenting behaviors vary quite substantially based on children's age. In fact, children's age is thought to be a primary determinant of media parenting behaviors. A meta-analysis of thirty-two studies of media parenting from 1992 to 2019 found that children's age was negatively associated with parental media control, possibly because "as children grow older, they obtain skills that allow them to avoid"[88] parental media control. A survey of 252 German-speaking Swiss parents of children ages 3–14 found that the older the child, the less the parent engaged in parental media monitoring and the more the parent engaged in joint media engagement, likely because parents feel a greater need to protect children from media content when they are younger.[89] This pattern existed even in the 1980s, when a study involving 7th and 10th graders found that children's age was negatively associated with both parent–child media conversations and parental media control of both TV and VCR content/usage.[90] Even with samples of just adolescents (ages 13–19), parental media monitoring, parental media control, and parent–child media conversations were all less likely to occur with older youth.[91] A longitudinal study involving children ages 3–10 found that parents' engagement in both parental media control and parent–child media conversations increased from ages 3–8, peaked around age 8, and then began to slowly decline through age 10.[92] Parents in the Czech Republic were significantly more likely to engage in parental media monitoring for children ages 5–8 than they were for children ages 14–17.[93] Among a Dutch sample of 8- to 18-year-olds and their parents, parental media control, parent–child media conversations, and joint media engagement with video games was more likely among younger youth.[94] Parental media monitoring of children's Internet use was also more likely for younger children among 9- to 16-year-olds[95] and among youth ages 11–18.[96] Among youth ages 13–18 in Belgium, the strongest and most consistent determinant of media parenting of children's Internet use was child age—age was negatively associated with parental media control, parental media monitoring, and parent–child media conversations.[97]

Gender

Parents engage in media parenting differently for daughters than they do with sons. A nationally representative sample of U.S. parents of children ages 8 and younger found that parents were more likely to read books and jointly use computers with boys and to jointly watch television with girls.[98] Parents tended to engage in more Internet-related parent–child media conversations with girls.[99] Female university students recalled that their parents engaged in significantly more frequent parent–child media conversations and joint media engagement than male university students recalled.[100] Parents in Brazil have been shown to engage in parental media control more often with girls than with boys.[101] On the other hand, parents of children ages 10–17 in Ireland reported that they engaged in parental media control and parent–child media conversations more with sons than with daughters after the beginning of the Covid-19 lockdown.[102] Russian parents of girls ages 13–15, however, were more likely than parents of boys to engage in both parent–child media conversations and parental media control of children's Internet use.[103] Parental media monitoring of girls' social media activity was more common than for boys' social media activity among parents of U.S. youth ages 10–14.[104] Parents were also more likely to engage in parental media control of video games for girls than for boys, but were more likely to jointly engage in and employ parent–child media conversations about video games with boys than with girls.[105]

Media Use

Children's media use may rightly be categorized as a home media environment contextual characteristic; nonetheless, media use can also be considered an attribute of children that leads to media parenting. Many of the same studies that explored the predictive value of other child characteristics also looked at the influence of children's media use. Again, an argument could be made from correlational research findings that media parenting changes children's media use (and it does), but an opposite argument can also be made that children's media use changes media parenting. Sciacca and colleagues argued, for example, that "frequent technology use is more difficult to monitor for parents, who therefore give up on rules and become more permissive instead."[106] On the other hand, a study in Pakistan found that parental media control was more frequent among adolescents categorized with "high internet addiction."[107] Parents of U.S. elementary school students were more likely to engage in parental media control the more time their children spent watching videotapes, and joint media engagement was more likely the more time children spent watching both TV and videotapes, though watching TV was related to less parental media control.[108] Adolescents' media use, a combination of time spent using video games and watching TV, was related to less of what the authors termed "cocooning" and more of "deference," which refer to parental media control and giving a child the freedom to make their own media decisions, respectively.[109] Padilla-Walker and Coyne argued there is

> utility in considering the role of the adolescent when examining media monitoring, as most research suggests that parents' monitoring is related to lower levels of media use, when it could be that adolescents' levels of media use are also driving parents' media monitoring. This is consistent with research suggesting the bidirectional nature of the parent-child relationship.[110]

Mental and Emotional Well-being

A few studies show that children's mental and emotional well-being may predict media parenting. For example, parents who perceive that their child has low self-control, conceptualized as a combination of factors such as high impulsiveness and self-centeredness, were more likely to engage in parental media control.[111] Similarly, parents of children with emotional problems were more likely to engage in parental media control and parent–child media conversations.[112] In a similar but reverse pattern, parents of adolescents with high levels of self-regulation were less likely to engage in parental media monitoring.[113]

Media Parenting Model (MPM)

Determining the types of and extent to which parents engage in any or all of the different media parenting behaviors is, of course, a science that takes time, replication, and continuous refinement. The best available collective science teaches us that no two parents are the same, no two contexts for parenting are the same, and no two children are the same. But we can begin to construct a model of media parenting to illustrate the determinants and outcomes of media parenting. As Figure 4.1 shows, we can represent the three main categories of characteristics that function together to determine media parenting for any given child by the left-most box. Just as Valkenburg and Peter illustrated their Differential Susceptibility to Media Effects model as a mixing console,[114] it is similarly useful to envision each characteristic, be it parent, context, or child (represented by the letters beneath each bar), as an individual fader or knob. When combined, all the characteristics determine the media parenting behaviors for a given parent. Likewise, not all media parenting behaviors are undertaken at once or at the same level as other media parenting behaviors, so media parenting can also be seen as the result of a unique mix of the various behaviors of which it is comprised. The rest of the model will be explained in upcoming chapters.

Media Parenting Profiles

Several researchers have taken the next logical step of creating profiles of media parents based on the location of the faders for each media parenting behavior. For example, Bradt and colleagues identified four clusters, or profiles, of parental media controllers in the context of online gaming among parents of Belgian adolescents, including parents who exclusively control, those who lack media control, those who combine types of media parenting, and those who support children's autonomy.[115] Other scholars identified four profiles of media parenting among parents of Chinese children ages 3–6, including mother-dominated mediation, father-dominated mediation, coordinated high-level mediation, and coordinated low-level mediation.[116] Researchers in Europe identified parents who prefer parent–child media conversations, those who prefer moderate levels of both parent–child media conversations and parental media control, and those who prefer high levels of parent–child media conversations and parental media control.[117] Other researchers identified all-rounders, active mediation preferred, restrictive mediation preferred, and passive media parents.[118] None of these profiles, however, truly summarizes the parental, contextual, and childhood characteristics that have been shown to predict parents' engagement in the various media parenting behaviors. In fact, given the five types of media parenting in the MPM, any number of profiles of media parents can be constructed, limited only by the number of parents or children currently on the planet. We could run different types of profile analyses each time we conduct a study, but that would simply result in different media parenting profiles with each study we conduct. So, instead of trying to define media parenting profiles by the types of media parenting in which parents engage, another approach is to create media parenting profiles based on the parent, context, and child characteristics most predictive of the various media parenting strategies. Future research could (and should) continuously refine these media parenting profiles, ultimately allowing us to target media parenting interventions to those parents who fail to engage in effective media parenting. To that end, the following section reflects an initial attempt to describe which parents are most likely to engage in the five media parenting strategies identified by the MPM, based on the extant research described in this chapter.

Parental Media Modeling

According to existing research, no characteristic, be it parent, context, or child, makes it more or less likely that parents will engage in parental media modeling. All parents are media models, either intentionally or unintentionally.

It is possible that parents purposely model media behavior in the attempt to set an example for their children, but more research is needed to understand the intentionality of parental media modeling and the characteristics that make it more or less likely.

Parental Media Monitoring

Engagement in parental media monitoring is most likely to occur when the following parent, context, and child characteristics are present:

- Parents who are confident in their parenting abilities
- Parents who are confident in their digital parenting ability
- Parents who believe media monitoring makes a difference
- Mothers
- Relatively more educated parents
- Hispanic parents
- Parents from individualistic cultures
- Children without screen media in their bedroom
- Parents of younger children
- Parents of girls
- Children who use media primarily for entertainment purposes
- Adolescents with high self-regulation

Parental Media Control

Parental media control is most likely to occur when the following parent, context, and child characteristics are present:

- Parents concerned about the potential effects of media
- Parents concerned about certain types of media content
- Parents with negative attitudes toward children's media use
- Parents with the ability to think critically about media
- Parents with more developed digital media skills
- Parents who are confident in their parenting abilities
- Parents who are confident in their ability to help their children navigate the media environment
- Parents who are confident in their own Internet skills
- Parents who believe parental media control makes a positive difference and is worth the effort
- Parents who value balance between children's media and non-media activities
- Parents who value protecting their children from outside influences
- Parents who are less concerned about children's autonomy and creativity
- Mothers

- Relatively less educated parents
- Relatively lower income parents
- Religious parents
- Protestant parents (vs. other Christians)
- Parents concerned about effects of political candidates on their children
- Parents from collectivistic cultures and collectivistic child-rearing cultures
- Parents with an interdependent self-construal
- Parents for whom English is a second language
- American parents (vs. Dutch)
- Australian parents (vs. Singaporean)
- Parents of larger families
- Non-married parents in Africa, but married parents in the United States
- Parents who are highly accessible to their children and who are highly engaged in children's lives
- Parents with an authoritative parenting style
- Parents in families characterized by socio-oriented family communication patterns
- Parents whose children have access to a home computer
- Children without a TV in their bedroom
- Parents who play video games more often
- Low media use parents
- Younger children, and children near age 8
- Daughters generally, but sons during Covid-19
- Youth with high Internet addiction
- Children who frequently watch videos
- Adolescents who use high levels of media
- Adolescents who use high levels of social media
- Children with low self-control
- Children with emotional problems
- Children with less developed digital skills

Parent–Child Media Conversations

Parent–child media conversations are most likely to occur when the following parent, context, and child characteristics are present:

- Parents concerned about potential media effects
- Parents with positive attitudes about media content
- Parents who can think critically about media
- Parents with positive attitudes toward media parenting
- Parents who are confident in their parenting abilities
- Parents who are confident in their ability to help their children navigate the media environment
- Parents who are confident in their ability to use the Internet

- Mothers
- Relatively more educated parents
- Relatively higher income parents
- Black, Hispanic, or White parents, depending on media content
- Religious parents
- Catholic parents (vs. other Christians)
- Parents high in political interest
- Parents from individualistic cultures
- Parents with an independent self-construal
- Parents whose first language is English
- Parents who identify as North American
- American parents (vs. Dutch)
- Australian parents (vs. Singaporean)
- Married parents
- Two-parent families
- Parents who are highly accessible to their children and who are highly engaged in children's lives
- Parents with a responsive parenting style
- Parents with an authoritative parenting style
- Families whose members interact openly
- Families characterized by a concept-orientation family communication pattern
- Parents who frequently play video games
- High media use parents
- Younger children, and children around age 8
- Daughters, but boys during Covid-19
- Children with emotional problems
- Children with more developed digital skills

Joint Media Engagement

Joint media engagement is most likely to occur when the following parent, context, and child characteristics are present:

- Parents who think the media could have a positive educational or socio-emotional effect on children
- Parents with more developed Internet skills
- Less religious parents
- Catholic and Protestant parents (vs. Latter-day Saints)
- Parents high in political interest
- Strongly partisan parents
- Parents from individualistic cultures, and from individualistic child-rearing cultures

- Parents who are highly accessible to their children and who are highly engaged in children's lives
- Families whose members value shared activities
- Families characterized by a socio-oriented family communication pattern
- Parents who watch high levels of TV
- Parents who frequently play video games
- High media use parents
- Boys who use computers or video games
- Girls, and girls who use TV
- High TV-using children
- Children who use media primarily for entertainment purposes

Knowing that certain characteristics make certain media parenting behaviors more likely allows researchers, educators, and policymakers to know which parents to target with media parenting interventions. This idea echoes the arguments of Densley and colleagues, who, in response to the results of their study, argued that the extent of parents' engagement in media parenting strategies signals "to practitioners and policymakers that there is a knowledge gap and that media use guidelines should be shared with parents who have attained less formal education, have lower socioeconomic status, and potentially those who do not regularly visit or have access to a pediatrician."[119] As data presented in this chapter reveals, the field of media parenting is now mature enough, with enough empirical evidence, for the field to create theoretically driven, scientifically based media parenting interventions capable of having a meaningful impact in the lives of children and families.

Chapter 6

CHILDREN'S MEDIA USE AND MEDIA PARENTING

We now move from a discussion about the predictors of media parenting to exploring the outcomes of media parenting. Children's media use is clearly the outcome of most historical research and is a concept that considers time spent with media, media content, and other media activities in which children engage. Hearkening back to the ultimate goal of parenting generally, parents understand that humans become, in part, by doing—this means that in the process of human being, we are often first what Dr. Russ Harris refers to as "human doings."[1] Harris argued that human behaviors move us either toward or away from the sort of life we want for ourselves. In terms of media use, then, children's media behaviors can either enhance life by making it "richer, fuller, and more meaningful,"[2] or make it worse because they "inhibit our growth, negatively impact our relationships, or impair our health and well-being."[3] Media parenting, then, becomes a behavior with the potential to help children make beneficial media choices in order to help children's doings facilitate their human being.

In this sense, media parenting is conceptualized as a predictor variable in the Media Parenting Model. The MPM (see Figure 4.1) shows this relationship as the box containing the five media parenting strategies leading to children's media use via path 2. Subsequent chapters will show how media parenting can also serve as a moderator of the relationship between children's media use and its outcomes (path 3). In addition, the effect of media parenting on children's media use is often conditioned on characteristics of the parent, context, and child (paths 4 and 5), and even by features of the media parenting behavior itself (paths 6 and 7).

Parental Media Modeling as a Predictor

As discussed in both Chapters 2 and 4, parents' media use serves as a strong model, and thus is a powerful predictor, of children's media use in terms of both time and content. The body of research on parental media modeling suggests that parents who are concerned about the amount of time children spend using media or the content to which children are exposed should first evaluate their own media use patterns and habits. This exercise in media literacy, which involves a critical and transparent assessment of one's own behaviors, leads seamlessly to the next implication of parental media modeling research: If parents want to change children's media use, they should first alter their own media use. Instead of belaboring this point, a simple illustration from nutrition research will suffice. A research team comprised of scholars from Florida International University, University of Miami, and Quaid-I-Azam University in Pakistan conducted a study with eighty-six primarily ethnic minority and low-income children ages 5–7 and their parents to determine if parents' food consumption habits were associated with their children's eating habits.[4] Not surprisingly, children whose parents were at a healthy weight were 3.7 times more likely to also be at a healthy weight, likely due to the association between parents' and children's eating habits. Parents who consumed the recommended daily amounts of fruits and vegetables were likely to have children who likewise ate the recommended amounts. In what could easily be mistaken for a conclusion about parental media modeling, the authors concluded, "The combination of healthy role modeling behaviors is associated with child healthy habits but also parents who meet criteria for individual recommendations impact their child's healthy habits in that domain."[5] In many life domains, the example of parents is powerful, and it is likely that no group is better positioned to persuade parents of this fact, with an eye toward helping parents adopt healthy media use behaviors as habit, than children and media researchers.

Parental Media Monitoring as a Predictor

We encounter a conundrum when it comes to parental media monitoring as a predictor of children's media use. Parental media monitoring is most often measured cross sectionally, making it difficult to determine whether the act of parental media monitoring somehow provides an impetus for children's future media use or whether the monitoring simply reveals children's past or current media use. With this in mind, let us explore the associations between parental media monitoring and children's media use.

Parental media monitoring, as explained in previous chapters, can take several forms. Focus group research suggests that common types of parental media monitoring include mandated surveillance and non-intrusive inspection, which refer to establishing rules that allow parents access to children's online accounts and to following their child on social media, respectively.[6] It includes efforts to learn which media children use, how often they use them, and with whom children interact via media.[7] It can also include the use of monitoring tools or technologies[8,9] and watching a child when they are using media.[10]

A potential confound in the parental media monitoring research relates to the number of studies employing scales to measure parental monitoring generally, with parental media monitoring comprising one or two items of those larger scales. This makes it difficult to determine the amount of variance in outcomes uniquely explained by parental media monitoring. This was the case, for example, in a study involving Finnish adolescents ages 11–15.[11] The study found that problematic social media use was most likely among adolescents who had experienced low parental monitoring, a construct, which when operationalized, included just one out of six total items that specifically tapped parental monitoring of adolescents' Internet activity. Similarly, among adolescents in Slovakia, parental monitoring was associated with lower levels of excessive Internet use, though just one of the items measuring parental monitoring related to parents' knowledge of what adolescents do in their spare time, including, presumably, with media.[12]

A handful of studies that specifically measured parental media monitoring, and not parental monitoring generally, have found little or no relationship between parental media monitoring and children's media use. For example, a study in the United Kingdom involving more than 1,500 youth ages 9–19 failed to find a significant relationship between parental media monitoring, which included behaviors such as checking their child's Internet history and email messages, and youths' exposure to violent content, pornographic content, privacy risks, or contact risks.[13] Similar non-significant relationships were found between parental media monitoring of youths' video game playing and adolescents' time spent playing video games.[14]

Other research, however, has found that parental media monitoring is related to reductions in certain types of media use. A national U.S. survey of adolescents ages 12–17 and one of their parents found that media parenting, which included measures of parental media monitoring, such as the frequency with which parents monitored or tracked adolescents' online activities, was related to less problematic Internet use.[15] As mentioned above, the authors likewise agreed that due to the correlational nature of the study, the direction of the relationship could not be determined. In Abu Dhabi, United Arab Emirates, parents' awareness of adolescents' social networking activities was related to a reduced risk of adolescents being a victim of online bullying; the study, however, did not explain how parents monitored or became aware of adolescents' social media use,[16] further complicating our understanding of the role of parental media monitoring due to the lack of conceptual clarity between parents' knowledge and the actual monitoring activities used to obtain that knowledge. Consistent with the MPM's conceptualization of parental media monitoring, a study in India involving adolescents ages 13–17 described "monitoring mediation" as parents' checking adolescents' browsing history, checking social media contacts and friends, monitoring social networking profiles and activities, and checking email.[17] The study also included "technical mediation," which included measures of parents' use of technology to track adolescents' social media activities. Findings showed that "monitoring mediation" was positively associated, and "technical mediation" was negatively associated, with adolescents' hedonistic smartphone use. More specifically, both mothers' and fathers' provision of "technical mediation" were related to lower hedonistic smartphone use, whereas only mothers' provision of "monitoring mediation" was related to higher levels of adolescents' hedonistic smartphone use, suggesting a conditional effect of parent gender, consistent with MPM path 5. In addition, a study involving more than three thousand Chinese youth ages 9–14 found that parental media monitoring behaviors such as checking children's emails or instant messages were positively associated with Internet addiction.[18] To further explain their findings, the authors suggested that future research should explore adolescents' level of self-control as a moderator of the relationship between parental media monitoring and Internet addiction, which would appear in MPM as path 5.

On the other hand, research also shows that parental media monitoring is associated with greater time spent with media and higher levels of exposure to certain types of media content. For example, among adolescents ages 13–18 in China, researchers operationalized "non-intrusive inspection" as parents' adding children to their social media friends lists, browsing children's personal profiles, and monitoring children's tweets and comments on social media.[19] In the study, while "non-intrusive inspection" was not associated with being a victim of cyberbullying, it was positively associated with the child being a perpetrator of cyberbullying, a highly specific type of media activity. The authors argued that "high-level non-intrusive inspection may give rise to a sense of oppression in teenagers, which leads teenagers to bypass such inspection and conceal personal information."[20] They also argued that "parents' well-meaning attempts to observe their children's online behaviors do not mean that children are willing to disclose what they are doing. Many teenagers adopt a variety of tactics, including wheedling, lying, demanding, and refusing, in an effort to assert their rights."[21] Interestingly, the study provided support for the use of a mixer analogy of media parenting, as the combination of low levels of parental media control, high levels of parent–child media conversations, and high levels of parental media monitoring ("non-intrusive inspection") reduced the risk of adolescents' involvement in cyberbullying. In another survey study involving U.S. youth ages 10–14 and a parent, researchers found that parental media monitoring, which included items measuring behaviors such as checking on the child's social networking or online community profile, was associated with parents' reports of a greater likelihood of the youth ever having sent a sext.[22] Again, however, the authors noted that "parents are more likely to monitor when risky behavior has already occurred" and that youth may perceive parental monitoring "as a privacy invasion and react by engaging in additional risk behaviors."[23]

What is clear from parental media monitoring research is that the role of parental media monitoring in children's media use remains somewhat unclear.

The literature does seem to suggest, however, that parental media monitoring is most successful when combined with other forms of media parenting, such as parent–child media conversations. In addition, research suggests that parental media monitoring may best serve its purpose when done with the child's knowledge of its occurrence. In addition to avoiding the psychological reactance that could occur with certain types of parental media monitoring, overt forms of parental media monitoring could also help to avoid the negative parent–child interactions and depressive symptoms that appear to emerge with covert types of parental monitoring.[24]

Parental Media Control as a Predictor

Next, research related to parental media control shows highly mixed results about its effectiveness. For example, a 2010 Common Sense Media study found that U.S. kids whose parents provided at least some media use rules consumed nearly three hours less media content per day than kids whose parents did not provide any rules.[25] Similarly, research involving Dutch adolescents found that parental media control of youths' Internet use was related to lower levels of adolescents' problematic social media use.[26] Parental media control was also related to fewer symptoms of social media disorder among Dutch adolescent girls ages 11–15.[27] A systematic review of research related to media parenting and problematic social media use concluded that parental media control functions best to reduce or prevent problematic social media use when it occurs before the development of the symptoms of problematic social media use (MPM path 2), and tends to backfire, or result in more symptoms, when it occurs during or after (MPM path 3) children's social media use.[28] Parental media control is negatively related to digital game addiction tendencies and digital device use among children ages 3–6 in Turkey,[29] but was not related to time spent on social media among young adolescents ages 11–13 in Australia.[30] In Hong Kong, parental media control of adolescents' social media use at Time 1, what the authors called "reactive restrictive mediation," was related to adolescents' social media addiction at Time 2.[31] Interestingly, this type of parental media control was actually effective at reducing adolescents' social media addiction when mothers exhibited demandingness, a positive general parenting behavior that refers to parents' regulation, control, and monitoring of children's behavior in order to help children adapt to society—in terms of the MPM, parental media control's impact on children's media use would be found on path 2, but maternal demandingness would be found on path 5. In another study, parental media control, however, was unrelated to the likelihood of German early adolescents ages 10–14 having a smartphone in bed with them.[32] But for very young children, parental media control at age 2 in the form of not allowing their child to use a tablet resulted in lower levels of child problematic media use two years later[33] and over time.[34] In fact, among young children ages

9 and younger, a systematic review determined that parental media control reduced the likelihood of developing problematic media use.[35] Also, among middle-school students in China, parental media control was related to less leisure-related Internet use.[36] And among U.S. youth ages 10–14, parental media control was related to less sending and receiving of sexts.[37]

One study provided a good example of the mixer analogy related to media parenting. Researchers in Ireland found that parent–child media conversations and parental media control interacted to predict children's time spent online during the Covid-19 pandemic.[38] Specifically, among youth ages 10–17 time spent online was highest with the combination of high parent–child media conversations and low parental media control, and time spent online decreased with the combination of high parental media control and low parent–child media conversations. The authors argued,

> It could be that, given the challenges with constantly restricting such frequent digital technology use that takes place on private devices during lockdown, parents resorted to a combination of active and restrictive strategies, having conversations with their child about online safety and what is appropriate to post online; and setting rules in an autonomy-supportive way, giving rationale and listening to the child's opinion. In turn, these strategies might have promoted further digital technology use by the child instead of limiting it, in a sort of bidirectional relationship. In short, child's digital technology use might be promoted by parents' negotiations and encouragement to explore online opportunities and to learn new skills, which might require the child to spend more time online. At the same time, a more frequent use of digital technology might prompt parents to combine active and restrictive mediation, to encourage the child to explore more online opportunities while still setting rules to prevent excessive use.[39]

Parents' inconsistent engagement in parental media control tends to have negative outcomes. For example, among Singaporean children ages 3–6, the more often parents resorted to inconsistent parental media control (measured by the single item, "I would tell my child that he/she is not allowed to use a smartphone, but my child knows that the next time, he/she will be allowed to use it"), the higher the level of their child's problematic smartphone use.[40] This relationship (MPM path 2) was especially true among mothers who relied on negative parent–child resolution tactics (MPM path 5), such as psychological aggression (e.g., threats of physical assault) and actual physical assault (e.g., spanking).

Reading between the lines of research related to parental media control, however, it is evident that as children age through adolescence, parental media control is inconsistent at best, and at worst prompts even more use of undesirable media content. In Iran, for instance, parental media control was less effective than parent–child media conversations at reducing older adolescents' exposure to certain Internet risks, but among younger adolescents each of the two types of media parenting tended to reduce exposure to those risks.[41] U.S. adolescents in 6th through 8th grades (mean age of 13) who reported greater parental media control also reported spending more time with television, books, magazines, and email (but not social media).[42] But even among young children, parental media control has inconsistent results. For example, among Greek parents of children ages 3–5, parental media control actually resulted in more digital media use among children, while parental media monitoring resulted in less digital media use, causing the authors to conclude that "setting rules about where, when, for how long and what to access, and applying consequences when these rules are not followed is not effective in decreasing time spent on digital media by children in contrast to keeping an eye on children as they use digital media."[43] On the other hand, for some youth, it is highly effective at reducing Internet use patterns that can be deemed excessive, as found in a twenty-five-country European study involving youth ages 11–16[44] and among 5th graders in Taiwan.[45]

Researchers have argued that parental media control may produce inconsistent results due to the varying levels of psychological reactance it induces, especially among adolescents, which in turn produces the unintended effect of increased media use.[46,47] A test of this proposition was conducted by White and colleagues, who found a clear connection between parental media control and each of the constructs involved with adolescents' psychological reactance.[48] Specifically, parental media control was related directly and indirectly (in serial) to increased viewing of restricted media content with friends through perceived freedom threat, state reactance, and reactance restoration.

The inconsistent findings related to parental media control may also be explained by research showing that the effects of parental media control may be conditioned on other factors. One such study involving more than three thousand Singaporean students found that parental media control was related to a reduced likelihood of pathological Internet use, but especially for those at higher levels of attachment, communication, and comfort at home, "implying that the effectiveness of restrictive mediation varies with the degree of warmth and support in the general family environment."[49] These conditional findings represent path 5 in the MPM. Another study found that parental media control itself was not sufficient to reduce the frequency of children's exposure to media violence.[50] In the study, both "controlling" and "inconsistent" parental media control were related to greater frequency of exposure to media violence, while "autonomy-supportive" parental media control was related to less frequent exposure to media violence. In other words, MPM path 2 was conditioned by a feature of the media parenting strategy, represented by MPM path 7. The authors of the study argued that "boomerang effects may be circumvented when parents restrict media in an autonomy-supportive style."[51] Conversely, when parental media control occurs as a reaction to adolescents' Internet use, children's Internet use tended to rise to the level of "problematic," which refers to the presence of Internet-use addiction-related symptoms.[52] The reactive nature of parental media control in these examples represents MPM path 7, as it is not the parental media control itself, but its timing or nature of the control, that appear to be problematic.

Inconsistent findings related to the effectiveness of parental media control may also be explained by the types of outcomes explored by individual studies. Chen and Shi conducted a meta-analysis of fifty-two studies published from 1987 to 2016 involving nearly seventy-five thousand participants, and found that parental media control was related to a reduced risk of both children's exposure to inappropriate content and to time spent on media, but it was also related to an increased likelihood of children being addicted to media.[53] In other words, time spent with media is different than exhibiting symptoms of addiction to media, suggesting that parental media control "may not be able to help children develop a less favorable or negative attitude toward media use,"[54] even if it happens to reduce the time spent with media.

Perhaps most importantly, even if it does function to reduce the time children spend with media or their exposure to undesirable media content, parental media control appears to lack the parenting power to help children exercise their agency to develop healthy media habits. In making this claim, I am not suggesting that parental media control research concludes that all parental media control is ineffective or inappropriate. But I am suggesting that research shows that parental media control alone cannot help children develop the skills necessary to make healthy media choices for themselves. This tension between rule setting and freedom allowance is summarized well by Roper:

> Freedom without limits can result in anxiety, aggression, a lack of self-control and a poor sense of responsibility. Children without limits fail to develop the capacity to deal with the frustration of not having their own way and as a result cope poorly in relationships, at school, and later at work. At the other extreme, excessive limits restrict personal development, undermine children's self-esteem, and prevent them from developing an inner sense of responsibility. Children who are excessively controlled and restricted do not learn to think for themselves and they learn to rely on authority figures to direct them. Aggression, lack of initiative and difficulty in dealing with authority may become lifelong problems. The ideal, then, is for parents to encourage freedom and individuality within moderate limits.[55]

In fact, Roper continued, "The goal of rule enforcement is to help children develop inner resources (healthy values, an ability to cope with feelings, and an ability to control one's behavior)."[56] Said differently, parental media control should be implemented and enforced in a way that supports children's autonomy. And the way to do this is to combine parental media control with parent–child media conversations and other forms of media parenting. Fikkers and colleagues argued that "autonomy-supportive restriction (characterized by providing a rationale for rules and taking the child's perspective seriously) may lead to successful internalization of regulations."[57] Thus, rules, enforcement, and compliance do not necessarily facilitate developing or becoming. It is only when developmentally appropriate rules are coupled with an equally appropriate degree of agency-supportive parenting that children can access their potential to become in a healthy way.

Parent–Child Media Conversations as a Predictor

Parent–child media conversations have consistently been shown to possess the ability to help reduce children's time spent with media and their exposure to potentially negative media content, and to increase the time children spend with relatively healthier media fare. It appears that next to parent–child media modeling, parent–child media conversations constitute the next most effective media parenting behavior in which parents can engage to support children's well-being.

Much of the most recent research conceptualizes children's time spent with media in terms of concern—instead of just measuring time spent online, researchers tend to operationalize time as problematic media use or as a tendency toward Internet addiction, or via some other related construct. Substantial research shows that parent–child media conversations can help reduce the risk of these excessive and problematic types of children's media use. For example, parent–child media conversations were related to both lower levels of children's smartphone use and children's digital game addiction tendency among children ages 3–6 in Turkey.[58] They were also related to a reduced likelihood of early adolescents (ages 10–14) having a smartphone in bed with them.[59] In addition, a study involving more than two thousand Chinese elementary school children ages 8–13 and their parents found that media parenting of the Internet, which included parental media control, joint media engagement, and parent–child media conversations, was negatively associated with problematic smartphone use.[60] Of note in this study is that the researchers also found that children's self-regulation was a significant mediator of the relationship between media parenting of the Internet and problematic smartphone use. In other words, in addition to its direct effect on problematic smartphone use, media parenting was also related to higher levels of self-regulation, which in turn was related to lower levels of problematic smartphone use. The MPM could represent this mediation effect with an extra variable/step along path 2. In another study, this one involving Chinese youth ages 12–15, parents' encouragement of children's media use was related to lower levels of compulsive Internet use, likely because the encouragement was indicative of a warm, collaborative parent–child relationship that served to guide children's media use.[61]

Parent–child media conversations can also influence the types of media activities in which children engage. For example, hedonistic smartphone use refers to using media for its sensory and emotional affordances, and is motivated by pleasure, enjoyment, and self-gratification.[62] Interestingly, time spent with media (social media, watching videos, and playing games) leads to desensitization of hedonic media effects,[63] making it easy to understand why parents would want to prevent hedonistic smartphone use in the first place. Accordingly, a survey of adolescents ages 13–17 in India found that parent–child media conversations, what the authors called "active mediation of safety," were negatively associated with adolescents' hedonistic smartphone use.[64] Parent–child media conversations were also negatively associated with a specific Internet activity, cyberbullying perpetration, among youth ages 13–18 in China.[65] Parent–child media conversations were also negatively associated with sending sexts among youth ages 10–14 in the United States.[66] A study involving middle school students in China found that parent–child media conversations were related to more use of media for educational/learning purposes.[67] The study also revealed that parent–child media conversations were related to lower levels of both Internet use and use of media for leisure purposes, but only for youth whose parents engaged in a supportive style of overall parenting. In the context of the MPM, the association between media parenting and children's media use (path 2) was conditioned on a contextual characteristic (path 5).

While much of the research shows that parent–child media conversations consistently result in positive outcomes, some studies fail to demonstrate a positive relationship between parent–child media conversations and children's media use. A meta-analysis of media parenting literature failed to find a significant association between parent–child media conversations and children's media use,[68] though the study did find that parent–child media conversations did seem to protect against the negative effects of exposure to certain forms of content, as in MPM path 3. The authors noted that the different operationalizations of parent–child media conversations likely played a role in the meta-analysis' null findings, and called for future research to "differentiate between the varying types of active mediation to explore in greater detail what the influences are on children and adolescents."[69]

Taken together, this research provides a compelling case that parents should individually and collectively raise the standard for the quantity and quality of parent–child media conversations if the hope is to guide children into behaviors and cognitions with the most potential for positive outcomes to their well-being. Given the clarity and consistency of the direction of research findings, it may seem surprising that more parents do not regularly and intentionally engage in frequent parent–child media conversations; a next phase of media parenting research should explore theoretically based ways to persuade parents to make a more concerted effort to proactively talk with their children about their relationship with media.

Joint Media Engagement as a Predictor

Children's media use patterns tend to model their parents' media use patterns, so it makes sense that children's media use also increases when it is done jointly with their parents. The relationship between joint media engagement and children's media use is consistent across media, largely regardless of age, gender, and geography. In addition, not only is joint media engagement positively associated with the time children spend with media, it is also related to the media content to which children are exposed.

In 2016, a group of researchers conducted a meta-analysis of the relationships between various forms of media parenting and children's outcomes, including children's time spent with media, and found that joint media engagement was significantly and positively associated with the amount of time children spend with media, a combination of TV, video game, Internet, movies/videos or multiple media use.[70] The authors concluded that children's media use increased not just because joint media engagement was simply added onto the time children spent with media, but actually encouraged additional media use beyond what children would have consumed had their parents not also jointly engaged in media use with them: "When consuming media with parents, children and adolescents see the rewards of such behavior (i.e., family time; relaxing in front of the TV, computer, etc.) and then consume additional media outside the direct supervision of parents."[71] In other words, as other researchers[72,73] and I have argued elsewhere, joint media engagement "may also signal to the child that the activity is important, valued by, and approved by the parent, and that the parent enjoys watching television together with the child. These perceptions can then trigger positive emotions related to the shared activity, thereby instigating a motivation in the child to engage more deeply"[74] and more frequently with media activities.

A study involving children ages 5–6 found a significant positive association between joint media engagement of television and both children's total weekly TV viewing time and the amount of time the TV was on in the home.[75] More specifically, families with frequent joint media engagement of TV reported the TV being on in their home for an average of nearly thirty-one hours per week, compared to about twenty-seven hours in other families. The study also found that joint media engagement of TV was associated with children's increased viewing of both children's and adult TV programming. This was also the case in a study involving tween girls—they watched significantly more TV when their parents watched TV with them.[76] On the other hand, among young children (ages 3–6) in China, joint media engagement was related to a reduced likelihood of engagement in problematic media use.[77] And though problematic media use was likewise related to children's screentime, when combined with the former study, the latter findings suggest that while joint media engagement may be associated with children's screentime, it is less likely to associate with screen time that becomes problematic or excessive.

A more nuanced view of joint media engagement emerged from a two-wave study involving more than 1,600 parent–adolescent (ages 9–18) dyads in China.[78] Results of the study showed that the purpose for joint media engagement made a difference. Specifically, joint media engagement of smart devices for learning purposes was negatively associated with future problematic smart device use, while joint media engagement of smart devices for entertainment purposes was positively associated with future problematic smart device use. In other words, the relationship between joint media engagement and children's media use was conditioned on parents' intent behind their joint media engagement, exemplifying MPM path 7. Padilla-Walker and colleagues likewise found that the intent of joint media engagement made a distinct difference in children's media use outcomes.[79] As part of their study, they conducted an exploratory factor analysis on the five items measuring parents' reports of joint media engagement with their adolescent child—three of the items loaded onto a factor they called "connective co-use," which refers to joint media engagement conducted with the intent to connect with their child. The other two items loaded onto a factor they called "passive co-use," referring to joint media engagement without a stated intent. When combined with high levels of parental media monitoring, "connective co-use" was related to the lowest levels of overall media time than any other combination of media parenting strategies. The same combination of high and moderate levels of parental media monitoring and joint media engagement for connection purposes was related to lower access to media in the bedroom than media parenting behavior combinations that included parental media control. We can make at least two conclusions from these findings: first, a combination of more than one form of media parenting may be necessary to curb children's media use, and second, the intent behind the media parenting strategy (MPM path 7) makes a difference. Why the intent of media parenting matters is not made clear in these studies, but it is possible that engaging in media parenting for a specific purpose changes the nature of the media parenting behavior in some important way, whether the changes in media parenting are a result of conscious consideration of a specific purpose, whether the changes are simply noticed by the child, or both.

Other factors appear to help determine the influence of joint media engagement on children's media consumption. A study involving both urban and rural Chinese youth ages 6–14 found that joint media engagement in the form of watching TV together was positively associated with frequency of children's TV viewing for urban children, but not rural children,[80] even though rural children watched less TV than urban children. These findings provide support for MPM path 5, with urban/rural home environment as a moderating context characteristic. Children's age may also moderate the influence of joint media engagement on media consumption. Woolf found that joint media engagement of prosocial media content between parents and their 12-year-old or younger children was related to higher levels of prosocial content viewing among the oldest children in the group (ages 10 and older).[81] Woolf argued that "viewing with parents may have raised older children's awareness of the content available for their age group. It may also have socialized children to prefer such content."[82] In addition, the type of programming being consumed also seems to alter the relationship between joint media engagement and amount of media consumption. One study involving children ages 3–7 in the United States found that children tended to watch more child-oriented informative and entertaining programs when they watched alone, but watched more adult-oriented informative, sports, comedy, drama, action-adventure, and variety-game programs when they watched with their parents.[83] Parental responsiveness is another characteristic that has a similar moderating effect on the relationship between joint media engagement and children's media use. A study involving adolescents in Hong Kong found that paternal joint media engagement was positively associated with adolescents' social media addiction when paternal responsiveness was low, and negatively associated with adolescents' social media addiction when paternal responsiveness was high.[84] The authors argued that "paternal responsiveness is often associated with playfulness, challenge, and encouragement of risk-taking. Highly responsive fathers tend to invest more time in playing with their children such as engaging in outdoor activities and sports, which may subsequently decrease a child's dependence on the Internet or social media."[85] The relationship between joint media engagement and children's media use has also been shown to depend on children's gender. For example, a study involving U.S. adolescents ages 11–14 found that joint media engagement of video games was related to more frequent video game playing among boys, but not among girls, even though levels of joint media engagement of video games did not differ for girls and boys, nor for family structure, ethnicity, or income.[86] Clark argued that such quality play time between parent and child is increasingly important in today's busy society, and that "new technologies have made digitally enhanced collaborative learning possible just as interactions between adults and children have become more two-way, child-centered, and less defined by hierarchical authority arrangements."[87]

In sum, joint media engagement relates to increased media consumption among children, though this relationship depends on a number of parent, context, and child characteristics. Parents can facilitate closeness with their child and children's exposure to prosocial programming via joint media engagement. They can also prevent children's exposure to certain types of content by reducing joint engagement with that content or by planning for their own exposure to that content to occur at times when children's joint exposure is not possible.

This chapter focused almost completely on screen time as an outcome of media parenting, almost as if altering children's screen time solves all problems associated with children's media use. The next several chapters will show, however, that a myopic focus on altering children's screen time assumes that media parenting can circumvent both societal norms about children's media use and the need for children to use media to meaningfully exist in a world dominated by media. Indeed, more and more researchers seem to use the term "ubiquitous" to describe children's media use, suggesting that eliminating children's media use is not practical, nor even wholly desirable. Of greater import may be the role of media parenting in altering children's responses to media use, and it is in this direction that the next several chapters now take us.

Chapter 7

PHYSICAL HEALTH AND MEDIA PARENTING

Both the embodied mind and the mind embodied perspectives of human nature espouse a strong connection between the mind, brain, and body. This connection is so strong, in fact, that some believe that research evidence demonstrates the existence of "a literal linkage of body and mind in the very structure of the brain."[1] From a mind embodied perspective, such a linkage does not assume the absence of human duality, for human duality does not suggest an absence of some sort of mortal linkage between mind, brain, and body. Without getting too deep into the science of brain mapping that shows how the thinking and planning parts of the brain are intricately connected to the motor regions of the brain that control movement,[2] it is sufficient to understand that the body, even in ways we may not currently understand, shows evidence of every thought produced by the mind. And vice versa, our minds reflect the experiences of the body. From a systems theory perspective, these assertions are at once logical, plausible, and practical. We see a corollary, for example, in the body's digestive system. What we put into our bodies—an external input— affects the way our minds and bodies work. It is second nature to many in the Western world that eating a high calorie diet full of simple sugars will result in a feeling of lethargy, increased fat deposits, and poorer mental health over time. Likewise, what we put into our minds, such as information contained in media messages, likewise affects how the brain and body function.

Like media messages, media parenting constitutes additional information encoded and stored in children's minds. And like ingredients in a recipe, both media and media parenting messages interact with each other and with all the other bits of information stored in children's minds to produce media exposure outcomes. This analogy is well reflected by a study I conducted among children ages 5–7 and 10–12 while I was a doctoral student at The Ohio State University.[3] In the study, each child watched a clip from the TV show *SpongeBob SquarePants*. Children were randomly assigned to one of four intervention conditions in which they listened to the experimenter (me) share a thirty-second message refuting the somewhat violent nature of the clip before watching the clip, in the middle of watching the clip, after they watched the clip, or not at all. After the experiment, children then answered questions about how much they liked the characters in the clip, how much they liked the program, and how much they thought other children like the characters in the clip. The younger children (ages 5–7) liked the violent characters most when they did not hear the message from the experimenter, liked the program least when they heard the message while watching the clip or after watching the clip, and thought others liked the violent characters least when they heard the message while watching the clip. The older children (ages 10–12) liked the characters in the clip least when they heard the message before or during the clip, and thought others liked the characters most when they heard the message after watching the clip. Note that a main difference in results between the younger group and the older group involved the timing of hearing the message from the experimenter. Children in the older group were least affected by the violence in the clip when they heard the message either before or during the clip, but children in the younger group were least affected by the violence in the clip when they heard the message either during or after watching the clip. My best explanation of these findings is that older children have the capacity to hold two things in their working memory at the same time—both the TV content and the experimenter's message about TV violence—allowing the message about TV violence the opportunity to help reinterpret the TV content. Younger children, on the other hand, responded best when they heard the message after watching the clip—because they have not yet developed as mature of an ability to hold multiple bits of information simultaneously in working memory, the message served best to reinterpret the media content when they heard it after watching the clip. Now, we could get into a much deeper discussion about what this means for the timing of media parenting (see MPM paths 6 and 7), but the point is that media parenting interacts with media messages (and other factors) to produce an outcome. In other words, the effect of media exposure is conditioned by, or dependent on, the media parenting engaged in by the parent. And said even more academically, media parenting moderates the relationship between children's media exposure and its outcomes. This moderation effect is illustrated by MPM path 3 and demonstrates that the combination of information provided by media content and media parenting work together to produce important outcomes.

Researchers also conceptualize children's media use as a mediator between media parenting and children's health outcomes. This process is reminiscent of the associations between media parenting and children's media use discussed in the previous chapter, with the added sequential eventual association of children's media use with children's health outcomes (the far right box in the MPM, see Figure 4.1). The premise of these types of mediation models is that reducing (or increasing) children's time spent with certain types of media content will serve to reduce (or increase) the negative (or positive) outcomes of exposure to that content simply because children are consuming the content less (or more), thereby reducing (or increasing) the opportunity for media content to have an effect. The rest of this chapter will discuss children's physical health as the ultimate outcome, with the combination of media use and media parenting as the predictors that either interact with each other or function in serial to influence children's physical health outcomes.

Body Composition, Physical Fitness, and Diet

An interesting example of a conceptual mediation model showing the role of both media parenting and children's media use in children's physical health comes from a 2020 study conducted by researchers in Taiwan involving more than one thousand parents of elementary school-age children.[4] Results of the survey showed that parental media modeling, operationalized as the number of hours per day the parent spent using the Internet, reading emails, online chatting, or gaming during their free time, was positively associated with children's screen time. In addition, parental media control, in the form of setting rules about how much time children can spend using screen media, was associated with lower levels of children's screen time. Children's screentime, in turn, was itself positively associated with overweight—it is unclear what type of mediation analysis was conducted, but based on these associations the authors concluded, "Given that child screen viewing was significantly related to child overweight, parental rules and appropriate screen viewing behavior may decrease the level of child screen viewing and indirectly reduce the risk of overweight for children."[5] In other words, children's body mass index (BMI) increases when parents model high levels of screentime, and decreases when parents set rules about children's media use, due to the effect of each media parenting strategy on children's screentime. Similarly, a longitudinal study of Australian children ages 4–5 at time 1 (and ages 8–9 at time 3) found that television viewing was positively associated with overweight/obese, and that parental media control of television reduced the likelihood of obesity by reducing television viewing.[6] The study also showed that parental media control also functioned to increase the frequency of moderate to vigorous exercise among children by reducing time spent viewing television. This type of mediation analysis was also conducted for data collected from a sample of Spanish parents of children with an average age around 9 years old.[7] Findings showed that family rules, which included rules about media use in the home, were associated with fewer hours of children watching TV. Children's TV hours were, in turn, positively associated with their BMI, meaning that parental media control can help reduce children's BMI by first reducing their screen time.

BMI is, of course, related to diet, and another study found that while children's media use did not predict BMI, media use was positively associated with their consumption of sugary drinks, candy, sweets, and salty snacks, and negatively associated with consumption of both fruits and vegetables.[8] Furthermore, the study found that parental media control was negatively associated with children's consumption of sugary drinks, candy, and sweets, regardless of how much TV children watched. Interaction analysis found that the positive relationship between TV viewing and salt snack consumption was strongest when parental media control was low, and that the relationship between TV viewing and both greater consumption of unhealthy foods and less consumption of healthy foods was strongest when joint media engagement and parent–child media discussions were high. Said differently, parental media control altered the relationship between children's TV viewing and eating habits in a healthy way, while joint media engagement and parent–child media discussions altered the relationship in a negative way. It is important to note that the study involved parents of young children, ages 2–4, and thus appears to mirror research showing that parental media control tends to result in positive outcomes among younger children. A study involving children ages 6–11 failed to find a significant moderating effect of parental media control on children's consumption of healthy/unhealthy foods following exposure to advertisements of each, and high levels of parent–child media discussions actually seemed to increase children's consumption of unhealthy snacks after watching food advertising.[9] On the other hand, a study involving 3rd and 4th grade children and their mothers in Indonesia found that parent–child food-related discussions, but not necessarily media-related discussions, attenuated the relationship between suburban children's media exposure and their fast-food consumption.[10] And among children ages 2–6, parental media control in the form of rules about television viewing was related to lower BMI among girls.[11]

Before people engage in behavior, they often engage in a consideration of their own ability to enact the behavior and of the behavior's ability to have positive results. A 2015 study of parents of children with an average age of 13 found that parents who believed that parent–child media conversations about food would help their child develop healthy eating habits were likely to also have positive beliefs about their ability to enact healthy dietary practices in the home, the latter of which was ultimately related to healthy family dietary behaviors.[12]

Another study, this one involving U.S. college students' recollections of their parents' media parenting behaviors when the college students' were younger, found that parent–child media conversations in the form of negative comments about television content were associated with higher taste ratings for healthier foods and lower taste ratings for unhealthy, highly advertised foods, which were, in turn, related to a healthier diet.[13]

It also appears that media parenting during childhood has effects that last well into adulthood. Nearly 1,400 Dutch adults ages 25–54 were asked to respond to a series of questions about their pre-adult years, including their weight and height at both age 20 and currently, from which BMI was calculated.[14] They also provided retrospective reports of how much time they remember their parents spent watching TV during participants' childhood, as well media parenting in which their parents engaged during the same approximate time period. Results showed that parents' time spent watching TV during participants' childhood was positively associated with participants' current BMI. In addition, parent–child media conversations during childhood were related to lower current BMI, and joint media engagement during childhood was related to higher current BMI—all the associations, however, were indirect. Specifically, parent TV viewing during participants' childhood was positively associated with participants' TV viewing during adolescence, which in turn was positively associated with both participants' BMI at age 20 and adult TV viewing, which were each positively associated with participants' current BMI. The negative association between parent–child media conversations and current BMI was mediated by participants' adult TV viewing, and the positive association between joint media engagement and current BMI was serially mediated by TV viewing during adolescence, and both BMI at age 20 and adult TV viewing.

While the handful of studies that have explored media parenting's potential to alter the association between children's media use and disordered eating and negative body image could be included in a discussion about media parenting and mental health, it also fits well here with our discussion of media parenting and physical health. For example, one study found that parent–child media conversations were related to adolescents' body satisfaction through adolescents' perception of parental caring.[15] The authors argued, "Watching television together and talking about television might convey to adolescents that their parents care about them, which could, in turn, strengthen their satisfaction with their bodies and improve their self-esteem."[16] On the other hand, another study found that parent–child media conversations about TV characters' appearance and body size consistently predicted negative emotions and body image disturbance, suggesting that these conversations encouraged adolescents' to process such media portrayals more deeply than they otherwise might have.[17] Lastly, one study found that adolescent girls' sense of empowerment was associated with lower levels of disordered eating pathology, and that parental involvement with their daughters' media use in the form of conversations and monitoring were related to higher levels of empowerment, while parental media control was related to lower levels of empowerment.[18] From this analysis, the authors concluded:

> The parental role is particularly important during this critical adolescent period, when health and illness behaviours may develop that hold significance not only for present but also for future well-being. Consistent with other research, our findings show that the role of the parent–adolescent relationship is significant for the development or prevention of disturbed behaviour, including disordered eating behaviour.[19]

Sleep

Media parenting has the potential to help children's subsequent sleep habits. For example, a study of more than 1,300 U.S. children in grades 3–5 found that media parenting at time 1, operationalized as a combination of both parent–child media conversations and parental media control, was indirectly associated with increased average weekly sleep time through its association with reduced total screen time.[20] Interestingly, average weekly sleep time then predicted lower BMI. Similarly, among German early adolescents ages 10–14, parent–child media conversations about smartphone use at time 1 were negatively associated with children having their smartphone in bed with them four months later.[21] Having a smartphone in bed was itself positively associated with daytime tiredness, which, in turn, was associated with lower levels of feeling healthy and energetic over time. Among middle schoolers in the U.S Pacific Northwest, parental media control at time 1 was negatively associated with bedtime media use at time 1 and time 2, and with daytime sleepiness at time 1, and was positively associated with nighttime sleep duration at times 1 and 2.[22] Parent–child media conversations at time 1 were also positively associated with sleep duration and negatively associated with daytime sleepiness at time 1, but not at time 2. Another study found cross-sectional associations between media parenting and adolescent sleep outcomes, but failed to find significant associations over time.[23] Cross sectionally, the study found that parental media control was associated with better sleep and less time spent using technology among adolescents, but a similar significant association over time was not found. The authors argued that "parental limit setting may not result in changes in technology use, nor sleep" (p. 378) among adolescent populations over time. This appears to be especially true among adolescents who are highly involved in social media use. In one study, adolescents ages 11–17 completed a computer-based questionnaire about the frequency of their social media use, perceived sleep quality, bedtime, and parents' rules about using the Internet and smartphone before bedtime.[24] Findings showed that among low frequency social media users, quality of sleep was highest when parents provided strict rules about media use before bed, but among high frequency social media users, quality of sleep was about the same for adolescents with and without strict rules. The authors provided three compelling potential explanations for these results:

> Highly engaged social media users, including users who report problematic social media use, experience more stress and fear of missing out when they are not allowed to check their social media late in the evening . . . Experiencing FOMO could prevent adolescents from falling asleep and/or lead to more restless sleep. A second explanation relates to perceived social norms and expectations, as adolescents may not stop their social media use as they may experience fear of social disapproval when violating norms on steady online availability and prompt responding. A third explanation may be that restrictive parental rules may provoke more conflicts with parents when adolescents are highly engaged in social media use and/or display signs of social media addiction . . . These parent–child conflicts (late in the

evening) may evoke emotional insecurity and physical and cognitive arousal, which may interfere with adolescents' healthy sleep patterns.[25]

A study of Australian adolescents, on the other hand, found that parental regulation, operationalized as a combination of parental media control, parental media monitoring, and parent–child media conversations, was negatively associated with both video gaming duration and school night bedtime, without a mediating effect of gaming duration on the relationship between parental regulation and bedtime.[26]

The success of media parenting as a strategy to improve children's sleep depends, then, on a few factors. First, parental media control seems to help improve the sleep of young children by reducing their time spent with media. Next, parental media control does not seem to benefit older children and adolescents as much, and it may even unintentionally result in opposite effects. And third, children seem to benefit most from media parenting when it involves a combination of types of media parenting, providing further support for the argument that parental media control alone lacks the power to induce long-term behavioral change in children.

Sexual Health

Children's sexual health is more behavior-oriented than sleep quality—children cannot simply choose to sleep better at night or feel more rested in the morning, but they do have some control over their sexual health behaviors. Thus, in the sense of altering the media's effect on children's sexual behaviors and their associated attitudes and other cognitions, media parenting has a relatively strong track record for certain groups of children. In fact, a meta-analysis of media parenting research representing fifty-seven studies and nearly sixty thousand research participants found that both parental media control and parent–child media conversations were negatively associated with child and adolescent sexual outcomes, conceptualized as sexual behavior such as kissing, petting, and any form of oral or vaginal intercourse.[27] The authors argued, "By implementing specific time and content rules about media, parents limit child exposure to media and assist in preventing unwanted early sex, pregnancy, and multiple partners for their child or adolescent,"[28] and that "casual, nonthreatening conversations about sex may have a greater influence on children and adolescents than the sex in the media, especially when children are taught to critically analyze the media through these conversations."[29]

These findings are also consistent with the handful of studies that asked emerging adults to think back to when they were growing up and to recall the media parenting in which their parents engaged. One study asked participants to recall media parenting and then measured their current level of sexual media content desirability (the extent to which they found 'sexy' media portrays desirable), expectancies (the extent to whey they thought alcohol disinhibited their sexual behavior), realism (the extent to which they thought beer ads were realistic portrayals of life), norms (the extent to which they thought their peers engage in risky behavior involving alcohol and sex), similarity (how similar they thought people in alcohol ads are to them and people they know), and wishful identification (how much they wanted to emulate characters in alcohol ads).[30] The study also measured critical orientation toward media and the extent to which participants engaged in risky sexual behaviors in the last four weeks. Analyses revealed that parent–child media conversations that critiqued media content were related to a reduction in engagement in risky sexual behaviors in several ways, including serially through critical thinking toward media, similarity, norms, identification, and expectancies; through desirability, norms, and expectancies; and through critical thinking toward media alone. Interestingly, parent–child media conversations that endorsed media content were negatively associated with critical thinking toward media, followed by each of the pathways to risky sexual behaviors outlined above. Two other studies with emerging adults asked participants to recall conversations they had with their parents about pornography while growing up. The first found that parent–child media conversations critical of pornography were negatively associated with emerging adults' pornography use through attitudes about pornography, and that these conversations protected the self-esteem of participants whose sexual partner views pornography.[31] The second found that these same types of conversations reduced future pornography use by instilling the salient belief that parents disapprove of viewing pornography.[32]

Parent–child media conversations are consistently predictive of positive sexual health outcomes among adolescents. Among Dutch adolescents ages 13–16, for example, one study found that parent–child media conversations about adolescents' consumption of sexual media content were related to less permissive sexual attitudes among girls, the measure of which asked adolescents to respond whether it was totally wrong or right to engage in certain behaviors, such as having sex with someone they just met, or having sex for sex and not because they are in love with the partner. The study's results, though, did not support a moderating effect of parent–child media conversations (which the authors called "instructive mediation") on the association between adolescents' media use and sexual behavior outcomes.[33] The authors argued:

> At first sight, this finding seems to contrast the outcomes of previous research and the general notion that instructive mediation may be an effective parenting strategy to modulate effects of popular media on adolescent development. However, our present findings do not necessarily imply that parents' use of instructive mediation is not a viable strategy for preventing the development of risky sexual attitudes and behaviors in adolescents. It may well be that the effects of instructive mediation and parental media critique are relevant, but mostly when delivered in warm, supportive family contexts.[34]

Among Hispanic adolescents ages 13–21, parent–child media conversations about adolescents' online privacy settings were related to greater odds of adolescents having private social media profiles and lower odds of ever engaging in sexting.[35] Among U.S. adolescents in grades 8, 9, and 10, media parenting operationalized as a combination of both joint media engagement of TV and parent–child media conversations about TV was related to less sexual experience and greater self-esteem, and among girls, greater body satisfaction; parental media control of TV use was also related to less sexual experience.[36]

A host of other outcomes related to media parenting of sexual content have been explored. Many of these involve the role of parental media control, and some relate to the role of joint media engagement and parental media monitoring. As with other types of media effects, parental media control is inconsistently effective, and joint media engagement tends to strengthen the effect of media exposure on child outcomes. For example, parental media control helped reduce the relationship between exposure to sexually suggestive media programming and adolescents' engagement in either oral sex or vaginal intercourse, as well as their intention to engage in intercourse in the next twelve months.[37] The study also found that while parent–child media conversations did the same for the relationship between general TV viewing and intentions to engage in oral sex, they actually seemed to strengthen the relationship between exposure to sexually suggestive broadcast programming and future intentions for oral sex, though this could be because those conversations do not happen until parents catch their child watching sexually suggestive broadcast programming. Among younger adolescents, parental media control was associated with less frequent sending and receiving sexts, parent–child media conversations were associated with less frequent sending sexts, and parental media monitoring was positively associated with sending sexts.[38] The latter result was likely due to the higher likelihood of finding evidence of sending sexts when parents engage in media monitoring and not necessarily because parental media monitoring is a predictor of sending sexts. In Scotland, parental media control in the form of restrictions on exposure to sexual media content was associated with a lower likelihood of adolescents ages 14–15 ever having engaged in sexual intercourse.[39] Among Swedish adolescents ages 13–16, parental media control by fathers was negatively associated with adolescents' online sexual activity, which included flirting, searching for a girlfriend/boyfriend, visiting pornographic websites, discussions about sex, posting attractive photos or movies, and webcam sex.[40] Among some groups of adolescents, research has shown that both parental media control and joint media engagement were negatively associated with adolescents' initiation of oral sex.[41] Another study found that joint media engagement of sexual television content was related to both engaging in sex at a younger age and with having more sexual partners among adolescents.[42] Results of the study also showed that a moderate amount of parental media control (neither low nor high) was associated with comparatively higher levels of contraceptive use and weaker beliefs that sex is a game. The authors suggested that moderate amounts of parental media control "send a message of caring and concern while simultaneously communicating trust and respect for the adolescents' preferences."[43] In Uganda, parental media control in the form of restricting high schoolers' time spent with media was related to a reduced likelihood of adolescents reporting having ever had sex.[44] But too much media control for Dutch adolescent girls has been shown to lead to more sexual experience, operationalized as a combination of dating, deep kissing, light petting, heaving petting, and sexual intercourse.[45]

To summarize, research shows that parent–child media conversations, especially when conducted in a warm, loving, respectful, and autonomy-supportive manner, have the potential to powerfully moderate the effect of exposure to sexual media content on sexual health outcomes among adolescents. Specifically, adolescents whose parents engage in consistent parent–child media conversations in the appropriate ways are less likely to experience or choose negative sexual health attitudes and behaviors. Parental media control likewise has the same power, but both adolescents' age and the dosage of that parental media control seems to make a significant difference in its effectiveness. Older adolescents, as with adolescents' media use in other contexts, may not respond as well to parental media control due to its potential to induce psychological reactance, especially when the parental media control is perceived as excessive or presented in an authoritarian parenting style.

Substance Use

The influence of media parenting on the relationship between children's media use and their use of alcohol and tobacco appears to follow a similar pattern as the effects of media parenting on children's sexual health outcomes. In fact, the same meta-analysis that showed media parenting's ability to reduce media's impact on sexual health outcomes showed that media parenting had a similar influence on substance use among children and adolescents.[46] The study's authors concluded that parent–child media conversations were effective at reducing desire for and use of substances: "The media, at times, presents attractive actors using substances in an enticing way without consequences, and unless parents use such instances to discuss the unrealistic and sometimes dangerous repercussions from substance use, children and adolescents walk away with impractical expectations."[47]

Parent–child media conversations also seem to reduce the association between certain types of risky media activities and children's substance use. For example, among young adolescents (mean age of 13), parent–child media conversations served to weaken the association between being a victim of cyberbullying and young adolescents' alcohol and illicit drug use, as well as the association between cyberbullying perpetration and illicit drug use.[48] But it appears that features or content of parent–child media conversations make a difference. One study found that parent–child media conversations that were critical of media messages were related to higher levels of critical thinking skills among youth (via retrospective reports of emerging adults), which in turn were related to less interaction with alcohol brands on social media and fewer expectations that drinking would have some positive effect on one's social life.[49] Conversely, parent–child media conversations that endorsed media portrayals of drinking alcohol were related to lower levels of youths' critical thinking skills, which ultimately predicted a greater likelihood of interactions with alcohol brands on social media and more expectations that drinking would have a positive effect on their social life. Similarly, one study found that alcohol expectancies were higher when parents endorsed media content, and were lower when parents refuted media content, thereby respectively altering the positive association between alcohol expectancies and alcohol use among high schoolers.[50] Likewise, parent–child media conversations characterized as positive appraisals of smokers in the media were associated with young adolescents' (ages 11–13) smoking intentions.[51] Among Dutch adolescents ages 12–17, parent–child media conversations that were critical of media content were indirectly related to lower levels of descriptive norms about peers' engagement in five risk behaviors, three of which were alcohol use, smoking, and drug use—parent–child media conversations critical of media content were first associated with reduced perceptions of similarity with media characters, which were in turn associated with lower descriptive norms.[52] The authors concluded that "media parenting may still play an important role during adolescence."[53] Thus, it is not just parent–child media conversations alone that alter children's responses to media content, but the nature of those conversations likewise makes a difference, represented by MPM path 6.

In addition, the age of children impacts media parenting's effectiveness at reducing substance-related outcomes. Among youth ages 9–13 in China, both parent–child media conversations about Internet use and parental media control of children's Internet use reduced, or moderated, the association between children's social media exposure to drinking and smoking and their tobacco and alcohol use, but no significant moderating effects were found for those ages 12–18.[54] The authors suggested that media parenting may not affect adolescents the same way it affects children because adolescents have greater and more frequent access to social media than children, and as a result are more likely to view tobacco and alcohol-related content on social media. They also suggested that adolescents' "desire to be autonomous often leads them to reject parental authority and take risks, particularly when their parents strictly restrict their media use."[55] Among young adolescents (average age of 12), parental media control in the form of restrictions on access to R-rated movies reduced exposure to alcohol content in the media, and was ultimately associated with lower levels of peer drinking, willingness to drink, drinking initiation, and frequency of alcohol use.[56] Also among young adolescents (mean age of 12) in Argentina, parental media control in the form of rules about adolescents' exposure to mature content online, in video games, on TV, and in movies/

DVDs was related to decreased odds of adolescents' use of tobacco, alcohol, and illicit drugs.[57] Among German adolescents younger than 15, parental media control in the form of restrictions on viewing movies rated appropriate only for those ages 16 and older was related to less exposure to movies depicting tobacco and alcohol use, which was itself related to lower levels of adolescents' smoking and alcohol use.[58] The authors concluded, "By exerting control on media access, parents may influence the type and amount of a particular social influence, e.g. media smoking and drinking depictions or media violence, and thereby influence risk for these behaviors,"[59] at least for younger adolescents. These findings are consistent with research among U.S. young adolescents and pre-adolescents (ages 9–12) that found that parents' prohibition on watching R-rated movies was related to a lower risk of drinking and smoking,[60] as well as with research among U.S. youth ages 11–14 showing that restrictions on watching R-rated movies were related to less susceptibility to smoking.[61] On the other hand, among older adolescents (mean age of 15) parental media monitoring in the form of asking questions about adolescents' media use was not related to a reduction in substance use.[62] In fact, parents who monitored their child's media use in this way reported high levels of adolescent substance use, and the authors suggested that these findings indicate that adolescents' substance use likely occurred prior to parents' engagement in media monitoring activities instead of in response to this type of media parenting.

Media parenting dosage also changes substance use outcomes. For example, one study found that young U.S. adolescents (mean age of 12) were most likely to abstain from using alcohol and marijuana when media parenting was offered in moderate doses, especially when combined with low levels of child device ownership.[63] In the study, media parenting was operationalized as a combination of several different behaviors, including parental media monitoring, parent–child media conversations, and parental media control, so it is difficult to distinguish the unique influence of the various media parenting behaviors. A separate study parsed media parenting behaviors apart in a more nuanced way. Young adolescents (mean age 12) were less likely to engage in substance use when their parents supervised their exposure to R-rated movies, and were more likely to initiate alcohol use when they watched R-rated movies despite parental restrictions.[64] While it is unclear if "supervision" referred to parental media monitoring or to joint media engagement, what is clear is that parental media control was effective only when combined with another media parenting strategy.

Conclusion

Media parenting in its various forms can influence children's physical health outcomes. The nature of that influence, whether it is intended or unintended, depends on a number of factors. Speaking in generalities, as we must with all social science research, children's physical health tends to benefit from media parenting that involves parent–child media conversations. Specifically, parent–child media conversations that endorse media portrayals seem to encourage the adoption of healthy behaviors, and parent–child media conversations that are critical of media content seem to discourage children's adoption of unhealthy behaviors. These conversations have the ability to reframe adolescents' perceptions of (1) the value, or the rightness or wrongness, of consuming media content with portrayals of unhealthy attitudes and behaviors and (2) the desirability of media content and characters. Like media effects processes, media parenting processes also work to alter the cognitions that precede behavior. This chapter has identified a few of those processes, including the role of parent–child media conversations in reducing the level of importance that children place on products, people, and stories they encounter in the media. These conversations can also work by reducing children's perceptions of the similarity between themselves and media characters. They can also change children's perceptions of the normative behaviors of people important to them. Parent–child media conversations can help children develop critical thinking skills, inform them of the persuasive nature of media content, and change children's beliefs about themselves and about their ability to enact healthy behaviors. These processes are captured by theories such as Protection Motivation Theory, Theory of Planned Behavior, and the Persuasion Knowledge Model, among others.

Parental media control appears to work through different processes. For children and younger adolescents, parental media control operates through both cognitive and non-cognitive means. Non-cognitively, parents can restrict access and exposure to unhealthy media content simply by being the person that holds the proverbial, or actual, remote. Cognitively, this could indicate to the child the value that parents place, or rather don't place, on media content with the potential to affect children's physical health outcomes. But as children grow older, these types of restrictions may increasingly be interpreted by adolescents as a lack of trust, as a lack of support of adolescents' budding autonomy, or as a lack of confidence in adolescents' ability to interpret media content in healthy ways. These cognitions may lead to, or serve as part of, the unintended process of psychological reactance, leading to an increased likelihood of adolescents' engagement in behavior that parents tried to prevent in the first place. Regardless of the process, however, it is once again clear that while parental media control might change media behavior, and thereby reduce effects of media exposure on children's physical health, it lacks the power to help children fully and independently make choices that will benefit their physical health. Said differently, simply changing children's behavior does not necessarily equip them with tools to navigate the media landscape themselves (which is another reason "parental mediation" is not an appropriate label for media parenting).

It is also appropriate at the close of this chapter to refer back to the start of this chapter. There, we discussed the ability of inputs (media parenting and media exposure) to affect outputs (physical health). It is equally important to note that causes of symptoms are different than the symptoms themselves, and that treating symptoms is not the same as treating the underlying cause of the symptoms. For example, taking a painkiller to eliminate pain associated with an ankle sprain does not actually fix the ankle sprain. It simply alters some of the symptoms of the ankle sprain. There may be health conditions for which a painkiller affects the underlying cause of a malady, such as inflammation or muscle tightness causing a headache, at least temporarily. But generally speaking, targeting symptoms of a health condition does not necessarily treat the cause of the condition. Similarly, limiting children's access or exposure to certain types of media content may prevent symptoms of exposure that children might have otherwise experienced, but it may not necessarily alter the cognitions that precede children's physical health behaviors and attitudes. If the goal is to help children become as physically healthy as possible, parents must target more than children's behaviors. They must target the thoughts and perceptions that drive the behavior in the first place. Employing a variety of media parenting strategies can help in these efforts.

Chapter 8

SOCIO-EMOTIONAL WELL-BEING AND MEDIA PARENTING

The American Psychological Association defines parenting as "all actions related to the raising of offspring."[1] It defines communication as "the transmission of information, which may be by verbal (oral or written) or nonverbal means."[2] Scholars and parents alike may find problems with and even challenge these definitions in whole or in part, but the intent of beginning this chapter by defining "parenting" and "communication" is not to initiate a philosophical debate about what constitutes each, but rather to put into words some assumptions about media parenting. If the goals of parenting, both generally and media-specific, are to help children be and become, then communication is the means by which parenting is enacted. In other words, parents cannot engage in parenting without communicating something to children. Even when parents choose not to engage in parenting (which could be considered a form of parenting itself), they communicate something to their child about either their motivation to parent, their ability to parent, the context in which their parenting takes place, or the child themselves. An argument could then be made that all parenting behaviors communicate something interpersonally to or with a child, whether that communication is intentional or unintentional, reciprocal or one-way, verbal or non-verbal, explicit or implied. Of course, parenting involves more than interpersonal communication—the act of ensuring that food is placed on the dinner table each night is not in and of itself an act of interpersonal communication, but it does communicate something to the child. Thus, parenting is a social activity with social consequences. And as this chapter will demonstrate, such a conceptualization of parenting, and media parenting specifically, is important to a discussion of children's socio-emotional well-being because the ability of children to successfully and skillfully navigate their social worlds and remain resilient in the face of life's stressors is strongly tied to the social and emotional lessons communicated through the social process of parenting. Because parenting is regarded as perhaps "the primary factor that shapes child and adolescent development to a large extent,"[3] and because "parents may have different socialization practices, thus introducing different developmental trajectories to children,"[4] media parenting practices can help shape children's social and emotional responses to media exposure.

In fact, media parenting can help children incorporate positive lessons about social relationships and emotional skills into their own interactions and can help mitigate the negative lessons about the same topics that children learn from media exposure.

The broad domain of socio-emotional well-being encompasses a multitude of competencies and skills, but it could be argued that all relate in some way to children's ability to establish and maintain healthy relationships with oneself and with others. Due to the wide array of these skills and competencies, media parenting research does not specifically address every aspect of socio-emotional well-being independently, but it does provide us with a solid foundation for understanding the role of media parenting in helping children develop several aspects of social and emotional competence.

Prosocial Behavior

Prosocial behavior is defined as voluntary "social behavior that benefits others"[5] or that is intended to benefit someone else,[6] such as helping, sharing, and consoling.[7] In their review of the effects of prosocial behavior on the person who engages in that behavior, Caprara and colleagues noted that prosocial children have better relationships with peers, perform better in school, and are less inclined to both aggression and externalizing behaviors.[8] Because of the importance of prosocial behavior in the development of positive relationships with self[9] and with others, media scholars have explored the role of media in the development of prosocial attitudes and behaviors. Longitudinally, prosocial media use is positively associated with helping behaviors through its relationship with empathy.[10] In addition, a meta-analysis of seventy-two studies found that prosocial media use was positively associated with both prosocial behavior, empathic concern, and prosocial thinking;[11] as a result, the authors called for parents to seek out prosocial media content and make it available to their children, a suggestion that refers to the role of parents in helping children enjoy the benefits of such positive media content.

A growing body of research, in fact, explores this role of parents, and research suggests that the development and enactment of children's prosocial competencies, in the form of thoughts and behaviors, can be facilitated through a combination of appropriate media use and media parenting. For example, a study involving more than 1,300 U.S. grade school children (mean age of 9) found that parental monitoring of media, operationalized in the study as a combination of rules about the time children spend with media and the media content they consume, and discussion about media content, significantly reduced children's total time spent with media and children's exposure to media violence.[12] Both pathways ultimately led to increases in children's prosocial behavior, such as the extent to which they help peers, consistent with MPM path 2. High levels of parent–child media conversations likewise strengthened the relationship between boys' (ages 3–6) engagement with Disney princesses (of which media exposure to Disney princesses comprised part) and boys' prosocial behaviors and body esteem.[13] Among children in the 4th–6th grades in the U.S. Upper Midwest, parent–child media conversations strengthened the association between prosocial media exposure and children's altruism and affection, especially among the youngest children in the sample,[14] consistent with MPM path 3. Similarly, and consistent with MPM path 2, among children ages 12–18 in Belgium parental media control in the form of autonomy-supportive provision of media rules was related to prosocial media exposure, which was itself positively related to prosocial behavior;[15] the same type of media parenting was also related to lower levels of antisocial media content exposure, and in turn, to less antisocial behavior. The study found that a different process, consistent with MPM path 3, was found for parent–child media conversations; specifically, autonomy-supportive parent–child media conversations strengthened the positive association between prosocial media content exposure and prosocial behavior. It is likewise important to note that a feature (autonomy-supportive) of both parental media control and parent–child media conversations made a difference, consistent with MPM paths 7 and 6, respectively. Similar patterns were found in a study involving nearly 1,200 U.S. adolescents (mean age of 14) that found a positive association between autonomy-supportive (MPM path 7) parent–child media conversations and prosocial behavior through exposure to prosocial media content (MPM path 2).[16] Autonomy-supportive parent–child media conversations and autonomy-supportive parental media control were also related to higher levels of prosocial behavior through media disclosure among U.S. adolescents ages 10–18, regardless of adolescents' age.[17] The authors argued that autonomy-supportive media parenting is "more effective than controlling approaches from early to late adolescence,"[18] and that "when parents use autonomy-supportive approaches, adolescents are active participants in the family system and are encouraged to express their own opinions and thoughts, while still understanding that parents' rules and expectations need to be maintained, which likely fosters internalization of parental values regarding media."[19] Consistent with this argument, research that failed to distinguish between autonomy-supportive and controlling types of media parenting tended to coincide with previous research that found unintentional or boomerang effects of parental media control. For example, a longitudinal study of U.S. young adolescents (mean age of 11 at time 1, and age 13 at time 3) found that parent–child media conversations related positively to children's prosocial behavior (as measured by the Kindness and Generosity subscale of the Value in Action Inventory of Strengths, which will be addressed later on in this book)[20] through their effect on children's self-regulation and sympathy, while parental media control had the opposite effect.[21] And among children ages 9–11 in Malaysia, "active co-use," conceptualized as a combination of joint media engagement and parent–child media conversations, was associated with fewer peer problems and more prosocial behavior. In the same study, parental media monitoring was associated with more prosocial behavior, and parental media control in the form of technological restrictions and rules about children's media use was unrelated to both peer problems and prosocial behavior.[22]

Other research shows that children may receive the positive benefits of prosocial media consumption only when parent–child media conversations are regular and consistent. For example, a study involving 127 children ages 2–6 found that children who watched ten episodes of *Daniel Tiger's Neighborhood* exhibited higher levels of empathy, self-efficacy, and emotion recognition, but only when parent–child media conversations regularly accompanied children's television viewing at home, and especially for younger and lower income children in the sample.[23] The authors argued that children whose parents engage in consistent parent–child media conversations "are more efficient TV viewers and can learn better from prosocial content."[24]

Parental media modeling also affects children's socio-emotional development. For example, phubbing uniquely affects children's prosocial behavior. Shi and colleagues found that parental phubbing was negatively associated with parent–child closeness, which ultimately resulted in lower levels of prosocial behavior, such as helping and sharing, among children ages 3–6 in China.[25] In another study related to parental media modeling, the media use of U.S. mothers of children aged about 18 months at time 1 of a three-year longitudinal study encouraged children's prosocial behavior.[26] Specifically, mothers' exposure to prosocial media content at time 1 was positively associated with children's exposure to prosocial media content at time 2, which was itself positively associated with children's prosocial behavior at time 3, constituting another example of the media parenting process demonstrated by MPM path 2. Even as young as infancy, children's emerging prosocial behavior is influenced by their parents' media use. Stockdale and colleagues argued that certain physiological changes, such as respiratory sinus arrhythmia (RSA), have been shown to relate to both attention and emotional regulation in children.[27] Their study found that infants/toddlers ages 1–3 with higher RSA while jointly engaging with media with a caregiver were those whose primary caregivers also engaged more with prosocial media, suggesting that "parents who are more drawn to prosocial media may also engage in more prosocial behaviors and model better regulatory processes for their children in relation to others' emotions," and that "parental prosocial media exposure might be a means for a parent to create a broader culture in the home that benefits children's emotion regulation."[28]

As just alluded to, joint media engagement can sometimes make a difference in children's socio-emotional outcomes. The Stockdale and colleagues' study also found that jointly watching a short clip from a prosocial children's program led to increases in children's RSA, an induced "physiological calming effect,"[29] though in a separate study, joint media engagement between infants and primary caregivers was not associated with children's prosocial behavior.[30] In another study involving U.S. parents of pre- and young adolescents ages

6–12, the likelihood of parents participating in joint media engagement of both adolescent-genre television programs and general audience television programs was associated with children's prosocial behavior.[31] Joint media engagement can even drastically alter media effects. For adolescent girls, joint media engagement in the form of co-playing video games was associated with higher levels of prosocial behavior toward family members, "which may be a function of higher relationship quality between daughters and parents who co-play."[32] Joint media engagement in the form of watching TV together was not related to perceptions of the social realism of programs featuring families among U.S. children in the 2nd, 6th, and 10th grades.[33] Joint media engagement in the form of watching general entertainment programs, but not informative programs, was negatively associated with the prosocial behavior of U.S. children ages 3–7.[34]

Antisocial Behavior

In addition to facilitating the adoption or internalization of prosocial media content, media parenting can also reduce or protect against antisocial outcomes associated with children's media exposure. Though antisocial behaviors consist of a wide range of behaviors, such as rule-breaking, crime, and other violations of social norms,[35] children and media researchers often focus on the antisocial behaviors of physical or relational aggression.

Physical Aggression

Consistent with MPM path 2, a study involving children in grades 3–5 in Minnesota and Iowa in the United States found that a combination of parental media control of time and content and parent–child media conversations reduced both children's total screen time and media violence exposure, each of which, in turn, was then associated with lower levels of children's physically aggressive behavior, such as hitting or kicking school peers.[36] In Anambra State, Nigeria, researchers concluded that a variety of media parenting behaviors moderate in a positive way the relationship between exposure to violent media and adolescents' aggressive behavior,[37] consistent with MPM path 3. In a study involving U.S. adolescents, researchers found that among three different types of media parenting, namely, autonomy-supportive parent–child media conversations, autonomy-supportive parental media control, and controlling parent–child media conversations, only autonomy-supportive parental media control was associated with lower levels of violent media content exposure, a precursor to adolescents' physical aggression.[38] Perhaps somewhat unexpectedly, both forms of parent–child media conversations were related to increased levels of violent content exposure, and the authors argued that "autonomy supportive parenting may be the most effective way to influence child behavior, but when exposure to negative content is a part of the discussion, restriction seems to be necessary for decreasing negative effects and behavioral outcomes."[39] These findings are consistent with research among Belgian adolescents that found that autonomy-supportive parent–child media conversations likewise failed to moderate the association between antisocial media content exposure and direct aggressive behavior, such as hitting or kicking.[40] Dutch adolescents also responded with decreased media violence exposure and reduced aggression to autonomy-supportive parental media control, while no form of parent–child media conversations were related to either outcome.[41] These counterintuitive results were "somewhat surprising"[42] to researchers, who argued:

> It may be that, despite its theoretical assertion, active mediation is less effective at reducing the effects of antisocial media content than restrictive mediation. One possible explanation for this difference is that the information active mediation conveys about the value of antisocial content is less evident to adolescents. By actively discussing the undesirability of such content, but not restricting their access, parents may still affirm that antisocial content is worthy of children's cognitive involvement.[43]

On the other hand, a meta-analysis found that parental media control was not significantly associated with children's aggression, comprised of physical, relational, and verbal forms of aggression; however, the study did find a significant negative association between parent–child media conversations and aggression, and a significant positive association between joint media engagement and aggression.[44] The authors suggested that a combination of parent–child media conversations and parental media control may actually be the most effective media parenting strategy, and that the autonomy level of both the child and the media parenting may be important considerations. In light of other research, these assertions appear meaningful. For example, in a U.S. study involving parents and their 2nd to 6th grade children, both parent–child media conversations and parental media control were associated with lower levels of children's general and TV-induced aggression.[45] Joint media engagement was also positively associated with TV-induced aggression. The author argued that data from the study suggest that both parent–child media conversations and parental media control seem to influence children's perceived importance of violent TV, thereby socializing children in a way that reduces their vulnerability to the effects of violent TV exposure. She also argued that joint media engagement of violent media content "communicates to children that the depicted content is important, useful, and should be attended to carefully"[46] and "that if mom and dad are willing to invest time in watching television and do not say anything bad about the material, then it must be important material that is worthy of their attention."[47] Atkin and Greenberg also found that parent–child media conversations in the form of comments intended to minimize the effect of antisocial programming were associated with lower levels of aggressive behavior among U.S. children in the 4th, 6th, and 8th grades,[48] but Liebeskind failed to find an association between media parenting strategies and the verbal and physical aggression of children ages 6–12,[49] suggesting that the survey measures involved were insufficient to capture the extent and nuances of media parenting behaviors.

Relational Aggression

Some research shows that media parenting may be related to an increase in some forms of relational aggression. A study involving U.S. adolescents and their parents found that exposure to relational aggression in the media was positively associated with actual relational aggression among girls, but only when parent–child media conversations were frequent.[50] Similarly, the study found that both parental media control and joint media engagement tended to strengthen the relationship between relational aggression exposure and actual relational aggression. The authors suggested that parent–child media conversations have the potential to backfire when the media content in question is a highly salient topic for children, which may especially be the case among adolescent girls in the context of relational aggression. Parent–child media conversations may motivate more thinking about relational aggression and encourage girls to pay more attention to relationally aggressive media content. These findings are in contrast to research that found that parent–child media conversations can attenuate the relationship between relational aggression exposure and relational aggression,[51] though the age of the children in the two studies should be noted as a potential moderator of the effect of parent--child media conversations. The consistency with which media parenting is enacted may be another potential moderator. For instance, Martins and colleagues found that inconsistent media parenting (both parental media control and parent–child media conversations) provided to U.S. adolescents was positively associated with adolescents' social media use; furthermore, inconsistent parental media control predicted parent–child conflict and higher levels of social media use, each of which predicted both online aggression perpetration and victimization.[52] And inconsistent parent–child media conversations led to more social media use, which then led to more online aggression perpetration and victimization. The autonomy-supportive nature of media parenting also makes a difference in the context of relational aggression. A study of U.S. youth ages 10–18 found that autonomy-supportive parent–child media conversations were related to lower levels of youths' media secrecy, conceptualized as how often youth keep secrets from their parents about their own media use.[53] This positive influence is important, because the study also found that media secrecy was related to both less prosocial behavior toward family members and to more engagement in relationally aggressive behaviors, such as calling others names behind their back.

Emotion/Self-Regulation

Self-regulation has been described as "a cornerstone of early childhood development across domains of behaviour,"[54] including in the domain of prosocial behavior. Specifically, prosocial behavior requires attentional regulation, as prosocial behavior can be instigated by noticing others' needs or desires.[55] It also requires children's ability to control and understand emotions.[56] Prosocial behavior may also promote or enhance the development of self-regulation.[57] And self-regulation has been shown to mediate the relationship between parenting and children's prosocial behavior.[58] As a result, children and media researchers have consistently explored the relation between media parenting and children's emotion regulation and self-regulation.

A valuable opportunity to explore this relationship presented itself during the Covid-19 pandemic, which was characterized by "a large amount of emotionally charged messaging."[59] In fact, the authors found that parent–child media conversations about news related to the outbreak of Covid-19 were related to higher emotion regulation, such as the ability to express both positive and negative emotions, and lower levels of emotional negativity, such as a tendency to have destructive outbursts of energy and exuberance, among Italian children ages 6–13. On the other hand, parental media control of news related to the Covid-19 outbreak was related to higher levels of emotional negativity, while joint media engagement was related to lower levels of emotion regulation. In the first year of a three-year longitudinal study of children ages 8–11, both parent–child media conversations and parental media control positively predicted children's subsequent self-regulation of Internet use and emotion regulation, and negatively predicted children's impulsivity.[60] Self-regulation is also strongly related to engagement in risky behavior,[61] and studies of risky behavior can serve as a sort of proxy for studies of self-regulation. For example, among youth ages 10–18 in Israel parental media control was related to higher levels of engagement in risky online behaviors, such as posting personal details, sending insulting messages, and meeting face to face with a stranger they met online.[62] Similarly, as "emotion recognition is a fundamental skill that promotes more effective regulation of emotions,"[63] research found that regular parent–child media conversations facilitated a significant positive association between watching prosocial programming and preschoolers' emotion recognition skills.[64] Parent–child media conversations can also help reduce children's negative emotional responses to news coverage of a violent news event, though primarily among the younger part of a sample of children ages 8–12.[65] But another study among children ages 5–6 found that both joint media engagement and parent–child media conversations were associated with higher levels of children's TV-related fears.[66] The authors suggested that media parenting in the study did not perform as expected because young children's abstract reasoning capacities may not be developed enough to benefit from reinterpretations of scary media content. It is also possible that media parenting interacts with children's developing emotion regulation skills, thereby influencing their emotional reactions to such content. A study of children ages 11–12 in Belgium found that parent–child media conversations while engaged in joint media engagement of news did not reduce children's fear in response to scary news images.[67] The study also found that parental media control was positively related with children's news-based fear responses. While neither of the two latter studies specifically measured emotion regulation in addition to emotions themselves, they do provide evidence that children's emotional responses to some types of media content are so strong that some media parenting for some children does not seem to help reduce, or rather, does not seem to help children manage strong induced emotions. Indeed, parent–child media conversations are "not a simple and magical solution to fear and sadness provoked by news but a very complex and diverse concept" and "that the precise content of the parental interventions is crucial."[68] De Cock continued,

> Some well-intended explanations may broaden the child's comprehension of the news event but do not necessarily help mitigate feelings of fear or may even magnify scary details. For parents to stress children should "avoid strange people" is an understandable suggestion when crime cases are shown on television but it does not necessarily reassure frightened children.[69]

Yang and colleagues found that parental media control was negatively associated with the executive function skills of preschoolers ages 3–6 in northern China.[70] The study also found that the amount of time preschoolers spent watching TV was related indirectly to higher levels of executive function through the time they spend watching classical children's cartoons and live educational viewing programs, but only when parental media control was relatively low. The authors argued that these findings have several implications, including the relatively prominent role of media content over only time spent with media in the development of children's executive function. But more directly related to media parenting, they suggested that parental media control may not strengthen the association between watching educational television and children's executive function because parental media control "is associated with an arbitrary parenting style, which involves depriving children's opportunities to regulate their own behavior and requiring them to adapt continually to another's perspective."[71] They also argued that parents of children with poor executive function may set more TV viewing rules for their children. While parental media control may not strengthen the association between viewing educational television and emotion regulation, joint media engagement of children's educational programming has been shown to improve the emotion regulation skills of both children and parents in the Middle East.[72] U.S. infants also exhibited greater levels of respiratory sinus arrhythmia, a marker of regulatory function in children, when they watched an educational video clip modeling emotion regulation together with a parent.[73]

Parents' media use habits—parental media modeling—also affect children's emotions. While we might rightly consider social anxiety to relate more to mental health than social well-being, social anxiety is characterized by strong emotions, such as fear, in social situations.[74] Using the Technology Interference in Life Examples Scale to operationalize parents' "technoference," Ji and colleagues found a positive association between technoference, or the frequency of parents using technology in the middle of parent–child interactions, and Chinese adolescents' social anxiety through parent–child attachment.[75] To put these findings in context, other research and theorizing suggests that parent–child attachment is an important predictor of emotion regulation, partly because low levels of parent–child attachment inhibit children's development of the ability to manage negative emotions.[76] It is possible, then, that emotion regulation might also serve as a mediator, likely in serial, of the relationship between unhealthy parental media modeling and children's negative feelings in social situations.

Parent–Child Relationship Quality and Conflict

The changing nature of the parent–child relationship across childhood can cause challenges in the family, including challenges with parent–child communication, parent–child conflict,[77] and parent–child closeness. Some level of parent–child conflict is "a normal part of development,"[78] but frequent parent–child conflict has a number of negative outcomes. A multitude of factors contribute to the extent of conflict in parent–child relationships, including child factors such as temperament, behavior problems, and autonomy development; parent factors such as hostility and mental health; and contextual factors such as ethnicity and socio-economic status.[79] Research also shows that media parenting may also serve as a contributing factor in parent–child conflict, though how and when media parenting is enacted seems to make a significant difference in the nature of that conflict. For example, a survey of parents of children ages 2–10 in Belgium found that children whose parents engaged in high levels of parental media control of children's tablet use experienced more frequent conflicts with their parents about the tablet, while children whose parents frequently engaged in joint media engagement of tablet use experienced less conflict.[80] In their study with youth ages 10–14, Valkenburg and colleagues found that media parenting in the form of both inconsistent and controlling parental media control was positively associated with family conflict, while autonomy-supportive parental media control was negatively associated with family conflict.[81] Similarly, the study found that autonomy-supportive parent–child media conversations were negatively associated with family conflict, but controlling parent–child media conversations were positively associated with family conflict. Kanter, Afifi, and Robbins recruited 118 college students (mean age of 19) and their parents to participate in an experiment in which some of the parents were asked to create a Facebook account and connect with/friend their child, while the remaining parents were not asked to do so.[82] Results of the study showed that parents' Facebook presence decreased parent–child conflict and enhanced parent–child closeness, especially among dyads who had experienced relatively more parent–child relationship conflict prior to the study (consistent with MPM path 4). And in a study involving nearly four thousand parents of kindergarteners in China, parents' phubbing was negatively associated with parent–child closeness, which ultimately resulted in lower levels of child prosocial behavior; interestingly, an authoritative parenting style tended to attenuate this relationship.[83] The authors argued, "When parents spend most of their time on screens, children may feel that they need to compete with their electronic devices for their parents' attention, and this competition for attention can lead to tension and conflict in the parent-child relationship, hindering the development of a sense of intimacy."[84] These findings coincide with findings from a study involving a nationally representative samples of U.S. adolescents ages 12–17 showing that parents' problematic Internet use was related to adolescents reporting a worse relationship with their parents.[85] Relatedly, U.S. college students were asked to think back to their time in high school (grades 9–12) as they answered survey questions about attitudes toward their parents (among other measures), and their parents answered questions about media parenting in which they engaged when their child was in high school.[86] Results showed that adolescents whose parents engaged in parental media control had less positive feelings about their parents. The study also found that those who remember their parents engaging in high levels of parental media control thought their parents felt less positively toward them, especially when their parents also failed to engage in high levels of parent–child media conversations, suggesting that parent–child media conversations "may protect children from the detrimental effect of restrictive mediation on adolescents' perceptions of their parents' attitudes toward them."[87] In another study, this one involving Chinese children ages 10–12, parent–child media conversations about children's mobile phone use were related to more positive parent–child relationships.[88]

Conclusion

As with other facets of childhood development, media parenting is a unique form of parenting that can have an influence on children's social and emotional development. Media parenting strategies that reduce children's exposure to antisocial media content can reduce children's adoption of, or participation in, similarly antisocial behaviors, including aggression. Likewise, media parenting strategies that promote children's exposure to prosocial media content can increase children's participation in prosocial behaviors. Parental media modeling can function to increase children's prosocial behavior or reduce parent–child relationship quality and children's emotion regulation skills, depending on the type of modeling performed. Research also demonstrates that not all media parenting strategies are the same, and that a single strategy can function differently when it is characterized by different features. Features such as the autonomy-supportive nature of media parenting, for example, seem to be especially impactful in determining the nature of media parenting's influence on child outcomes. Finally, joint media engagement of prosocial media content can lead to prosocial behaviors, but joint media engagement of entertainment or antisocial content can have the opposite outcome.

It is once again clear that parent–child media conversations tend to be most effective at helping children benefit from prosocial media content and resist the effects of antisocial media content. For some children with some types of content, however, parent–child media conversations and parental media control may both be necessary, especially if they each support children's autonomy. Parental media control by itself appears to be less related to children's socio-emotional development. And importantly, research demonstrates that the appropriate forms of media parenting, to be effective, must be practiced consistently enough that they become part of the family culture.

Let us now once again briefly return to the discussion in Chapter 1 about the nature of children and the distinction between a human being and being human. Let us remember that according to a mind embodied perspective of human nature, the most important outcome of childhood socialization is not the development of attitudes, behaviors, or skills necessary for successful adaptation to living in society. Rather, what is truly at stake is the development of the child's mind. It can be argued that the attitudes, behaviors, and skills that we talk about when it comes to children's socio-emotional development, such as the ability to regulate one's emotions, a child's engagement in sharing a toy with another child, or healthy conflict resolution skills, are simply a reflection of the health of the mind. The mind's health, in these terms, is not limited to one's mental health, though mental health certainly plays a role. A healthy mind is not merely reflective of the presence of positive social relationships or the absence of unhealthy relationships. It is more than the brain's reaction to the nutrition and exercise that serve as bodily inputs. The health of the mind is even more than all these things combined. It may be that the real test of the health of the mind is not actually measurable by current methods, for how does one validly and reliably answer the question "Am I more human today than I was yesterday?" Or in the context of media parenting, "Is my child more human today than they were yesterday?" as a result of media parenting. Being human involves human connection with each other, which is the underlying goal of all research devoted to socio-emotional development. Beauregard's suggestion that it is "socially hazardous"[89] to reduce humans to their neurobiology applies directly to a discussion of media parenting and children's social development. It is one thing to teach a child not to hit or kick to resolve conflict and to store those lessons in the synapses of memory and locations of the brain associated with moral reasoning, but it is quite another thing for a child to gain a sense deep in her soul that she and every person she encounters has inestimable worth and potential, a concept of human nature that may constitute the highest levels of moral reasoning and development. We must then ask whether there is room in communication research and practice[90] and in the social sciences generally for a concept reminiscent of the "Imago Dei" in many world religions. Or more scientifically speaking, is there room in communication research and practice and in the social sciences for an acceptance that the mind might exist independent of the brain, suggesting that the aim of human development is the development of the mind and not just the training of the brain? If we are willing to accept that, then it becomes much easier to accept the idea that our job as researchers and scientists might actually be to prescribe how people *should* live, how parents *should* parent, how children (and adults for that matter) *should* interact with others. As scientists, it makes us a bit squeamish to think about making subjective pronouncements about the right way to live. Perhaps our brains (and stomachs) have been conditioned to have such a reaction. But the simple fact that we study aggression and violence and interpersonal relationship quality and media parenting tells us that, at least on some level, we believe in the rightness or wrongness of ways of living, and that those beliefs motivate our research, even if that research is simply an attempt to identify that certain ways of living have certain outcomes. These motivations give meaning, and reflect an inherent belief that the goal of parenting, be it media parenting or otherwise, is to help children be and become, and that becoming a parent in its fullest sense is a process of seeing children as capable of both being and becoming, and that through communication parents can be and become what their child needs them to be.

Chapter 9

MENTAL HEALTH AND MEDIA PARENTING

About 14 percent of youth ages 10–19 worldwide experience a mental health disorder.[1] Other estimates suggest that up to 20 percent of adolescents ages 12–18 worldwide suffer from what can properly be called a diagnosable mental health disorder.[2] What's more, about 40–50 percent of these adolescents, for one or more reasons, fail to receive timely, professional mental health treatment.[3,4] While it is difficult to disentangle the myriad causes and symptoms of mental health problems and the barriers to helping youth receive appropriate professional treatment, evidence suggests there is a link between loneliness, media use, and symptoms of both anxiety and depression. In a day when many youth have access to media technologies that provide opportunities to connect with others in ways unlike those of any previous generation, "studies indicate that loneliness and isolation are more widespread than many of the other major health issues of our day, including smoking, diabetes, and obesity, and with comparable levels of risk to health and premature death."[5] At its best, media use can provide connections that can help alleviate symptoms of loneliness and mental health distress,[6] and at its worst, can serve among the causes of suicidal thoughts and behaviors.[7]

Perhaps just as significant is research demonstrating a strong, significant relationship between certain types of parent–child interactions and lower levels of mental health problems, including depression, anxiety, psychosis, suicidal ideation, post-traumatic stress symptoms, addictive Internet use/gaming,[8] and loneliness.[9] Indeed, parenting can be expected to "directly influence child development, functioning, and mental health in favorable or unfavorable manners, depending on the quality and appropriateness of parenting behavior."[10] In their review, Achtergarde and colleagues found that parenting characterized by warmth, support, and acceptance tends to relate to better child mental health, while a lack of those attributes, along with parenting that is critical or rejecting in nature, contributes to poorer mental health.[11] The authors argued that certain parenting behaviors, such as how they model behavior, enact rules, and communicate with their child, all relate to children's mental well-being (not coincidentally, you'll notice, these behaviors correspond to several media parenting behaviors). The relationship between parenting and children's mental well-being is so strong, in fact, that interventions such as Parent–Child Interaction Therapy, which is intended to build a positive parent–child relationship, and thereby reduce children's problem behavior and internalizing symptoms, have become regular parts of clinical practice targeting the mental health of children.[12,13,14,15] Thus, we can expect media parenting behaviors to likewise influence the mental health and associated media use of children.

Media Parenting

Before reviewing the literature related to media parenting and mental health, it is important to clarify that not all outcomes of media parenting and children's media use that will be discussed are necessarily clinical symptoms or diagnoses of mental health disorders. As we know, there are strong connections between mental health, self-regulation, emotional well-being, and even physical health; therefore, many of the outcomes noted in this section could very well be included in another chapter of this book. Whether they are included here or elsewhere in this book matters less than ensuring that they are discussed somewhere in order to give them the consideration they warrant. For example, one study involving children as young as 8 (mean age of 13) found that parental media control was positively associated with kids' online self-regulation (i.e., the ability to manage how much time they spend online) and emotion regulation, and negatively associated with their impulsivity two years later.[16] These outcomes are notable because, as the authors noted, they have been linked to pathological gaming and other risky online behaviors, as well as to the ability to cope with distressing emotions. So, with the understanding that some of the research that will now be reviewed might more appropriately fall under a mental well-being umbrella instead of a mental health umbrella, let us explore the various connections between media parenting and children's mental well-being.

To begin, it must be acknowledged that some research has failed to find a connection between media parenting and youths' mental well-being. Barry and colleagues, for example, surveyed 113 U.S. parent–adolescent dyads about their social media use, parental media monitoring, and symptoms of several mental health disorders.[17] The study failed to find a significant relationship between parental media monitoring and symptoms of inattention and hyperactivity/impulsivity, oppositional defiant disorder, conduct disorder, anxiety, and depression. On the other hand, studies from around the world fairly consistently show that media parenting can promote the mental well-being of children. Australian pre-adolescents ages 10–12 reported fewer depressive symptoms when their parents had greater control over the amount of time pre-adolescents spent on social media—the relationship between parental media control and fewer depressive symptoms was mediated through both time spent on social media and appearance comparisons,[18] consistent with MPM path 2. That is, when parents had greater control over the time their pre-adolescent children spent on social media, pre-adolescents spent less time on social media, which in turn related to less frequent comparisons of one's appearance to that of people on social media, which ultimately related to fewer depressive symptoms. The same type of parental media control was also related to greater life satisfaction among pre-adolescents, likely because "those parents also engage in other useful forms of mediation and engagement in the child's life."[19] Wright found that both joint media engagement and parent–child media conversations were negatively related to adolescents' (ages 13–15) cyberbullying victimization and both depression and anxiety one year later.[20] Wright suggested that joint media engagement "allows parents and their children to discuss appropriate online content and strategies for dealing with such content"[21] and that parent–child media conversations represent "discussions between parents and children concerning online risks, thus making these children more likely to act in ways that minimize their exposure to such risks."[22] Also consistent with MPM path 2, a U.S. national study involving youth ages 10–20 found that autonomy-supportive parental media control was related to less social media and video game use, which ultimately resulted in lower levels of depression (for social media use) and of both depression and anxiety (for video games).[23] In addition, consistent with MPM path 3, the cybervictimization of U.S. adolescents ages 12–17 diagnosed with autism spectrum disorder was less likely to relate to depression among those whose parents engaged in high frequency media parenting, leading the author to conclude that "parents should also recognize that their mediation of technology use and social support might protect against cyber victimization and depression," that media parenting could "lead to continuous dialogue between parent and adolescent regarding online risks and opportunities," and that media parenting efforts "contribute to adolescents' beliefs that someone is there for them."[24] Among Taiwanese junior high school students, parental media control was negatively associated with Internet addiction and engagement in cyberbullying.[25] Similarly, among Dutch adolescents, parental media control that was either autonomy-supportive or controlling in nature was negatively associated with violent media use, and through violent media use to lower levels of ADHD-related behaviors.[26] Research conducted in England involving more than sixteen thousand adolescents ages 10–18 found that having a public social media account (an account that does not require a follow request, friend request, or permission in order to access the account's content) was positively associated with experiencing symptoms of both anxiety and depression.[27] In the study, adolescents who reported relatively higher levels of parent–child media conversations and parental media control were actually more likely than adolescents reporting no media parenting to have experienced anxiety and depression. These findings appear to contradict past research, but the authors suggested that these findings implicated that adolescents experiencing anxiety and depression may have reported behavior from their caregivers that indicated caregiver recognition of the adolescent's mental distress, prompting the implementation of parental guidance and regulation approaches in addressing what may have been perceived by caregivers as the exacerbating effect of their children's social media use on anxiety and depression.[28]

They also argued that this conclusion is warranted due to the finding of a negative association between parent–child media conversations and both anxiety and depression, as well as to the finding of no significant relationship between parental media control and symptoms of anxiety and depression. In Israel, though it did not measure media parenting directly, a study found that negative parenting (i.e., hostility, lack of control, and physical control) during the Covid-19 pandemic was related to an increased risk of children's digital media addiction, which in turn related to increased emotional and behavioral difficulties such as emotional symptoms, conduct problems, hyperactivity-inattention, and peer problems.[29] In Russia, children ages 13–15 reported greater happiness when their parents engaged in high levels of parent–child media conversations and moderate levels of parental media control.[30] In the northeast United States, adolescents' mobile phone use and TV viewing were both related to depression one year later, but parental media control of TV use was shown to reduce depression one year later.[31] Parental media modeling in the form of phubbing directly predicted depression in youth ages 11–18 in China, and indirectly through lower levels of youths' basic psychological needs satisfaction and lower self-esteem.[32] In a review of eighteen studies involving youth ages 8–18, Rega and colleagues concluded that media parenting, especially parent–child media conversations and joint media engagement, "seemed to protect against cyberbullying and related psychopathological symptoms, such as depression and anxiety."[33] And a Gallup survey published in late 2023 found that while U.S. teenagers' time spent on social media predicted lower mental health, parental media control reduced social media time, and the authors concluded that "screen time has no association with an index of mental health problems for teens who demonstrate high levels of self-control and enjoy a strong relationship with parents who supervise them."[34] In other words, general parenting and media parenting are part of the recipe to reduce the negative effect of children's media use on their mental health.

Parent and Child Mental Health

In addition to highlighting the influence of media parenting on children's media use and its outcomes, the Media Parenting Model also postulates that both parent and child characteristics play a role in the ultimate outcomes of children's media use. Of particular importance to a discussion about children's mental health as an outcome of the interaction between media parenting and children's media use are parent and child mental health characteristics and how they affect parent–child interactions.

Children of parents who suffer from mental health problems are more likely to experience their own mental health problems.[35,36,37,38,39] While research about the reasons for this connection is ongoing, some studies suggest that experiencing mental health problems affects parents' ability to engage in parenting behaviors and establish a relationship with their child that is conducive to the child's healthy mental well-being. For example, one study analyzed data from 124 families with a mentally ill parent and 127 families with a parent without mental illness and found that parents without a mental illness had significantly higher quality interactions with their adolescents (ages 11–16) than parents with a mental illness, and that parents with a mental illness also monitored their children less.[40] Thus, beyond any obvious biological reason for the intergenerational transmission of the propensity to mental health problems, parent–child interactions suffered as a result of parents' mental health distress. In other words, a parent's mental health distress affected their parenting. Parents' mental illness symptomatology increased parental unresponsiveness and other difficulties in parent–child interactions.[41] Parents with a mental illness reported lower levels of joint problem-solving, organization, and emotional climate.[42] Parents' mental health distress can also manifest in low levels of children's attachment and higher levels of parental withdrawal.[43] It can disrupt the parent–child relationship, the level of parents' responsiveness to children, and parents' emotional availability.[44] It can set a poor example of how to regulate one's mood,[45] limit the level of autonomy granting, and increase the level of parental overprotectiveness.[46] A systematic review concluded that parents with mental health problems had difficulty setting boundaries, maintaining discipline, managing routines, balancing their own needs with the needs of their children, maintaining a close emotional connection with their child, differentiating their own feelings from those of their children, and communicating with their child.[47] Parents with a mental illness also had difficulty enacting appropriate discipline and establishing clear boundaries between their own emotional well-being and the emotional well-being of their children, and tended to experience role reversal with their children (where the older children perform parenting behaviors for the younger children or even the parent themselves).[48] Ackerson concluded that parents who experience mental illness "have the same desires to care for their children and to perform well in the parent role as other parents. . . . However, they must cope with a disorder that at times challenges their ability to effectively carry out the parenting role."[49]

To put this in context, nearly one billion people worldwide are estimated to be living with a mental illness.[50] It is difficult to estimate the number of adults worldwide who are parents; while parenting customs differ around the world and fertility rates continue to decline in much of the world,[51] for this exercise we will use the United States as a comparative baseline. In the United States alone, estimates suggest that 59.3 million adults live with a mental illness, or about 23.1 percent of all U.S. adults.[52] Of these, about 69 percent are parents,[53] meaning more than forty million U.S. parents can be expected to currently experience a mental illness. If the world has a population of around 8.2 billion, about 5.7 billion of those are 18 or older.[54] If 69 percent of those 5.7 billion are parents, that means about 3.9 billion adults worldwide are parents. And if 23 percent of parents worldwide live with a mental illness, that means that around nine hundred million parents around the world live with a mental illness. Now, these estimates are obviously crude extrapolations, but the point remains that hundreds of millions of parents of all ages experience mental illness. Significantly for this discussion, this also means that a sizable portion of the world's children may be exposed to less positive parenting and more negative parenting than they otherwise might if mental illness were not a problem among parents. But it is a problem, and some might claim it is an epidemic. And the epidemic reaches all corners of parenting, even, presumably, media parenting. "Presumably" is used purposely here to note that we need research about how parents' mental health affects their engagement in media parenting, including research exploring the pathways through which parents' mental health affects media parenting and its outcomes.

Knowing that parents' mental health affects their parenting, possibly their media parenting, and ultimately, their children's mental health, it is also helpful to discuss how children's mental health might influence parenting. Research shows that parents of seriously ill (but not necessarily mentally ill) children place high value on ensuring that their child feels loved, making sure their child receives the appropriate medical attention, and advocating for their child with medical staff.[55] Despite these values, research also shows that families with children who had a chronic physical illness were characterized by lower levels of parental responsiveness/warmth and higher levels of parental demandingness/monitoring and overprotection.[56] In other words, the well-being of children can make it more difficult for parents to be the kind of parents they want to be.

A 2023 study provides evidence that children's well-being affects parenting behaviors. In the study, parents and their offspring from 137 families (though the average age of the "offspring" was 25.7, children were as young as 7.5 years old) participated in a task in which they were instructed to discuss and reach consensus on a topic, and their interactions during the task were recorded and coded.[57] Participants also completed surveys measuring both internalizing problems (such as withdrawal, somatic complaints, and anxiety/depression) and externalizing problems (such as aggression and rule breaking). Analysis found that offspring externalizing problems predicted lower levels of warmth displayed by mothers during the conflict/discussion task. The authors argued:

> Offspring's externalizing behaviors might provoke annoyance and dissatisfaction in one's interaction partner, which in turn could result in receiving less warmth and patience during communication.... However, it

could also be argued that offspring with externalizing problems might need more restrictive parenting, including setting clear boundaries and rules, which might come with a more directive communication style during the mother–offspring interactions and could have been rated as less warm.[58]

In other words, children can affect the parenting practices of their own parents by reducing the level of positive parenting in which their parents engage. Though it found a connection between externalizing problems and parenting behavior, the study did not find a connection between internalizing problems and parenting behavior. But a study by Serbin and colleagues involving low-income children ages 7–13 in Canada found that children's internalizing problems actually increased positive parenting over time and that children's externalizing problems predicted lower levels of positive parenting over time.[59] A meta-analysis also revealed that children's externalizing behavior was related to parents' subsequent psychological distress and incompetent parenting.[60] Externalizing problems of Finnish school children were also related to a parenting style characterized by behavioral control, and internalizing problems were predictive of parenting characterized by psychological control, especially among fathers.[61] Regarding the latter finding, the authors speculated,

> Perhaps fathers try to impact on children's internalizing problems through psychological means rather than affection or directly setting limits. In middle childhood, mothers may come to expect and accept socially withdrawn children's internalizing behaviours. Fathers, however, may become less tolerant of emotional arousal, expecting children to manage their anxious, depressed or withdrawn behaviours. In attempting to decrease internalizing problems, fathers may feel more helplessness and tell their children that they are ashamed of their emotional problems.[62]

Another study provides evidence that children's poor mental health can lead to parents' feelings of parenting incompetence and poorer parents' mental health. Farmer and colleagues found that parents of children who received services for emotional and mental well-being, compared to parents of those who had not, reported more depression, worry, fatigue, and relationship difficulties in the family.[63] They also felt less competent about their ability to handle their children's psychological problems. Parents of children with a mental health disorder also experienced poorer quality of life compared to parents of other children.[64] While none of these studies suggest that children's mental health affects media parenting behaviors specifically, they certainly point to the plausibility of such a relationship. In fact, it could be reasoned that media parenting may be even more affected by children's mental health than other parenting behaviors since children's media use, especially as children progress through adolescence, becomes a behavior about which parents know progressively less, and over which they have less and less control. Of note is research showing that general parental monitoring during adolescence is characterized by reductions in both adolescent disclosure and parents' knowledge about their children,[65] and research on media parenting tends to follow similar patterns.[66,67,68]

Children's Mental Health and Media Use

The discussion about media and mental health in Chapter 3 focused mainly on children's media use as a predictor of children's mental health problems. While evidence for the direction of this relationship is abundant, it is equally plausible that children's mental health problems may predict their media use. In turn, this mental health-instigated media use may then affect both general and media parenting. In an attempt to better understand the direction of the relationship between media use and mental health, Makarin said, "There may be hundreds of papers that present correlations between social media and well-being, and many of them are great and highly informative, but we still know little about which way the effect runs."[69] Makarin co-authored a study that explored this directionality and found that the introduction of Facebook on U.S. college campuses predicted more symptoms of mental health problems, such as depression symptoms.[70] But the study also found that college students who were susceptible to mental illness were more likely to seek professional mental health services after the introduction of Facebook at their school. Another study found that people experiencing anxiety were more likely to interact with others on social media.[71] Thus, it is safe to conclude, as other researchers have done, that "media use and behavioral difficulties are interrelated and that the effects of both might mutually reinforce each other to impact child development negatively,"[72] that "social media use and common emotional and mental outcomes work together in a transactional fashion"[73] and that "opting to substitute digital media for interpersonal communication to avoid feared situations may become cyclically reinforced over time, making the person even more avoidant and worsening the symptoms and severity of social anxiety disorder."[74]

As with all research in the social sciences, not every study reaches the same conclusion. In fact, research exists that fails to show that adolescents' poor mental health predicts certain types of media use.[75] And while a systematic review concluded that time spent using, activity on, investment in, and addiction to social media each correlated with depression, anxiety, and psychological distress, the authors were quick to point out that the relationships were too complex to make general conclusions, and that from the data they reviewed "it is not possible to decide whether social media use causes depression, anxiety, and psychological distress, or whether those with depression, anxiety and psychological distress are more likely to spend time on social media."[76] Yet, other research suggests that youths' gender, age, emotion regulation skills, and quality of support network all play a role in predicting both media use and mental health outcomes.[77] These inconsistencies, lack of clarity, and other intervening variables in the research further strengthen the need for more research to understand the implications of these potentially reciprocal, transactive relationships for media parenting. One obvious hypothesis that emerges from this brief discussion is that children's media use mediates the relationship between children's mental health and media parenting. We've already seen that both children's media use and their mental health affect parenting, and it makes sense that theoretical and statistical mediation is occurring. And if the relationship can work in the opposite direction, parenting, as we've also seen, can influence children's mental health, which may in turn affect their media use. The time is right to more fully explore the interactions between children's mental health, their media use, and media parenting.

Media and Parent–Child Communication About Mental Health

From everything discussed in this chapter, we can conclude that mental health, media, and parenting interact in a variety of ways. Sometimes behavior drives mental health. Other times mental health drives behavior. But through it all run a few unmistakable threads. First, more can (and should) be done to help children and youth suffering from mental health distress. Second, parent–child interactions generally, as well as those related to media specifically, can influence children's mental well-being. And third, media use likewise plays a role in children's mental well-being. Many times, as researchers, we seek to unravel disparate threads of research to answer a single research question, but in the case of children's mental health, parenting, and media, it may be helpful to weave the three together to generate an understanding of parents' role in navigating the complex, media-centered lives of today's youth.

Among the many things that can be done to support the mental health of children and youth is to help them receive appropriate, professional treatment. Similarly to adolescents' reluctance to disclose their specific media use to their parents,[78] many adolescents are also reluctant to disclose their mental health challenges to a parent.[79] Unwillingness to disclose mental health information to one's parents has been attributed to (1) adolescents' lack of knowledge about mental health issues, (2) adolescents' perception that their parents do not or cannot understand what it feels like to experience symptoms of mental illness, (3) adolescents' fear that their parents will respond negatively to the disclosure of mental health information, (4) their perception that their relationship with their parents is not good enough to warrant disclosure, and (5) the perception that their mental health problems are not severe enough to justify the risks of disclosure.[80] Thus, while media parenting does not immediately jump out from this list of barriers to parent–child communication about mental health, it is possible that both media use and media parenting play some sort of ancillary role in the development of these barriers. More research is needed, to be sure, but adolescents' media use has been shown to relate to many of the barriers noted above. For instance, specialized media can be used to enhance health literacy[81] and mental health literacy, even among marginalized populations.[82] Media can also be used to shape, perpetuate, and reduce negative perceptions of mental illness.[83] The portrayal of mental illness in the media also influences the likelihood of seeking professional mental health help for those with a mental illness.[84] Some research has even found that media can be used to help encourage adolescents' disclosure of sensitive information—adolescent girls who watched a YouTube vlog with a self-efficacy message related to sexual assault disclosure had higher sexual assault disclosure efficacy, especially among girls who identified with the vlog's character.[85] It appears plausible, then, that media content can be strategically used, and promoted by parents, to help youth overcome barriers to parent–child communication about stigmatized identities or other health topics, though much more research is needed.

Conclusion

Media use, media parenting, and mental health affect each other in ways both known and unknown. Risk factors for children's mental health include all three—their own media use, the parenting they receive, and their parents' mental health. Children's mental health can likewise influence their parents' mental well-being, the parenting behaviors in which their parents engage, their own media use behaviors, as well as the outcomes of their own media use. Media use, media parenting, and other forms of parent–child interactions can also be used to help manage youths' mental health, alter the mental health outcomes of media use, encourage mental health treatment-seeking behaviors, and overcome barriers to youths' disclosure to parents of mental health problems. The kaleidoscope of variables that influence children's mental health is vast, making them all the more relevant for the allocation of time and resources to learning more about how they interact. And the more we learn about these interactions, the better equipped we will be to help support the mental well-being of children. Speaking of the role of public television in a statement to members of the U.S. Senate in 1969, Fred Rogers said something that applies just as equally now, well into the twenty-first century, to media and parenting: "If we . . . can only make it clear that feelings are mentionable and manageable, we will have done a great service for mental health."[86] That still remains the goal.

Chapter 10

COGNITIVE DEVELOPMENT, ACADEMIC PERFORMANCE, AND MEDIA PARENTING

During an interview with a writer for *The New York Dramatic Mirror* in 1913, Thomas Edison was asked, "What is your estimation of the future educational value of pictures?" In response, Edison predicted:

> Books will soon be obsolete in the public schools. Scholars will be instructed through the eye. It is possible to teach every branch of human knowledge with the motion picture. Our school system will be completely changed inside of ten years. We have been working for some time on the school pictures. We have been studying and reproducing the life of the fly, mosquito, silk weaving moth, brown moth, gypsy moth, butterflies, scale and various other insects, as well as chemical crystallization. It proves conclusively the worth of motion pictures in chemistry, physics and other branches of study, making the scientific truths, difficult to understand from textbooks, plain and clear to children.[1]

While Edison was wrong about the place of books in education, he was correct about the value of motion pictures, and his words have echoes of a prophecy about YouTube. Fifty-six years after Edison's prediction, another man sat in front of the Senate Subcommittee on Communications to lobby against a presidential budget cut for public broadcasting. At the hearing, Fred Rogers, who "saw the potential and possibility of media to help children,"[2] said:

> I'm very much concerned, as I know you are, about what's being delivered to our children in this country. And I've worked in the field of child development for six years now, trying to understand the inner needs of children. We deal with such things as, as the inner drama of childhood. We don't have to bop somebody over the head to make drama on the screen. We deal with such things as getting a haircut, or the feelings about brothers and sisters, and the kind of anger that arises in simple family situations. And we speak to it constructively.[3]

Rogers achieved his objective that day, and today, more than one hundred years after Edison's predictions and more than fifty years after Rogers' plea, children's learning is increasingly facilitated by a multitude of digital media platforms. But with the help of decades of research, we now know that children get the most out of any type of educational content—be it taught face to face by a school teacher or visually by an online sketch—when their parents are involved in the learning process. As has been known, or at least surmised, for centuries, parents are often in the best position to support children's learning, regardless of the medium that presents the content. Some accounts suggest that shortly after the first Europeans settled what is now Massachusetts in the United States, laws about public education were established because citizens feared that parents were not adequately performing the role of educator for their children. The first of these laws was passed in 1642 by the Massachusetts General Court and required that parents and "masters" should not allow "barbarism in any of their families as not to endeavour to teach, by themselves or others, their children and apprentices, so much learning, as may enable them perfectly to read the English tongue, and knowledge of the capital laws" because "many parents and masters are too indulgent and negligent of their duty in that kind."[4] In the ensuing years, the Massachusetts General Court was apparently not satisfied with parents' engagement in the teaching of their children, as just five years later they passed a follow-up law often known as the "Old Deluder Satan Act"[5] requiring all towns with at least 50 families to hire a teacher for the town's children, to be paid for by parents, and for towns with at least one hundred families to establish a grammar school. The first line of the law states the justification for its creation: "It being one chief project of that old deluder, Satan, to keep men from the knowledge of the Scriptures,"[6] suggesting that parents were not fulfilling their responsibility to teach their children to read the scriptures. It appears that similar concerns of parental and societal neglect of children's learning were experienced in Europe, as suggested by Frederick the Great's 1763 decree:

> Whereas, to our great displeasure, we have perceived that schools and the instruction of youth in the country have come to be greatly neglected, and that by the inexperience of many sacristans and schoolmasters, the young people grow up in stupidity and ignorance, it is our well-considered and serious pleasure, that instruction in the country, throughout all our provinces, should be placed on a better footing and be better organized than heretofore.[7]

And as early as 1530, the reformer Martin Luther lamented the negligence of families in educating their children: "Because I see that the common man is indifferent to the maintenance of schools, and wholly withholds his children from instruction, and gives himself solely to food and belly-care, and besides will not or cannot consider what an abominable, un-Christian thing he purposes in this, and what a great, murderous damage he is doing in all the world for the Devil's service, I have determined to put out this admonition to you,"[8] that civil authorities should assist parents by providing education and an educational system for children. "Count it to be one of the highest virtues on earth," Luther continued, "to train faithfully the children of other people, which so very few, yea almost no one, does for his own."[9]

The positions of the Massachusetts General Court, Frederick the Great, and Luther all shared the common primary motivation of educating children for the welfare of children's souls. In each case, the welfare of children's souls was perceived as being tied to, and a result of, their ability to read and study scripture. An argument could be made that today, hundreds of years later, the primary motivation of parents and policymakers to educate children has not changed—the hope is to support children's development into good humans. We could semantically enter the estuary of "hard-core religious fundamentalists on one side and equally hard-core scientific fundamentalists on the other,"[10] to repeat a quote from Chapter 1, or we could simply equate the concept of human development through education with the development of the soul through education. Both positions espouse the development of the mind as the purpose of children's education. Martin Luther King Jr., for example, believed that an educated mind is one that has developed the gifts of both reason and morality:

> We must remember that intelligence is not enough. Intelligence plus character—that is the goal of a true education. The complete education gives one not only power of concentration, but worthy objectives upon which to concentrate. The broad education will, therefore, transmit to one not only the accumulated knowledge of the race but also the accumulated experience of social living.[11]

Writing for Time, Mallory Hutchings-Tryon, a historian and doctoral student at the University of Washington with a master's degree from Columbia University, argued that "the belief that schools have a responsibility to teach moral, ethical, and religious values—often encompassed by the term 'civic morality'—is older than public schools themselves . . . Before there were schoolhouses, communities monitored the moral teaching in the home."[12] In the twentieth century, she argued, debates arose about the role of publicly funded institutions in teaching moral values to citizens. And speaking of the ongoing debates about teaching morality in the U.S. public education system, she continued, "Using public education to teach universal values and strengthen society has always been central in the development of our education system. Our historical and current problem is that we cannot agree *what* our nation's universal values are and *who we need* to strengthen our society."

But while citizens, politicians, and pundits continue to wrangle with what should or should not be taught to America's children, research is clear and unequivocal that parents' involvement is essential to the education of children,[13,14,15,16] be it academic or moral. And while there are many "powerful social and economic factors that still prevent many parents from fully participating in schooling,"[17] evidence suggests that what parents do in the home is of primary import to childhood learning. In fact, it is not the role of parents to support formal schooling, but the role of formal schooling to support parents,[18] for "the true goal of parents, communities, and societies have always been education goals, and hence a multiplicity of learning goals. Schooling is just one of the many instruments in achieving an education."[19] We rightly talk of schoolteachers as educators, but it is important to remember that the primary educator of children is the parent, who is supported in countless ways by well-meaning adults in extended families, schools, churches, and other community groups. In support of this argument, it is interesting to note that parental engagement in children's learning in the home is far more predictive of learning outcomes than parental involvement in school-based activities.[20]

Boonk and colleagues provided a comprehensive review of seventy-five studies published from 2003 to 2017 that explored the role of parental involvement in youth academic achievement.[21] They concluded that parental involvement predicts a multitude of measures of children's math and reading achievement, literacy skills, science achievement, overall learning performance, language achievement, grade point average, history achievement, and social sciences performance. The review also found that the types of parental involvement that appeared to be the most effective included reading at home, engaging in learning activities at home, having high expectations for learning, providing an appropriate learning environment and learning materials, autonomy-supportive involvement with homework, reinforcement of learning at home, and parent–child educational discussions.

So, while society has long wrestled with implementing strategies to assist in the education of children, the onus for children's learning has remained on parents, primarily because parents' influence on children's learning is so powerful. There is every reason to extol the benefits of public education and its outcomes for both individuals and society, but there is also reason to lament the position of parents in children's education in contemporary society. Today, parents are considered supporters of the public educational system and its educators, when evidence suggests that the ideal direction of support should mainly be the opposite. And further complicating the "ideal" structure of education are the limitless opportunities and risks of children's access and exposure to amounts of information heretofore unavailable to children. But instead of providing an abdication of parents' role in children's learning, the place of both public education and media in the lives of children makes the participation of parents in the process of children's learning more desperately important than ever. In 1991, Ernest Boyer wrote what is often known as the Carnegie Report. In it, he suggested that television, next to parents, could help support children's preparation for formal schooling: "Next to parents, television is, perhaps, a child's most influential teacher."[22] Thus, predictably, some of the earliest and most influential work in the sphere of media parenting concerns the powerful part that parents play in helping children learn from media content intended to supplement their formal education.

Comprehension

Media parenting has the potential to help children comprehend media content. For example, parent–child media conversations characterized as dialogic questioning have been shown to help children's learning from media content. Dialogic questioning involves asking questions to help children engage with media content, and is associated with both story comprehension and vocabulary among preschoolers who jointly watched storybook videos with a parent.[23] Parent–child media conversations were also related to increased comprehension of an episode of *Swiss Family Robinson* among kindergarteners and 1st graders in the northeast United States,[24] especially for boys.[25] Parent–child media conversations during joint media engagement were positively associated with kindergarteners' curiosity, especially among children from low-SES backgrounds.[26] Parental media control in the form of restrictions on viewing were also positively associated with TV plot comprehension among first and 2nd graders in the United States,[27] and the authors suggested that parental media control may help children develop a critical attitude toward content they consume and encourage more investment of mental effort to comprehending the content, which could then lead to enhanced content comprehension. Joint media engagement, even without the support of other types of media parenting, also has the potential to alter children's comprehension of media content. For example, young children from low-SES backgrounds who watched *Sesame Street* with a coviewing parent had higher comprehension scores than their counterparts whose parents were not encouraged to watch the show with their child.[28] The author argued that joint media engagement may function to increase the levels of physiological arousal among children, a proposition supported by subsequent research.[29] Joint media engagement may also imply to children that what they are watching is approved by or important to parents,[30] thereby encouraging children's mental engagement with the content. Lessons facilitated by video chat were more effective at improving children's learning the more responsive and engaged the coviewer was.[31] And children who watched a cartoon with an adult were more likely to recall more content than other children.[32]

School Performance/Academic Achievement

In addition to facilitating children's comprehension of media content, media parenting has the potential to turn comprehension into school performance and academic achievement. Liebeskind, for example, found that children's (ages 6–12) performance in English was better at higher levels of joint media engagement and parent–child media conversations of child-oriented programming.[33] The study also found that children's performance in math and their overall academic achievement were higher the more their parents participated in joint media engagement. Media parenting in the form of a combination of both parental media control and parent–child media conversations (called 'parental monitoring of media' in the study) was related to better grades among U.S. children (mean age of 9).[34] Consistent with MPM paths 1 and 2, another study found that parental autonomy support was related to Chinese adolescents' academic performance through parent–child conversations about media.[35] In other words, adolescents whose parents allowed them relatively greater levels of freedom of choice and opinion were also more likely to have parents who engaged in relatively more frequent parent–child media conversations about adolescents' use of the Internet, which ultimately related to higher levels of perceived academic performance. The authors suggested that parent–child media conversations can help youth develop self-regulation and the ability to use the Internet effectively for acquiring knowledge. They also suggested that parent–child media conversations can improve youths' attitudes about academics, which can result in improved academic performance. Ball and Bogatz found that children who watched *Sesame Street* at home learned more from the program than children who watched at school, likely because children who watched the show the most were more likely to have parents who watched the show with them.[36] Children who watched a program with their parent were also more likely to say they liked the program because of the things they could learn from it.[37] In another study, Israeli kindergarten children ages 5–6 were taught to use one of two types of computer software programs, and their teacher engaged with them in one of three ways while using the computer program.[38] Children scored higher on measures of abstract thinking, planning, vocabulary, visuo-motor coordination, and reflective thinking when their computer use was accompanied by "adult mediation," which consisted of adult–child conversations aimed at helping the child focus on the problem at hand, sharing positive evaluations of the software content, associating the lessons with other experiences, being flexible in problem-solving, thinking about the thinking process, regulating behavior, and encouraging the child. The authors concluded:

> One of the most basic characteristics of mediation is the active role played by the adult mediator who continuously attempts to adjust elements available in the immediate environment or beyond it (using his own experiences) and makes those compatible with the child's needs, abilities and interests. The probability that an experience will constitute a learning experience for a child increases when adult intervention is adapted to the specific task at hand and to the characteristics of the child's functioning and thinking at a given time.[39]

Language/Literacy/Math/Science

Research suggests that a combination of media parenting strategies is most effective at helping children acquire essential academic skills, such as the acquisition of language, literacy, math, and science knowledge and skills. For example, in some children's educational media programming the characters address child viewers directly, what is known as "breaking the fourth wall." In her book *Preschool Clues*, Angela Santomero, the creator of *Blue's Clues* and other successful children's programs, said,

> One of the key ways to be interactive is when a character breaks the fourth wall by leaning in, looking directly at the camera, and talking to the viewer at home. The character is acknowledging the presence of the home viewer and respectfully communicating, actively listening, and seeming to affirm what they have to say. This interactive format is the key to preschoolers mastering the curriculum.[40]

What Santomero did not say, however, is that research shows that even when programs break the fourth wall, it often takes a parent's involvement for the lesson to stick. This was shown in a study by Strouse and colleagues that involved eighty-eight 2-year-olds.[41] The children watched a video with an actress that provided contingent responses to children, while the parents of the children either modeled responsiveness to the actress's requests for participation, or not. Results of the study showed that children whose parent modeled responsiveness to the actress had higher subsequent word learning. In other words, the lessons from the content were more likely to help children learn new words when a parent watched the program and interacted with both their child and the content. The authors suggested that parent modeling indicated to the child that a lesson was occurring, directed children's attention to the content, and facilitated deeper processing of the content. This type of discussion and explanation, sometimes combined with joint media engagement, was also related to reading recognition skills of U.S. kindergarteners and 1st graders,[42] receptive and expressive word learning among Israeli kindergartners,[43] emergent literacy among high-SES Israeli children ages 5-6,[44] math understanding among U.S. preschoolers,[45] and recall of information about opera among children ages 9-12 in the Netherlands.[46] In South Korea, parent–child interactions (a mix of media parenting strategies) involving newspapers and newspaper content were related to the reading motivation and subsequent academic achievement of elementary school children.[47] And in the United States, children ages 3 and 5 better learned vocabulary from watching *Sesame Street* when they watched with a parent.[48] Even parental media control alone seems to help children's domain-specific learning: parental media control was positively associated with science achievement indirectly through use of technology for learning (watching science TV shows and browsing the Internet for science-related content) among 8th graders (mean age of 14) in China.[49] Among high-SES Chinese preschoolers, a measure of media parenting that combined parental media control, parent–child media conversations, joint media engagement, and parental media monitoring, was associated with higher levels of digital literacy;[50] however, another study involving Chinese adolescents found that both parent–child media conversations and parental media monitoring were positively associated with adolescents' digital literacy, but joint media engagement was negatively associated with digital literacy.[51] And as U.S. adolescents exhibited higher levels of skepticism of news media, the more their parents engaged in parent–child media conversations with them.[52]

Cognitive Development

An argument could be made that studying factors contributing to children's academic performance is not nearly as important as learning more about factors that accelerate children's cognitive development. Evidence suggests that certain cognitive abilities, when present at sufficient levels, significantly predict academic performance.[53] Indeed, "conventional opinions and most research on the relation between cognitive abilities and academic achievement have treated cognitive abilities as foundational constructs, presupposing that cognitive abilities are primary and cause academic outcomes."[54] But additional evidence, on the other hand, suggests that academic performance and cognitive development have a bidirectional relationship—that is, cognitive abilities support academic achievement, and education supports cognitive development, especially among young children.[55] Regardless of the directionality of the relationship, it is equally important and informative to discuss the role of media parenting in both academic performance and cognitive development, though, as will be shown, substantially less (although valuable) research explicitly explores cognitive development as a media parenting outcome. Of note, many outcomes of media parenting, as shown in this and previous chapters, are characterized by researchers as being essential predictors or outcomes of cognitive development, or of child development generally, but few appear to measure actual cognitive development constructs, such as being able to distinguish fantasy from reality, perceptions of object permanence, theory of mind, egocentrism, perspective taking, metacognition, conservation, inductive and deductive reasoning, and abstract reasoning. Three examples that do measure such constructs seem relevant to this discussion. First, parent–child media conversations can help increase the disparity between children's perceptions of actual reality and televised reality among Korean adolescents.[56] Next, among Chinese 5-year-olds, joint media engagement in the form of watching a video together was related to improved memory and what the authors called "overall cognition," which consisted of several measures of children's ability to relate concepts to each other.[57] And, third, among South Korean children ages 0–5, daily joint media engagement was positively associated with cognitive development, conceptualized as changes in cognitive structure over time, but the authors cautioned that "TV viewing should not be actively promoted for brain development, however, when it happens, it may be beneficial for caregivers to watch TV interactively with young children."[58]

Brain Development

Brain development is another related, potentially significant outcome of media parenting. Research shows that both media use and parenting impact brain development in some very foundational ways. For example, screen media use has been shown to relate to lower levels of microstructural organization and myelination of brain white matter tracts in areas of the brain associated with language and emergent literacy skills among preschoolers,[59] lower cortical thickness and sulcal depth in areas of the brain associated with primary visual and higher order processing among preschoolers,[60] lower connectivity between a region of the brain related to reading and other brain regions in children ages 8–12,[61] lower neural sensitivity in several areas in the brain among youth age 12 with habitual social media checking behaviors,[62] and reduced gray matter volume in certain parts of the brain among adolescents and emerging adults who play video games at the level of Internet gaming disorder.[63] In other words, screen use has the potential to change the actual structure of children's developing brains.

Parenting also affects children's developing brains in a number of ways. For example, among children with a history of parental maltreatment and symptoms of post-traumatic stress disorder, stress was associated with hippocampus reduction.[64] Maltreated children and adolescents with PTSD also had smaller intracranial and cerebral volumes, leading researchers to conclude that "the overwhelming stress of maltreatment experiences in childhood is associated with adverse brain development."[65] Maternal aggression was also associated with delayed patterns of adolescent boys' cortical development, which itself is associated with executive function.[66] On the other hand, positive parenting predicted the development of the amygdala and prefrontal cortex among adolescents.[67] And perhaps highly relevant to media parenting, positive parenting inhibited the relationship between childhood stress and decreased hippocampal volumes among youth ages 10–17, leading to the authors' conclusion that "high-quality parenting is associated with resilience in youth through adulthood."[68] Others likewise argued that positive parenting has the potential to enhance adolescents' emotion regulation through altering the functional connectivity between the hippocampus and certain regions of the prefrontal cortex.[69] Said differently, parenting, like media use, has the power to alter children's brain development.

Because both media and parenting can affect the brain in such striking ways, it is logical to suggest that it is possible for media parenting to have similar effects. Perhaps, like positive parenting, media parenting can alter the effects of media use on brain development, as in MPM path 3. Or perhaps media parenting can alter brain development by altering children's media use itself in the first place, as in MPM path 2. And it is possible that features of media parenting, such as its valence,[70] may correspond with the moderating influence of valenced parenting (positive vs. negative), as in MPM paths 6 and 7.

Conclusion

We have now reviewed a quite substantial body of research related to the effects of media parenting on children's physical health, mental health, socio-emotional well-being, and cognitive development/academic performance. It is evident and unmistakable that media parenting is powerful, and has the vigor to affect all the same areas of children's lives that are also influenced by media. We can thus conclude, similar to Belsky and de Haans' conclusions about parenting, that before it influences children's behavior, media parenting first influences the brain:

> Unless one believes in magic, it is difficult to conclude on the basis of the evidence available that parenting does not affect the developing brain, in terms of either structure or function—or both. After all, how else would parenting or any experience for that matter influence a developing organism's behaviour, cognitions, emotions and even, in some instances, physiology and health? . . . If parenting and other developmental experiences influenced the developing brain but such effects did not extend to functioning in the real world, would there be any reason for policymakers and practitioners to regard evidence of such as important or especially meaningful?[71]

That is not to say that it is more important to establish media parenting's effect on the brain in lieu of its effect on other outcomes. As Belsky and de Hann continued, "Chronicling of links between parenting and brain structure and function, including of course causal not just statistical-associational ones, is no more important, from the perspective of either basic or applied science, than documenting such links between parenting and children's development more generally."[72] What is most important is a child's well-being, and that has many antecedents. A human's well-being is

> determined by the interaction of psychological, social, and cultural factors with biochemistry and physiology. Our physiology and biochemistry are

not separate and distinct from the rest of our life and our experiences. The mind—a manifest functioning of the brain—and the other body systems interact in ways critical for health, illness, and well-being.[73]

Whether what Ray claimed about the source of the mind is true or not (and I think the reader can guess what I believe by now), what is true is that the mind, brain, and body work together to establish the nature of human well-being, and that all three are influenced by our environments, including both media and parenting inputs.

In fact, Ray argues, scientists and health professionals increasingly agree that the body largely manifests the well-being of the mind. And like healthcare professionals who are "very good at treating disease but often not as good at treating the person,"[74] I sometimes wonder if our focus on the child developmental outcomes of media, parenting, and media parenting comes at the expense of a focus on the health of the mind. Speaking about caring for patients with cardiovascular problems, Levine and colleagues continued, "The mind, heart, and body are interconnected and interdependent" and that a growing body of research suggests that "the psychological health of a person (a person's mind) can positively or negatively affect cardiovascular health, cardiovascular risk factors, risk for CVD events, and cardiovascular prognosis over time. The intertwined relationship between heart, body, and mind can be called the mind-heart-body connection."[75] The mind they had in mind was clearly a reference to mental well-being, but seen through the mind embodied perspective of human nature, it could also refer once again to our need to refocus our research on the person, and not just on the obvious and oft-measured manifestations of brain-body interactions. We need to focus more on, to use the heart clinicians' language, what can be called the mind–brain–body connection and the role that all three play in the development of the human child and the latent humanity within each.

Chapter 11

MEDIA PARENTING METHODS AND MEASURES

Media parenting has the potential to powerfully guide children's media use and media use outcomes. Decades of research plainly show that media parenting relates to children's screen use, physical health, socio-emotional well-being, mental health, and cognitive development and academic performance. Media parenting, of course, cannot be expected to have uniform effects for all children, as parent characteristics, child characteristics, context characteristics, and features of media parenting all contribute to outcomes of media parenting, as shown in the Media Parenting Model. But, we now have a mountain of evidence showing that media parenting can function to help curb negative media effects and facilitate positive media effects. Media parenting works.

Knowing *that* something works, however, is different from understanding *how* it works. Investigating whether or not something works, in the research sense, is known as descriptive research. Descriptive research describes what happened or what is happening. But it does not tell us *how* something came, or comes, to pass. Theoretical research, on the other hand, helps us understand how something happens. A relevant analogy involving cars is insightful. Everyone who drives a car knows that when a car functions as intended, the car will accelerate when the accelerator pedal is pressed. Similarly, drivers know that turning the ignition key or pushing the ignition button starts the car, and that the car cannot be driven without the ignition of the engine. As every car owner knows, the process of igniting the engine and driving down the road is interrupted by any number of mechanical or electrical failures, but if car owners, like myself, do not understand how a car engine works, we hire a mechanic to help get the car back on the road. Mechanics have acquired a specific and valuable skill set and knowledge base that allows them to understand how an engine works, and thus, discover why a car fails to function as intended. Knowing *that* a car works and *how* it works, or does not, are both important.

Descriptive research and theoretical research may also be understood by the alternative labels of *applied* and *basic* research, respectively. Jaccard and Jacoby defined applied research as research intended "to address and hopefully solve an immediate real-world problem," and basic research as research with "the purpose of extending the boundaries of our collective body of understanding, not for the purpose of addressing a pressing problem."[1] They also described (while admittedly oversimplifying) that "basic researchers use theories whereas applied researchers do not."[2] Like the example of understanding cars, both applied and basic research are valuable. In the context of media parenting, applied research has logically preceded basic research, and has advanced our knowledge as a discipline. Levine and Markowitz said,

> One can imagine empirically documenting an effect or phenomenon whose explanation is not yet understood. While this might not count as a theoretical advancement under most uses of the term, it might nevertheless make a valuable contribution to knowledge. If nothing else, we typically need to know what needs explaining before we go about explaining it.[3]

As early as 2003, scholars lamented the atheoretical, almost universally applied nature of media parenting research. Nathanson, whose use of "mediation" should be understood as "media parenting," said,

> Most previous work on mediation has not helped us understand why certain strategies are effective and others are not. This limitation is the inevitable result of research that does not derive mediation strategies from theories which suggest that the strategies will be effective. As a result, when mediation succeeds or fails, we have no available explanatory framework that can account for the results.[4]

Having read Nathanson's argument during my time as her doctoral student, I followed up her argument in a 2013 article:

> This does not mean that scholars' efforts in the meantime to provide parents with information for their applied mediation activities are in vain and unproductive. Just as it is illogical to withhold beneficial treatment for a terminally ill patient simply because a cure is not available, it does not make sense to withhold active mediation just because we are still learning about how it works.[5]

Also in 2013, Valkenburg and colleagues wrote that one could "reasonably presuppose that parental mediation theories would borrow insights from general parenting theories. Remarkably, however, an integration of parenting theories into the field of parental mediation has largely been lacking."[6]

To be clear, in my view, media parenting (nor its predecessor, "parental mediation") is not a theory, and may more accurately be called a model or framework. If theories explain relationships between constructs, then models or frameworks provide an organizational structure for the information related to the constructs. Thus, the Media Parenting Model (MPM) is designed to organize the knowledge gained about media parenting and to point out where theory might appropriately be used to explain the relationships identified by the MPM's various pathways. The development of a model like the MPM may be a necessary step in what we might call the theory-building process. But media parenting is no more a theory than is "parenting" itself; however, just as there are theories of parenting, there can also be theories of media parenting, theories that explain why certain media parenting behaviors are related to certain predictors and outcomes.

If a media parenting theory is to be developed, we may find that the first iterations of it may come from the application of one or more theories from other disciplines, such as social psychology or human development. Regardless, the study of media parenting has matured to the point that we now know much about what needs explaining, and it is time to start explaining it through methodical application of theory. It is time for children and media researchers to become the mechanics for media parents so we can help them reach their parenting goals. In saying that, I do not mean that all media parenting research has been atheoretical, especially in recent years. The reason behind this call for a focus on pivoting toward more intentionally theoretical, basic research is explained well by Levine and Markowitz, who said that an

> underappreciated function of theory is research agenda setting. Just as the media might tell us which news topics and frames are important, so too does theory tell us what we need to study, how to study it, and what to expect ... Theory provides a straight-forward way to come up with a hypothesis and an approach to testing it ... Theory tells us what to prioritize.[7]

Therefore, when we talk about media parenting methods and measures, a discussion about both what we have studied in the past and how we have studied it is important. Previous chapters have already explored, in depth, what has been studied in the context of media parenting. I believe that as a group of scholars, we have studied many worthwhile topics, and have done so with empirical rigor and honorable intentions. I would not change anything about the research we have published to date, and I am proud to count myself among those who have, perhaps in some small way, made a contribution to knowledge in this area. Knowing what we have studied and seeing that it is good, therefore, leads us to embark on the next leg of this exploration—a discussion about the methods and measures that have been used to study media parenting and its outcomes, along with what theory suggests we should study next.

Primary among the methods that have been used to study the predictors and outcomes of media parenting are quantitative surveys that operationalize media parenting using one of many validated scales or indices. This collective body of research exhibits an overwhelming empirical bent and has not received much interest from critical/cultural or rhetorical scholars. This is not to say that there is no place for interpretive research related to parent–child dialogue, parent–child power relationships, the representation of the parent–child relationship in media, gender role communication, the construction of parent and child identities, and the performance of listening in the parent–child relationship. Being a positivist, I am admittedly rather ignorant of the topics of study and methods employed by rhetorical and critical/cultural scholars. It is only to say that most media parenting research is either positivist in nature, or when it is interpretive in nature, focus groups and interviews are about as far as scholarship goes to explore the subjective experiences of parents and children. Ultimately, these methods are a reflection of the question that has overwhelmingly motivated media parenting research in the first place: Does it work?

To answer that question, there are nearly as many ways that media parenting has been operationalized as there are studies about the topic. Some scholars have developed and validated scales, and most research has either used those scales, employed self-created indices, or adapted the scales/indices used by other researchers as a proxy for the establishment of validity. Two of the most prominent media parenting scales were developed by Dr. Patti Valkenburg and her research colleagues in the Netherlands. The first of these was published in 1999 and was described as "a scale to assess three styles of television mediation: instructive mediation, restrictive mediation, and social coviewing."[8] The group was motivated to develop and validate the scale because "to investigate the short- and long-term effects of television mediation in a survey context investigators need a reliable instrument that measures the different styles of television mediation used by parents. With unreliable scales, effect sizes are attenuated, and results may be less convincing than otherwise."[9] The scale consists of fifteen items (of which several were adapted from previous research) in three subscales, with each subscale comprised of five items each. The three subscales included the three titular types of media parenting of children's television use, and correspond to parent–child media conversations, parental media control, and joint media engagement, respectively. According to Google Scholar, the manuscript introducing the scale had been cited 1,168 times at the writing of this chapter.

Not long after the publication of the 1999 scale, children's Internet use began to be more commonplace, so that by 2008 researchers had begun to develop measures of children's online media use and media parenting thereof. Primary among these was a scale developed by Livingstone and Helsper.[10] They identified parental media monitoring, which they called simply "monitoring," as a distinct media parenting activity among parents of adolescents. This publication had been cited 1,902 times as of this writing, according to Google Scholar. A subsequent scale developed by Nikken and Jansz focused on media parenting of children's Internet use among toddlers and young children, and used items from previous research and adapted them to children's online activities.[11]

The second oft-employed Valkenburgian media parenting scale was published in 2013, and was developed, at least partly, in response to the digitalization of children's media use beyond traditional television and to tailor a scale specifically to adolescents.[12] The scale, called the Perceived Parental Media Mediation Scale (PPMMS), focuses on active mediation and restrictive mediation, or in new media parenting terminology, parent–child media conversations and parental media control. Items for the scale are largely based on the aforementioned 1999 scale, as well as another previously used scale to tap into features of both types of media parenting, namely the autonomy-supportive, controlling, or inconsistent nature of each media parenting behavior. The final scale consists of twenty-eight items and had been cited 390 times as of this writing.

Nimrod and colleagues also developed a sixteen-item scale to measure media parenting of both non-interactive and interactive media use by grandparents of young children.[13] Like other prominent scales, this scale was created by adapting items from previous scales and combining them with newly created items. Another scale was created to measure parent–child media conversations and parental media control of adolescents' interactions with others online.[14] Similarly, the Media Parenting Scale for Parents of School-Aged Children was built on operationalizations of parent–child media conversations and parental media control from more than ten previous survey instruments.[15] The authors of the latter study created their scale in an attempt to "reflect current conceptualizations in the field, and, at the same time, would overcome most problems of currently existing scales (e.g., mixing good and bad practices, focusing on only one device or one activity, and a lack of balance between active and restrictive approaches."[16] Another study created a scale based on past measures to measure media parenting of adolescents' Internet use.[17] The scale identified six separate types of media parenting (that overlap with each other in the context of the MPM's conceptualization of media parenting). Finally, lamenting the "inconsistent findings about validity of parental mediation scales for children's Internet use,"[18] researchers assessed the validity of ten media parenting measurement scales and concluded that "the reviewed studies showed no consistent evidence" for the content validity of the scales, suggesting a lack of conformity between the scales and the conceptual distinctions/definitions of the various types of media parenting.

As can be seen in this brief review of media parenting measurement tools, "in the field of media parenting, most measurement tools are self-generated for the purpose of one or a few studies."[19] And despite concerns expressed by researchers about the content validity of existing scales, evidence from the noted scale development research shows that media parenting scholars appear to be measuring what we say we're measuring. And these scales have allowed the field to identify many types of media parenting, which have been coalesced in this book into the Media Parenting Model.

As might be expected, media parenting researchers have been well- and consistently trained to develop and employ empirical methods to the study of phenomena in question. But, just as there exists a distinction between knowing *that* something works and *how* it works, there likewise exists a distinction between measuring what we say we're measuring and measuring what we *should* be measuring. Theory can help bridge this gap. The process of theory building can provide a connection between the necessary descriptive, observational research with our hunches for why something has occurred by systematizing "the provision of explanation" and "proposing causal processes."[20] And one way that theory can help the media parenting literature, which is rife with variation in operationalization and inconsistency across the research board, is by "critiquing prior operationalizations that have conceptual as well as methodological implications."[21] Specifically, Slater and Gleason argued that

> efforts that seek to integrate or compare competing definitions of a construct, identify conceptual slippage that may have led to confusion in earlier research, or compare alternate operationalizations that may have led to conflicting inferences about theory in past research will typically have substantially greater value than those that simply further multiply the many conceptualizations already being used.[22]

For example, this chapter notes an apparent lack of uniformity or consensus in how researchers measure the construct of parent–child media conversations, likely at least partly due to the multitude of labels used to describe these types of conversations. Theory can help provide focus and structure to our combined research efforts, and can help bring order and understanding to the processes at work when parents engage in conversations about media with their children. For instance, I've argued elsewhere that extant research suggests that parent–child media conversations work because they help alter children's attitudes about media and media content.[23] And Dillard explained that an attempt to alter another's opinion or behavior is the very definition of persuasion.[24] Thus, looking to theories of persuasion and testing their boundary conditions can help us better define parent–child media conversations, understand how they work to change children's cognitions and affect, operationalize parent–child media conversations in terms that can be systematically tested among children in varied and disparate contexts and life circumstances, and ultimately, help us establish a cohesive body of research with the prescriptive power to improve the actual act of media parenting for those currently in the parenting trenches.

To illustrate, a good example of the appropriate use of theory to better understand why parents might engage in parent–child media conversations is found in a study conducted by Sharma and Lee.[25] Protection motivation theory posits that people make decisions about coping with danger by appraising the threat of the danger and their own ability to cope with the threat, and includes constructs such as perceived threat severity, perceived threat vulnerability, response efficacy, and self-efficacy.[26] Though they were not the first to apply protection motivation theory to media parenting, Sharma and Lee argued that media parenting behaviors could be predicted by the various constructs within the framework of the theory.[27] As such, the theory told them what constructs to operationalize, and having done so, they found that perceived severity, response efficacy, and self-efficacy each independently predicted engagement in parent–child media conversations among U.S. parents of youth ages 10–17. Based on the test of the theory, the authors concluded (in the language of parental mediation, instead of media parenting),

> When parents worry about the severity of the threat their kids may have from digital media usage, they use all the possible mediation strategies, such as restrictive and active, and educate their kids about digital media. Also, parents who have confidence in their ability to manage the risk of their kid's use of technology will use both restrictive and active mediation strategies.[28]

In other words, the study provides insight about the parent characteristics that help determine the media parenting strategies in which parents engage, consistent with MPM path 1, and we understand in part, for some parents in some contexts, why they choose to engage in certain media parenting behaviors.

Similar theoretical work can help us understand media parenting outcomes. To explore the reasons why coviewing has certain effects, for example, a research team of which I was part viewed joint media engagement (coviewing) within a framework of social facilitation.[29] Social facilitation theory asserts that people perform simple tasks better in front of other people because having an audience induces higher levels of physiological arousal.[30] And since joint media engagement of television is really no more nor less than performing a simple task (watching TV) in front of one's parent, we tested whether children who watched with a parent experienced higher levels of physiological arousal than children who watched alone, among U.S. children ages 6–13. The study found that this was, indeed, the case, especially among younger children whose parents regularly engage in joint media engagement of television. As a result of these findings, we argued that "parents can have an impact on children without children's awareness that their cognitions and mental processes are being affected."[31] Furthermore, the study provided evidence that social facilitation theory's boundaries can include media-related tasks. Thus, consistent with MPM path 3, we now understand a little bit more why one form of media parenting can moderate outcomes of children's television exposure.

Theory, therefore, can help us identify the variables we *should* be measuring to understand why parents engage (or don't engage) in media parenting, and why or how media parenting functions to alter children's media use and its effects. The word *should* in the previous sentence is a deliberate choice with big implications for media parenting research. Part of the allure of a career as a researcher is the freedom to choose a research topic, as well as the ability to choose the method and measures most appropriate for the pursuit of knowledge about that topic. The professional autonomy granted by the value of academic freedom (the definition of which could be debated, but that is beyond the scope of this discussion) is a privilege that is highly valued by academics. But an argument could be made that along with academic freedom comes academic responsibility, suggesting that academic researchers and their research are accountable to other researchers and to the society that finances their paychecks. A survey of social science academics from a variety of disciplines found that many consider academic freedom to be more than an absence of constraints on research and teaching and *should* include some level of responsibility on the part of researchers.[32] According to the study, this responsibility includes the "integrity to conduct research for the public good" and "the obligation of academics to make social and political commentary."[33] Children and media researchers, then, should be expected to conduct research that will benefit the lives of children themselves; else, why are we engaged in research in the first place? If we are accountable to any person, institution, or group, it is to children and those who care for them. In this way, the word *should* is more appropriate than it is extreme, suggesting that it is both appropriate and expected to have a conversation about what we *should* research, even beyond what theory prescribes.

Mind Embodied

And thereupon sits the practical value and importance of the ideas that researchers have about the nature of human children, bringing us back, full circle, to the ideas introduced at the beginning of this book about who children are and what the ultimate goals of parenting are. If the ultimate goal of children and media research is to explore the socially learned (or otherwise developed) traits of human beings, then what we *should* study doesn't really matter, as long as it improves our understanding of the younger human beings of our species. But if the goal of children and media research is to provide parents with knowledge about how to help their children in the process of being human, then what we *should* study is a decision of great consequence, especially in the choice of research topics and methods used to inquire about the topic.

For starters, considering humans as minds embodied, instead of embodied minds, encourages scholars to enrich current quantitative methods, especially psychophysiological methods, with qualitative methods capable of capturing experiences as lived by human subjects. If the self (the mind or the *who* of a person) is the amalgamation of "how we come to experience a coherent 'me,'"[34] it cannot necessarily be measured through physical evidence of its existence; it can only be measured as retold by those who experience the self. If the *who* is experienced and not performed, it is not measurable using the neuroscientific tools being used under the current, dominant communication research paradigm. It can only be measured by hearing the stories and experiences of the actors of those who lived them. It is quantified, then, only upon reflection and in the sharing of those reflections.

If, as Fred Rogers stated, "who you are inside is what helps you make and do everything in life,"[35] it is perhaps this self, this coherent individual, that drives our thought processes, our attitudes, desires, motivations, and behaviors—or at the very least, the self (or mind) works in conjunction with the brain to create these outcomes. It is possible, then, that to better understand human behavior and the drivers of those behaviors, we must first understand the *who* of our research subjects. If the *who* predicts the *what*, perhaps our research methods should acquiesce more often to the necessary inclusion of interpretive methods to answer some of our pressing research questions.

As scientists, rather than distance ourselves from having to deal with a concept (the mind) with which we may be uncomfortable, the mind embodied perspective suggests that we allow ourselves to explore the impact of the *who* on communication phenomena, and vice versa through the sharing and analysis of experiences as individuals experience them. In other words, my call for allowing for the possibility of the mind embodied, in contrast to the embodied mind, is a call for the employment of research methods that elicit the sharing of the lived experiences of research subjects, and the subsequent qualitative analysis of the language used to share those stories. Such an approach is not antithetical to Colombetti's (2014) treatise on neurophenomenology, which encourages scientists to explore both quantitatively and qualitatively the human experience in order to discover "the extent to which mind reflects the organizational properties of the living organism."[36] A mind embodied approach would also employ attributes of the mind as an independent variable in order to discover the opposite, namely, the extent to which human biology reflects properties of the mind. Thus, in order to better understand media parenting processes and effects, we may need to back up and conduct research that helps us better understand *who* children are and the attributes of their minds, as well as parents' perceptions about the ways that social influences might interact with children's minds, character, and their search for meaning.

A mind embodied approach to human communication also has implications for the study of media parenting and its role in children's well-being, including their physical, mental, and socio-emotional health. In the earlier days of health communication as a sub-field, Zook lamented researchers' hyperfocused emphasis on the "biological primacy"[37] of human well-being, instead of allowing for other, broader contributors to and definitions of health, including the role of humans' search for meaning. To view one's health as solely an object to be acted upon, he argued, limits the human experience to merely maintaining survival while discounting "the pursuit of authentic being-in-the-world."[38] In other words, human well-being is a composite of more than just biological health and, in fact, may be more about finding meaning than about biological health itself. Well-being, he argued, is best measured, communicated, and experienced by the individual experiencing intrusions upon that well-being, and that the pursuit of a meaningful, authentic life differs not only among individuals, but in different stages of individuals' own health-related experiences. He concluded that "the centrality of meaning in ontological health shifts attention from biology to biography at the individual level, and from science to cultural history on the collective level."[39] The past several decades have, of course, seen an increased devotion to less strictly biological forms of well-being, such as mental health and healthy social relationships. The central assumption of human communication research, however, has remained largely within the biologically oriented, embodied mind realm. Thus, a fuller understanding of the role of media parenting in children's well-being may, at least in part, depend on the topics, methods, and measures we choose to explore the interactions between well-being and being human. It is possible that the latter—being human—is influenced by the former—well-being—suggesting that being human is the outcome of primary importance that *should* drive our research choices.

To the children and media researcher, such a readjustment in what one's health really entails means that the researcher must consider the backgrounds, lived experiences, and life possibilities—those aspects of life and health that are not as readily apparent—as held by children involved in a communication event, such as exposure to a media message. These considerations can only be discovered in the sharing of one's background, experiences, and beliefs and perceptions about life possibilities in the context of interpersonal relationships between both parties in the media parenting encounter. In other words, it is not enough to know which parts of a media message or media parenting message children pay attention to. Nor is it enough to know that certain messages, whether they come from parents or the media, cause certain emotions or thoughts. To be most effective, media parenting efforts in the realm of children's well-being must be based on insightful inquiry that can only be obtained by non-biological means. That is, stories must be told and aspirations explained, and individuals' search for meaning and for an authentic life must be discovered if we want media parenting to influence the well-being of children to the fullest extent. The search for meaning and an authentic life fits squarely within a mind embodied approach to the human condition.

Perhaps nowhere in the realm of media parenting (and communication generally) might insightful inquiry and one's search for meaning have greater implications than for mental health. If, as a mind embodied approach would suggest, the brain is characterized by plasticity, in that the mind can alter the biology of the brain, the positive results of both psychotherapy are possible only because of the mind's capacity for intentionality, consciousness, and mental causation. Beauregard concluded that "the mental functions and processes involved in the various types of psychotherapy exert a significant influence on the functioning and plasticity of the brain."[40] In other words, it may be largely due to the ability of the mind as its own agentic entity separate from the body and brain that psychotherapy has the potential to help those suffering from mental health disorders—an individual's ability to mindfully exert influence over their brain appears to be key to managing and maintaining optimal mental health. It behooves mental health professionals, their patients, and parents then, to consider beliefs about their own and their child's dualistic nature in the design, implementation, and evaluation of mental health interventions. Alignment of the therapeutic approach, in the case of health professionals, and of research methods and measures, in the case of children and media researchers, with the dualism-related beliefs of the person suffering from a mental health disorder has the potential to influence the beliefs in their own ability to successfully manage their mental health, as well as their beliefs in the ability of the therapy or parental recommendations to have positive results. In addition, the way mental health treatment and recovery are discussed in the media by health communicators and parents has the potential to help those suffering from mental health challenges overcome barriers to mental health disclosure if it is couched in terms of empowerment and efficacy due to the ability of the mind to alter dysfunctional brain processes.

This argument is strengthened by research in the provider-patient relationship context. A study involving more than 1,800 medical professionals, paramedical health-care workers, and other professionals found that 42 percent of participants agreed that the mind and the brain are separate, 40 percent agreed that a spiritual part of humans survives after death, and 40 percent agreed that individuals have souls that are separate from the body.[41] Furthermore, and more importantly to a discussion about media parenting, the authors argued that "the persistence of dualistic attitudes toward mind and brain has direct implications for clinical practice,"[42] and it *should* likewise have direct implications for media parenting practice. These direct implications were demonstrated in a study showing that a sizable majority of students in a variety of disciplines, including psychology, biology, theology, philosophy, chemistry, and physics believed that dualistic perspectives would influence both doctors' and psychologists' diagnostic or investigative method, choice of treatment method, and the way they deal with patients.[43] These beliefs may similarly affect the media parenting choices made by parents, as well as the media parenting preferences of children. It is thus advisable for children and media researchers to approach our questions with a focus more on how both parents and children view themselves in relation to the mind and the implications that these views might have on outcomes of media parenting. This may be especially true considering that, at least in the United States, 83 percent of all adults believe people have a soul or spirit in addition to their physical body.[44]

A mind embodied approach to media parenting research also has implications for how we seek to understand children's experiences with media portrayals of the human body. For example, the effect of media portrayals of the human body may affect children's self- or other-objectification, an arguably important individual health matter due to its emphasis on the body over the person. Objectification "occurs whenever a person's body, body parts, or sexual functions are separated out from his or her person, reduced to the status of mere instruments."[45] To regard another human being only as an object is to ignore their personhood in a way that their body *is* the person in the eye of the beholder, whether that person is oneself or someone else. An embodied mind approach to studying the processes and effects of exposure to objectifying images could measure the body's physiological response to such exposure. I would like to offer up for consideration, however, that relying solely on psychophysiological methods based on an embodied mind approach essentially objectifies the media consumer. A mind embodied approach to studying the processes and effects associated with exposure to objectifying images would supplement our knowledge of the body's physical reaction to such images with knowledge about how exposure to these images is received by the person as they are experienced. A mind embodied approach would allow researchers to explore the ways in which a child, with the assistance of media parenting, seeks to alter the effects of exposure to objectifying images. In our efforts to ameliorate any tendency toward objectification in the minds of young viewers, we could learn more about viewers' responses to objectifying stimuli by making efforts to not objectify them through limiting the research methods we use.

Intellectual Humility

Next, a change in language from embodied mind to mind embodied is an acceptance of, and if not an acceptance of, an allowance of the possibility that current scientific approaches may not hold a monopoly on the discovery of meaning in the context of parents, children, and media (and any other discipline that explores the human condition). Indeed, a mind embodied approach effectively discourages social scientists from believing their way of knowing is somehow better than ways of knowing pursued by average "folk," for it is perhaps through the basic assumptions of the embodied mind approach that we have restricted our ability to find meaning related to the *who*, both as an independent and dependent variable in media parenting research and in communication research broadly.

In other words, a mind embodied perspective that allows for the possibility that human consciousness might exist outside, or on the borders of, the realms of objective, quantifiable evidence encourages the social scientist to have an increasingly open mind about the process of discovering truth. I am not suggesting that any attempts to discover truth via psychophysiological means are necessarily undertaken by the intellectually arrogant, but rather that having an open mind about the place of the mind in the human condition may encourage a level of intellectual humility that is associated with both knowledge and traits related to knowledge acquisition.[46] In essence, when coupled with the position that the mind embodied perspective encourages the use of complementary, interpretive methods, having an open mind toward the perspective would allow both the body and the mind to speak for themselves, to provide data based on both "hard" data and subjective experiential data, rather than lumping the workings of the mind and the body into the data associated only with biological responses. It is one thing to know that thoughts or emotions are experienced. It is quite another thing to know how a human experienced them. A mind embodied approach encourages the latter.

Conclusion

In discussions with colleagues and students, I get the sense that we are never completely satisfied with any single research study we conduct and publish. To look back at one's dissertation or early career publications is an exercise in seeing holes in our thinking. And years from now, I imagine we will be able to conduct the same exercise and perceive similar problems with the research we are conducting today. The process of learning from our mistakes can be painful, but it is also a beautiful part of individual scholarly development. For a research discipline, it can also be both a painful and beautiful part of the development of a field of research, such as media parenting. It is true that a greater part of this chapter is devoted to identifying shortcomings in our research and offering suggestions for improvement, and I suppose that reading this may be much like reading comments from 'reviewer number two.' But looking through the body of media parenting research, I do not see problems that need fixing. I simply see opportunities for things we can do better in future research in our choice of topics and the methods and measures we employ to study those topics, so that we might help parents become increasingly effective in their media parenting efforts.

We now know much about media parenting because of the rigorous research conducted by many over several decades. But relative to what we know about the predictors and outcomes of media parenting, we know strikingly little about the processes at play when parents engage in media parenting. Theory, as we've discussed, and a little philosophy, can help guide our media parenting research-related choices. The application of theory, by which I mean the study of phenomena within a framework of theories from both within and outside the fields of communication and human development, will tell us something of what to study and how to study it. As we do this, let us bear in mind that "simply doing research that is consistent with a theory does not advance theory,"[47] and thus, does less to advance our field of inquiry than does actually testing the processes stipulated by a theory. Advancing our knowledge of communication phenomena requires that we "do more theory testing."[48]

Thinking about, and perhaps, reevaluating our individual and collective assumptions about the nature of children and their being human can also direct our research interests and methodological choices in directions we may not otherwise tread. We may find that this type of self-introspection as researchers will expand the possibilities of what and how we choose to study. The field would benefit from more researchers who deliberately choose to explore parents' and children's subjective experiences with media and media parenting, and from choosing research methods best equipped to elicit this type of data, especially as these experiences relate to well-being and mind-body interactions. Such mind embodied philosophizing also makes clearer both the distinctions and interrelations between the body and the person of the child. Physical health is then seen as separate from, and intertwined with, the person. Mental health is perceived as separate from, yet related to, the person. Social skills are seen as emanating from the person, but are not necessarily the person. Our research then moves away from an arguably voyeuristic fixation on the body and its responses and moves toward a focus on the person and the personhood of children and parents who are our research subjects. The field has ample room for small or large pivots in this direction. There is even room for additional embodied mind-oriented research by those who think everything said about a mind embodied perspective of human nature is moralistic hogwash, as well as for all those in the middle.

Chapter 12

PRESCRIPTIVE MODELS OF MEDIA PARENTING

Several years before the Covid-19 pandemic, Elizabeth Bass, the founding director of the Alan Alda Center for Communicating Science at Stony Brook University, said,

> Lay people are yearning for information they can understand. They need explanations in plain language that fit their level of knowledge and anxiety, the chance to air options and risks with someone they can trust. They want someone to hear the uncertainty in their voice and respond to it, to anticipate the areas of likely confusion and deal with misconceptions and fears that may never be voiced. This is true whether the people are patients, relatives of patients, or just 21st century humans trying to make sense of successive waves of diet trends, child-rearing advice, and as-seen-on-TV prescription drugs.[1]

In addition to conducting research, then, it is the duty of children and media researchers to communicate the science in which we participate to parents. But it is often unrealistic to engage parents in a one- or two-hour conversation, let alone enroll them for 3–5 years in our academic programs or for a semester in one of our classes. In addition, sifting through the research, making sense of it, and coming to some logical and reasonable conclusions, as I have attempted to do in this book, is hard enough for one trained to do this type of knowledge work for a living. But we must communicate to parents about our research to equip them with the knowledge they need to become the powerful media parents that today's generation of children requires and deserve.

To that end, the following discussion shares the results of a quasi-scientific content analysis of the media parenting research shared in this book. It is quasi-scientific because I will not report reliability statistics; nor did I conduct a thematic analysis based on established procedures. I have simply categorized and summarized the media parenting research with the intent to make it easily digestible to even a lay audience. And in Piagetian spirit, I have organized the findings from media parenting research by approximate age groups, as a proxy for the sensorimotor, preoperational, concrete operational, and formal operational stages of childhood cognitive development, while simultaneously attempting to align the age groups/stages of development with the most common developmental groupings used by media parenting researchers. Age groupings are approximations and may include some overlap. Then, under each age grouping, media parenting research is summarized and organized by outcomes that correspond with this book's chapter topics, as long as research about each topic for that age/developmental group is available. Note, again, that in attempting to organize and provide summative conclusions about media parenting research, not all media parenting efforts function the same for every child—this discussion should be used as a heuristic to guide researcher–parent communication, literature exploration, and future research. The following age-group summaries of media parenting research, then, lead to the Media Parenting Typology found in Figure 12.1 that serves as a prescriptive guide for what type of media parenting should be used for different groups of children.

Early Childhood/Toddlers (Ages 0–2)

Time and Content

One focus of media parenting research involving children ages 0–2/3 is the identification of ways to prevent their excessive and problematic use of media and to prevent a tendency toward any type of behavior that might be considered evidence of media addiction. Parental media modeling behaviors that can reduce young children's media use and direct children toward content supportive of their well-being include reductions in parents' (especially mothers') own time spent with screen media generally, increases in their own exposure to prosocial media, and reductions in their own exposure to aggressive or violent media content. Parents should engage in parent–child media conversations in which they discuss content, comment, ask questions, explain media content, compare media content to real life, and interpret media content. Parental media control that has proven effective includes parental rules about the amount of time young children spend in front of screens, intermittently and intentionally removing access to devices by disconnecting them, and not allowing young children to use devices, such as phones and tablets, without parental supervision.

Socio-Emotional Well-Being

To encourage children's engagement in prosocial behavior, such as sharing and helping, as well as their emotion regulation abilities, media parenting research suggests that parents should watch prosocial media content themselves and jointly with their young child.

Cognitive Development/Academic Performance

Cognitive and academic outcomes of research interest include media message comprehension, message recall, acquisition of vocabulary, development of curiosity, mental engagement with media content, and word learning. Media parenting research shows that these outcomes can be facilitated by joint media engagement in the form of watching educational programs together, engaging in parent–child media conversations in which the parent asks questions to help the child engage with media content and in which the parent is responsive to the child's communication, and by establishing rules and restrictions about the amount of time young children spend with media.

Preschoolers/Young Children (Ages 3–6)

Time and Content

Among children ages 3–6, several media parenting strategies have been shown to be effective at reducing children's screen time and directing them to prosocial and educational media content. Research findings suggest that parental media modeling should aim to reduce the time parents spend with screen media. Parents should watch children's programming together with their child, and they should be consistent in setting rules and restrictions about children's screen time and exposure to content parents deem inappropriate.

Physical Health

Media parenting research identifies media parenting strategies to help reduce children's overweight and obesity and maintain a healthy BMI; reduce consumption of sugary drinks, candy, and sweets; and increase their consumption of healthy foods. Research suggests that media parenting can function to these ends when parents reduce their own time on the Internet, emailing, chatting, and gaming. Parents should also set rules about screen time and which shows children can watch. In addition, parents should avoid making food salient by avoiding media content that focuses on food and by avoiding conversations highly focused on the media's portrayal of food.

Socio-Emotional Well-Being

Outcomes of research interest include increasing children's prosocial behavior, such as helping behavior and sharing; the development of empathy, self-efficacy, and emotion recognition skills; reducing media-induced fear; and increasing parent–child closeness. These outcomes are most likely when media parenting includes parental media modeling that avoids phubbing. Parents should also avoid joint engagement with entertainment-only programs and fear-inducing content. Parents should engage in watching prosocial and educational media content together with their child. Parent–child media conversations should be frequent and should attempt to help children understand what they see in the media, and should be consistent and regular, especially for younger children in this developmental group and for children from low-income backgrounds.

Cognitive Development/Academic Performance

Facets of cognitive and academic development of research interest include children's skills related to abstract thinking, planning, vocabulary, visuo-motor coordination, reflexive thinking, reading recognition, receptive and expressive word learning, emergent literacy, math understanding, digital literacy, memory, and the ability to relate concepts to each other. For children in this developmental group, media parenting should include a combination of joint media engagement and parent–child media conversations. Specifically, research suggests that parents should watch educational programs together with their child, and parent–child media conversations should include appropriate positive evaluations of content, associations between the content and other experiences, encouragement of the child, and efforts to help the child think about the thinking process. These conversations should also be responsive to children's actions and communication and should help them interact with the content.

Pre/Early Adolescents (Ages 7–12)

Time and Content

Research provides insight into how media parenting can reduce pre/early adolescents' tendency to media addiction and compulsive media use, decrease the frequency of taking one's phone to bed, reduce media use for leisure purposes, reduce engagement in sexting (sending or receiving), reduce media violence exposure, reduce Internet use, increase the use of media for education and learning, and increase prosocial content viewing. According to media parenting research, parents can help accomplish these aims by reducing their own time spent with media. They should jointly engage with prosocial media with the purpose of increasing their own learning and educating their child. They should have parent–child media conversations in which they explain online content and clarify its appropriateness, explain why some apps and functions of mobile phones are good or bad, encourage pre/early adolescents to explore and learn new things on the phone on their own, discuss what their child should and should not do on their phone, and discuss what kinds of things should or should not be shared online. They should set some media use rules about the extent and timing of media use, such as allowing media use after pre/early adolescents finish their homework, but not in the hour before bed and not when interacting with others, and should restrict the uploading and downloading (sharing) of photos or videos, especially with those they do not know offline. These rules, however, should be proactive and consistent, and not reactive to pre/early adolescents' media use. They should support pre/early adolescents' autonomy by supplementing them with explanations of the reasons behind the rules and should not be controlling (done with anger or threats of punishment) or inconsistent.

Physical Health

Research provides evidence about how media parenting can encourage pre/early adolescents' moderate to vigorous exercise, reduce BMI, and help them consume more healthy food and less unhealthy food. Also, media parenting can help pre/early adolescents set healthy sleep habits, such as decreasing their use of smartphones in bed. Media parenting can help reduce engagement in sexual behaviors such as kissing, petting, and participation in oral or vaginal intercourse. It can reduce pornography use and pre/early adolescents' smoking, tobacco use, and alcohol use. To facilitate these outcomes, parental media monitoring should include moderate doses of asking pre/early adolescents' questions about their media use. Parent–child media conversations should be moderate in dosage—not too much and not too little—and should include conversations that are critical of content the parent perceives as inappropriate. Conversations about portrayals of food should be limited as they tend to make food more salient to children. Setting some media use rules can also help, such as rules about time spent using media and about content viewed, especially in the child's bedroom, limiting the number of TVs in the home, and watching during family meals, and restricting access to adult/R-rated movies and mature online content. Rules should also be used moderately and should be combined with other media parenting strategies.

Socio-Emotional Well-Being

Media parenting can improve pre/early adolescents' prosocial behavior, such as helping peers, altruism, and showing affection and sympathy; increase emotion regulation and parent–child closeness; reduce peer problems and physically aggressive behavior such as hitting or kicking; reduce fear of the world and of scary news; and reduce parent–child conflict and family conflict. Media parenting research suggests parents should jointly engage in watching the news with pre/early adolescents, though joint media engagement should avoid violent or aggressive content and should be supplemented with parent–child media conversations. These conversations should help pre/early adolescents understand what they see in the media and help interpret media content. Parental media control can be helpful when it supports pre/early adolescents' autonomy, but can be harmful or have no effect when it is inconsistent and controlling.

Mental Health

For pre- and young adolescents, media parenting can help reduce symptoms of depression and anxiety and encourage greater life satisfaction. This is accomplished through joint media engagement with social media, having parent–child media conversations about how to use social media and warning about social media's risks, and by rules that limit pre/early adolescents' time spent on social media.

Cognitive Development/Academic Performance

Media parenting can have positive effects on pre/early adolescents' academic performance and academic achievement. Watching educational programming together, supplemented by parent–child media conversations that point things out, direct, help them understand, and encourage pre/early adolescents' exploration of academic topics, seems to be especially effective.

Adolescents (Ages 13–17)

Time and Content

Outcomes of interest for adolescents include reductions in their tendency to media addiction and compulsive/problematic levels of media use, less frequent taking of a phone to bed, less hedonistic smartphone use, less cyberbullying perpetration and victimization, more use of media for education and learning, and less sending and receiving of sexts. To these ends, research suggests parents should reduce their overall time spent with screen media, reduce time spent on social media, reduce excessive smartphone use, avoid phubbing, and increase their time spent consuming news content. Parents may track their adolescent children's social media activities, as long as adolescents are aware of the tracking. Parents should also combine parental media monitoring with low levels of parental media control and high levels of parent–child media conversations. Parents should engage in joint media engagement with the intent to help their child learn and connect with them. This joint media engagement should be combined with responsive parent–child media conversations. Parent–child media conversations are highly encouraged and should be collaborative in nature. They should explain the positive and negative uses and features of mobile technologies. Parents should also discuss with their adolescent what should and should not be disclosed on social media, explain the dangers of social media, and encourage them to stop using social media if they feel uncomfortable or scared. To influence adolescents' media time and content consumption, some parental media control can help, as long as it is preventive and not reactive. At least some media rules can be used, such as rules about what content adolescents should/should not share and upload, and the rules should be combined with parent–child media conversations and parental warmth and support in order to prevent boomerang effects. Rules should support adolescents' autonomy and seem to work best for younger adolescents.

Physical Health

Physical health outcomes of research interest include consumption and enjoyment of healthy foods, reduced consumption of unhealthy foods, increased body satisfaction, reduced body image disturbance, and disordered eating pathology, establishment of healthy sleep patterns, less engagement in sexual behavior and risky sexual behavior, establishment of healthy sex-related cognitions, and less permissive sexual attitudes, reduction in pornography use, and reduction of the desire for and use of substances such as alcohol, tobacco, and drugs. These outcomes are most likely when parents reduce their own media use, are aware of their child's media use, and avoid joint media engagement in the form of watching inappropriate content together. Parent–child media conversations should be frequent and should include parents' negative comments about undesirable media content, discussions about why some content/programs are wrong, and discussions about the adolescent's media use generally. Especially for girls, parents should avoid starting conversations about media characters' appearance and body size, as they can encourage deeper processing of content and negative emotions. Conversations should be critical of media messages to build critical thinking and media literacy skills, be critical of pornography use, and be critical of the risky behaviors of media characters. They should include discussions about how to use the Internet and warnings about its risks, especially with younger adolescents; discussions about the unreality of media portrayals; and discussions showing support for adolescents' media choice autonomy. For younger adolescents, some rules about the use of mature media content can be helpful, but overall, more rules about media use tend to reduce adolescents' sense of empowerment and autonomy; therefore, when used, rules should support autonomy and be combined with parental media monitoring and parent–child media conversations, including conversations about the rules.

Socio-Emotional Well-Being

Media parenting can encourage prosocial behavior, such as being kind and caring about others' feelings. It can reduce antisocial, aggressive behavior, such as hitting or kicking, as well as relational aggression, such as making up stories about others to get them in trouble, spreading rumors about others, and calling others names behind their backs. It can reduce the perpetration and victimization of online aggression, and can reduce risky online behavior, such as posting of personal details, sending insulting messages, and meeting face to face with strangers that adolescents meet online. It can reduce social anxiety and parent–child/family conflict and can support parent–child closeness. To these ends, parents should avoid unrelated media use during interactions with their adolescent children, and should themselves avoid excessive media use. Parents should connect with their adolescent children on social media and play video games together. When consuming media together, parents should avoid aggressive or violent content, and for girls, should avoid content depicting relational aggression. Parent–child media conversations should be frequent and should focus on the realism of media depictions. These conversations should support adolescents' autonomy by asking them about their opinions. They should be combined with autonomy-supportive rules. Also, for girls, conversations about relational aggression in the media, a topic that can be highly salient for girls, may backfire. Parent–child media conversations generally, though, should be regular and consistent. Likewise, parental media control should be consistent, should not be controlling, should support adolescents' autonomy, and should be combined with parent–child media conversations.

Mental Health

Media parenting can help reduce adolescents' depression, anxiety, and ADHD-related behaviors, and can facilitate greater happiness. This can be accomplished through parents' avoidance of phubbing and by getting help for their own mental health problems. Parents should engage in media conversations with their child that can be characterized as a continuous dialogue. Parents should encourage adolescents to explore and learn things online, and they should talk with adolescents about the types of content they see online. Parents should suggest ways to safely use the Internet and can recommend media content about maintaining one's mental health. As with other adolescent outcomes, parental media control should be moderate, overt, and autonomy supportive.

Cognitive Development/Academic Performance

Research suggests that autonomy-supportive parent–child media conversations and autonomy-supportive parental media control can support adolescents' academic performance, academic achievement, positive attitudes about academics, media literacy, and accurate perceptions of the distinction between TV reality and actual reality.

The Media Parenting Typology

Let us now tie these conclusions back to the Media Parenting Model (MPM). You'll remember that the MPM is illustrated by a mixer analogy (see Figure 4.1), and the exercise in conclusions discussed in this chapter allows us to make recommendations about the types and extent of media parenting that research shows give the best odds of resulting in positive childhood well-being. The Media Parenting Typology (see Figure 12.1) can be viewed as a zoomed-in version of the "media parenting" box that lies between paths 1 and 2 of the MPM. Both the MPM and the Media Parenting Typology are intended to be revised, updated, and refined over time as more media parenting research is published and our understanding grows.

To understand the Media Parenting Typology, for example, the first row shows the types and extent of media parenting that research shows are most beneficial for achieving healthy media use habits among children in different age groups. We can conclude, for example, that parental media control should be high for children ages 0–2 and 3–6, moderate for children ages 7–12, and low for children ages 13–17. No mixer bars are available in the physical health and mental health categories for children ages 0–2 for any type of media parenting because there is simply not enough research to come to defensible conclusions in those categories for children in that age group. The MPM Typology can also be understood by column. For example, for adolescents ages 13–17, media parenting should always include high levels of both parental media modeling and parent–child media conversations. On the other hand, while joint media engagement among adolescents should be high to facilitate healthy media use habits, it should be low to help children experience positive physical health benefits from their media use. Lastly, the Media Parenting Typology contains summary or overall, conclusions/recommendations about media parenting for the four age group categories. For children of all ages, media parenting research shows that both parental media modeling and parent–child media conversations should be high. For children ages 6 and younger, parental media control should be high, but as children progress through early adolescence and adolescence, parental media control should decrease accordingly. Both parental media monitoring and joint media engagement should be moderate for children of all ages.

Media Parenting Science Communication

The previous discussion centers on the research findings about effective media parenting strategies for different ages of children and for different groups of outcomes. It is a brief summary of decades of research and provides practical insights into media parenting behaviors that researchers should communicate to parents. But the manner in which these insights are communicated to parents is also an important consideration. It is not good enough simply to communicate these facts; indeed, these facts should be communicated in a way that is palatable to parents themselves. The aforementioned Elizabeth Bass also argued:

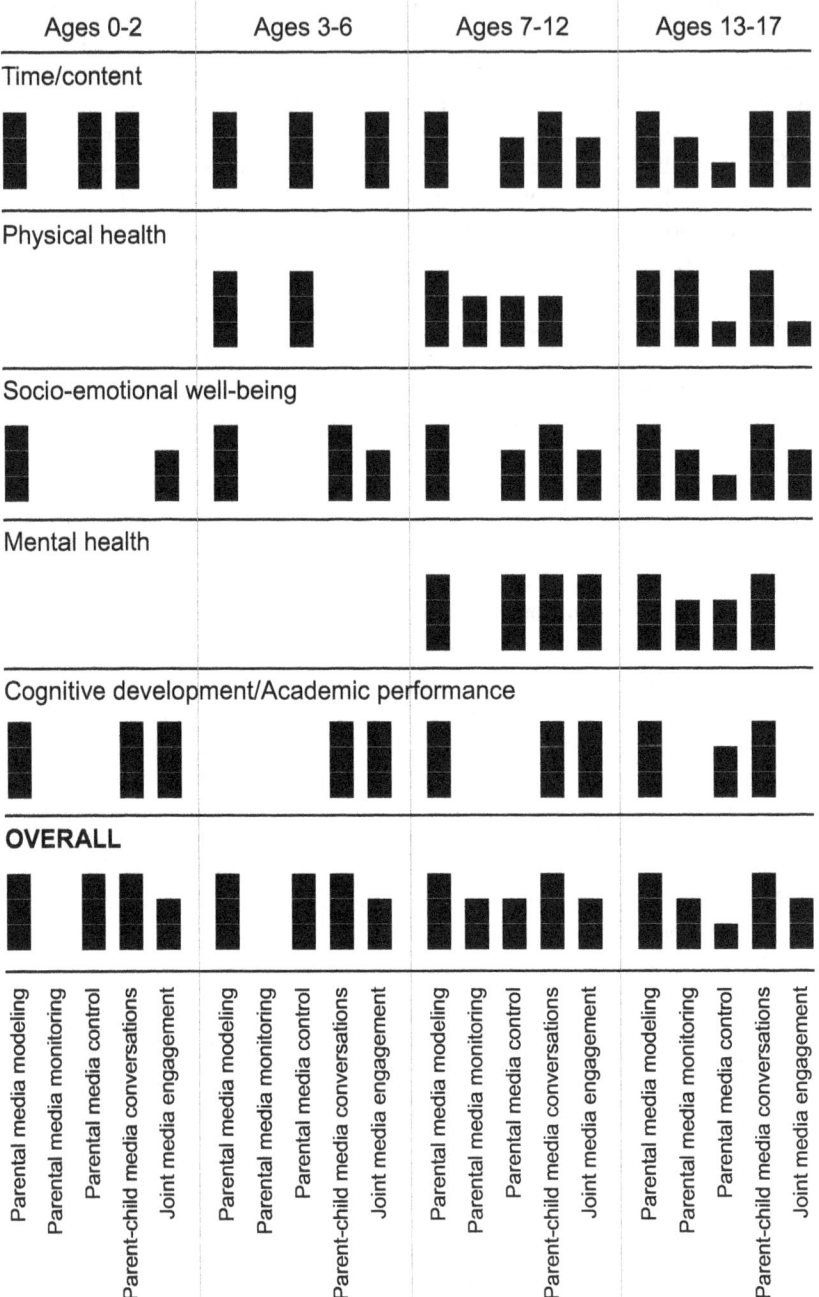

Figure 12.1 Media Parenting Typology.

> Effective communication involves far more than stating facts, even if the facts are true. Communication is a 2-way process that requires understanding, context, and judgment. It is always a conversation, even when only 1 person is speaking. In this duet, the harder role is the experts', because they must try to get into the mind of the other. They must make an imaginative leap, setting aside the language and assumptions they have worked so hard to acquire, and remembering what it was like not to know.[2]

For media parenting experts to get into the minds of parents, she suggested, we must set aside our assumptions about how and what parents think about their children. And this may include setting aside strongly held assumptions about the nature of children. Regardless of whether or not humans are dual beings, if a proportion of both the lay, non-scientific population of the world,[3,4] as well as a sizable proportion of scientists,[5] believe in concepts such as the mind or soul's ability to survive after death, it is incumbent upon scientists, media parenting scholars included, to communicate knowledge in a way that takes into account the mind embodied worldview of the audience. To not do so is a disservice to both the audience and our efforts to communicate knowledge in a persuasive manner. Demertzi and colleagues argued:

> Efforts to enhance the public understanding of science are creating lively dialog between scientists and a wider public. Nevertheless, the conceptual clarification of the relationship between mind and brain remains a challenge for scientists and philosophers, as we have inherited concepts and assumptions that may not do justice to their intimate connection.[6]

Several studies show that while many people are interested in brain processes, they are slow to believe that behavior is entirely determined by those brain processes, but is more likely to be regarded as driven by relationships with those close to them.[7,8] Furthermore, these conceptions seem to be driven by whether or not people have had experiences in which they have had to grapple with the underlying, brain-related causes of a disorder.[9] O'Connor and Joffe concluded that "neuroscientific ideas that reach the public sphere do not encounter passive receptacles of information, but active audiences who approach it through the lens of pre-existing worldviews, assumptions and agendas."[10]

As communicators of science, then, might it make more sense to couch our research in terms of the embodied mind to those who subscribe to the embodied mind approach, and in terms of the mind embodied to those who subscribe to the mind embodied approach? To fail to do so delegitimizes the research of fellow social scientists who have found that messages are most persuasive when they are within the audience's latitude of acceptance.[11] If we as media parenting researchers are not willing to employ the findings of some of our own and our colleagues' social influence research in such a way, we should also not expect either lay or scientific audiences (our colleagues) to employ strategies recommended by our own research when it is communicated in non-strategic ways. Science communication, then, need not come at the expense of assuming that the worldview of our audience is, or must be, consistent with our personal assumptions about the nature of the human mind. Indeed, Demertzi and colleagues found that dualism beliefs are widespread enough that they "exert an influence on scientific thought."[12] They further argued that "whether or not dualistic views are correct, their continuing influence should be acknowledged,"[13] and, I would argue, especially in our efforts to disseminate media parenting research to parents.

CONCLUSION

A ROADMAP FOR FUTURE RESEARCH

More research is needed, and more will always be needed. Thus, in addition to providing conclusions about which types of media parenting work best for which children, the Media Parenting Typology (see Figure 12.1) shows us, by lack of data in many row/column combinations, where more research is needed in several domains of child development. The absence of data in a cell does not indicate that no research to date has been performed for that media parenting strategy, in that developmental domain, or for that group of children. Rather, the absence of data indicates that more research is needed before we can establish generalizable conclusions about the combination of factors for each cell. The empty cells, thus, begin to tell a story about where we might focus future research efforts to help make our understanding of media parenting more complete.

The Media Parenting Typology, for example, reveals that more research is needed to understand how all five types of media parenting relate to the physical and mental health outcomes of children ages 0–2. Perhaps this type of research is limited simply because it takes time for children to develop noticeable problems with physical health and mental health, or because children in this age group do not consume enough media content to have a measurable effect on outcomes in the noted developmental domains. Whatever the reason, these areas of children's well-being appear ripe for additional empirical study. The same can be said for the physical and mental health of children ages 3–6, and also for the socio-emotional well-being of children ages 0–6. In addition, for children ages 12 and younger, we seem to know relatively little about the role of parental media monitoring for outcomes in several developmental domains. It is possible that little research made it into these parental media monitoring rows due to the narrower conceptualization of monitoring provided by the Media Parenting Model, suggesting that research employing operationalizations of the more precise concepts is needed and worthwhile. The Media Parenting Typology shows that other areas are also ready for additional scholarly exploration. What is not shown in the Media Parenting Typology, but what can be deciphered by the Media Parenting Model itself and which may prove worthy of consideration by media parenting researchers, is research related to the persuasion of a greater number of parents to engage in appropriate media parenting strategies. If media parenting characteristics are predictive of engagement in media parenting, it is not a far leap to suggest that the discipline can do more to determine what can be done to help parents adopt, acquire, or develop the characteristics that would make them more likely to perform appropriate media parenting. Furthermore, it is possible that certain parent characteristics may lend themselves more to certain types of media parenting, and future research can help parse apart these nuances. This is by no means an exhaustive list of ideas for future research, but it is mentioned to help media parenting researchers make use of both the MPM and the Media Parenting Typology as we develop our own research programs and determine how we might best support families.

Recommending directions for future research is relatively easy when using an organizational tool like the Media Parenting Typology. But suggesting future research that falls outside the tidy confines of such a tool becomes an exercise in subjectivity and an author's expression of personal interest. Scholarship in many disciplines, however, can bolster calls for research on topics that might lie outside the norms of any discipline. Relatedly, I have talked at length about the mind embodied perspective of human nature and have openly acknowledged its contradictions with the commonly accepted research paradigms of communication research, generally, and of media parenting research, specifically. Though with all that I have said in this book about children as "being human" instead of "human beings," about thinking more about "who" children are and their development into moral human beings, I have, until now, encouraged reading between the lines about what those ideas really mean. I have also suggested that we develop and use methods and measures that can more fully capture children's development into the kind of people that parents hope children are and will become, all without suggesting that empirical social sciences are even capable of capturing the becoming child within a mind embodied paradigm. Therefore, in addition to offering such a view of human nature and how to study it, a discussion to transform these vagaries into concrete concepts seems reasonable.

Together, the mind embodied perspective and the Media Parenting Typology make clear that media parenting research has largely avoided developmental topics related to moral psychology. Please do not misunderstand—the work of many excellent scholars has helped us understand children's moral development, especially using a "cognitive approach" by exploring how children "process moral quandaries and the types of resulting decisions they make."[1] Noftle explains that while massively useful, a cognitive approach to moral psychology dismisses the idea of studying moral characteristics. Furthermore, Noftle argues that research about personality moved away from moral characteristics because they were most often discussed in religious circles instead of in the scientific community. Many secularists seem to "prefer terminology that does not have a moral valence, such as social and emotional skills, noncognitive skills, or 21st-century skills or competencies."[2] In other words, one result of the domination of secular objectivity in the social sciences is that we have somehow undermined the important place of individual and collective virtue in life. This is not a discussion about the nature of virtue, but "given that the scientific world views no place in the natural world for moral values and moral purposes," we are indeed relatively unable to "account for the compelling force morality has on us."[3] If character is a collection of traits that are at once stable and enduring, and capable of change over time and across situations, that comprise "an individual's disposition to think, feel, and behave in an ethical versus unethical manner,"[4] science, and scientists, must reconcile the infatuation with the exclusion of moral characteristics with the fact that "how an individual defines what is right and what is wrong, either consciously or unconsciously, is paramount to understanding how that person will behave."[5] Significantly, early forms of moral development and the growth of character are influenced by the interactions children have with their parents,[6] and perhaps especially by parent–child conversations.

Noftle suggests an approach to studying moral character that provides a rather clean reconciliation.[7] He argues that the VIA Classification of 24 Character Strengths, originally developed by Peterson and Seligman[8] is a compilation of "the core characteristics valued by moral philosophers and religious thinkers across time and cultures."[9] The VIA, which stands for Values in Action, identifies six primary human virtues: wisdom, courage, humanity, justice, temperance, and transcendence.[10] A number of "character strengths" comprise each virtue. For example, the virtue of wisdom consists of the character strengths of creativity, curiosity, judgment, love of learning, and perspective. Transcendence involves appreciation of beauty and excellence, gratitude, hope, humor, and spirituality. In all, twenty-four strengths are operationalized. In addition, researchers may discover that additional character strengths and virtues, such as patience, as well as components of "bad" character, may provide fruitful insights about human nature.[11] Children and media scholars who peruse the list of character strengths will undoubtedly see overlap between some character strengths and outcomes they have explored in normative developmental domains, such as social intelligence and self-regulation.

While the mind, the self, the who, the soul, the being of children may prove ambiguous and appear incapable of capture via scientific means, we do have tools at our disposal,[12] such as the Values in Action Inventory of Strengths, that do more to approximate the attributes of children that are of far greater weight than the behavioral tendencies or skills/knowledge acquisition variables commonly used as dependent variables across a wide swath of our current research. These character strengths are more indicative of the substantive elements of life that provide meaning and purpose than our normative focus on aggressive behavior or engagement in cooperation with peers. The latter outcomes are, of course, important, but an argument can be made that they are evidence of underlying character strengths, such as love, loyalty, warmth, and genuineness. Thus, my call for research to be conducted within a mind embodied perspective of human nature is essentially a plea for children and media researchers to more fully explore the role of media, parenting, and media parenting in the development of children's character, those attributes that make them tick as human beings, that equate to what children *are* instead of what they think, feel, and do. It is my belief, though I provide no additional evidence of the same than the arguments I have heretofore presented, that a better understanding of children's character—of who they are—will only serve to enrich our similarly important inquiries in both traditional and nontraditional domains of children's development. I believe that it will be only when we make this shift and our study of children becomes more a study of "the content of their character"[13] and its precursors that the field of children and media will be able to go beyond a fanatical focus on predicting human behaviors to understanding the mind of a child, the nature of who they really are, and how to strive for the well-being of children more effectively.

In Chaim Potok's novel *My Name is Asher Lev*,[14] the titular character's father, Aryeh, frequently travels on behalf of their Jewish rebbe to assist and advocate for other Hasidic Jews in need. As his father travels, Asher feels a sense of loss, confusion, and even abandonment. One day between work trips, Aryeh said to his son, "You look so unhappy these days, Asher." Asher responded, "I'm sorry, Papa." Aryeh continued, "It bothers you that I am away so much?" To which Asher replied, "Yes, Papa." Then, in a statement of profound irony, Aryeh concluded, "It bothered me, too, when my father, may he rest in peace, was away. But I do not know how else the work can be done. To touch a person's heart, you must see a person's face. One cannot reach a soul through a telephone." A parent has a unique responsibility. No other person with any other title can touch the heart of a child or reach the soul of a child as frequently and as powerfully as their parent. It takes much of a parent's heart and mind, supported by many others, to effectively accomplish such a great work. Because media parenting scholars hold such an important space in the family's wider ecology, we too must continue our work in ways that allow us to touch parents' hearts and reach parents' souls. As they reach for their children, we can and must reach parents. These connections likely will not happen over the telephone or by traveling throughout the world, but they will happen as our media parenting research reflects our efforts to study the right things in the right ways and with the right perspective.

NOTES

Chapter 1

1. United Nations Human Rights, Office of the High Commissioner, *Convention on the Rights of the Child*, 1989, https://www.Ohchr.Org/En/Instruments-Mechanisms/Instruments/Convention-Rights-Child.
2. Dafna Lemish, *Children and Media: A Global Perspective* (West Sussex, UK: John Wiley & Sons, 2015), 3.
3. United Nations Human Rights, *Convention on the Rights of the Child*.
4. "Child," Merriam-Webster Dictionary, accessed April 1, 2025, https://www.merriam-webster.com/dictionary/child.
5. Sheila Greene and Elizabeth Nixon, *Children as Agents in Their Worlds: A Psychological–Relational Perspective* (Abingdon, Oxon, England: Routledge, 2020).
6. United Nations Department of Economic and Social Affairs, Population Division, *World Population Prospects 2022: Summary of Results*, 2022, https://www.un.org/development/desa/pd/sites/www.un.org.development.desa.pd/files/wpp2022_summary_of_results.pdf.
7. Federal Interagency Forum on Child and Family Statistics, *America's Children: Key National Indicators of Well-Being, 2023*, 2023, https://www.childstats.gov/americaschildren23/demo.asp.
8. Casey Family Programs, *Strategy Brief: Strong Families*, 2022, 1, https://www.casey.org/media/22.07-QFF-SF-Data-and-equity.pdf.
9. Albert Bandura, "Model of Causality in Social Learning Theory," in *Cognition and Psychotherapy*, ed. Michael J. Mahoney and Arthur Freeman (Plenum Press, 1985), 81–99.
10. Jay Tolson, "Is There Room for the Soul?," *CBS News*, October 16, 2006, https://www.cbsnews.com/news/is-there-room-for-the-soul/.
11. Warren Weaver, "Recent Contributions to the Mathematical Theory of Communication," in *The Mathematical Theory of Communication*, ed. Claude E. Shannon and Warren Weaver (Urbana, Illinois: University of Illinois Press, 1964), 1–28.
12. Annie Lang, "Discipline in Crisis? The Shifting Paradigm of Mass Communication Research," *Communication Theory* 23, no. 1 (2013): 10–24, https://doi.org/10.1111/comt.12000.
13. Annie Lang, Robert F. Potter, and Paul Bolls, "Where Psychophysiology Meets the Media: Taking the Effects Out of Mass Media Research," in *Media Effects: Advances in Theory and Research*, ed. Jennings Bryant and Mary Beth Oliver (New York, NY: Routledge, 2009), 185–206.
14. Lang, "Discipline in Crisis?"
15. Lang, "Discipline in Crisis?"

16 Thomas S. Kuhn, *The Structure of Scientific Revolutions* (Chicago, Illinois: The University of Chicago Press, 1996).
17 Lang, "Discipline in Crisis?," 10.
18 Lang, Potter, and Bolls, "Where Psychophysiology Meets the Media."
19 Robert Hanna and Michelle Maiese, *Embodied Minds in Action* (Oxford, UK: Oxford University Press, 2009), 2.
20 Annie Lang and Rachel L. Bailey, "Understanding Information Selection and Encoding from a Dynamic, Energy Saving, Evolved, Embodied, Embedded Perspective," *Human Communication Research* 41, no. 1 (2014): 2, https://doi.org/10.1111/hcre.12040.
21 Albert Bandura, "Social Cognitive Theory of Mass Communication," in *Media Effects: Advances in Theory and Research*, ed. Jennings Bryant and Mary Beth Oliver (New York, NY: Routledge, 2009), 94.
22 Lang, Potter, and Bolls, "Where Psychophysiology Meets the Media," 186.
23 Lang, Potter, and Bolls, "Where Psychophysiology Meets the Media," 186.
24 Tim Ingold, "Why We Disagree About Human Nature," review of *Why We Disagree About Human Nature*, by Elizabeth Hannon and Tim Lewens, *Notre Dame Philosophical Reviews*, May 3, 2019, https://ndpr.nd.edu/reviews/why-we-disagree-about-human-nature/.
25 Ingold, "Why We Disagree About Human Nature."
26 Kuhn, *The Structure of Scientific Revolutions*, 10.
27 Émile Durkheim, "The Dualism of Human Nature and Its Social Conditions," *Durkheimian Studies* 11, no. 1 (2005), https://doi.org/10.3167/175223005783472211.
28 Rebekah Richert and Paul Harris, "The Ghost in My Body: Children's Developing Concept of the Soul," *Journal of Cognition and Culture* 6, no. 3–4 (2006): 409–27, https://doi.org/10.1163/156853706778554913.
29 Paul Bloom, *Descartes' Baby: How the Science of Child Development Explains What Makes Us Human* (New York, NY: Basic Books/Hachette Book Group, 2004).
30 Lang, Potter, and Bolls, "Where Psychophysiology Meets the Media," 186.
31 Annie Lang and David Ewoldsen, "Beyond Effects: Conceptualizing Communication as Dynamic, Complex, Nonlinear, and Fundamental," in *Rethinking Communication*, ed. S. Allan (New York, NY: Hampton Press, 2010), 111–22.
32 Albert Bandura, "Human Agency in Social Cognitive Theory," *American Psychologist* 44, no. 9 (1989): 1181, https://doi.org/10.1037/0003-066x.44.9.1175.
33 Lang, "Discipline in Crisis?," 11.
34 Jennings Bryant and Dolf Zillman, "A Retrospective and Prospective Look at Media Effects," in *The Sage Handbook of Media Processes and Effects*, ed. Robin L. Nabi and Mary Beth Oliver (Sage, 2009), 9–17.
35 Bryant and Zillman, "A Retrospective and Prospective Look at Media Effects," 16.
36 Gerald Nosich, "What Is Ignorance?" *The University of Arizona: Q-Cubed*, accessed April 2, 2025, https://ignorance.medicine.arizona.edu/about-us/what-ignorance.
37 Jeffrey M. Schwartz et al., "Quantum Physics in Neuroscience and Psychology: A Neurophysical Model of Mind-Brain Interaction," *Philosophical Transactions of the*

Royal Society B 360, no. 1458 (2005): 1309–27, https://doi.org/10.1098/rstb.2004 .1598.
38 Bandura, "Human Agency in Social Cognitive Theory," 1175.
39 Bandura, "Human Agency in Social Cognitive Theory," 1181.
40 Albert Bandura, "Toward a Psychology of Human Agency," *Perspectives on Psychological Science* 1, no. 2 (2006): 165, https://doi.org/10.1111/j.1745-6916 .2006.00011.x.
41 Bandura, "Toward a Psychology of Human Agency," 165.
42 Bandura, "Toward a Psychology of Human Agency," 167.
43 Mario Beauregard, "Mind Does Really Matter: Evidence from Neuroimaging Studies of Emotional Self-regulation, Psychotherapy, and Placebo Effect," *Progress in Neurobiology* 81, no. 4 (2007): 232–33, https://doi.org/10.1016/j.pneurobio.2007 .01.005.
44 Beauregard, "Mind Does Really Matter," 233.
45 Lisa Feldman Barrett, "The Future of Psychology: Connecting Mind to Brain," *Perspectives on Psychological Science* 4, no. 4 (2009): 327, https://doi.org/10.1111/j .1745-6924.2009.01134.x.
46 Jonathan Sacks, *Not in God's Name: Confronting Religious Violence* (New York, NY: Schocken Books, 2015), 13.
47 Jo Orsatti and Kai Riemer, "Identity-Making: A Multimodal Approach for Researching Identity in Social Media," Paper, 23rd European Conference on Information Systems, Munster, 2015, 4.
48 Athena Demertzi et al., "Dualism Persists in the Science of Mind," *Annals of the New York Academy of Sciences* 1157, no. 1 (2009): 1–9, https://doi.org/10.1111/j .1749-6632.2008.04117.x.
49 Edward J. Larson and Larry Witham, "Scientists Are Still Keeping the Faith," *Nature* 386, no. 6624 (1997): 435–6, https://doi.org/10.1038/386435a0.
50 Cliodhna O'Connor and Helene Joffe, "How Has Neuroscience Affected Lay Understandings of Personhood? A Review of the Evidence," *Public Understanding of Science* 22, no. 3 (2013): 263, https://doi.org/10.1177/0963662513476812.
51 Peter Berger, "The Desecularization of the World: A Global Overview," in *The Desecularization of the World: Resurgent Religion and World Politics*, ed. Peter L. Berger (Eerdmans, 1999), 1–18.
52 Ingold, "Why We Disagree About Human Nature."
53 James Jaccard and Jacob Jacoby, *Theory Construction and Model-Building Skills: A Practical Guide for Social Scientists* (New York, NY: The Guilford Press, 2010), 23.
54 Gunilla Hallden, "The Child as Project and the Child as Being: Parents' Ideas as Frames of Reference," *Children & Society* 5, no. 4 (1991): 334, https://doi.org/10 .1111/j.1099-0860.1991.tb00499.x.
55 Scott A. Miller, "Parents' Beliefs About Children," *Psychology* (2023), https://doi .org/10.1093/obo/9780199828340-0317.
56 W.-Y. Lin, "From Human Nature Belief to Parenting Behavior: Mediation Process Hypothesis," *Chinese Journal of Psychology* 47, no. 3 (2005): 231.
57 Jerome Bruner, "Culture and Human Development: A New Look," *Human Development* 33, no. 6 (1990): 344–55, https://doi.org/10.1159/000276535.
58 "Folk Psychology," APA Dictionary of Psychology, April 19, 2018. https:// dictionary.apa.org/folk-psychology.

59 Lin, "From Human Nature Belief to Parenting Behavior."
60 Naomi J. Aldrich et al., "Evaluating Associations Between Parental Mind-Mindedness and Children's Developmental Capacities Through Meta-Analysis," *Developmental Review* 60 (2021): 100946, https://doi.org/10.1016/j.dr.2021.100946.
61 Gaby Illingworth, "Maternal Mind-Mindedness: A Cognitive-Behavioural Trait or a Relational Construct?" (PhD thesis, Oxford Brookes University, 2014), 6.
62 Karen Wells, *Childhood in a Global Perspective* (Cambridge, UK: Polity Press, 2009), 2.
63 Bloom, *Descartes' Baby*.
64 Kara Weisman et al., "Similarities and Differences in Concepts of Mental Life Among Adults and Children in Five Cultures," *Nature Human Behaviour* 5, no. 10 (2021): 1358–68, https://doi.org/10.1038/s41562-021-01184-8.
65 Joseph Stone and Joseph Church, *Childhood and Adolescence: A Psychology of the Growing Person* (New York, NY: Random House, 1973), 205.
66 Rachel Minkin and Juliana Menasce Horowitz, "Parenting in America Today: Mental Health Concerns Top the List of Worries for Parents; Most Say Being a Parent Is Harder Than They Expected," *Pew Research Social & Demographic Trends*, January 24, 2023, https://www.pewresearch.org/social-trends/2023/01/24/parenting-in-america-today/.
67 Hallden, "The Child as Project and the Child as Being."
68 Hallden, "The Child as Project and the Child as Being," 341.
69 Lisha Liu et al., "Developing Children's Humanity: The Unique and Interactive Role of Parents' and Peers' Humanity," *Educational Psychology* 43, no. 8 (2023): 967–88, https://doi.org/10.1080/01443410.2023.2272068.

Chapter 2

1 Jennifer Keishin Armstrong, "The Evolution of the Family Sitcom," *Peabody Finds*, accessed April 29, 2025, https://peabodyawards.com/stories/the-evolution-of-the-family-sitcom/.
2 Lynn Spigel, *TV Snapshots: An Archive of Everyday Life* (Durham, NC: Duke University Press, 2022), 26.
3 Spigel, *TV Snapshots*, 32.
4 Spigel, *TV Snapshots*, 36.
5 Hermann Bausinger, "Media, Technology and Daily Life," *Media, Culture and Society* 6 (1984): 349, https://doi.org/10.1177/016344378400600403.
6 Bausinger, "Media, Technology and Daily Life," 349.
7 Urie Bronfenbrenner, *The Ecology of Human Development: Experiments by Nature and Design* (Cambridge, Massachusetts: Harvard University Press, 1979).
8 Gordon Jack, "Ecological Perspectives in Assessing Children and Families," in *The Child's World: Assessing Children in Need*, ed. Jan Horwatch (London, UK: Jessica Kingsley Publishers, 2001), 56.
9 Michael P. Sheldrick et al., "Associations Between the Home Physical Environment and Children's Home-Based Physical Activity and Sitting,"

International Journal of Environmental Research and Public Health 16, no. 21 (2019): 4178, https://doi.org/10.3390/ijerph16214178.

10 Theodora Pouliou et al., "Environmental Influences on Children's Physical Activity," *Journal of Epidemiology & Community Health* 69, no. 1 (2014): 77–85, https://doi.org/10.1136/jech-2014-204287.

11 C. R. Bates et al., "Links Between the Organization of the Family Home Environment and Child Obesity: A Systematic Review," *Obesity Reviews* 19, no. 5 (2018): 716–27, https://doi.org/10.1111/obr.12662.

12 S. M. P. L. Gerards and S. P. J. Kremers, "The Role of Food Parenting Skills and the Home Food Environment in Children's Weight Gain and Obesity," *Current Obesity Reports* 4, no. 1 (2015): 30–6, https://doi.org/10.1007/s13679-015-0139-x.

13 Patricia East et al., "Home and Family Environment Related to Development of Obesity: A 21-Year Longitudinal Study," *Childhood Obesity* 15, no. 3 (2019): 156–66, https://doi.org/10.1089/chi.2018.0222.

14 Amanda C. Bennett et al., "The Association of Child Mental Health Conditions and Parent Mental Health Status Among U.S. Children, 2007," *Maternal and Child Health Journal* 16, no. 6 (2011): 1266–75, https://doi.org/10.1007/s10995-011-0888-4.

15 Md Jamal Uddin et al., "Is the Association Between Parents' Mental Illness and Child Psychopathology Mediated via Home Environment and Caregiver's Psychosocial Functioning? A Mediation Analysis of the Danish High Risk and Resilience Study—VIA7, a Population-Based Cohort Study," *Schizophrenia Bulletin Open* 2, no. 1 (2021), https://doi.org/10.1093/schizbullopen/sgab024.

16 Laura M. Glynn et al., "A Predictable Home Environment May Protect Child Mental Health During the Covid-19 Pandemic," *Neurobiology of Stress* 14 (2021): 100291, https://doi.org/10.1016/j.ynstr.2020.100291.

17 Samantha Krauss et al., "Family Environment and Self-esteem Development: A Longitudinal Study From Age 10 to 16," *Journal of Personality and Social Psychology* 119, no. 2 (2019): 457–78, https://doi.org/10.1037/pspp0000263.

18 Khaled Sarsour et al., "Family Socioeconomic Status and Child Executive Functions: The Roles of Language, Home Environment, and Single Parenthood," *Journal of the International Neuropsychological Society* 17, no. 1 (2011): 120–32.

19 Samantha Marsh et al., "The Relationship Between Household Chaos and Child, Parent, and Family Outcomes: A Systematic Scoping Review," *BMC Public Health* 20, no. 1 (2020), https://doi.org/10.1186/s12889-020-08587-8.

20 Robert H. Bradley and Robert F. Corwyn, "Socioeconomic Status and Child Development," *Annual Review of Psychology* 53, no. 1 (2002): 371–99, https://doi.org/10.1146/annurev.psych.53.100901.135233.

21 Amy Jordan, "The Role of Media in Children's Development: An Ecological Perspective," *Developmental and Behavioral Pediatrics* 25, no. 3 (2004): 197.

22 Donald F. Roberts et al., *Generation M: Media in the Lives of 8–18 Year-Olds*. Kaiser Family Foundation, 2004, https://www.kff.org/wp-content/uploads/2013/01/generation-m-media-in-the-lives-of-8-18-year-olds-report-section-3.pdf.

23 Alexis R. Lauricella and Drew P. Cingel, "Parental Influence on Youth Media Use," *Journal of Child and Family Studies* 29, no. 7 (2020): 1927–37, https://doi.org/10.1007/s10826-020-01724-2.

24 Alexis R. Lauricella et al., "Young Children's Screen Time: The Complex Role of Parent and Child Factors," *Journal of Applied Developmental Psychology* 36 (2015): 11–17, https://doi.org/10.1016/j.appdev.2014.12.001.

25 Amy Bleakley et al., "The Relationship Between Parents' and Children's Television Viewing," *Pediatrics* 132, no. 2 (2013): e364–71, https://doi.org/10.1542/peds.2012-3415.

26 Russell Jago et al., "Parent and Child Screen-Viewing Time and Home Media Environment," *American Journal of Preventive Medicine* 43, no. 2 (2012): 150–8, https://doi.org/10.1016/j.amepre.2012.04.012.

27 Caroline Fitzpatrick et al., "Do Parent Media Habits Contribute to Child Global Development?," *Frontiers in Psychology* 14 (2024), https://doi.org/10.3389/fpsyg.2023.1279893.

28 Sarah Overgaard Sørensen et al., "Recreational Screen Media Use Among Danish Children Aged 6–11 Years: Influence of Parental Screen Media Habits and Attitudes," *Scandinavian Journal of Public Health* 51, no. 8 (2022): 1173–81, https://doi.org/10.1177/14034948221103463.

29 Jasmine Fardouly et al., "Investigating Longitudinal and Bidirectional Relationships Between Parental Factors and Time Spent on Social Media During Early Adolescence," *New Media & Society* 26, no. 3 (2022): 1610–26, https://doi.org/10.1177/14614448221076155.

30 Il Bong Mun and Seyoung Lee, "How Does Parental Smartphone Addiction Affect Adolescent Smartphone Addiction?: Testing the Mediating Roles of Parental Rejection and Adolescent Depression," *Cyberpsychology, Behavior, and Social Networking* 24, no. 6 (2020): 399–406, https://doi.org/10.1089/cyber.2020.0096.

31 Sarah E. Vaala and Amy Bleakley, "Monitoring, Mediating, and Modeling: Parental Influence on Adolescent Computer and Internet Use in the United States," *Journal of Children and Media* 9, no. 1 (2015): 40–57, https://doi.org/10.1080/17482798.2015.997103.

32 Laura M. Padilla-Walker et al., "Longitudinal Associations Between Parents' Prosocial Behavior and Media Use and Young Children's Prosocial Development: The Mediating Role of Children's Media Use," *Infancy* 29, no. 2 (2023): 95–112, https://doi.org/10.1111/infa.12576.

33 Chance York and Rosanne M. Scholl, "Youth Antecedents to News Media Consumption," *Journalism & Mass Communication Quarterly* 92, no. 3 (2015): 681–99, https://doi.org/10.1177/1077699015588191.

34 Stephanie Edgerly et al., "Do Parents Still Model News Consumption? Socializing News Use Among Adolescents in a Multi-device World," *New Media & Society* 20, no. 4 (2017): 1263–81, https://doi.org/10.1177/1461444816688451.

35 Sarah Pila et al., "The Power of Parent Attitudes: Examination of Parent Attitudes Toward Traditional and Emerging Technology," *Human Behavior and Emerging Technologies* 3, no. 4 (2021): 540–51, https://doi.org/10.1002/hbe2.279.

36 Drew P. Cingel and Marina Krcmar, "Predicting Media Use in Very Young Children: The Role of Demographics and Parent Attitudes," *Communication Studies* 64, no. 4 (2013): 374–94, https://doi.org/10.1080/10510974.2013.770408.

37 Hye Eun Lee et al., "The Influence of Parent Media Use, Parent Attitude on Media, and Parenting Style on Children's Media Use," *Children* 9, no. 1 (2022): 37, https://doi.org/10.3390/children9010037.

38 Shayl F. Griffith, "Parent Beliefs and Child Media Use: Stress and Digital Skills as Moderators," *Journal of Applied Developmental Psychology* 86 (2023): 101535, https://doi.org/10.1016/j.appdev.2023.101535.
39 Rachel Barr et al., "Amount, Content and Context of Infant Media Exposure: A Parental Questionnaire and Diary Analysis," *International Journal of Early Years Education* 18, no. 2 (2010): 107–22, https://doi.org/10.1080/09669760.2010.494431.
40 Molly Hammer et al., "New Technology, New Role of Parents: How Parents' Beliefs and Behavior Affect Students' Digital Media Self-efficacy," *Computers in Human Behavior* 116 (2020): 106642, https://doi.org/10.1016/j.chb.2020.106642.
41 Lauricella and Cingel, "Parental Influence on Youth Media Use."
42 Victoria Rideout et al., "The Common Sense Census: Media Use by Tweens and Teens, 2021," Common Sense, 2021, https://www.commonsensemedia.org/sites/default/files/research/report/8-18-census-integrated-report-final-web_0.pdf.
43 Jenny S. Radesky et al., "Young Children's Use of Smartphones and Tablets," *Pediatrics* 146, no. 1 (2020), https://doi.org/10.1542/peds.2019-3518.
44 Hui-Lien Chou and Chien Chou, "A Quantitative Analysis of Factors Related to Taiwan Teenagers' Smartphone Addiction Tendency Using a Random Sample of Parent-child Dyads," *Computers in Human Behavior* 99 (2019): 335–44, https://doi.org/10.1016/j.chb.2019.05.032.
45 Sarah E. Vaala et al., "The Media Environments and Television-Viewing Diets of Infants and Toddlers: Findings from a National Survey of Parents," *Zero to Three* 33, no. 4 (2013): 18–24, https://eric.ed.gov/?id=EJ1125720.
46 Jean L. Wiecha et al., "Household Television Access: Associations With Screen Time, Reading, and Homework Among Youth," *Ambulatory Pediatrics* 1, no. 5 (2001): 244–51, https://doi.org/10.1367/1539-4409(2001)001<0244:HTAAWS>2.0.CO;2.
47 Jenny S. Radesky et al., "Constant Companion: A Week in the Life of a Young Person's Smartphone Use," *Common Sense Media*, 2023, 1.
48 Rideout et al., "The Common Sense Census: Media Use by Tweens and Teens, 2021."
49 Pew Research Center, "Teens, Social Media and Technology 2023," December 11, 2023, https://www.pewresearch.org/internet/2023/12/11/teens-social-media-and-technology-2023/.
50 Rideout et al., "The Common Sense Census: Media Use by Tweens and Teens, 2021."
51 Victoria Rideout and Michael B. Robb, "The Common Sense Census: Media Use by Kids Age Zero to Eight," Common Sense, 2022.
52 Rideout et al., "The Common Sense Census: Media Use by Tweens and Teens, 2021."
53 Pew, "Teens, Social Media and Technology 2023."
54 Rideout and Robb, "The Common Sense Census."
55 Ofcom, *Children and Parents: Media Use and Attitudes Report*, 2023.
56 Rideout et al., "The Common Sense Census."
57 Rideout and Robb, "The Common Sense Census."
58 Rideout et al., "The Common Sense Census."
59 Pew, "Teens, Social Media and Technology 2023."

60 Rideout and Robb. "The Common Sense Census."
61 Ofcom, *Children and Parents: Media Use and Attitudes Report.*
62 Rideout et al., "The Common Sense Census."
63 Jason M. Nagata et al., "Social Epidemiology of Early Adolescent Problematic Screen Use in the United States," *Pediatric Research* 92, no. 5 (2022): 1443–9, https://doi.org/10.1038/s41390-022-02176-8.
64 Rideout et al., "The Common Sense Census."
65 Pew, "Teens, Social Media and Technology 2023."
66 Rideout et al., "The Common Sense Census."
67 Pew, "Teens, Social Media and Technology 2023."
68 Jonathan Y. Bernard et al., "Predictors of Screen Viewing Time in Young Singaporean Children: The GUSTO Cohort," *International Journal of Behavioral Nutrition and Physical Activity* 14, no. 1 (2017), https://doi.org/10.1186/s12966-017-0562-3.
69 Itziar Hoyos Cillero and Russell Jago, "Systematic Review of Correlates of Screen-viewing Among Young Children," *Preventive Medicine* 51, no. 1 (2010): 3–10, https://doi.org/10.1016/j.ypmed.2010.04.012.
70 Bita Shalani et al., "Correlates of Screen Time in Children and Adolescents: A Systematic Review Study," *Journal of Modern Rehabilitation* (2021), https://doi.org/10.18502/jmr.v15i4.7740.
71 Torunn H. Totland et al., "Adolescents' Prospective Screen Time by Gender and Parental Education, the Mediation of Parental Influences," *International Journal of Behavioral Nutrition and Physical Activity* 10, no. 1 (2013): 89, https://doi.org/10.1186/1479-5868-10-89.
72 Brae Anne McArthur et al., "Trajectories of Screen Use During Early Childhood: Predictors and Associated Behavior and Learning Outcomes," *Computers in Human Behavior* 113 (2020): 106501, https://doi.org/10.1016/j.chb.2020.106501.
73 Niko Männikkö et al., "Parental Socioeconomic Status, Adolescents' Screen Time and Sports Participation Through Externalizing and Internalizing Characteristics," *Heliyon* 6, no. 2 (2020): e03415, https://doi.org/10.1016/j.heliyon.2020.e03415.
74 Rideout and Robb. "The Common Sense Census: Media Use by Kids Age Zero to Eight."
75 Mai-Han Trinh et al., "Association of Trajectory and Covariates of Children's Screen Media Time," *JAMA Pediatrics* 174, no. 1 (2019): 71, https://doi.org/10.1001/jamapediatrics.2019.4488.
76 Cingel and Krcmar, "Predicting Media Use in Very Young Children."
77 M. K. Gebremariam et al., "Associations Between Socioeconomic Position and Correlates of Sedentary Behaviour Among Youth: A Systematic Review," *Obesity Reviews* 16, no. 11 (2015): 988–1000, https://doi.org/10.1111/obr.12314.
78 John J. Davies and Douglas A. Gentile, "Responses to Children's Media Use in Families With and Without Siblings: A Family Development Perspective," *Family Relations* 61, no. 3 (2012): 410–25, https://doi.org/10.1111/j.1741-3729.2012.00703.x.
79 Sarah Bagley et al., "Family Structure and Children's Television Viewing and Physical Activity," *Medicine & Science in Sports & Exercise* 38, no. 5 (2006): 910–18, https://doi.org/10.1249/01.mss.0000218132.68268.f4.

80 Louise L. Hardy et al., "Family and Home Correlates of Television Viewing in 12–13 Year Old Adolescents: The Nepean Study," *International Journal of Behavioral Nutrition and Physical Activity* 3, no. 1 (2006): 24, https://doi.org/10.1186/1479-5868-3-24.

81 Meena Chandra et al., "Screen Time of Infants in Sydney, Australia: A Birth Cohort Study," *BMJ Open* 6, no. 10 (2016): e012342, https://doi.org/10.1136/bmjopen-2016-012342.

82 Jasmine Rai et al., "Demographic, Parental and Home Environment Correlates of Traditional and Mobile Screen Time in Preschool-aged Children," *Child: Care, Health and Development* 48, no. 4 (2022): 544–51, https://doi.org/10.1111/cch.12958.

83 Bi Ying Hu et al., "Relationship Between Screen Time and Chinese Children's Cognitive and Social Development," *Journal of Research in Childhood Education* 34, no. 2 (2020): 183–207, https://doi.org/10.1080/02568543.2019.1702600.

84 J. Granich et al., "Understanding Children's Sedentary Behaviour: A Qualitative Study of the Family Home Environment," *Health Education Research* 25, no. 2 (2008): 199–210, https://doi.org/10.1093/her/cyn025.

85 Kjartan Ólafsson et al., "Is Big Brother More at Risk Than Little Sister? The Sibling Factor in Online Risk and Opportunity," *New Media & Society* 20, no. 4 (2017): 1360–79, https://doi.org/10.1177/1461444817691531.

86 Leonie H. Bogl et al., "Like Me, Like You—Relative Importance of Peers and Siblings on Children's Fast Food Consumption and Screen Time but Not Sports Club Participation Depends on Age," *International Journal of Behavioral Nutrition and Physical Activity* 17, no. 1 (2020), https://doi.org/10.1186/s12966-020-00953-4.

87 Marie Danet, "Parental Concerns About Their School-aged Children's Use of Digital Devices," *Journal of Child and Family Studies* 29, no. 10 (2020): 2890–904, https://doi.org/10.1007/s10826-020-01760-y.

88 Jesper Pedersen et al., "Recreational Screen Media Use in Danish School-aged Children and the Role of Parental Education, Family Structures, and Household Screen Media Rules," *Preventive Medicine* 155 (2021): 106908, https://doi.org/10.1016/j.ypmed.2021.106908.

89 Amund Langøy et al., "Associations Between Family Structure and Young People's Physical Activity and Screen Time Behaviors," *BMC Public Health* 19, no. 1 (2019), https://doi.org/10.1186/s12889-019-6740-2.

90 Rachel McMillan et al., "Family Structure as a Predictor of Screen Time Among Youth," *PeerJ* 3 (2015): e1048, https://doi.org/10.7717/peerj.1048.

91 Nagata et al., "Social Epidemiology of Early Adolescent Problematic Screen Use in the United States."

92 Bagley et al., "Family Structure and Children's Television Viewing and Physical Activity."

93 Cingel and Krcmar, "Predicting Media Use in Very Young Children."

94 Stephen Whiting et al., "Physical Activity, Screen Time, and Sleep Duration of Children Aged 6–9 Years in 25 Countries: An Analysis Within the WHO European Childhood Obesity Surveillance Initiative (COSI) 2015–2017," *Obesity Facts* 14, no. 1 (2020): 32–44, https://doi.org/10.1159/000511263.

95 Julie Latomme et al., "The Association Between Children's and Parents' Co-TV Viewing and Their Total Screen Time in Six European Countries: Cross-Sectional Data from the Feel4diabetes-Study," *International Journal of Environmental Research and Public Health* 15, no. 11 (2018): 2599, https://doi.org/10.3390/ijerph15112599.

96 Eun-Young Lee et al., "Levels and Correlates of Physical Activity and Screen Time Among Early Years Children (2–5 Years): Cross-Cultural Comparisons Between Canadian and South Korean Data," *Child: Care, Health and Development* 47, no. 3 (2021): 377–86, https://doi.org/10.1111/cch.12850.

97 Killian Mullan and Sandra L. Hofferth, "A Comparative Time-Diary Analysis of UK and US Children's Screen Time and Device Use," *Child Indicators Research* 15, no. 3 (2021): 795–818, https://doi.org/10.1007/s12187-021-09884-3.

98 Gwyther Rees, "Children's Activities and Time Use: Variations Between and Within 16 Countries," *Children and Youth Services Review* 80 (2017): 78–87, https://doi.org/10.1016/j.childyouth.2017.06.057.

99 Bernard et al., "Predictors of Screen Viewing Time in Young Singaporean Children."

100 Amanda Santos et al., "Screen Time Between Portuguese and Brazilian Children: A Cross-Cultural Study," *Motriz: Revista de Educação Fisica* 23, no. 2 (2017): e101636, http://dx.doi.org/10.1590/S1980-6574201700020006.

101 Hugues Sampasa-Kanyinga et al., "Social Media Use and Parent–child Relationship: A Cross-sectional Study of Adolescents," *Journal of Community Psychology* 48, no. 3 (2019): 793–803, https://doi.org/10.1002/jcop.22293.

102 Yaron Sela et al., "Family Environment and Problematic Internet Use Among Adolescents: The Mediating Roles of Depression and Fear of Missing Out," *Computers in Human Behavior* 106 (2019): 106226, https://doi.org/10.1016/j.chb.2019.106226.

103 Laura M. Padilla-Walker et al., "Getting a High-Speed Family Connection: Associations Between Family Media Use and Family Connection," *Family Relations* 61, no. 3 (2012): 426–40, https://doi.org/10.1111/j.1741-3729.2012.00710.x.

104 Padilla-Walker et al., "Getting a High-Speed Family Connection," 437.

105 Sook-Jung Lee et al., "Predicting Children's Media Use in the USA: Differences in Cross-sectional and Longitudinal Analysis," *British Journal of Developmental Psychology* 27, no. 1 (2009): 123–43, https://doi.org/10.1348/026151008x401336.

106 Tassi Yunga Celine Seh, "Children's Excessive Internet Use and its Relationship to the Family Bond: The Case of Helsinki, Finland" (Master's thesis, Catholic University and University Institute of Lisbon, 2023).

107 Dorothée Hefner et al., "Rules? Role Model? Relationship? The Impact of Parents on Their Children's Problematic Mobile Phone Involvement," *Media Psychology* 22, no. 1 (2018): 82–108, https://doi.org/10.1080/15213269.2018.1433544.

108 Roger Silverstone et al., "Families, Technologies and Consumption: The Household and Information and Communication Technologies," discussion paper at Centre for Research into Innovation, Culture & Technology, Uxbridge, 1989.

109 Silverstone et al., "Families, Technologies, and Consumption," 1989, 22.

110 Lara Perez-Felkner, "Socialization in Childhood and Adolescence," in *Handbook of Social Psychology*, 2nd ed., ed. John DeLamater and Amanda Ward (Dordrecht, the Netherlands: Springer 2013), 123.
111 Jennifer E. Lansford, "Annual Research Review: Cross-Cultural Similarities and Differences in Parenting," *Journal of Child Psychology and Psychiatry* 63, no. 4 (2021): 466–79, https://doi.org/10.1111/jcpp.13539.
112 Lansford, "Annual Research Review."
113 Lemish, *Children and Media*, 22.

Chapter 3

1 Salima Kerai et al., "Screen Time and Developmental Health: Results From an Early Childhood Study in Canada," *BMC Public Health* 22, no. 1 (2022), https://doi.org/10.1186/s12889-022-12701-3.
2 Vivi Irzalinda and Melly Latifah, "Screen Time and Early Childhood Well-Being: A Systematic Literature Review Approach," *Journal of Family Sciences* (2023): 18–34, https://doi.org/10.29244/jfs.vi.49792.
3 Neza Stiglic and Russell M. Viner, "Effects of Screentime on the Health and Wellbeing of Children and Adolescents: A Systematic Review of Reviews," *BMJ Open* 9, no. 1 (2019): e023191, https://doi.org/10.1136/bmjopen-2018-023191.
4 Julie Cullen et al., "Impact of Digital Screen Use on Health and Wellbeing of Children and Adolescents: A Narrative Review," *New Zealand Journal of Physiotherapy* 52, no. 1 (2024): 62–77, https://doi.org/10.15619/nzjp.v52i1.364.
5 Chao Li et al., "The Relationships Between Screen Use and Health Indicators Among Infants, Toddlers, and Preschoolers: A Meta-Analysis and Systematic Review," *International Journal of Environmental Research and Public Health* 17, no. 19 (2020): 7324, https://doi.org/10.3390/ijerph17197324.
6 Youjie Zhang et al., "Screen Time and Health Issues in Chinese School-aged Children and Adolescents: A Systematic Review and Meta-Analysis," *BMC Public Health* 22, no. 1 (2022), https://doi.org/10.1186/s12889-022-13155-3.
7 Yiling Wu et al., "Screen Time and Body Mass Index Among Children and Adolescents: A Systematic Review and Meta-Analysis," *Frontiers in Pediatrics* 10 (2022), https://doi.org/10.3389/fped.2022.822108.
8 Purya Haghjoo et al., "Screen Time Increases Overweight and Obesity Risk Among Adolescents: A Systematic Review and Dose-Response Meta-Analysis," *BMC Primary Care* 23, no. 1 (2022), https://doi.org/10.1186/s12875-022-01761-4.
9 Emma Boyland et al., "Association of Food and Nonalcoholic Beverage Marketing with Children and Adolescents' Eating Behaviors and Health," *JAMA Pediatrics* 176, no. 7 (2022): e221037, https://doi.org/10.1001/jamapediatrics.2022.1037.
10 Madhvi Tripathi and Shailendra Kumar Mishra, "Screen Time and Adiposity Among Children and Adolescents: A Systematic Review," *Journal of Public Health* 28, no. 3 (2019): 227–44, https://doi.org/10.1007/s10389-019-01043-x.

11 Crystal R. Smit et al., "The Impact of Social Media Influencers on Children's Dietary Behaviors," *Frontiers in Psychology* 10 (2020), https://doi.org/10.3389/fpsyg.2019.02975.
12 Hugues Sampasa-Kanyinga et al., "Sex Differences in the Relationship Between Social Media Use, Short Sleep Duration, and Body Mass Index Among Adolescents," *Sleep Health* 6, no. 5 (2020): 601–8, https://doi.org/10.1016/j.sleh.2020.01.017.
13 Kathryn Backholer et al., "Differential Exposure to, and Potential Impact of, Unhealthy Advertising to Children by Socio-economic and Ethnic Groups: A Systematic Review of the Evidence," *Obesity Reviews* 22, no. 3 (2020), https://doi.org/10.1111/obr.13144.
14 Zihao He et al., "Effects of Smartphone-Based Interventions on Physical Activity in Children and Adolescents: Systematic Review and Meta-Analysis," *JMIR Mhealth and Uhealth* 9, no. 2 (2021): e22601, https://doi.org/10.2196/22601.
15 Leanne M. Mauriello et al., "Results of a Multi-media Multiple Behavior Obesity Prevention Program for Adolescents," *Preventive Medicine* 51, no. 6 (2010): 451–6, https://doi.org/10.1016/j.ypmed.2010.08.004.
16 Michelle S. H. Hsu et al., "Effectiveness and Behavioral Mechanisms of Social Media Interventions for Positive Nutrition Behaviors in Adolescents: A Systematic Review," *Journal of Adolescent Health* 63, no. 5 (2018): 531–45, https://doi.org/10.1016/j.jadohealth.2018.06.009.
17 Sabine Herget et al., "High-Intensity Interval Training for Overweight Adolescents: Program Acceptance of a Media Supported Intervention and Changes in Body Composition," *International Journal of Environmental Research and Public Health* 13, no. 11 (2016): 1099, https://doi.org/10.3390/ijerph13111099.
18 Taylor Rose et al., "A Systematic Review of Digital Interventions for Improving the Diet and Physical Activity Behaviors of Adolescents," *Journal of Adolescent Health* 61, no. 6 (2017): 669–77, https://doi.org/10.1016/j.jadohealth.2017.05.024.
19 Sabine Pawellek et al., "Strategien und Effekte digitaler Interventionen bei der Übergewichts- und Adipositastherapie von Kindern und Jugendlichen – ein systematischer Review," *Bundesgesundheitsblatt Gesundheitsforschung Gesundheitsschutz* 65, no. 5 (2022): 624–34, https://doi.org/10.1007/s00103-022-03512-3.
20 Xanne Janssen et al., "Associations of Screen Time, Sedentary Time and Physical Activity with Sleep in Under 5s: A Systematic Review and Meta-Analysis," *Sleep Medicine Reviews* 49 (2019): 101226, https://doi.org/10.1016/j.smrv.2019.101226.
21 Li et al., "The Relationships Between Screen Use and Health Indicators Among Infants, Toddlers, and Preschoolers."
22 Qiu-Ye Lan et al., "Sleep Duration in Preschool Children and Impact of Screen Time," *Sleep Medicine* 76 (2020): 48–54, https://doi.org/10.1016/j.sleep.2020.09.024.
23 Lisbeth Lund et al., "Electronic Media Use and Sleep in Children and Adolescents in Western Countries: A Systematic Review," *BMC Public Health* 21, no. 1 (2021), https://doi.org/10.1186/s12889-021-11640-9.
24 Garrett Hisler et al., "Associations Between Screen Time and Short Sleep Duration Among Adolescents Varies by Media Type: Evidence From a Cohort

Study," *Sleep Medicine* 66 (2019): 92–102, https://doi.org/10.1016/j.sleep.2019.08.007.

25 Nate S. Bergfeld and Jan Van Den Bulck, "It's Not All About the Likes: Social Media Affordances with Nighttime, Problematic, and Adverse Use as Predictors of Adolescent Sleep Indicators," *Sleep Health* 7, no. 5 (2021): 548–55, https://doi.org/10.1016/j.sleh.2021.05.009.

26 Nicole E. Carmona et al., "A Transdiagnostic Self-management Web-Based App for Sleep Disturbance in Adolescents and Young Adults: Feasibility and Acceptability Study," *JMIR Formative Research* 5, no. 11 (2021): e25392, https://doi.org/10.2196/25392.

27 Aliza Werner-Seidler et al., "Pilot Evaluation of the Sleep Ninja: A Smartphone Application for Adolescent Insomnia Symptoms," *BMJ Open* 9, no. 5 (2019): e026502, https://doi.org/10.1136/bmjopen-2018–026502.

28 Arika Yoshizaki et al., "Improving Children's Sleep Habits Using an Interactive Smartphone App: Community-Based Intervention Study," *JMIR mHealth and uHealth* 11 (2023): e40836, https://doi.org/10.2196/40836.

29 Raquel Nogueira Avelar e Silva et al., "Early Sexual Intercourse: Prospective Associations with Adolescents Physical Activity and Screen Time," *PLoS ONE* 11, no. 8 (2016): e0158648, https://doi.org/10.1371/journal.pone.0158648.

30 Elissa M. Barr et al., "The Relationship Between Screen Time and Sexual Behaviors Among Middle School Students," *Health Educator* 46, no. 1 (2014): 6–13, https://eric.ed.gov/?id=EJ1046859.

31 Megan Landry et al., "Social Media and Sexual Behavior Among Adolescents: Is There a Link?" *JMIR Public Health and Surveillance* 3, no. 2 (2017): e28, https://doi.org/10.2196/publichealth.7149.

32 Rebecca L. Collins et al., "Sexual Media and Childhood Well-being and Health," *Pediatrics* 140, no. Supplement_2 (2017): S162–6, https://doi.org/10.1542/peds.2016-1758x.

33 Naomi Gazendam et al., "Individual and Social Determinants of Early Sexual Activity: A Study of Gender-based Differences Using the 2018 Canadian Health Behaviour in School-aged Children Study (HBSC)," *PLoS ONE* 15, no. 9 (2020): e0238515, https://doi.org/10.1371/journal.pone.0238515.

34 Wen-Hsu Lin et al., "Exposure to Sexually Explicit Media in Early Adolescence Is Related to Risky Sexual Behavior in Emerging Adulthood," *PLoS ONE* 15, no. 4 (2020): e0230242, https://doi.org/10.1371/journal.pone.0230242.

35 Elena Martellozzo et al., "'I Wasn't Sure it was Normal to Watch it . . . ': A Quantitative and Qualitative Examination of the Impact of Online Pornography on the Values, Attitudes, Beliefs and Behaviours of Children and Young People," Middlesex University, NSPCC, OCC, 2017, https://doi.org/10/6084/m9.figshare.3382393.

36 Tracy M. Scull et al., "A Media Literacy Education Approach to High School Sexual Health Education: Immediate Effects of 'Media Aware' on Adolescents' Media, Sexual Health, and Communication Outcomes," *Journal of Youth and Adolescence* 51, no. 4 (2022): 708–23, https://doi.org/10.1007/s10964-021-01567-0.

37 Lynn E. Fiellin et al., "Video Game Intervention for Sexual Risk Reduction in Minority Adolescents: Randomized Controlled Trial," *Journal of Medical Internet Research* 19, no. 9 (2017): e314, https://doi.org/10.2196/jmir.8148.
38 Ross Shegog et al., "It's Your Game-Tech: Toward Sexual Health in the Digital Age," *Creative Education* 5, no. 15 (2014): 1428–47, https://doi.org/10.4236/ce.2014.515161.
39 Chelly Maes et al., "#(Me)Too Much? The Role of Sexualizing Online Media in Adolescents' Resistance Towards the MeToo-movement and Acceptance of Rape Myths," *Journal of Adolescence* 77, no. 1 (2019): 59–69, https://doi.org/10.1016/j.adolescence.2019.10.005.
40 Anna Vannucci et al., "Social Media Use and Risky Behaviors in Adolescents: A Meta-Analysis," *Journal of Adolescence* 79, no. 1 (2020): 258–74, https://doi.org/10.1016/j.adolescence.2020.01.014.
41 David Jernigan et al., "Alcohol Marketing and Youth Alcohol Consumption: A Systematic Review of Longitudinal Studies Published Since 2008," *Addiction* 112, no. S1 (2016): 7–20, https://doi.org/10.1111/add.13591.
42 Elizabeth J. D'Amico et al., "Gateway to Curiosity: Medical Marijuana Ads and Intention and Use During Middle School," *Psychology of Addictive Behaviors* 29, no. 3 (2015): 613–19, https://doi.org/10.1037/adb0000094.
43 Scott I. Donaldson et al., "Association Between Exposure to Tobacco Content on Social Media and Tobacco Use," *JAMA Pediatrics* 176, no. 9 (2022): 878, https://doi.org/10.1001/jamapediatrics.2022.2223.
44 Ting Luo et al., "Using Social Media for Smoking Cessation Interventions: A Systematic Review," *Perspectives in Public Health* 141, no. 1 (2020): 50–63, https://doi.org/10.1177/1757913920906845.
45 Alison Hutton et al., "mHealth Interventions to Reduce Alcohol Use in Young People: A Systematic Review of the Literature," *Comprehensive Child and Adolescent Nursing* 43, no. 3 (2019): 171–202, https://doi.org/10.1080/24694193.2019.1616008.
46 Jamilah Ahmad et al., "Impact of Social Media-based Intervention in Reducing Youths' Propensity to Engage in Drug Abuse in Nigeria," *Evaluation and Program Planning* 94 (2022): 102122, https://doi.org/10.1016/j.evalprogplan.2022.102122.
47 Patricia Van Den Berg et al., "Is Dieting Advice from Magazines Helpful or Harmful? Five-Year Associations with Weight-Control Behaviors and Psychological Outcomes in Adolescents," *Pediatrics* 119, no. 1 (2007): e30–7, https://doi.org/10.1542/peds.2006-0978.
48 Miguel Angel Martínez-González et al., "Parental Factors, Mass Media Influences, and the Onset of Eating Disorders in a Prospective Population-Based Cohort," *Pediatrics* 111, no. 2 (2003): 315–20, https://doi.org/10.1542/peds.111.2.315.
49 Huw Goodwin et al., "Sociocultural Correlates of Compulsive Exercise: Is the Environment Important in Fostering a Compulsivity Towards Exercise Among Adolescents?" *Body Image* 8, no. 4 (2011): 390–5, https://doi.org/10.1016/j.bodyim.2011.05.006.
50 Hannah K. Jarman et al., "Social Media, Body Satisfaction and Well-being Among Adolescents: A Mediation Model of Appearance-Ideal Internalization

and Comparison," *Body Image* 36 (2020): 139–48, https://doi.org/10.1016/j.bodyim.2020.11.005.

51 Kathrin Karsay et al., "'I (Don't) Respect My Body': Investigating the Role of Mass Media Use and Self-Objectification on Adolescents' Positive Body Image in a Cross-National Study," *Mass Communication & Society* 24, no. 1 (2020): 57–84, https://doi.org/10.1080/15205436.2020.1827432.

52 Jolien De Coen et al., "Media Influence Components as Predictors of Children's Body Image and Eating Problems: A Longitudinal Study of Boys and Girls During Middle Childhood," *Body Image* 37 (2021): 204–13, https://doi.org/10.1016/j.bodyim.2021.03.001.

53 Jason M. Nagata et al., "Contemporary Screen Time Modalities Among Children 9–10 Years Old and Binge-eating Disorder at One-Year Follow-up: A Prospective Cohort Study," *International Journal of Eating Disorders* 54, no. 5 (2021): 887–92, https://doi.org/10.1002/eat.23489.

54 Sarah M. Coyne et al., "A Meta-analysis of Prosocial Media on Prosocial Behavior, Aggression, and Empathic Concern: A Multidimensional Approach," *Developmental Psychology* 54, no. 2 (2017): 331–47, https://doi.org/10.1037/dev0000412.

55 Rebecca N. H. De Leeuw and Christa A. Van Der Laan, "Helping Behavior in Disney Animated Movies and Children's Helping Behavior in the Netherlands," *Journal of Children and Media* 12, no. 2 (2017): 159–74, https://doi.org/10.1080/17482798.2017.1409245.

56 Dimitri A. Christakis et al., "Modifying Media Content for Preschool Children: A Randomized Controlled Trial," *Pediatrics* 131, no. 3 (2013): 431–8, https://doi.org/10.1542/peds.2012-1493.

57 Marie-Louise Mares and Zhongdang Pan, "Effects of Sesame Street: A Meta-analysis of Children's Learning in 15 Countries," *Journal of Applied Developmental Psychology* 34, no. 3 (2013): 140–51, https://doi.org/10.1016/j.appdev.2013.01.001.

58 Eric E. Rasmussen et al., "Promoting Preschoolers' Emotional Competence Through Prosocial TV and Mobile App Use," *Media Psychology* 22, no. 1 (2018): 1–22, https://doi.org/10.1080/15213269.2018.1476890.

59 Rebecca Dredge and Lara Schreurs, "Social Media Use and Offline Interpersonal Outcomes During Youth: A Systematic Literature Review," *Mass Communication & Society* 23, no. 6 (2020): 885–911, https://doi.org/10.1080/15205436.2020.1810277.

60 Silje Steinsbekk et al., "The New Social Landscape: Relationships Among Social Media Use, Social Skills, and Offline Friendships from Age 10–18 Years," *Computers in Human Behavior* 156 (2024): 108235, https://doi.org/10.1016/j.chb.2024.108235.

61 Shunsen Huang et al., "Beyond Screen Time: Exploring the Associations Between Types of Smartphone Use Content and Adolescents' Social Relationships," *International Journal of Environmental Research and Public Health* 19, no. 15 (2022): 8940, https://doi.org/10.3390/ijerph19158940.

62 Hege Sjolie et al., "Attachments or Affiliations? The Impact of Social Media on the Quality of Peer Relationships—A Qualitative Study Among Norwegian High

School Students," *Youth & Society* 56, no. 4 (2023): 673–92, https://doi.org/10.1177/0044118x231171180.
63 American Academy of Pediatrics, *AAP-AACAP-CHA Declaration of a National Emergency in Child and Adolescent Mental Health*, 2021, https://www.aap.org/en/advocacy/child-and-adolescent-healthy-mental-development/aap-aacap-cha-declaration-of-a-national-emergency-in-child-and-adolescent-mental-health/.
64 U.S. Department of Health and Human Services, *Social Media and Youth Mental Health: The U.S. Surgeon General's Advisory*, 2023, https://www.hhs.gov/sites/default/files/sg-youth-mental-health-social-media-advisory.pdf, 4.
65 National Center for Health Statistics, *National Health Interview Survey-Teen*, 2024, https://www.cdc.gov/nchs/nhis/teen/index.html.
66 Nicole Racine et al., "Global Prevalence of Depressive and Anxiety Symptoms in Children and Adolescents During COVID-19," *JAMA Pediatrics* 175, no. 11 (2021): 1142–50, https://doi.org/10.1001/jamapediatrics.2021.2482.
67 Jean M. Twenge et al., "Worldwide Increases in Adolescent Loneliness," *Journal of Adolescence* 93, no. 1 (2021): 257–69, https://doi.org/10.1016/j.adolescence.2021.06.006.
68 Sylia Wilson and Nathalie M. Dumornay, "Rising Rates of Adolescent Depression in the United States: Challenges and Opportunities in the 2020s," *Journal of Adolescent Health* 70, no. 3 (2022): 354–5, https://doi.org/10.1016/j.jadohealth.2021.12.003.
69 Rideout et al., "The Common Sense Census."
70 Victoria Rideout and Michael B. Robb, "Social Media, Social Life: Teens Reveal Their Experiences," Common Sense Media, 2018.
71 Emily A. Vogels and Risa Gelles-Watnick, "Teens and Social Media: Key Findings from Pew Research Center Surveys," *Pew Research Center*, April 24, 2023, https://www.pewresearch.org/short-reads/2023/04/24/teens-and-social-media-key-findings-from-pew-research-center-surveys/.
72 "Patti Valkenburg Gives Seminar at Stanford Policy Center," *Patti Valkenburg*, May 3, 2024, https://www.pattivalkenburg.nl/news/patti-valkenburg-gives-seminar-at-stanford-policy-center.
73 Elizabeth Hoge et al., "Digital Media, Anxiety, and Depression in Children," *Pediatrics* 140, no. Supplement_2 (2017): S76–80, https://doi.org/10.1542/peds.2016-1758g.
74 Igor Pantic et al, "Association Between Online Social Networking and Depression in High School Students: Behavioral Physiology Viewpoint," *Psychiatria Danubina* 24, no. 1 (2012): 90–3.
75 Jacqueline Nesi and Mitchell J. Prinstein, "Using Social Media for Social Comparison and Feedback-Seeking: Gender and Popularity Moderate Associations with Depressive Symptoms," *Journal of Abnormal Child Psychology* 43, no. 8 (2015): 1427–38, https://doi.org/10.1007/s10802-015-0020-0.
76 Hoge et al., "Digital Media, Anxiety, and Depression in Children," S77.
77 Hoge et al., "Digital Media, Anxiety, and Depression in Children," S78.

78 Eric E. Rasmussen et al., "The Serially Mediated Relationship Between Emerging Adults' Social Media Use and Mental Well-being," *Computers in Human Behavior* 102 (2020): 206–13, https://doi.org/10.1016/j.chb.2019.08.019.
79 David S. Bickham et al., "Media Use and Depression: Exposure, Household Rules, and Symptoms Among Young Adolescents in the USA," *International Journal of Public Health* 60, no. 2 (2015): 147–55, https://doi.org/10.1007/s00038-014-0647-6.
80 Rachel Eirich et al., "Association of Screen Time with Internalizing and Externalizing Behavior Problems in Children 12 Years or Younger," *JAMA Psychiatry* 79, no. 5 (2022): 393–405, https://doi.org/10.1001/jamapsychiatry.2022.0155.
81 Twenge et al., "Worldwide Increases in Adolescent Loneliness."
82 Sakshi Prasad et al., "Anxiety and Depression Amongst Youth as Adverse Effects of Using Social Media: A Review," *Annals of Medicine and Surgery* 85, no. 8 (2023): 3974–81, https://doi.org/10.1097/ms9.0000000000001066.
83 Jacqueline Nesi et al., "Patterns of Social Media Use Among Adolescents Who Are Psychiatrically Hospitalized," *Journal of the American Academy of Child & Adolescent Psychiatry* 58, no. 6 (2019): 635–9.e1, https://doi.org/10.1016/j.jaac.2019.03.009.
84 Hilde Thygesen et al., "Social Media Use and Its Associations with Mental Health 9 Months After the COVID-19 Outbreak: A Cross-National Study," *Frontiers in Public Health* 9 (2022), https://doi.org/10.3389/fpubh.2021.752004.
85 Laura Marciano et al., "Digital Media Use and Adolescents' Mental Health During the Covid-19 Pandemic: A Systematic Review and Meta-Analysis," *Frontiers in Public Health* 9 (2022), https://doi.org/10.3389/fpubh.2021.793868.
86 Michelle O'Reilly et al., "Potential of Social Media in Promoting Mental Health in Adolescents," *Health Promotion International* 34, no. 5 (2018): 981–91, https://doi.org/10.1093/heapro/day056.
87 Sandra Bucci et al., "The Digital Revolution and its Impact on Mental Health Care," *Psychology and Psychotherapy Theory Research and Practice* 92, no. 2 (2019): 277–97, https://doi.org/10.1111/papt.12222.
88 Verolien Cauberghe et al., "How Adolescents Use Social Media to Cope with Feelings of Loneliness and Anxiety During COVID-19 Lockdown," *Cyberpsychology Behavior and Social Networking* 24, no. 4 (2020): 250–7, https://doi.org/10.1089/cyber.2020.0478.
89 Mengguo Jing et al., "Screen Media Exposure and Young Children's Vocabulary Learning and Development: A Meta-Analysis," *Child Development* 94, no. 5 (2023): 1398–418, https://doi.org/10.1111/cdev.13927.
90 Sheri Madigan et al., "Associations Between Screen Use and Child Language Skills," *JAMA Pediatrics* 174, no. 7 (2020): 665–75, https://doi.org/10.1001/jamapediatrics.2020.0327.
91 Erin K. Howie et al., "Associations Between Meeting Sleep, Physical Activity or Screen Time Behaviour Guidelines and Academic Performance in Australian School Children," *BMC Public Health* 20, no. 1 (2020), https://doi.org/10.1186/s12889-020-08620-w.

92 Konstantina Louka and Stamatios Papadakis, "Enhancing Computational Thinking in Early Childhood Education Through 'ScratchJr' Integration," *Heliyon* 10, no. 10 (2024): e30482, https://doi.org/10.1016/j.heliyon.2024.e30482.
93 Stefanie Vanbecelaere et al., "The Effects of Two Digital Educational Games on Cognitive and Non-Cognitive Math and Reading Outcomes," *Computers & Education* 143 (2019): 103680, https://doi.org/10.1016/j.compedu.2019.103680.
94 Elizabeth McCarthy et al., "Learning Math with Curious George and the Odd Squad: Transmedia in the Classroom," *Technology Knowledge and Learning* 23, no. 2 (2018): 223–46, https://doi.org/10.1007/s10758-018-9361-4.
95 Patti M. Valkenburg and Jochen Peter, "The Differential Susceptibility to Media Effects Model," *Journal of Communication* 63, no. 2 (2013): 221–43, https://doi.org/10.1111/jcom.12024.
96 Jessica Taylor Piotrowski and Patti M. Valkenburg, "Finding Orchids in a Field of Dandelions: Understanding Children's Differential Susceptibility to Media Effects," *American Behavioral Scientist* 59, no. 14 (2015): 1777, https://doi.org/10.1177/0002764215596552.
97 Jennings Bryant and Dorina Miron, "Theory and Research in Mass Communication," *Journal of Communication* 54, no. 4 (2004): 662–704, https://doi.org/10.1111/j.1460-2466.2004.tb02650.x.
98 Chung Joo Chung et al., "An Analysis on Communication Theory and Discipline," *Scientometrics* 95, no. 3 (2012): 985–1002, https://doi.org/10.1007/s11192-012-0869-4.
99 Rasha Kamhawi and David Weaver, "Mass Communication Research Trends From 1980 to 1999," *Journalism & Mass Communication Quarterly* 80, no. 1 (2003): 7–27, https://doi.org/10.1177/107769900308000102.
100 James W. Potter, *Media Effects* (Thousand Oaks, California: Sage Publications, 2012).
101 Nathan Walter et al., "The Ebb and Flow of Communication Research: Seven Decades of Publication Trends and Research Priorities," *Journal of Communication* 68, no. 2 (2018): 424–40, https://doi.org/10.1093/joc/jqx015.
102 Jean Piaget, "Piaget's Theory," in *Handbook of Child Psychology: Vol. I History, Theory, and Methods*, ed. Paul H. Mussen and William Kessen (New York, NY: John Wiley, 1983), 41–102.

Chapter 4

1 Bronfenbrenner, *The Ecology of Human Development*.
2 S. Genner and D. Süss, "Socialization as Media Effect," in *The International Encyclopedia of Media Effects*, ed. P. Rössler, C. A. Hoffner, and L. Zoonen (Chichester, England: Wiley-Blackwell, 2017), 1–15.
3 Joan E. Grusec and Maayan Davidov, "Analyzing Socialization from a Domain-Specific Perspective," in *Handbook of Socialization: Theory and Research*, 2nd ed., ed. Joan E. Grusec and Paul D. Hastings (New York, NY: Guilford Press, 2015), 158–81.

4. Marjorie J. Hogan, "Parents and Other Adults: Models and Monitors of Healthy Media Habits," in *Handbook of Children and the Media*, ed. Dorothy G. Singer and Jerome L. Singer (Thousand Oaks, California: Sage Publications, 2001), 663–80.
5. Beatrice Sciacca et al., "Parental Mediation in Pandemic: Predictors and Relationship with Children's Digital Skills and Time Spent Online in Ireland," *Computers in Human Behavior* 127 (2021): 107081, https://doi.org/10.1016/j.chb.2021.107081.
6. Sciacca et al., "Parental Mediation in Pandemic," 1.
7. Lang and Ewoldsen, "Beyond effects," 112.
8. Lev S. Vygotsky, *Mind in Society: The Development of Higher Psychological Processes* (Cambridge, Massachusetts: Harvard University Press, 1978).
9. Lev S. Vygotsky, *Thought and Language: Translation Newly Revised and Edited by Alex Kozulin* (Cambridge, Massachusetts: The MIT Press, 1986).
10. Yuriy Karpov, "Vygotsky's Concept of Mediation," *Journal of Cognitive Education and Psychology* 3, no. 1 (2003): 46.
11. Alex Inkeles, "Social Change and Social Character: The Role of Parental Mediation," *Journal of Social Issues* 11, no. 2 (1955): 12–23, https://doi.org/10.1111/j.1540-4560.1955.tb00311.x.
12. Ine Beyens and Kathleen Beullens, "Parent–Child Conflict About Children's Tablet Use: The Role of Parental Mediation," *New Media & Society* 19, no. 12 (2016): 2075–93, https://doi.org/10.1177/1461444816655099.
13. Eric E. Rasmussen, "Proactive Vs. Retroactive Mediation: Effects of Mediation's Timing on Children's Reactions to Popular Cartoon Violence," *Human Communication Research* 40, no. 3 (2014): 396–413, https://doi.org/10.1111/hcre.12030.
14. Marc H. Bornstein et al., "The Future of Parenting Programs: An Introduction," *Parenting* 22, no. 3 (2022): 190, https://doi.org/10.1080/15295192.2022.2086808.
15. Bornstein et al., "The Future of Parenting Programs," 190.
16. Bleakley et al., "The Relationship Between Parents' and Children's Television Viewing."
17. Lauricella et al., "Young Children's Screen Time."
18. Xiaoyun Li et al., "Maternal Phubbing and Problematic Media Use in Preschoolers: The Independent and Interactive Moderating Role of Children's Negative Affectivity and Effortful Control," *Psychology Research and Behavior Management* 17 (2024): 3083–100, https://doi.org/10.2147/prbm.s471208.
19. Li et al., "Maternal Phubbing and Problematic Media Use in Preschoolers."
20. Jia Wang et al., "How Parental Mediation and Parental Phubbing Affect Preschool Children's Screen Media Use: A Response Surface Analysis," *Cyberpsychology Behavior and Social Networking* 27, no. 9 (2024): 651–7, https://doi.org/10.1089/cyber.2023.0638.
21. Amy I. Nathanson, "Mediation of Children's Television Viewing: Working Toward Conceptual Clarity and Common Understanding," in *Communication Yearbook 25*, ed. William B. Gudykunst (Mahwah, New Jersey: Lawrence Erlbaum Associates, 2001), 115–51.
22. Purva D Lanjekar et al., "The Effect of Parenting and the Parent-Child Relationship on a Child's Cognitive Development: A Literature Review," *Cureus*, 2022, https://doi.org/10.7759/cureus.30574.

23 Lanjekar et al., "The Effect of Parenting and the Parent-Child Relationship on a Child's Cognitive Development."
24 María Cruz López-de-Ayala-López and Leslie Haddon, "The Parental Mediation Strategies of Parents with Young Children," *Media@LSE Working Paper Series* 50 (2018): 1–26.
25 Albert Bandura, *Social Learning Theory* (Englewood Cliffs, New Jersey: Prentice Hall, 1977).
26 Lara A. Wood et al., "Whom Do Children Copy? Model-based Biases in Social Learning," *Developmental Review* 33, no. 4 (2013): 341–56, https://doi.org/10.1016/j.dr.2013.08.002.
27 Wood et al., "Whom Do Children Copy?"
28 Lauricella and Cingel, "Parental Influence on Youth Media Use."
29 Lauricella and Cingel, "Parental Influence on Youth Media Use."
30 Thomas J. Dishion and Robert J. McMahon, "Parental Monitoring and the Prevention of Child and Adolescent Problem Behavior: A Conceptual and Empirical Formulation," *Clinical Child and Family Psychology Review* 1, no. 1 (1998): 61, https://doi.org/10.1023/a:1021800432380.
31 Margaret Kerr et al., "A Reinterpretation of Parental Monitoring in Longitudinal Perspective," *Journal of Research on Adolescence* 20, no. 1 (2010): 39–64, https://doi.org/10.1111/j.1532-7795.2009.00623.x.
32 Kristen C. Jacobson and Lisa J. Crockett, "Parental Monitoring and Adolescent Adjustment: An Ecological Perspective," *Journal of Research on Adolescence* 10, no. 1 (2000): 65–97, https://doi.org/10.1207/sjra1001_4.
33 Patricia J. Dittus et al., "Parental Monitoring and its Associations with Adolescent Sexual Risk Behavior: A Meta-Analysis," *Pediatrics* 136, no. 6 (2015): e1587–99, https://doi.org/10.1542/peds.2015-0305.
34 Jill Ryan et al., "The Effects of Parental Monitoring and Communication on Adolescent Substance Use and Risky Sexual Activity: A Systematic Review," *The Open Family Studies Journal* 7, no. suppl 1_m3 (2015): 12–27, http://hdl.handle.net/10566/2422.
35 Jungup Lee and Karen A. Randolph, "Effects of Parental Monitoring on Aggressive Behavior Among Youth in the United States and South Korea: A Cross-National Study," *Children and Youth Services Review* 55 (2015): 1–9, https://doi.org/10.1016/j.childyouth.2015.05.008.
36 Robert D. Laird et al., "Revisiting Parental Monitoring: Evidence That Parental Solicitation Can Be Effective When Needed Most," *Journal of Youth and Adolescence* 39, no. 12 (2009): 1431–41, https://doi.org/10.1007/s10964-009-9453-5.
37 Stacey S. Tiberio et al., "Parental Monitoring of Children's Media Consumption," *JAMA Pediatrics* 168, no. 5 (2014): 414, https://doi.org/10.1001/jamapediatrics.2013.5483.
38 Douglas A. Gentile et al., "Protective Effects of Parental Monitoring of Children's Media Use," *JAMA Pediatrics* 168, no. 5 (2014): 479, https://doi.org/10.1001/jamapediatrics.2014.146.
39 Laura M. Padilla-Walker et al., "The Protective Role of Parental Media Monitoring Style from Early to Late Adolescence," *Journal of Youth and Adolescence* 47, no. 2 (2017): 445–59, https://doi.org/10.1007/s10964-017-0722-4.

40　Lacey N. Wallace, "Associations Between Parental Monitoring and Parents' Social Media Use and Social Media Perceptions," *Social Sciences & Humanities Open* 6, no. 1 (2022): 100294, https://doi.org/10.1016/j.ssaho.2022.100294.
41　William E. Pelham et al., "What Is Parental Monitoring?" *Clinical Child and Family Psychology Review* 27, no. 2 (2024): 586, https://doi.org/10.1007/s10567-024-00490-7.
42　Fumiko Kakihara and Lauree Tilton-Weaver, "Adolescents' Interpretations of Parental Control: Differentiated by Domain and Types of Control," *Child Development* 80, no. 6 (2009): 1722, https://doi.org/10.1111/j.1467-8624.2009.01364.x.
43　Judith G. Smetana and Christopher Daddis, "Domain-Specific Antecedents of Parental Psychological Control and Monitoring: The Role of Parenting Beliefs and Practices," *Child Development* 73, no. 2 (2002): 563, https://doi.org/10.1111/1467-8624.00424.
44　Fumiko Kakihara et al., "The Relationship of Parental Control to Youth Adjustment: Do Youths' Feelings About Their Parents Play a Role?" *Journal of Youth and Adolescence* 39, no. 12 (2009): 1442–56, https://doi.org/10.1007/s10964-009-9479-8.
45　Berna Akcinar and Nazli Baydar, "Parental Control Is Not Unconditionally Detrimental for Externalizing Behaviors in Early Childhood," *International Journal of Behavioral Development* 38, no. 2 (2014): 118–27, https://doi.org/10.1177/0165025413513701.
46　Brian K. Barber et al., "Associations Between Parental Psychological and Behavioral Control and Youth Internalized and Externalized Behaviors," *Child Development* 65, no. 4 (1994): 1120–36, https://doi.org/10.1111/j.1467-8624.1994.tb00807.x.
47　Akcinar and Baydar, "Parental Control Is Not Unconditionally Detrimental for Externalizing Behaviors in Early Childhood," 119.
48　Daniel Fu Keung Wong et al., "Is Parental Control Beneficial or Harmful to the Development of Young Children in Hong Kong?," *Journal of Child and Family Studies* 28, no. 3 (2018): 831–8, https://doi.org/10.1007/s10826-018-1301-3.
49　Cristiano Inguglia et al., "The Role of Parental Control and Coping Strategies on Adolescents' Problem Behaviors," *Current Psychology* 41, no. 3 (2020): 1287–300, https://doi.org/10.1007/s12144-020-00648-w.
50　Alyssa R. Williams and Cliff McKinney, "Indirect Effects of Parental Psychological Control on Emerging Adult Psychological Problems," *Journal of Child and Family Studies* 33, no. 4 (2023): 1058–69, https://doi.org/10.1007/s10826-023-02623-y.
51　Fuyun Yan et al., "Relationship Between Parental Psychological Control and Problem Behaviours in Youths: A Three-Level Meta-analysis," *Children and Youth Services Review* 112 (2020): 104900, https://doi.org/10.1016/j.childyouth.2020.104900.
52　Annemiek Karreman et al., "Parenting and Self-regulation in Preschoolers: A Meta-Analysis," *Infant and Child Development* 15, no. 6 (2006): 561–79, https://doi.org/10.1002/icd.478.
53　Amy I. Nathanson, "Identifying and Explaining the Relationship Between Parental Mediation and Children's Aggression," *Communication Research* 26, no. 2 (1999): 124–43, https://doi.org/10.1177/009365099026002002.

54 Stijn Van Petegem et al., "Parents' Degree and Style of Restrictive Mediation of Young Children's Digital Gaming: Associations with Parental Attitudes and Perceived Child Adjustment," *Journal of Child and Family Studies* 28, no. 5 (2019): 1379–91, https://doi.org/10.1007/s10826-019-01368-x.
55 Vivian Hsueh Hua Chen and Grace S. Chng, "Active and Restrictive Parental Mediation Over Time: Effects on Youths' Self-Regulatory Competencies and Impulsivity," *Computers & Education* 98 (2016): 206–12, https://doi.org/10.1016/j.compedu.2016.03.012.
56 Fong-Ching Chang et al., "Children's Use of Mobile Devices, Smartphone Addiction and Parental Mediation in Taiwan," *Computers in Human Behavior* 93 (2018): 25–32, https://doi.org/10.1016/j.chb.2018.11.048.
57 Shawna R. White et al., "Restrictive Mediation and Unintended Effects: Serial Multiple Mediation Analysis Explaining the Role of Reactance in US Adolescents," *Journal of Children and Media* 9, no. 4 (2015): 510–27, https://doi.org/10.1080/17482798.2015.1088873.
58 Leslie A. Baxter et al., "Parent-Child Perceptions of Parental Behavioral Control Through Rule-Setting for Risky Health Choices During Adolescence," *Journal of Family Communication* 9, no. 4 (2009): 253, https://doi.org/10.1080/15267430903255920.
59 Baxter et al., "Parent-Child Perceptions of Parental Behavioral Control Through Rule-Setting for Risky Health Choices During Adolescence."
60 Virginia Satir, *The New Peoplemaking* (Mountain View, California: Science & Behavior Books, 1988).
61 Moniek Buijzen and Claartje Mens, "Adult Mediation of Television Advertising Effects," *Journal of Children and Media* 1, no. 2 (2007): 177–91, https://doi.org/10.1080/17482790701339233.
62 Katrien Symons et al., "A Factorial Validation of Parental Mediation Strategies with Regard to Internet Use," *Psychologica Belgica* 57, no. 2 (2017): 93–111, https://doi.org/10.5334/pb.372.
63 Nili Steinfeld, "Parental Mediation of Adolescent Internet Use: Combining Strategies to Promote Awareness, Autonomy and Self-Regulation in Preparing Youth for Life on the Web," *Education and Information Technologies* 26, no. 2 (2020): 1899, https://doi.org/10.1007/s10639-020-10342-w.
64 Kathryn Greene, "An Integrated Model of Health Disclosure Decision-Making," in *Uncertainty, Information Management, and Disclosure Decisions*, ed. Tamara D. Afifi and Walid A. Afifi (New York, NY: Routledge, 2009), 226–53.
65 Roger Bakeman and Lauren B. Adamson, "Coordinating Attention to People and Objects in Mother-Infant and Peer-Infant Interaction," *Child Development* 55, no. 4 (1984): 1278, https://doi.org/10.2307/1129997.
66 Lauren B. Adamson et al., "The Development of Symbol-Infused Joint Engagement," *Child Development* 75, no. 4 (2004): 1171–87, https://doi.org/10.1111/j.1467-8624.2004.00732.x.
67 Bakeman and Adamson, "Coordinating Attention to People and Objects in Mother-Infant and Peer-Infant Interaction."
68 Connie B. Smith et al., "Interactional Predictors of Early Language," *First Language* 8, no. 23 (1988): 143–56, https://doi.org/10.1177/014272378800802304.

69 L. J. Conway et al., "The Role of Joint Engagement in the Development of Language in a Community-Derived Sample of Slow-to-Talk Children," *Journal of Child Language* 45, no. 6 (2018): 1275–93, https://doi.org/10.1017/s030500091800017x.
70 Josef Perner, *Understanding the Representational Mind* (Cambridge, Massachusetts: MIT Press, 1993).
71 Frances Gardner et al., "The Role of Mother-Child Joint Play in the Early Development of Children's Conduct Problems: A Longitudinal Observational Study," *Social Development* 12, no. 3 (2003): 361–78, https://doi.org/10.1111/1467-9507.00238.
72 Eric W. Lindsey and Jacquelyn Mize, "Parent-Child Physical and Pretense Play: Links to Children's Social Competence," *Merrill-Palmer Quarterly* 46, no. 4 (2000): 565–91, https://www.jstor.org/stable/23092565.
73 Sandi D. Wallace and Jake Harwood, "Associations Between Shared Musical Engagement and Parent–Child Relational Quality: The Mediating Roles of Interpersonal Coordination and Empathy," *Journal of Family Communication* 18, no. 3 (2018): 202–16, https://doi.org/10.1080/15267431.2018.1466783.
74 Lori Takeuchi et al, "The New Co-viewing: Designing for Learning through Joint Media Engagement," The Joan Ganz Cooney Center at Sesame Workshop and LIFE Center, 2011.
75 Carrie A. Ewin et al., "The Impact of Joint Media Engagement on Parent–Child Interactions: A Systematic Review," *Human Behavior and Emerging Technologies* 3, no. 2 (2020): 231, https://doi.org/10.1002/hbe2.203.
76 Takeuchi et al., "The New Co-viewing," 9.
77 Tiffany A. Pempek et al., "The Impact of Infant-Directed Videos on Parent–child Interaction," *Journal of Applied Developmental Psychology* 32, no. 1 (2010): 10–19, https://doi.org/10.1016/j.appdev.2010.10.001.
78 Takeuchi et al., "The New Co-viewing," 9.
79 Ewin et al, "The Impact of Joint Media Engagement on Parent–Child Interactions."
80 Eric E. Rasmussen, "Theoretical Underpinnings of Reducing the Media's Negative Effect on Children: Person-Centered, Negative-Evaluative Mediation within a Persuasion Framework," in *Communication Yearbook 37*, ed. Elisia L. Cohen (New York, NY: Routledge, 2013), 379–406.
81 Tatek Abebe, "Reconceptualising Children's Agency as Continuum and Interdependence," *Social Sciences* 8, no. 3 (2019): 5, https://doi.org/10.3390/socsci8030081.
82 Elsbeth Robson, Stephen Bell, and Natascha Klocker, "Conceptualising Agency in the Lives of Rural Young People," in *Global Perspectives on Rural Childhood and Youth: Young Rural Lives*, ed. Ruth Panelli, Samantha Punch, and Elsbeth Robson (New York, NY: Routledge, 2007), 135–48.

Chapter 5

1 Jay Belsky, "The Determinants of Parenting: A Process Model," *Child Development* 55, no. 1 (1984): 83, https://doi.org/10.2307/1129836.

2. Eric E. Rasmussen et al., "Parental Mediation of US Youths' Exposure to Televised Relational Aggression," *Journal of Children and Media* 12, no. 2 (2017): 192–210, https://doi.org/10.1080/17482798.2017.1405829.
3. Rebecca L. Densley et al., "Media Parenting in a Pandemic: Understanding U.S. Parents' Motivations for Parental Mediation During the COVID-19 Lockdown," *Journal of Children and Media* (2024): 1–20, https://doi.org/10.1080/17482798.2024.2409669.
4. Saskia Böcking and Tabea Böcking, "Parental Mediation of Television," *Journal of Children and Media* 3, no. 3 (2009): 286–302, https://doi.org/10.1080/17482790902999959.
5. Sciacca et al., "Parental Mediation in Pandemic."
6. Van Petegem et al., "Parents' Degree and Style of Restrictive Mediation of Young Children's Digital Gaming."
7. Sook-Jung Lee, "Parental Restrictive Mediation of Children's Internet Use: Effective for What and for Whom?" *New Media & Society* 15, no. 4 (2012): 466–81, https://doi.org/10.1177/1461444812452412.
8. Ron Warren, "Parental Mediation of Preschool Children's Television Viewing," *Journal of Broadcasting & Electronic Media* 47, no. 3 (2003): 399, https://doi.org/10.1207/s15506878jobem4703_5.
9. Peter Nikken and Jeroen Jansz, "Parental Mediation of Children's Videogame Playing: A Comparison of the Reports by Parents and Children," *Learning Media and Technology* 31, no. 2 (2006): 181–202, https://doi.org/10.1080/17439880600756803.
10. Patricia Aufderheide, "Media Literacy: A Report of the National Leadership Conference on Media Literacy," Queenstown, Maryland: Aspen Institute, 1993.
11. Center for Media Literacy, *Empowerment Through Education*, 2015, http://www.medialit.org/readingroom/empowerment-through-education.
12. Eric Rasmussen et al., "Predicting Parental Mediation Behaviors: The Direct and Indirect Influence of Parents' Critical Thinking About Media and Attitudes About Parent-Child Interactions," *Journal of Media Literacy Education* 8, no. 2 (2017): 1–22, https://doi.org/10.23860/jmle-2016-08-02-01.
13. Sciacca et al, "Parental Mediation in Pandemic."
14. Sonia Livingstone et al., "Maximizing Opportunities and Minimizing Risks for Children Online: The Role of Digital Skills in Emerging Strategies of Parental Mediation," *Journal of Communication* 67, no. 1 (2017): 82–105, https://doi.org/10.1111/jcom.12277.
15. Peter Nikken and Jeroen Jansz, "Developing Scales to Measure Parental Mediation of Young Children's Internet Use," *Learning Media and Technology* 39, no. 2 (2013): 250–66, https://doi.org/10.1080/17439884.2013.782038.
16. Sarosh Iqbal et al., "Predictors of Parental Mediation in Teenagers' Internet Use: A Cross-sectional Study of Female Caregivers in Lahore, Pakistan," *BMC Public Health* 21, no. 1 (2021), https://doi.org/10.1186/s12889-021-10349-z.
17. Lenka Dedkova and David Smahel, "Online Parental Mediation: Associations of Family Members' Characteristics to Individual Engagement in Active Mediation and Monitoring," *Journal of Family Issues* 41, no. 8 (2019): 1112–36, https://doi.org/10.1177/0192513x19888255.
18. Lee, "Parental Restrictive Mediation of Children's Internet Use."

19 Wonsun Shin and May O. Lwin, "Parental Mediation of Children's Digital Media Use in High Digital Penetration Countries: Perspectives from Singapore and Australia," *Asian Journal of Communication* 32, no. 4 (2022): 309–26, https://doi.org/10.1080/01292986.2022.2026992.
20 Shin and Lwin, "Parental Mediation of Children's Digital Media Use in High Digital Penetration Countries."
21 Wonsun Shin, "Empowered Parents: The Role of Self-efficacy in Parental Mediation of Children's Smartphone Use in the United States," *Journal of Children and Media* (2018): 1–13, https://doi.org/10.1080/17482798.2018.1486331.
22 Sanne Holvoet et al., "Predicting Parental Mediation of Personalized Advertising and Online Data Collection Practices Targeting Teenagers," *Journal of Broadcasting & Electronic Media* 66, no. 2 (2022): 213–34, https://doi.org/10.1080/08838151.2022.2051511.
23 Terese Glatz et al., "Internet-specific Parental Self-efficacy: Developmental Differences and Links to Internet-specific Mediation," *Computers in Human Behavior* 84 (2018): 8–17, https://doi.org/10.1016/j.chb.2018.02.014.
24 Pengfei Zhao et al., "Digital Parenting Divides: The Role of Parental Capital and Digital Parenting Readiness in Parental Digital Mediation," *Journal of Computer-Mediated Communication* 28, no. 5 (2023), https://doi.org/10.1093/jcmc/zmad032.
25 Rachel Young et al., "Barriers to Mediation Among U.S. Parents of Adolescents: A Mixed-Methods Study of Why Parents Do Not Monitor or Restrict Digital Media Use," *Computers in Human Behavior* 153 (2023): 6, https://doi.org/10.1016/j.chb.2023.108093.
26 Claudia Van Kruistum and Roel Van Steensel, "The Tacit Dimension of Parental Mediation," *Cyberpsychology Journal of Psychosocial Research on Cyberspace* 11, no. 3 (2017), https://doi.org/10.5817/cp2017-3-3.
27 Young et al, "Barriers to Mediation Among U.S. Parents of Adolescents," 6.
28 Lindsay Taraban and Daniel S. Shaw, "Parenting in Context: Revisiting Belsky's Classic Process of Parenting Model in Early Childhood," *Developmental Review* 48 (2018): 74–75, https://doi.org/10.1016/j.dr.2018.03.006.
29 Dedkova and Smahal, "Online Parental Mediation."
30 Meyran Boniel-Nissim et al., "Parental Mediation Regarding Children's Pornography Exposure: The Role of Parenting Style, Protection Motivation and Gender," *The Journal of Sex Research* 57, no. 1 (2019): 42–51, https://doi.org/10.1080/00224499.2019.1590795.
31 Alexis R. Lauricella et al., "The Common Sense Census: Plugged-in Parents of Tweens and Teens," 2016, Common Sense Media.
32 Nikken and Jansz, "Developing Scales to Measure Parental Mediation of Young Children's Internet Use."
33 Patti M. Valkenburg et al., "Developing a Scale to Assess Three Styles of Television Mediation: 'Instructive Mediation,' 'Restrictive Mediation,' and 'Social Coviewing,'" *Journal of Broadcasting & Electronic Media* 43, no. 1 (1999): 52–66, https://doi.org/10.1080/08838159909364474.
34 Beáta Nagy et al., "Parental Mediation in the Age of Mobile Technology," *Children & Society* 37, no. 2 (2022): 424–51, https://doi.org/10.1111/chso.12599.

35 Teresa Koch et al., "Socioeconomic Status and Young People's Digital Maturity: The Role of Parental Mediation," *Computers in Human Behavior* 154 (2024): 3, https://doi.org/10.1016/j.chb.2024.108157.
36 Juan Li et al., "Chinese Parental Mediation, Predictors, and Associations with Children's Problematic Media Use: A Latent Profile Analysis," *Early Education and Development* (2024): 1–18, https://doi.org/10.1080/10409289.2024.2360867.
37 Ifeanyi Adigwe et al., "Investigating the Relationship Between Socio- demographic Variables of Parents, Digital Literacy and Parental Mediation Practices in the Digital Age: Nigeria in Focus," *E-Learning and Digital Media* (2024), https://doi.org/10.1177/20427530241232495.
38 Nikken and Jansz, "Developing Scales to Measure Parental Mediation of Young Children's Internet Use."
39 Sonia Livingstone et al, "How Parents of Young Children Manage Digital Devices at Home: The Role of Income, Education and Parental Style," EU Kids Online, 2015.
40 Nagy et al., "Parental Mediation in the Age of Mobile Technology."
41 Peter Nikken and Suzanna J. Opree, "Guiding Young Children's Digital Media Use: SES-Differences in Mediation Concerns and Competence," *Journal of Child and Family Studies* 27, no. 6 (2018): 1844–57, https://doi.org/10.1007/s10826-018-1018-3.
42 Vikki S. Katz et al., "Connecting with Technology in Lower-income US Families," *New Media & Society* 20, no. 7 (2017): 2509–33, https://doi.org/10.1177/1461444817726319.
43 Lauricella et al., "The Common Sense Census: Plugged-in Parents of Tweens and Teens."
44 Katz et al, "Connecting with Technology in Lower-Income US Families."
45 Sabrina L. Connell et al., "Parental Co-Use of Media Technology with Their Young Children in the USA," *Journal of Children and Media* 9, no. 1 (2015): 5–21, https://doi.org/10.1080/17482798.2015.997440.
46 Shari Barkin et al., "Parental Media Mediation Styles for Children Aged 2 to 11 Years," *Archives of Pediatrics and Adolescent Medicine* 160, no. 4 (2006): 395, https://doi.org/10.1001/archpedi.160.4.395.
47 Elizabeth Behm-Morawitz et al., "Parent–Child Communication About Gender and Race Through the Films 'Black Panther' and 'Wonder Woman': The Roles of Parental Mediation and Media Literacy," *Psychology of Popular Media* 11, no. 4 (2022): 382–94, https://doi.org/10.1037/ppm0000405.
48 Pavel Izrael, "Religiousness, Values, and Parental Mediation of Children's Television Viewing in Slovakia," *Journal of Children and Media* 7, no. 4 (2013): 507–24, https://doi.org/10.1080/17482798.2013.827129.
49 Padilla-Walker et al., "Parents and Adolescents Growing Up in the Digital Age."
50 Laura M. Padilla-Walker and Ross A. Thompson, "Combating Conflicting Messages of Values: A Closer Look at Parental Strategies," *Social Development* 14, no. 2 (2005): 305–23, https://doi.org/10.1111/j.1467-9507.2005.00303.x.
51 Laura M. Padilla-Walker et al., "Parents and Adolescents Growing up in the Digital Age: Latent Growth Curve Analysis of Proactive Media Monitoring," *Journal of Adolescence* 35, no. 5 (2012): 1153–65, https://doi.org/10.1016/j.adolescence.2012.03.005.

52 Christopher Layton and David Hansen, "Religion and Gender in the Impact of Parental Mediation on Self-censorship and Attitudes Toward Mediation," *Journal of Undergraduate Research* 2013, no. 1 (2013), https://scholarsarchive.byu.edu/jur/vol2013/iss1/170/.
53 Amy I. Nathanson and William P. Eveland, "Parental Mediation During the U.S. 2016 Presidential Election Campaign: How Parents Criticized, Restricted, and Co-viewed News Coverage," *Communication Monographs* 86, no. 2 (2018): 184–204, https://doi.org/10.1080/03637751.2018.1527035.
54 Steven Holiday et al., "Coming Attractions: Parental Mediation Responses to Transgender and Cisgender Film Trailer Content Targeting Adolescents," *Sexuality & Culture* 22, no. 4 (2018): 1154–70, https://doi.org/10.1007/s12119-018-9517-3.
55 Uttara Manohar, "The Role of Culture in Parental Mediation" (MA thesis, The Ohio State University, 2011).
56 Janelle Bouknight et al., "Parental Mediation and Acculturation," *Global Media Journal* 19, no. 37 (2021): 1–8.
57 Stefan Mertens and Leen D'Haenens, "Parental Mediation of Internet Use and Cultural Values Across Europe: Investigating the Predictive Power of the Hofstedian Paradigm," *Communications* 39, no. 4 (2014), https://doi.org/10.1515/commun-2014-0018.
58 Marina Krcmar and Drew P. Cingel, "Examining Two Theoretical Models Predicting American and Dutch Parents' Mediation of Adolescent Social Media Use," *Journal of Family Communication* 16, no. 3 (2016): 248, https://doi.org/10.1080/15267431.2016.1181632.
59 Shin and Lwin, "Parental Mediation of Children's Digital Media Use in High Digital Penetration Countries."
60 Lucyna Kirwil, "Parental Mediation of Children's Internet Use in Different European Countries," *Journal of Children and Media* 3, no. 4 (2009): 394–409, https://doi.org/10.1080/17482790903233440.
61 Veronika Kalmus et al., "Towards More Active Parenting: Trends in Parental Mediation of Children's Internet Use in European Countries," *Children & Society* 36, no. 5 (2022): 1026–42, https://doi.org/10.1111/chso.12553.
62 Nathalie Sonck et al., "Determinants of Internet Mediation: A Comparison of the Reports by Dutch Parents and Children," *Journal of Children and Media* 7, no. 1 (2013): 96–113, https://doi.org/10.1080/17482798.2012.739806.
63 Nelly Elias et al., "From Experiencing Parental Mediation as a Child to Practicing it as a Parent: An Exploratory Study With Israeli Mothers," *Journal of Children and Media* 18, no. 2 (2024): 50–9, https://doi.org/10.1080/17482798.2023.2265513.
64 Adigwe et al., "Investigating the Relationship Between Socio-Demographic Variables of Parents, Digital Literacy and Parental Mediation Practices in the Digital Age."
65 Erica Weintraub Austin et al., "How and Why Parents Take on the Tube," *Journal of Broadcasting & Electronic Media* 43, no. 2 (1999): 175–92, https://doi.org/10.1080/08838159909364483.

66 Douglas A. Gentile et al., "Do You See What I See? Parent and Child Reports of Parental Monitoring of Media," *Family Relations* 61, no. 3 (2012): 470–87, https://doi.org/10.1111/j.1741-3729.2012.00709.x.
67 Ine Beyens et al., "Developmental Trajectories of Parental Mediation Across Early and Middle Childhood," *Human Communication Research* 45, no. 2 (2018): 226–50, https://doi.org/10.1093/hcr/hqy016.
68 Wang et al., "A Meta-Analysis of Factors Predicting Parental Mediation of Children's Media Use Based on Studies Published Between 1992–2019."
69 Ron Warren, "Parental Mediation of Preschool Children's Television Viewing."
70 Ron Warren, "Parental Mediation of Children's Television Viewing in Low-Income Families," *Journal of Communication* 55, no. 4 (2005): 847–63, https://doi.org/10.1111/j.1460-2466.2005.tb03026.x.
71 Nicole Martins et al., "Playing by the Rules: Parental Mediation of Video Game Play," *Journal of Family Issues* 38, no. 9 (2015): 1215–38, https://doi.org/10.1177/0192513x15613822.
72 Beyens et al., "Developmental Trajectories of Parental Mediation Across Early and Middle Childhood."
73 Laura M. Padilla-Walker and Sarah M. Coyne, "'Turn That Thing off!' Parent and Adolescent Predictors of Proactive Media Monitoring," *Journal of Adolescence* 34, no. 4 (2010): 705–15, https://doi.org/10.1016/j.adolescence.2010.09.002.
74 Boniel-Nissim et al., "Parental Mediation Regarding Children's Pornography Exposure."
75 Böcking and Böcking, "Parental Mediation of Television."
76 Seon-Kyoung An and Doohwang Lee, "An Integrated Model of Parental Mediation: The Effect of Family Communication on Children's Perception of Television Reality and Negative Viewing Effects," *Asian Journal of Communication* 20, no. 4 (2010): 389–403, https://doi.org/10.1080/01292986.2010.496864.
77 Böcking and Böcking, "Parental Mediation of Television."
78 Yuki Fujioka and Erica Weintraub Austin, "The Relationship of Family Communication Patterns to Parental Mediation Styles," *Communication Research* 29, no. 6 (2002): 642–65, https://doi.org/10.1177/009365002237830.
79 Manohar, "The Role of Culture in Parental Mediation."
80 Dina L. G. Borzekowski and Thomas N. Robinson, "Conversations, Control and Couch-Time," *Journal of Children and Media* 1, no. 2 (2007): 162–76, https://doi.org/10.1080/17482790701339183.
81 Barkin et al., "Parental Media Mediation Styles for Children Aged 2 to 11 Years."
82 David J. Atkin et al., "The Home Ecology of Children's Television Viewing: Parental Mediation and the New Video Environment," *Journal of Communication* 41, no. 3 (1991): 40–52, https://doi.org/10.1111/j.1460-2466.1991.tb02322.x.
83 Peter Nikken and Marjon Schols, "How and Why Parents Guide the Media Use of Young Children," *Journal of Child and Family Studies* 24, no. 11 (2015): 3423–35, https://doi.org/10.1007/s10826-015-0144-4.
84 Borzekowski and Robinson, "Conversations, Control, and Couch-Time."
85 Nikken and Jansz, "Parental Mediation of Children's Videogame Playing."
86 Hailey G. Holmgren et al., "Patterns of Parent Media Use: The Influence of Parent Media Use Profiles on Parental Mediation, Technoference, and Problematic

Media Use," *Computers in Human Behavior* 161 (2024): 108410, https://doi.org/10.1016/j.chb.2024.108410.
87 Connell et al., "Parental Co-Use of Media Technology with Their Young Children in the USA."
88 Wang et al., "A Meta-Analysis of Factors Predicting Parental Mediation of Children's Media Use Based on Studies Published Between 1992–2019."
89 Böcking and Böcking, "Parental Mediation of Television."
90 Carolyn A. Lin and David J. Atkin, "Parental Mediation and Rulemaking for Adolescent Use of Television and VCRs," *Journal of Broadcasting & Electronic Media* 33, no. 1 (1989): 53–67, https://doi.org/10.1080/08838158909364061.
91 Iqbal et al., "Predictors of Parental Mediation in Teenagers' Internet Use."
92 Beyens et al., "Developmental Trajectories of Parental Mediation Across Early and Middle Childhood."
93 Dedkova and Smahel, "Online Parental Mediation."
94 Nikken and Jansz, "Parental Mediation of Children's Videogame Playing."
95 Sonck et al., "Determinants of Internet Mediation."
96 Glatz et al., "Internet-Specific Parental Self-Efficacy."
97 Symons et al., "A Factorial Validation of Parental Mediation Strategies with Regard to Internet Use."
98 Connell et al., "Parental Co-Use of Media Technology with Their Young Children in the USA."
99 Sonck et al., "Determinants of Internet Mediation."
100 Layton and Hansen, "Religion and Gender in the Impact of Parental Mediation on Self-Censorship and Attitudes Toward Mediation."
101 Tania Cabello-Hutt et al., "Online Opportunities and Risks for Children and Adolescents: The Role of Digital Skills, Age, Gender and Parental Mediation in Brazil," *New Media & Society* 20, no. 7 (2017): 2411–31, https://doi.org/10.1177/1461444817724168.
102 Sciacca et al., "Parental Mediation in Pandemic."
103 Natalia Rudnova et al., "Characteristics of Parental Digital Mediation: Predictors, Strategies, and Differences Among Children Experiencing Various Parental Mediation Strategies," *Education Sciences* 13, no. 1 (2023): 57, https://doi.org/10.3390/educsci13010057.
104 Erin Corcoran et al., "Youth Sexting and Associations with Parental Media Mediation," *Computers in Human Behavior* 132 (2022): 107263, https://doi.org/10.1016/j.chb.2022.107263.
105 Martins et al., "Playing by the Rules."
106 Sciacca et al, "Parental Mediation in Pandemic," 9.
107 Iqbal et al., "Predictors of Parental Mediation in Teenagers' Internet Use," 317.
108 Borzekowski and Robinson, "Conversations, Control, and Couch-Time."
109 Padilla-Walker and Coyne, "'Turn That Thing Off!'"
110 Padilla-Walker and Coyne, "'Turn That Thing Off!'" 713.
111 Lee, "Parental Restrictive Mediation of Children's Internet Use."
112 Beyens et al., "Developmental Trajectories of Parental Mediation Across Early and Middle Childhood."
113 Padilla-Walker and Coyne, "'Turn That Thing Off!'"
114 Valkenburg and Peter, "The Differential Susceptibility to Media Effects Model."

115 Lowie Bradt et al., "Does Parents' Perceived Style of Setting Limits to Gaming Matter? The Interplay Between Profiles of Parental Mediation and BIS/BAS Sensitivity in Problematic Gaming and Online Gambling," *Journal of Adolescence* 96, no. 3 (2023): 580–97, https://doi.org/10.1002/jad.12271.

116 Li et al., "Chinese Parental Mediation, Predictors, and Associations with Children's Problematic Media Use."

117 Kalmus et al., "Towards More Active Parenting."

118 Ellen J. Helsper et al., "Country Classification: Opportunities, Risks, Harm, and Parental Mediation," *EU Kids Online*, 2013.

119 Densley et al., "Media Parenting in a Pandemic," 16.

Chapter 6

1 Russ Harris, *The Happiness Trap* (Boulder, Colorado: Shambhala Publications, 2022), 12.

2 Harris, *The Happiness Trap*, 13.

3 Harris, *The Happiness Trap*, 13.

4 Jennifer Coto et al., "Parents as Role Models: Associations Between Parent and Young Children's Weight, Dietary Intake, and Physical Activity in a Minority Sample," *Maternal and Child Health Journal* 23, no. 7 (2019): 943–50, https://doi.org/10.1007/s10995-018-02722-z.

5 Coto et al., "Parents as Role Models," 948.

6 Shirley Ho et al., "Development and Validation of a Parental Social Media Mediation Scale Across Child and Parent Samples," *Internet Research* 30, no. 2 (2019): 677–94, https://doi.org/10.1108/intr-02-2018-0061.

7 Kimberly D. Douglas et al., "Exploring Parents' Intentions to Monitor and Mediate Adolescent Social Media Use and Implications for School Nurses," *The Journal of School Nursing* 39, no. 3 (2020): 248–61, https://doi.org/10.1177/1059840520983286.

8 Douglas et al., "Exploring Parents' Intentions to Monitor and Mediate Adolescent Social Media Use and Implications for School Nurses."

9 Marit Sukk and Andra Siibak, "Caring Dataveillance and the Construction of 'Good Parenting': Estonian Parents' and Pre-teens' Reflections on the Use of Tracking Technologies," *Communications* 46, no. 3 (2021): 446–67, https://doi.org/10.1515/commun-2021-0045.

10 Katrien Symons et al., "Parental Knowledge of Adolescents' Online Content and Contact Risks," *Journal of Youth and Adolescence* 46, no. 2 (2016): 401–16, https://doi.org/10.1007/s10964-016-0599-7.

11 Leena Paakkari et al., "Problematic Social Media Use and Health Among Adolescents," *International Journal of Environmental Research and Public Health* 18, no. 4 (2021): 1885, https://doi.org/10.3390/ijerph18041885.

12 Anna Faltýnková et al., "The Associations Between Family-related Factors and Excessive Internet Use in Adolescents," *International Journal of Environmental Research and Public Health* 17, no. 5 (2020): 1754, https://doi.org/10.3390/ijerph17051754.

13. Sonia Livingstone and Ellen J. Helsper, "Parental Mediation of Children's Internet Use," *Journal of Broadcasting & Electronic Media* 52, no. 4 (2008): 581–99, https://doi.org/10.1080/08838150802437396.
14. Lisa J. Smith et al., "Parental Influences on Adolescent Video Game Play: A Study of Accessibility, Rules, Limit Setting, Monitoring, and Cybersafety," *Cyberpsychology Behavior and Social Networking* 18, no. 5 (2015): 273–79, https://doi.org/10.1089/cyber.2014.0611.
15. Amy Bleakley et al., "The Role of Parents in Problematic Internet Use Among US Adolescents," *Media and Communication*, 2016, https://www.cogitatiopress.com/mediaandcommunication/article/view/523/359.
16. Masood Badri et al., "School Children's Use of Digital Devices, Social Media and Parental Knowledge and Involvement – the Case of Abu Dhabi," *Education and Information Technologies* 22, no. 5 (2016): 2645–64, https://doi.org/10.1007/s10639-016-9557-y.
17. Nandhini Priya and P. Uma Maheswari, "Influence of Different Parental Mediation Strategies on Adolescents' Hedonistic Smartphone Use: Parent–Adolescent Reports," *Mobile Media & Communication*, 2024, https://doi.org/10.1177/20501579241260649.
18. Xiaojing Li et al., "Associations Between Parental Mediation and Adolescents' Internet Addiction: The Role of Parent-Child Relationship and Adolescents' Grades," *Frontiers in Psychology* 13 (2022), https://doi.org/10.3389/fpsyg.2022.1061631.
19. Liang Chen et al., "The Interactive Effects of Parental Mediation Strategies in Preventing Cyberbullying on Social Media," *Psychology Research and Behavior Management* 16 (2023): 1009–22, https://doi.org/10.2147/prbm.s386968.
20. Chen et al., "The Interactive Effects of Parental Mediation Strategies in Preventing Cyberbullying on Social Media," 1018.
21. Chen et al., "The Interactive Effects of Parental Mediation Strategies in Preventing Cyberbullying on Social Media," 1018.
22. Corcoran et al., "Youth Sexting and Associations with Parental Media Mediation."
23. Corcoran et al., "Youth Sexting and Associations with Parental Media Mediation," 7.
24. Wendy M. Rote and Judith G. Smetana, "Within-family Dyadic Patterns of Parental Monitoring and Adolescent Information Management," *Developmental Psychology* 54, no. 12 (2018): 2302–15, https://doi.org/10.1037/dev0000615.
25. Victoria J. Rideout et al., "Generation M^2: Media in the Lives of 8- to 18-year-olds," Henry J. Kaiser, Menlo Park, California: Family Foundation, 2010.
26. Suzanne M. Geurts et al., "Rules, Role Models or Overall Climate at Home? Relative Associations of Different Family Aspects with Adolescents' Problematic Social Media Use," *Comprehensive Psychiatry* 116 (2022): 152318, https://doi.org/10.1016/j.comppsych.2022.152318.
27. Ina M. Koning et al., "Bidirectional Effects of Internet-specific Parenting Practices and Compulsive Social Media and Internet Game Use," *Journal of Behavioral Addictions* 7, no. 3 (2018): 624–32, https://doi.org/10.1556/2006.7.2018.68.
28. Helen G. M. Vossen et al., "Parenting and Problematic Social Media Use: A Systematic Review," *Current Addiction Reports* 11, no. 3 (2024): 511–27, https://doi.org/10.1007/s40429-024-00559-x.

29 Ceren Çalhan and İdris Göksu, "An Effort to Understand Parents' Media Mediation Roles and Early Childhood Children's Digital Game Addiction Tendency: A Descriptive Correlational Survey Study," *Education and Information Technologies* 29, no. 14 (2024): 17825–65, https://doi.org/10.1007/s10639-024-12544-y.

30 Fardouly et al., "Investigating Longitudinal and Bidirectional Relationships Between Parental Factors and Time Spent on Social Media During Early Adolescence."

31 Lu Yu and Xiaohua Zhou, "Social Media Addiction Among Hong Kong Adolescents Before and After the Pandemic: The Effects of Parenting Behaviors," *Computers in Human Behavior* 156 (2024): 108233, https://doi.org/10.1016/j.chb.2024.108233.

32 Kathrin Karsay et al., "Sleeping with the Smartphone: A Panel Study Investigating Parental Mediation, Adolescents' Tiredness, and Physical Well-being," *Behaviour and Information Technology* 42, no. 11 (2022): 1833–44, https://doi.org/10.1080/0144929x.2022.2100277.

33 Jane Shawcroft et al., "Structures for Screens: Longitudinal Associations Between Parental Media Rules and Problematic Media Use in Early Childhood," *Technology Mind and Behavior* 3, no. 2 (2023), https://doi.org/10.1037/tmb0000104.

34 Sarah M. Coyne et al., "Masters of Media: A Longitudinal Study of Parental Media Efficacy, Media Monitoring, and Child Problematic Media Use Across Early Childhood in the United States," *Journal of Children and Media* 17, no. 3 (2023): 318–35, https://doi.org/10.1080/17482798.2023.2200958.

35 Valeria Rega et al., "Problematic Media Use Among Children up to the Age of 10: A Systematic Literature Review," *International Journal of Environmental Research and Public Health* 20, no. 10 (2023): 5854, https://doi.org/10.3390/ijerph20105854.

36 Wei Ren and Xiaowen Zhu, "Parental Mediation and Adolescents' Internet Use: The Moderating Role of Parenting Style," *Journal of Youth and Adolescence* 51, no. 8 (2022): 1483–96, https://doi.org/10.1007/s10964-022-01600-w.

37 Corcoran et al., "Youth Sexting and Associations with Parental Media Mediation."

38 Sciacca et al., "Parental Mediation in Pandemic."

39 Sciacca et al., "Parental Mediation in Pandemic," 10.

40 Hwajin Yang et al., "Inconsistent Media Mediation and Problematic Smartphone Use in Preschoolers: Maternal Conflict Resolution Styles as Moderators," *Children* 9, no. 6 (2022): 816, https://doi.org/10.3390/children9060816.

41 Mohammad Taghi Abbasi Shavazi et al., "Family, Mediation & Internet Risks: The Study of the Relation between Parental Mediation Strategies and Adolescents' Exposure to Internet Risks," *Cultural Studies & Communication* (2022), https://www.jcsc.ir/article_702031.html?lang=en.

42 María E. Len-Ríos et al., "Early Adolescents as Publics: A National Survey of Teens with Social Media Accounts, Their Media Use Preferences, Parental Mediation, and Perceived Internet Literacy," *Public Relations Review* 42, no. 1 (2015): 101–8, https://doi.org/10.1016/j.pubrev.2015.10.003.

43 Anastasia Psalti and Kostas Zafiropoulos, "The Role of Parents in Digital Media Use by Preschool-age Children in Greece," *Zenodo (CERN European Organization for Nuclear Research)*, 2023, https://doi.org/10.5281/zenodo.7812927.

44 Veronika Kalmus et al., "Does It Matter What Mama Says: Evaluating the Role of Parental Mediation in European Adolescents' Excessive Internet Use," *Children & Society* 29, no. 2 (2013): 122–33, https://doi.org/10.1111/chso.12020.
45 Chang et al., "Children's Use of Mobile Devices, Smartphone Addiction and Parental Mediation in Taiwan."
46 Amy I. Nathanson, "The Unintended Effects of Parental Mediation of Television on Adolescents," *Media Psychology* 4, no. 3 (2002): 207–30, https://doi.org/10.1207/s1532785xmep0403_01.
47 Peter Nikken and Hanneke De Graaf, "Reciprocal Relationships Between Friends' and Parental Mediation of Adolescents' Media Use and Their Sexual Attitudes and Behavior," *Journal of Youth and Adolescence* 42, no. 11 (2012): 1696–707, https://doi.org/10.1007/s10964-012-9873-5.
48 White et al., "Restrictive Mediation and Unintended Effects."
49 Grace S. Chng et al., "Moderating Effects of the Family Environment for Parental Mediation and Pathological Internet Use in Youths," *Cyberpsychology Behavior and Social Networking* 18, no. 1 (2014): 30, https://doi.org/10.1089/cyber.2014.0368.
50 Karin M. Fikkers et al., "A Matter of Style? Exploring the Effects of Parental Mediation Styles on Early Adolescents' Media Violence Exposure and Aggression," *Computers in Human Behavior* 70 (2017): 407–15, https://doi.org/10.1016/j.chb.2017.01.029.
51 Fikkers et al., "A Matter of Style?," 413.
52 Geurts et al., "Rules, Role Models or Overall Climate at Home?"
53 Liang Chen and Jingyuan Shi, "Reducing Harm from Media: A Meta-analysis of Parental Mediation," *Journalism & Mass Communication Quarterly* 96, no. 1 (2018): 173–93, https://doi.org/10.1177/1077699018754908.
54 Chen and Shi, "Reducing Harm from Media," 185.
55 Mona Roper, "Positive Parenting," *Article 19* 2, no. 3 (2006): 2.
56 Roper, "Positive Parenting," 3.
57 Fikkers et al., "A Matter of Style?," 413.
58 Çalhan and Göksu, "An Effort to Understand Parents' Media Mediation Roles and Early Childhood Children's Digital Game Addiction Tendency."
59 Karsay et al, "Sleeping with the Smartphone."
60 Qinxue Liu and Jiayin Wu, "What Children Learn in a Digital Home: The Complex Influence of Parental Mediation and Smartphone Interference," *Education and Information Technologies* 29, no. 5 (2023): 6273–91, https://doi.org/10.1007/s10639-023-12071-2.
61 Okwach Alphonce Akungu et al., "Longitudinal Association of Adolescents' Perceptions of Parental Mediations and Compulsive Internet Use," *Computers in Human Behavior* 150 (2023): 107989, https://doi.org/10.1016/j.chb.2023.107989.
62 Priya and Maheswari, "Influence of Different Parental Mediation Strategies on Adolescents' Hedonistic Smartphone Use."
63 Georgia Christodoulou et al., "Anhedonia, Screen Time, and Substance Use in Early Adolescents: A Longitudinal Mediation Analysis," *Journal of Adolescence* 78, no. 1 (2019): 24–32, https://doi.org/10.1016/j.adolescence.2019.11.007.
64 Priya and Maheswari, "Influence of Different Parental Mediation Strategies on Adolescents' Hedonistic Smartphone Use."

65. Chen et al., "The Interactive Effects of Parental Mediation Strategies in Preventing Cyberbullying on Social Media."
66. Corcoran et al., "Youth Sexting and Associations with Parental Media Mediation."
67. Ren and Zhu, "Parental Mediation and Adolescents' Internet Use: The Moderating Role of Parenting Style."
68. Kevin M. Collier, et al., "Does Parental Mediation of Media Influence Child Outcomes? A Meta-Analysis on Media Time, Aggression, Substance Use, and Sexual Behavior," *Developmental Psychology* 52, no. 5 (2016): 798–812.
69. Collier et al., "Does Parental Mediation of Media Influence Child Outcomes?" 808.
70. Collier et al., "Does Parental Mediation of Media Influence Child Outcomes?"
71. Collier et al., "Does Parental Mediation of Media Influence Child Outcomes?" 808.
72. Jennifer L. Chakroff and Amy I. Nathanson, "Parent and School Interventions: Mediation and Media Literacy," in *The Handbook of Children, Media, and Development*, ed. Sandra L. Calvert and Barbara J. Wilson (West Sussex, UK: Blackwell, 2008), 552–76.
73. Nathanson, "Mediation of Children's Television Viewing."
74. Eric E. Rasmussen et al., "Explaining Parental Coviewing: The Role of Social Facilitation and Arousal," *Communication Monographs* 84, no. 3 (2016): 367, https://doi.org/10.1080/03637751.2016.1259532.
75. E. J. Paavonen et al., "Do Parental Co-viewing and Discussions Mitigate TV-induced Fears in Young Children?" *Child: Care, Health and Development* 35, no. 6 (2009): 773–80, https://doi.org/10.1111/j.1365-2214.2009.01009.x.
76. Kirsten Krahnstoever Davison et al., "Links Between Parents' and Girls' Television Viewing Behaviors: A Longitudinal Examination," *The Journal of Pediatrics* 147, no. 4 (2005): 436–42, https://doi.org/10.1016/j.jpeds.2005.05.002.
77. Juan Li et al., "Translation and Validation of the Chinese Version of the Problematic Media Use Measure," *Early Education and Development* 35, no. 1 (2023): 26–41, https://doi.org/10.1080/10409289.2023.2193856.
78. Shunsen Huang et al., "Does Parental Media Mediation Make a Difference for Adolescents? Evidence From an Empirical Cohort Study of Parent-Adolescent Dyads," *Heliyon* 9, no. 4 (2023): e14897, https://doi.org/10.1016/j.heliyon.2023.e14897.
79. Padilla-Walker et al., "The Protective Role of Parental Media Monitoring Style from Early to Late Adolescence."
80. Tao Sun, "Parental Mediation of Children's TV Viewing in China: An Urban-Rural Comparison," *Young Consumers Insight and Ideas for Responsible Marketers* 10, no. 3 (2009): 188–98, https://doi.org/10.1108/17473610910986008.
81. Kimberly Duyck Woolf, "Children, Parents and Prosocial Television for Children: Accounting for Viewing and Looking for Effects" (PhD diss., University of Pennsylvania, 2019).
82. Woolf, "Children," 271.
83. Michelle St. Peters et al., "Television and Families: What Do Young Children Watch with Their Parents?" *Child Development* 62, no. 6 (1991): 1409–23, https://doi.org/10.2307/1130815.

84 Yu and Zhou, "Social Media Addiction Among Hong Kong Adolescents Before and After the Pandemic."
85 Yu and Zhou, "Social Media Addiction Among Hong Kong Adolescents Before and After the Pandemic," 7.
86 Sarah M. Coyne et al., "Game on . . . Girls: Associations Between Co-playing Video Games and Adolescent Behavioral and Family Outcomes," *Journal of Adolescent Health* 49, no. 2 (2011): 160–5, https://doi.org/10.1016/j.jadohealth.2010.11.249.
87 Lynn Schofield Clark, "Parental Mediation Theory for the Digital Age," *Communication Theory* 21, no. 4 (2011): 334, https://doi.org/10.1111/j.1468-2885.2011.01391.x.

Chapter 7

1 Tamara Bhandari, "Mind-Body Connection Is Built into Brain, Study Suggests," *WashU Medicine*, April 19, 2023, https://medicine.washu.edu/news/mind-body-connection-is-built-into-brain-study-suggests/.
2 Evan M. Gordon et al., "A Somato-Cognitive Action Network Alternates with Effector Regions in Motor Cortex," *Nature* 617, no. 7960 (2023): 351–9, https://doi.org/10.1038/s41586-023-05964-2.
3 Rasmussen, "Proactive vs. Retroactive Mediation."
4 Yi-Ching Lin et al., "Exploring Mediation Roles of Child Screen-Viewing Between Parental Factors and Child Overweight in Taiwan," *International Journal of Environmental Research and Public Health* 17, no. 6 (2020): 1878, https://doi.org/10.3390/ijerph17061878.
5 Lin et al, "Exploring Mediation Roles of Child Screen-Viewing Between Parental Factors and Child Overweight in Taiwan," 8.
6 Leonie Rutherford et al., "Screen Media, Parenting Practices, and the Family Environment in Australia: A Longitudinal Study of Young Children's Media Use, Lifestyles, and Outcomes for Healthy Weight," *Journal of Children and Media* 9, no. 1 (2015): 22–39, https://doi.org/10.1080/17482798.2015.997101.
7 Miguel Giménez Garcia-Conde et al., "Parental Attitudes to Childhood Overweight: The Multiple Paths Through Healthy Eating, Screen Use, and Sleeping Time," *International Journal of Environmental Research and Public Health* 17, no. 21 (2020): 7885, https://doi.org/10.3390/ijerph17217885.
8 Kristen Harrison and Janet M. Liechty, "US Preschoolers' Media Exposure and Dietary Habits: The Primacy of Television and the Limits of Parental Mediation," *Journal of Children and Media* 6, no. 1 (2011): 18–36, https://doi.org/10.1080/17482798.2011.633402.
9 Brigitte Naderer et al., "Shaping Children's Healthy Eating Habits with Food Placements? Food Placements of High and Low Nutritional Value in Cartoons, Children's BMI, Food-related Parental Mediation Strategies, and Food Choice," *Appetite* 120 (2017): 644–53, https://doi.org/10.1016/j.appet.2017.10.023.
10 May O. Lwin et al., "Media Exposure and Parental Mediation on Fast-Food Consumption among Children in Metropolitan and Suburban Indonesia," *PubMed* 26, no. 5 (2017): 899–905, https://doi.org/10.6133/apjcn.122016.04.

11. Heidi Vandebosch and Katrien Van Cleemput, "Television Viewing and Obesity Among Pre-school Children: The Role of Parents," *Communications* 32, no. 4 (2007): 417–46, https://doi.org/10.1515/commun.2007.031.
12. Erica Weintraub Austin et al., "The Role of Parents' Critical Thinking About Media in Shaping Expectancies, Efficacy and Nutrition Behaviors for Families," *Health Communication* 30, no. 12 (2015): 1256–68, https://doi.org/10.1080/10410236.2014.930550.
13. Jennifer L. Harris and John A. Bargh, "Television Viewing and Unhealthy Diet: Implications for Children and Media Interventions," *Health Communication* 24, no. 7 (2009): 660–73, https://doi.org/10.1080/10410230903242267.
14. Natascha Notten et al., "Parents, Television and Children's Weight Status," *Journal of Children and Media* 7, no. 2 (2012): 235–52, https://doi.org/10.1080/17482798.2012.712917.
15. Deborah Schooler et al., "Setting Rules or Sitting Down: Parental Mediation of Television Consumption and Adolescent Self-Esteem, Body Image, and Sexuality," *Sexuality Research and Social Policy* 3, no. 4 (2006): 49–62, https://doi.org/10.1525/srsp.2006.3.4.49.
16. Schooler et al., "Setting Rules or Sitting Down," 58.
17. Amy I. Nathanson and Renée A. Botta, "Shaping the Effects of Television on Adolescents' Body Image Disturbance," *Communication Research* 30, no. 3 (2003): 304–31, https://doi.org/10.1177/0093650203030003003.
18. Yael Latzer et al., "Disordered Eating and Media Exposure Among Adolescent Girls: The Role of Parental Involvement and Sense of Empowerment," *International Journal of Adolescence and Youth* 20, no. 3 (2015): 375–91, https://doi.org/10.1080/02673843.2015.1014925.
19. Latzer et al., "Disordered Eating and Media Exposure Among Adolescent Girls," 385.
20. Gentile et al., "Protective Effects of Parental Monitoring of Children's Media Use," 479.
21. Karsay et al., "Sleeping with the Smartphone."
22. Heather Leonard and Atika Khurana, "Parenting Behaviors and Family Conflict as Predictors of Adolescent Sleep and Bedtime Media Use," *Journal of Youth and Adolescence* 51, no. 8 (2022): 1611–21, https://doi.org/10.1007/s10964-022-01614-4.
23. C. Richardson et al., "A Longitudinal Investigation of Sleep and Technology Use in Early Adolescence: Does Parental Control of Technology Use Protect Adolescent Sleep?," *Sleep Medicine* 84 (2021): 368–79, https://doi.org/10.1016/j.sleep.2021.06.003.
24. Regina J. J. M. Van Den Eijnden et al., "Social Media Use and Adolescents' Sleep: A Longitudinal Study on the Protective Role of Parental Rules Regarding Internet Use Before Sleep," *International Journal of Environmental Research and Public Health* 18, no. 3 (2021): 1346, https://doi.org/10.3390/ijerph18031346.
25. Van Den Eijnden et al., "Social Media Use and Adolescents' Sleep," 9.
26. Lisa J. Smith et al., "Intrinsic and Extrinsic Predictors of Video-gaming Behaviour and Adolescent Bedtimes: The Relationship Between Flow States, Self-perceived Risk-taking, Device Accessibility, Parental Regulation of Media and Bedtime," *Sleep Medicine* 30 (2016): 64–70, https://doi.org/10.1016/j.sleep.2016.01.009.

27 Kevin M Collier et al., "Does Parental Mediation of Media Influence Child Outcomes? A Meta-Analysis on Media Time, Aggression, Substance Use, and Sexual Behavior," *Developmental Psychology* 52, no. 5 (2016): 798–812, https://doi.org/10.1037/dev0000108.
28 Collier et al., "Does Parental Mediation of Media Influence Child Outcomes?," 806–7.
29 Collier et al., "Does Parental Mediation of Media Influence Child Outcomes?," 808.
30 Marie Louise Radanielina-Hita, "Parental Mediation of Media Messages Does Matter: More Interaction About Objectionable Content Is Associated with Emerging Adults' Sexual Attitudes and Behaviors," *Health Communication* 30, no. 8 (2014): 784–98, https://doi.org/10.1080/10410236.2014.900527.
31 Eric E. Rasmussen et al., "Emerging Adults' Responses to Active Mediation of Pornography During Adolescence," *Journal of Children and Media* 9, no. 2 (2015): 160–76, https://doi.org/10.1080/17482798.2014.997769.
32 Eric E. Rasmussen et al., "The Relation Between Norm Accessibility, Pornography Use, and Parental Mediation Among Emerging Adults," *Media Psychology* 19, no. 3 (2016): 431–54, https://doi.org/10.1080/15213269.2015.1054944.
33 Geertjan Overbeek et al., "Buffer or Brake? The Role of Sexuality-Specific Parenting in Adolescents' Sexualized Media Consumption and Sexual Development," *Journal of Youth and Adolescence* 47, no. 7 (2018): 1427–39, https://doi.org/10.1007/s10964-018-0828-3.
34 Overbeek et al., "Buffer or Brake?" 1436.
35 Dina L. Romo et al., "Social Media Use and its Association with Sexual Risk and Parental Monitoring Among a Primarily Hispanic Adolescent Population," *Journal of Pediatric and Adolescent Gynecology* 30, no. 4 (2017): 466–73, https://doi.org/10.1016/j.jpag.2017.02.004.
36 Schooler et al., "Setting Rules or Sitting Down."
37 Deborah A. Fisher et al., "Televised Sexual Content and Parental Mediation: Influences on Adolescent Sexuality," *Media Psychology* 12, no. 2 (2009): 121–47, https://doi.org/10.1080/15213260902849901.
38 Corcoran et al., "Youth Sexting and Associations with Parental Media Mediation."
39 Alison Parkes et al., "Are Sexual Media Exposure, Parental Restrictions on Media Use and Co-viewing TV and DVDs With Parents and Friends Associated with Teenagers' Early Sexual Behaviour?," *Journal of Adolescence* 36, no. 6 (2013): 1121–33, https://doi.org/10.1016/j.adolescence.2013.08.019.
40 Emma Sorbring et al., "Parental Attitudes and Young People's Online Sexual Activities," *Sex Education* 15, no. 2 (2014): 129–43, https://doi.org/10.1080/14681811.2014.981332.
41 Melina Bersamin et al., "Parenting Practices and Adolescent Sexual Behavior: A Longitudinal Study," *Journal of Marriage and Family* 70, no. 1 (2008): 97–112, https://doi.org/10.1111/j.1741-3737.2007.00464.x.
42 Wenxiu Guo and Amy I. Nathanson, "The Effects of Parental Mediation of Sexual Content on the Sexual Knowledge, Attitudes, and Behaviors of Adolescents in the US," *Journal of Children and Media* 5, no. 4 (2011): 358–78, https://doi.org/10.1080/17482798.2011.587141.

43 Guo et al., "The Effects of Parental Mediation of Sexual Content on the Sexual Knowledge, Attitudes, and Behaviors of Adolescents in the US," 369.
44 Ann Neville Miller et al., "The Relationship Between Parental Mediation of Adolescent Media Use and Ugandan Adolescents' Sexual Attitudes and Behavior," *Howard Journal of Communications* 29, no. 2 (2017): 165–78, https://doi.org/10.1080/10646175.2017.1354788.
45 Nikken and De Graaf, "Reciprocal Relationships Between Friends' and Parental Mediation of Adolescents' Media Use and Their Sexual Attitudes and Behavior."
46 Collier et al., "Does Parental Mediation of Media Influence Child Outcomes?"
47 Collier et al., "Does Parental Mediation of Media Influence Child Outcomes?," 807–8.
48 Michelle F. Wright and Sebastian Wachs, "Does Parental Mediation of Technology Use Moderate the Associations Between Cyber Aggression Involvement and Substance Use? A Three-Year Longitudinal Study," *International Journal of Environmental Research and Public Health* 16, no. 13 (2019): 2425, https://doi.org/10.3390/ijerph16132425.
49 Marie Louise Radanielina Hita et al., "Parental Mediation in the Digital Era: Increasing Children's Critical Thinking May Help Decrease Positive Attitudes Toward Alcohol," *Journal of Health Communication* 23, no. 1 (2017): 98–108, https://doi.org/10.1080/10810730.2017.1411997.
50 Erica Weintraub Austin et al., "The Role of Interpretation Processes and Parental Discussion in the Media's Effects on Adolescents' Use of Alcohol," *Pediatrics* 105, no. 2 (2000): 343–49, https://doi.org/10.1542/peds.105.2.343.
51 Judith McCool et al., "Do Parents Have Any Influence Over How Young People Appraise Tobacco Images in the Media?" *Journal of Adolescent Health* 48, no. 2 (2010): 170–5, https://doi.org/10.1016/j.jadohealth.2010.06.012.
52 Anne Sadza et al., "Let's Talk About Risks. Parental And Peer Mediation and Their Relation to Adolescents' Perceptions of On- and Off-Screen Risk Behavior," *Communications* 49, no. 2 (2022): 175–98, https://doi.org/10.1515/commun-2021-0143.
53 Sadza et al., "Let's Talk About Risks," 191.
54 Liang-Shuang Yao et al., "Parental Mediation Moderates the Association Between Social Media Exposure and Tobacco and Alcohol Use: Differences Between Elementary and Middle School Students," *Journal of Studies on Alcohol and Drugs* 83, no. 2 (2022): 267–75, https://doi.org/10.15288/jsad.2022.83.267.
55 Yao et al., "Parental Mediation Moderates the Association Between Social Media Exposure and Tobacco and Alcohol Use," 273.
56 Kristina M. Jackson et al., "Mechanisms Underlying Associations Between Media Alcohol Exposure, Parenting, and Early Adolescent Drinking: A Moderated Sequential Mediation Model," *Journal of Youth and Adolescence* 50, no. 9 (2021): 1896–910, https://doi.org/10.1007/s10964-020-01373-0.
57 Raul Mejia et al., "Parental Restriction of Mature-rated Media and its Association With Substance Use Among Argentinean Adolescents," *Academic Pediatrics* 16, no. 3 (2015): 282–9, https://doi.org/10.1016/j.acap.2015.11.004.
58 Reiner Hanewinkel et al., "Longitudinal Study of Parental Movie Restriction on Teen Smoking and Drinking in Germany," *Addiction* 103, no. 10 (2008): 1722–30, https://doi.org/10.1111/j.1360-0443.2008.02308.x.

59 Hanewinkel et al., "Longitudinal Study of Parental Movie Restriction on Teen Smoking and Drinking in Germany," 1728.
60 Madeline A. Dalton et al., "Parental Rules and Monitoring of Children's Movie Viewing Associated with Children's Risk for Smoking and Drinking," *Pediatrics* 118, no. 5 (2006): 1932–42, https://doi.org/10.1542/peds.2005-3082.
61 Ellen M. Thompson and Albert C. Gunther, "Cigarettes and Cinema: Does Parental Restriction of R-Rated Movie Viewing Reduce Adolescent Smoking Susceptibility?" *Journal of Adolescent Health* 40, no. 2 (2006): 181.e1–6, https://doi.org/10.1016/j.jadohealth.2006.09.017.
62 Jessie Rudi and Jodi Dworkin, "Is Technology-Mediated Parental Monitoring Related to Adolescent Substance Use?" *Substance Use & Misuse* 53, no. 8 (2018): 1331–41, https://doi.org/10.1080/10826084.2017.1408653.
63 Melissa J. Cox et al., "Profiles of Parenting in the Digital Age: Associations with Adolescent Alcohol and Marijuana Use," *Journal of Studies on Alcohol and Drugs* 82, no. 4 (2021): 460–9, https://doi.org/10.15288/jsad.2021.82.460.
64 Cox et al., "Profiles of Parenting in the Digital Age."

Chapter 8

1 APA Dictionary of Psychology, "Folk Psychology," November 15, 2023, https://dictionary.apa.org/folk-psychology.
2 APA Dictionary of Psychology, "Communication," April 19, 2018, https://dictionary.apa.org/folk-psychology.
3 Xiaoqin Zhu et al., "Editorial: Parental Influence on Child Social and Emotional Functioning," *Frontiers in Psychology* 15 (2024): 1, https://doi.org/10.3389/fpsyg.2024.1392772.
4 Zhu et al., "Editorial," 1.
5 Eveline A. Crone and Michelle Achterberg, "Prosocial Development in Adolescence," *Current Opinion in Psychology* 44 (2021): 220, https://doi.org/10.1016/j.copsyc.2021.09.020.
6 Nancy Eisenberg, *Altruistic Emotion, Cognition, and Behavior* (Hillsdale, New Jersey: Lawrence Erlbaum, 1986).
7 Nancy Eisenberg et al., "Empathy-Related Responding: Associations with Prosocial Behavior, Aggression, and Intergroup Relations," *Social Issues and Policy Review* 4, no. 1 (2010): 143–80, https://doi.org/10.1111/j.1751-2409.2010.01020.x.
8 Gian Vittorio Caprara et al., "Positive Effects of Promoting Prosocial Behavior in Early Adolescence," *International Journal of Behavioral Development* 38, no. 4 (2014): 386–96, https://doi.org/10.1177/0165025414531464.
9 Xinyuan Fu et al., "Longitudinal Relations Between Adolescents' Self-Esteem and Prosocial Behavior Toward Strangers, Friends and Family," *Journal of Adolescence* 57, no. 1 (2017): 90–8, https://doi.org/10.1016/j.adolescence.2017.04.002.
10 Sara Prot et al., "Long-Term Relations Among Prosocial-Media Use, Empathy, and Prosocial Behavior," *Psychological Science* 25, no. 2 (2013): 358–68, https://doi.org/10.1177/0956797613503854.
11 Coyne et al., "A Meta-Analysis of Prosocial Media on Prosocial Behavior, Aggression, and Empathic Concern."

12. Gentile et al., "Protective Effects of Parental Monitoring of Children's Media Use," 479.
13. Sarah M. Coyne et al., "Pretty as a Princess: Longitudinal Effects of Engagement with Disney Princesses on Gender Stereotypes, Body Esteem, and Prosocial Behavior in Children," *Child Development* 87, no. 6 (2016): 1909–25, https://doi.org/10.1111/cdev.12569.
14. Charles K. Atkin and Bradley S. Greenberg, "Parental Mediation of Children's Social Behavior Learning from Television," Report No. 4, U.S. Office of Child Development, 1977, https://eric.ed.gov/?id=ED151808.
15. Anneleen Meeus et al., "Managing Positive and Negative Media Effects Among Adolescents: Parental Mediation Matters—But Not Always," *Journal of Family Communication* 18, no. 4 (2018): 270–85, https://doi.org/10.1080/15267431.2018.1487443.
16. Hailey G. Holmgren et al., "Parental Media Monitoring, Prosocial Violent Media Exposure, and Adolescents' Prosocial and Aggressive Behaviors," *Aggressive Behavior* 45, no. 6 (2019): 671–81, https://doi.org/10.1002/ab.21861.
17. Laura M. Padilla-Walker et al., "Associations Between Parental Media Monitoring Style, Information Management, and Prosocial and Aggressive Behaviors," *Journal of Social and Personal Relationships* 37, no. 1 (2019): 180–200, https://doi.org/10.1177/0265407519859653.
18. Padilla-Walker et al., "Associations Between Parental Media Monitoring Style, Information Management, and Prosocial and Aggressive Behaviors," 191.
19. Padilla-Walker et al., "Associations Between Parental Media Monitoring Style, Information Management, and Prosocial and Aggressive Behaviors," 192.
20. Christopher Peterson and Martin E. P. Seligman, *Character Strengths and Virtues: A Handbook and Classification* (Oxford, England: Oxford University Press, 2004).
21. Laura M. Padilla-Walker et al., "Longitudinal Relations Between Parental Media Monitoring and Adolescent Aggression, Prosocial Behavior, and Externalizing Problems," *Journal of Adolescence* 46, no. 1 (2015): 86–97, https://doi.org/10.1016/j.adolescence.2015.11.002.
22. Crystal Ling and Hon Kai Yee, "Parental Mediation: Its Impact on Contexts of Emotional Behavioral Adjustment Among Children in Kota Kinabalu District," *Cogent Social Sciences* 7, no. 1 (2021), https://doi.org/10.1080/23311886.2020.1870070.
23. Eric E. Rasmussen et al., "Relation Between Active Mediation, Exposure to Daniel Tiger's Neighborhood, and US Preschoolers' Social and Emotional Development," *Journal of Children and Media* 10, no. 4 (2016): 443–61, https://doi.org/10.1080/17482798.2016.1203806.
24. Rasmussen et al., "Relation Between Active Mediation, Exposure to Daniel Tiger's Neighborhood, and US Preschoolers' Social and Emotional Development," 455.
25. Dasheng Shi et al., "The Association Between Parents Phubbing and Prosocial Behavior Among Chinese Preschool Children: A Moderated Mediation Model," *Frontiers in Psychology* 15 (2024), https://doi.org/10.3389/fpsyg.2024.1338055.
26. Padilla-Walker et al., "Longitudinal Associations Between Parents' Prosocial Behavior and Media Use and Young Children's Prosocial Development."
27. Laura A. Stockdale et al., "Infants' Physiological Responses to Emotionally Salient Media with Links to Parent and Child, Empathy, Prosocial Behaviors and Media

Use," *Computers in Human Behavior* 139 (2022): 107497, https://doi.org/10.1016/j.chb.2022.107497.

28. Stockdale et al., "Infants' Physiological Responses to Emotionally Salient Media with Links to Parent and Child, Empathy, Prosocial Behaviors and Media Use," 8–9.
29. Stockdale et al., "Infants' Physiological Responses to Emotionally Salient Media with Links to Parent and Child, Empathy, Prosocial Behaviors and Media Use," 7.
30. Sara Catherine Brown, "Will TV Impact if I Help You? Prosocial Media, Joint Media Engagement, and Infant Prosocial Development During the Second Year," (MA thesis, Brigham Young University, 2020), ProQuest (28187302).
31. Kara M. Liebeskind, "The Exploration of U.S. Parents' Television Mediation Through Genre-Specific Scenarios," *Journal of Children and Media* 9, no. 1 (2015): 113–32, https://doi.org/10.1080/17482798.2015.997100.
32. Coyne et al., "Game on . . . Girls," 165.
33. Aimee Dorr et al., "Parent-Child Coviewing of Television," *Journal of Broadcasting & Electronic Media* 33, no. 1 (1989): 35–51, https://doi.org/10.1080/08838158909364060.
34. M. S. Peters, "Television and Families: Parental Coviewing and Young Children's Language Development, Social Behaviour, and Television Processing," *Resources in Education* 25, no. 3 (1990), http://files.eric.ed.gov/fulltext/ED312040.pdf.
35. A. M. Klahr et al., "Developmental Psychopathology," in *Elsevier eBooks*, 2012, 697–701, https://doi.org/10.1016/b978-0-12-375000-6.00132-4.
36. Gentile et al., "Protective Effects of Parental Monitoring of Children's Media Use," 479.
37. Emenike N. Anyaegbunam et al., "Parental Mediation as a Moderator of the Relationship Between Violent Media Contents Exposure and Aggressive Behaviour of In-School Adolescents," *Global Journal of Health Science* 11, no. 14 (2019): 1, https://doi.org/10.5539/gjhs.v11n14p1.
38. Holmgren et al., "Parental Media Monitoring, Prosocial Violent Media Exposure, and Adolescents' Prosocial and Aggressive Behaviors."
39. Holmgren et al., "Parental Media Monitoring, Prosocial Violent Media Exposure, and Adolescents' Prosocial and Aggressive Behaviors," 679.
40. Meeus et al., "Managing Positive and Negative Media Effects Among Adolescents."
41. Fikkers, Piotrowski, and Valkenburg, "A Matter of Style?"
42. Meeus et al., "Managing Positive and Negative Media Effects Among Adolescents," 281.
43. Meeus et al., "Managing Positive and Negative Media Effects Among Adolescents," 281.
44. Collier et al., "Does Parental Mediation of Media Influence Child Outcomes?"
45. Nathanson, "Identifying and Explaining the Relationship Between Parental Mediation and Children's Aggression."
46. Nathanson, "Identifying and Explaining the Relationship Between Parental Mediation and Children's Aggression," 129.
47. Nathanson, "Identifying and Explaining the Relationship Between Parental Mediation and Children's Aggression," 129.
48. Atkin and Greenberg, "Parental Mediation of Children's Social Behavior Learning from Television."

49 Liebeskind, "The Exploration of U.S. Parents' Television Mediation Through Genre-Specific Scenarios."
50 Eric E. Rasmussen et al., "Parental Mediation of US Youths' Exposure to Televised Relational Aggression," *Journal of Children and Media* 12, no. 2 (2017): 192–210, https://doi.org/10.1080/17482798.2017.1405829.
51 Rasmussen et al., "Parental Mediation of US Youths' Exposure to Televised Relational Aggression."
52 Nicole Martins et al., "Mixed Messages: Inconsistent Parental Mediation Indirectly Predicts Teens' Online Relational Aggression," *Journal of Family Communication* 19, no. 4 (2019): 311–28, https://doi.org/10.1080/15267431.2019.1649264.
53 Padilla-Walker et al., "Associations Between Parental Media Monitoring Style, Information Management, and Prosocial and Aggressive Behaviors."
54 Kate E. Williams and Donna Berthelsen, "The Development of Prosocial Behaviour in Early Childhood: Contributions of Early Parenting and Self-Regulation," *International Journal of Early Childhood* 49, no. 1 (2017): 75, https://doi.org/10.1007/s13158-017-0185-5.
55 Williams and Berthelsen, "The Development of Prosocial Behaviour in Early Childhood."
56 Laura M. Padilla-Walker and Katherine J. Christensen, "Empathy and Self-Regulation as Mediators Between Parenting and Adolescents' Prosocial Behavior Toward Strangers, Friends, and Family," *Journal of Research on Adolescence* 21, no. 3 (2010): 545–51, https://doi.org/10.1111/j.1532-7795.2010.00695.x.
57 Nancy Eisenberg et al., "The Relations of Children's Dispositional Prosocial Behavior to Emotionality, Regulation, and Social Functioning," *Child Development* 67, no. 3 (1996): 974–92, https://doi.org/10.1111/j.1467-8624.1996.tb01777.x.
58 Padilla-Walker and Christensen, "Empathy and Self-Regulation as Mediators Between Parenting and Adolescents' Prosocial Behavior Toward Strangers, Friends, and Family."
59 Mara Morelli et al., "Parental Mediation of COVID-19 News and Children's Emotion Regulation During Lockdown," *Journal of Child and Family Studies* 31, no. 6 (2022): 1522, https://doi.org/10.1007/s10826-022-02266-5.
60 Chen and Chng, "Active and Restrictive Parental Mediation Over Time."
61 Emily C.E. Magar et al., "Self-Regulation and Risk-Taking," *Personality and Individual Differences* 45, no. 2 (2008): 153–9, https://doi.org/10.1016/j.paid.2008.03.014.
62 Hagit Sasson and Gustavo Mesch, "Parental Mediation, Peer Norms and Risky Online Behavior Among Adolescents," *Computers in Human Behavior* 33 (2014): 32–8, https://doi.org/10.1016/j.chb.2013.12.025.
63 Catherine St-Amand-Guitard, "Emotion Recognition and Emotional Self-Regulation in Students with LDs," *LD@school*, April 14, 2023, https://www.ldatschool.ca/ate-emotion-recognition-regulation/#:~:text=Emotion%20recognition%20is%20a%20fundamental,Feldman%20&%20Matjasko%2C%202005).
64 Rasmussen et al., "Relation Between Active Mediation, Exposure to Daniel Tiger's Neighborhood, and US Preschoolers' Social and Emotional Development."

65 Moniek Buijzen et al., "Parental Mediation of Children's Emotional Responses to a Violent News Event," *Communication Research* 34, no. 2 (2007): 212–30, https://doi.org/10.1177/0093650206298070.
66 Paavonen et al., "Do Parental Co-viewing and Discussions Mitigate TV-induced Fears in Young Children?"
67 Rozane De Cock, "Mediating Flemish Children's Reactions of Fear and Sadness to Television News and its Limitations," *Journal of Children and Media* 6, no. 4 (2012): 485–501, https://doi.org/10.1080/17482798.2012.740414.
68 De Cock, "Mediating Flemish Children's Reactions of Fear and Sadness to Television News and its Limitations," 498.
69 De Cock, "Mediating Flemish Children's Reactions of Fear and Sadness to Television News and its Limitations," 498.
70 Xiaohui Yang et al., "The Relations Between Television Exposure and Executive Function in Chinese Preschoolers: The Moderated Role of Parental Mediation Behaviors," *Frontiers in Psychology* 8 (2017), https://doi.org/10.3389/fpsyg.2017.01833.
71 Yang et al., "The Relations Between Television Exposure and Executive Function in Chinese Preschoolers," 10.
72 Kim Foulds, "Co-Viewing Mass Media to Support Children and Parents' Emotional ABCs: An Evaluation of Ahlan Simsim," *Early Childhood Education Journal* 51, no. 8 (2022): 1479–88, https://doi.org/10.1007/s10643-022-01408-0.
73 Chris L. Porter et al., "'Katerina Gets Mad': Infants' Physiological and Behavioral Responses to Co-viewing Educational, Self-Regulatory Media," *Developmental Psychobiology* 64, no. 8 (2022), https://doi.org/10.1002/dev.22337.
74 Eleanor Leigh and David M. Clark, "Understanding Social Anxiety Disorder in Adolescents and Improving Treatment Outcomes: Applying the Cognitive Model of Clark and Wells (1995)," *Clinical Child and Family Psychology Review* 21, no. 3 (2018): 388–414, https://doi.org/10.1007/s10567-018-0258-5.
75 Xiaoqing Ji et al., "The Serial Mediation Role of Parent-Child Attachment and Empathy in the Relationship Between Parental Technoference and Social Anxiety," *Current Psychology* 43, no. 29 (2024): 24418–28, https://doi.org/10.1007/s12144-024-06109-y.
76 Laura E. Brumariu, "Parent-Child Attachment and Emotion Regulation," *New Directions for Child and Adolescent Development* 2015, no. 148 (2015): 31–45, https://doi.org/10.1002/cad.20098.
77 Susan Branje et al., "Parent-Child Communication During Adolescence," in *The Routledge Handbook of Family Communication*, 2nd ed., ed. Anita L. Vangelisti (New York, NY: Routledge, 2012), 271–86.
78 Jessica Melching, "Exploring Parent-Adolescent Conflict: An Examination of Correlates and Longitudinal Predictors in Early Adolescence" (MS thesis, The University of New Orleans, 2011), 1.
79 Melching, "Exploring Parent-Adolescent Conflict."
80 Beyens and Beullens, "Parent–Child Conflict About Children's Tablet Use."
81 Patti M. Valkenburg et al., "Developing and Validating the Perceived Parental Media Mediation Scale: A Self-Determination Perspective," *Human Communication Research* 39, no. 4 (2013): 445–69, https://doi.org/10.1111/hcre.12010.

82 Maggie Kanter et al., "The Impact of Parents 'Friending' Their Young Adult Child on Facebook on Perceptions of Parental Privacy Invasions and Parent-Child Relationship Quality," *Journal of Communication* 62, no. 5 (2012): 900–17, https://doi.org/10.1111/j.1460-2466.2012.01669.x.

83 Shi et al., "The Association Between Parents Phubbing and Prosocial Behavior Among Chinese Preschool Children."

84 Shi et al., "The Association Between Parents Phubbing and Prosocial Behavior Among Chinese Preschool Children," 8.

85 Alanna Peebles and Y. Anthony Chen, "Parental Internet Practices in the Family System: Restrictive Mediation, Problematic Internet Use, and Adolescents' Age-Related Variations in Perceptions of Parent-Child Relationship Quality," *Journal of Social and Personal Relationships* 41, no. 6 (2023): 1347–69, https://doi.org/10.1177/02654075231221581.

86 Nathanson, "The Unintended Effects of Parental Mediation of Television on Adolescents."

87 Nathanson, "The Unintended Effects of Parental Mediation of Television on Adolescents," 220.

88 Yi Yang et al., "The Relations Between Parental Active Mediation, Parent-Child Relationships and Children's Problematic Mobile Phone Use: A Longitudinal Study," *Media Psychology* 25, no. 4 (2021): 513–30, https://doi.org/10.1080/15213269.2021.1981945.

89 Beauregard, "Mind Does Really Matter," 233.

90 Nance McCown, "Recognizing the Imago Dei in Employee Publics: A Challenge for Christian Public Relations Scholars, Faculty, and Practitioners," *Journal of Communication & Religion* 43, no. 1 (2020): 75–88, https://doi.org/10.5840/jcr20204315.

Chapter 9

1 World Health Organization, *Mental Health of Adolescents*, 2024, https://www.who.int/news-room/fact-sheets/detail/adolescent-mental-health.

2 World Health Organization, *Adolescent Mental Health,* 2019, https://www.who.int/news-room/fact-sheets/detail/adolescent-mental-health.

3 U.S. Department of Health and Human Services, *Key Substance Use and Mental Health Indicators in the United States: Results from the 2016 National Survey on Drug Use and Health*, 2017.

4 Daniel G. Whitney and Mark D. Peterson, "US National and State-Level Prevalence of Mental Health Disorders and Disparities of Mental Health Care Use in Children," *JAMA Pediatrics* 173, no. 4 (2019): 389, https://doi.org/10.1001/jamapediatrics.2018.5399.

5 U.S. Department of Health and Human Services, *Our Epidemic of Loneliness and Isolation*, 2023, 9.

6 Osman Ulvi et al., "Social Media Use and Mental Health: A Global Analysis," *Epidemiologia* 3, no. 1 (2022): 11–25, https://doi.org/10.3390/epidemiologia3010002.

7. Natalia Macrynikola et al., "Does Social Media Use Confer Suicide Risk? A Systematic Review of the Evidence," *Computers in Human Behavior Reports* 3 (2021): 100094, https://doi.org/10.1016/j.chbr.2021.100094.
8. Holger Zapf et al., "A Systematic Review of the Association Between Parent-Child Communication and Adolescent Mental Health," *JCPP Advances* 4, no. 2 (2023), https://doi.org/10.1002/jcv2.12205.
9. Aynur Bütün Ayhan and Utku Beyazit, "The Associations Between Loneliness and Self-Esteem in Children and Neglectful Behaviors of Their Parents," *Child Indicators Research* 14, no. 5 (2021): 1863–79, https://doi.org/10.1007/s12187-021-09818-z.
10. Sandra Achtergarde et al., "Parenting and Child Mental Health," *The Family Journal* 23, no. 2 (2014): 167, https://doi.org/10.1177/1066480714564316.
11. Achtergarde et al., "Parenting and Child Mental Health."
12. Susan M. Bögels et al., "Mindful Parenting in Mental Health Care: Effects on Parental and Child Psychopathology, Parental Stress, Parenting, Coparenting, and Marital Functioning," *Mindfulness* 5, no. 5 (2013): 536–51, https://doi.org/10.1007/s12671-013-0209-7.
13. Laurel A. Brabson, Carrie B. Jackson, Brittany K. Liebsack, and Amy D. Herschell, "PCIT: Summary of 40 Years of Research," in *Handbook of Parent-Child Interaction Therapy for Children on the Autism Spectrum*, ed. Cheryl Bodiford McNeil, Lauren Borduin Quetsch, and Cynthia M. Anderson (Cham, Switzerland: Springer, 2018): 251–75.
14. Geneviève A. Mageau et al., "How-to-Parenting-Program: Change in Parenting and Child Mental Health Over One Year," *Journal of Child and Family Studies* 31, no. 12 (2022): 3498–513, https://doi.org/10.1007/s10826-022-02442-7.
15. Kristen M. McCabe et al., "The Relation Between Parent Mental Health and Child Internalizing Symptoms in Parent–Child Interaction Therapy," *Journal of Child and Family Studies* 31, no. 8 (2022): 2065–76, https://doi.org/10.1007/s10826-022-02254-9.
16. Chen and Chng, "Active and Restrictive Parental Mediation Over Time."
17. Christopher T. Barry et al., "Adolescent Social Media Use and Mental Health from Adolescent and Parent Perspectives," *Journal of Adolescence* 61, no. 1 (2017): 1–11, https://doi.org/10.1016/j.adolescence.2017.08.005.
18. Jasmine Fardouly et al., "Parental Control of the Time Preadolescents Spend on Social Media: Links with Preadolescents' Social Media Appearance Comparisons and Mental Health," *Journal of Youth and Adolescence* 47, no. 7 (2018): 1456–68, https://doi.org/10.1007/s10964-018-0870-1.
19. Fardouly et al., "Parental Control of the Time Preadolescents Spend on Social Media," 1465.
20. Michelle Wright, "Cyberbullying Victimization Through Social Networking Sites and Adjustment Difficulties: The Role of Parental Mediation," *Journal of the Association for Information Systems* 19, no. 2 (2018), https://aisel.aisnet.org/jais/vol19/iss2/1/.
21. Wright, "Cyberbullying Victimization Through Social Networking Sites and Adjustment Difficulties," 119.
22. Wright, "Cyberbullying Victimization Through Social Networking Sites and Adjustment Difficulties," 119.

23 Laura M. Padilla-Walker et al., "Associations Between Parental Media Monitoring, Media Use, and Internalizing Symptoms During Adolescence," *Psychology of Popular Media* 9, no. 4 (2019): 481–92, https://doi.org/10.1037/ppm0000256.
24 Michelle F. Wright, "Cyber Victimization and Depression Among Adolescents with Autism Spectrum Disorder: The Buffering Effects of Parental Mediation and Social Support," *Journal of Child & Adolescent Trauma* 11, no. 1 (2017): 22–23, https://doi.org/10.1007/s40653-017-0169-5.
25 Fong-Ching Chang et al., "The Relationship Between Parental Mediation and Internet Addiction Among Adolescents, and the Association with Cyberbullying and Depression," *Comprehensive Psychiatry* 57 (2014): 21–28, https://doi.org/10.1016/j.comppsych.2014.11.013.
26 Sanne Nikkelen et al., "Media Violence and Adolescents' ADHD-Related Behaviors: The Role of Parental Mediation," *Journal of Broadcasting & Electronic Media* 60, no. 4 (2016): 657–75, https://doi.org/10.1080/08838151.2016.1234476.
27 Wakithi Siza Mabaso et al., "Exploring the Relationship Between Public Social Media Accounts, Adolescent Mental Health, and Parental Guidance in England: Large Cross-Sectional School Survey Study," *Journal of Medical Internet Research* 26 (2024): e57154, https://doi.org/10.2196/57154.
28 Mabaso et al., "Exploring the Relationship Between Public Social Media Accounts, Adolescent Mental Health, and Parental Guidance in England."
29 Bar Shutzman and Naama Gershy, "Children's Excessive Digital Media Use, Mental Health Problems and the Protective Role of Parenting During COVID-19," *Computers in Human Behavior* 139 (2022): 107559, https://doi.org/10.1016/j.chb.2022.107559.
30 Rudnova et al., "Characteristics of Parental Digital Mediation," 57.
31 Bickham et al., "Media Use and Depression."
32 Xiaofang Xiao and Xifu Zheng, "The Effect of Parental Phubbing on Depression in Chinese Junior High School Students: The Mediating Roles of Basic Psychological Needs Satisfaction and Self-Esteem," *Frontiers in Psychology* 13 (2022), https://doi.org/10.3389/fpsyg.2022.868354.
33 Valeria Rega et al., "Parental Mediation and Cyberbullying: A Narrative Literature Review," *Marriage & Family Review* 58, no. 6 (2022): 495, https://doi.org/10.1080/01494929.2022.2069199.
34 Jonathan Rothwell, "How Parenting and Self-Control Mediate the Link Between Social Media Use and Youth Mental Health," Institute for Family Studies, 2023, 3.
35 Stephen M. Amrock and Michael Weitzman, "Parental Psychological Distress and Children's Mental Health: Results of a National Survey," *Academic Pediatrics* 14, no. 4 (2014): 375–81, https://doi.org/10.1016/j.acap.2014.02.005.
36 Bennett et al., "The Association of Child Mental Health Conditions and Parent Mental Health Status Among U.S. Children, 2007."
37 Clemens M. H. Hosman et al., "Prevention of Emotional Problems and Psychiatric Risks in Children of Parents with a Mental Illness in the Netherlands: I. the Scientific Basis to a Comprehensive Approach," *Australian E-Journal for the Advancement of Mental Health* 8, no. 3 (2009): 250–63, https://doi.org/10.5172/jamh.8.3.250.
38 Robert S. Kahn et al., "Combined Effect of Mothers' and Fathers' Mental Health Symptoms on Children's Behavioral and Emotional Well-Being," *Archives of*

Pediatrics and Adolescent Medicine 158, no. 8 (2004): 721, https://doi.org/10.1001/archpedi.158.8.721.

39 Mark Olfson et al., "Parental Depression, Child Mental Health Problems, and Health Care Utilization," *Medical Care* 41, no. 6 (2003): 716–21, https://doi.org/10.1097/01.mlr.0000064642.41278.48.

40 Linda M. A. Van Loon et al., "The Relation Between Parental Mental Illness and Adolescent Mental Health: The Role of Family Factors," *Journal of Child and Family Studies* 23, no. 7 (2013): 1201–14, https://doi.org/10.1007/s10826-013-9781-7.

41 Ylva Parfitt et al., "The Impact of Parents' Mental Health on Parent–Baby Interaction: A Prospective Study," *Infant Behavior and Development* 36, no. 4 (2013): 599–608, https://doi.org/10.1016/j.infbeh.2013.06.003.

42 Marlit Sell et al., "Family Functioning in Families Affected by Parental Mental Illness: Parent, Child, and Clinician Ratings," *International Journal of Environmental Research and Public Health* 18, no. 15 (2021): 7985, https://doi.org/10.3390/ijerph18157985.

43 Brenda M. Gladstone et al., "Children's Experiences of Parental Mental Illness: A Literature Review," *Early Intervention in Psychiatry* 5, no. 4 (2011): 271–89, https://doi.org/10.1111/j.1751-7893.2011.00287.x.

44 Andrea Reupert and Darryl Maybery, "What Do We Know About Families Where Parents Have a Mental Illness? A Systematic Review," *Child & Youth Services* 37, no. 2 (2015): 98–111, https://doi.org/10.1080/0145935x.2016.1104037.

45 Brynna Kroll, "Living with an Elephant: Growing up With Parental Substance Misuse," *Child & Family Social Work* 9, no. 2 (2004): 129–40, https://doi.org/10.1111/j.1365-2206.2004.00325.x.

46 Friederike C. Gerull and Ronald M. Rapee, "Mother Knows Best: Effects of Maternal Modelling on the Acquisition of Fear and Avoidance Behaviour in Toddlers," *Behaviour Research and Therapy* 40, no. 3 (2002): 279–87, https://doi.org/10.1016/s0005-7967(01)00013-4.

47 C. I. Harries et al., "Parenting and Serious Mental Illness (SMI): A Systematic Review and Metasynthesis," *Clinical Child and Family Psychology Review* 26, no. 2 (2023): 303–42, https://doi.org/10.1007/s10567-023-00427-6.

48 Barry J. Ackerson, "Coping with the Dual Demands of Severe Mental Illness and Parenting: The Parents' Perspective," *Families in Society: The Journal of Contemporary Social Services* 84, no. 1 (2003): 109–18, https://doi.org/10.1606/1044-3894.69.

49 Ackerson, "Coping with the Dual Demands of Severe Mental Illness and Parenting," 117.

50 World Health Organization, *Mental Disorders*, 2022, https://www.who.int/news-room/fact-sheets/detail/mental-disorders.

51 United States Census Bureau, *Global Population Estimates Vary but Trends Are Clear: Population Growth is Slowing*, 2023, https://www.census.gov/library/stories/2023/11/world-population-estimated-eight-billion.html.

52 National Institute of Mental Health, *Mental Illness*, 2024, https://www.nimh.nih.gov/health/statistics/mental-illness.

53 Megan Brenan, "Americans' Preference for Larger Families Highest Since 1971," *Gallup*, September 25, 2023, https://news.gallup.com/poll/511238/americans-preference-larger-families-highest-1971.aspx.
54 UNICEF, *How Many Children Are There in the World?*, 2023, https://data.unicef.org/how-many/how-many-children-under-18-are-in-the-world/.
55 Chris Feudtner et al., "Good-Parent Beliefs of Parents of Seriously Ill Children," *JAMA Pediatrics* 169, no. 1 (2014): 39, https://doi.org/10.1001/jamapediatrics.2014.2341.
56 Martin Pinquart, "Do the Parent–Child Relationship and Parenting Behaviors Differ Between Families with a Child with and without Chronic Illness? A Meta-Analysis," *Journal of Pediatric Psychology* 38, no. 7 (2013): 708–21, https://doi.org/10.1093/jpepsy/jst020.
57 Marie-Louise J. Kullberg et al., "Linking Internalizing and Externalizing Problems to Warmth and Negativity in Observed Dyadic Parent–Offspring Communication," *Family Relations* 72, no. 5 (2023): 2777–99, https://doi.org/10.1111/fare.12847.
58 Kullberg et al., "Linking Internalizing and Externalizing Problems to Warmth and Negativity in Observed Dyadic Parent–Offspring Communication," 2792.
59 Lisa A. Serbin et al., "The Impact of Children's Internalizing and Externalizing Problems on Parenting: Transactional Processes and Reciprocal Change Over Time," *Development and Psychopathology* 27, no. 4_1 (2015): 969–86, https://doi.org/10.1017/s0954579415000632.
60 Ni Yan et al., "Reconsidering the Relation Between Parental Functioning and Child Externalizing Behaviors: A Meta-Analysis on Child-driven Effects," *Journal of Family Psychology* 35, no. 2 (2020): 225–35, https://doi.org/10.1037/fam0000805.
61 Maryam Zarra-Nezhad et al., "The Impact of Children's Socioemotional Development on Parenting Styles: The Moderating Effect of Social Withdrawal," *Early Child Development and Care* 192, no. 7 (2020): 1032–44, https://doi.org/10.1080/03004430.2020.1835879.
62 Zarra-Nezhad et al., "The Impact of Children's Socioemotional Development on Parenting Styles," 1040–1.
63 Elizabeth M. Z. Farmer et al., "Impact of Children's Mental Health Problems on Families," *Journal of Emotional and Behavioral Disorders* 5, no. 4 (1997): 230–8, https://doi.org/10.1177/106342669700500406.
64 M. Dey et al., "Quality of Life of Parents of Mentally-Ill Children: A Systematic Review and Meta-Analysis," *Epidemiology and Psychiatric Sciences* 28, no. 5 (2018): 563–77, https://doi.org/10.1017/s2045796018000409.
65 Francesca Lionetti et al., "The Development of Parental Monitoring During Adolescence: A Meta-Analysis," *European Journal of Developmental Psychology* 16, no. 5 (2018): 552–80, https://doi.org/10.1080/17405629.2018.1476233.
66 Michaela Geržičáková et al., "What Do Parents Know About Children's Risky Online Experiences? The Role of Parental Mediation Strategies," *Computers in Human Behavior* 141 (2022): 107626, https://doi.org/10.1016/j.chb.2022.107626.
67 Albert Kienfie Liau et al., "Parental Awareness and Monitoring of Adolescent Internet Use," *Current Psychology* 27, no. 4 (2008): 217–33, https://doi.org/10.1007/s12144-008-9038-6.

68. Symons et al., "Parental Knowledge of Adolescents' Online Content and Contact Risks."
69. Dylan Walsh, "Study: Social Media Use Linked to Decline in Mental Health," *MIT Management Sloan School*, September 14, 2022, https://mitsloan.mit.edu/ideas-made-to-matter/study-social-media-use-linked-to-decline-mental-health.
70. Luca Braghieri et al., "Social Media and Mental Health," *SSRN Electronic Journal*, 2021, https://doi.org/10.2139/ssrn.3919760.
71. Sarmistha Dutta et al., "Measuring the Impact of Anxiety on Online Social Interactions," *Proceedings of the International AAAI Conference on Web and Social Media* 12, no. 1 (2018), https://doi.org/10.1609/icwsm.v12i1.15081.
72. Tanja Poulain et al., "Reciprocal Associations Between Electronic Media Use and Behavioral Difficulties in Preschoolers," *International Journal of Environmental Research and Public Health* 15, no. 4 (2018): 10, https://doi.org/10.3390/ijerph15040814.
73. Rasmussen et al., "The Serially Mediated Relationship Between Emerging Adults' Social Media Use and Mental Well-Being," 211.
74. Hoge et al., "Digital Media, Anxiety, and Depression in Children," S78.
75. Joseph Ciarrochi et al., "The Development of Compulsive Internet Use and Mental Health: A Four-year Study of Adolescence," *Developmental Psychology* 52, no. 2 (2015): 272–83, https://doi.org/10.1037/dev0000070.
76. Betul Keles et al., "A Systematic Review: The Influence of Social Media on Depression, Anxiety and Psychological Distress in Adolescents," *International Journal of Adolescence and Youth* 25, no. 1 (2019): 89, https://doi.org/10.1080/02673843.2019.1590851.
77. Arianna Sala et al., "Social Media Use and Adolescents' Mental Health and Well-Being: An Umbrella Review," *Computers in Human Behavior Reports* 14 (2024): 100404, https://doi.org/10.1016/j.chbr.2024.100404.
78. Pamela Wisniewski et al., "Parents Just Don't Understand: Why Teens Don't Talk to Parents About Their Online Risk Experiences," in *CSCQ '17: Proceedings of the 2017 ACM Conference on Computer Supported Cooperative Work and Social Computing*, Portland, Oregon, 2017, 523–40.
79. Aubrey V. Herrera et al., "How Mental Health Interviews Conducted Alone, in the Presence of an Adult, a Child or Both Affects Adolescents' Reporting of Psychological Symptoms and Risky Behaviors," *Journal of Youth and Adolescence* 46, no. 2 (2016): 417–28, https://doi.org/10.1007/s10964-016-0418-1.
80. Eric E. Rasmussen et al., "Adolescents' Disclosure of Mental Illness to Parents: Preferences and Barriers," *Health Communication* 37, no. 3 (2020): 346–55, https://doi.org/10.1080/10410236.2020.1839201.
81. Stefania Mancone et al., "Integrating Digital and Interactive Approaches in Adolescent Health Literacy: A Comprehensive Review," *Frontiers in Public Health* 12 (2024), https://doi.org/10.3389/fpubh.2024.1387874.
82. Maria Y. Hernandez and Kurt C. Organista, "Entertainment–Education? A Fotonovela? A New Strategy to Improve Depression Literacy and Help-Seeking Behaviors in At-Risk Immigrant Latinas," *American Journal of Community Psychology* 52, no. 3–4 (2013): 224–35, https://doi.org/10.1007/s10464-013-9587-1.

83 Anat Klin and Dafna Lemish, "Mental Disorders Stigma in the Media: Review of Studies on Production, Content, and Influences," *Journal of Health Communication* 13, no. 5 (2008): 434–49, https://doi.org/10.1080/10810730802198813.
84 Jane Pirkis et al., "On-Screen Portrayals of Mental Illness: Extent, Nature, and Impacts," *Journal of Health Communication* 11, no. 5 (2006): 523–41, https://doi.org/10.1080/10810730600755889.
85 Rachel E. Riggs and Eric E. Rasmussen, "The Influence of Video-Modeled Sexual Assault Disclosure and Self-Efficacy Messages on Sexual Assault Disclosure Efficacy of Adolescent Girls," *Journal of Health Communication* (2021): 1–10, https://doi.org/10.1080/10810730.2021.1943729.
86 "Mister Fred Rogers: Senate Statement on PBS Funding," *American Rhetoric*, last modified April 26, 2024, https://www.americanrhetoric.com/speeches/fredrogerssenatetestimonypbs.htm.

Chapter 10

1 Frederick James Smith, "The Evolution of the Motion Picture," *The New York Dramatic Mirror*, July 9, 1913.
2 "Our Story," Fred Rogers Productions, accessed April 18, 2025, https://www.fredrogers.org/our-story/.
3 American Rhetoric, "Mister Fred Rogers."
4 *The Charters and General Laws of the Colony and Province of Massachusetts Bay* (T.B. Waite & Co, 1814), 73–74.
5 David Carleton, "Old Deluder Satan Act of 1647," *Free Speech Center at Middle Tennessee State University*, January 1, 2009, https://firstamendment.mtsu.edu/article/old-deluder-satan-act-of-1647.
6 *The Laws and Liberties of Massachusetts: Old Deluder Satan Law of 1647* (Harvard University Press, 1929).
7 Ellwood P. Cubberley, *Readings in the History of Education* (Boston, Massachusetts: Houghton Mifflin Company, 1920).
8 Martin Luther, "A Sermon or Discourse of Martin Luther: That Children Be Kept at School," *The Open Court*, 423–32, https://opensiuc.lib.siu.edu/cgi/viewcontent.cgi?article=1067&context=ocj.
9 Luther, "A Sermon or Discourse of Martin Luther," 432.
10 Tolson, "Is There Room for the Soul?"
11 Martin Luther King, Jr., "The Purpose of Education," *Maroon Tiger*, January 1, 1947, https://kinginstitute.stanford.edu/king-papers/documents/purpose-education#fn1.
12 Mallory Hutchings-Tryon, "Yes, School Should Teach Morality. But Whose Morals?," *Time*, January 9, 2024, https://time.com/6451192/history-civic-morality-schools/.
13 Xitao Fan and Michael Chen, "Parental Involvement and Students' Academic Achievement: A Meta-Analysis," *Educational Psychology Review* 13 (2001): 1–22, https://doi.org/10.1023/A:1009048817385.

14 Nancy E. Hill and Diana F. Tyson, "Parental Involvement in Middle School: A Meta-Analytic Assessment of the Strategies that Promote Achievement," *Developmental Psychology* 45, no. 3 (2009): 740–63, https://doi.org/10.1037/a0015362.
15 William H. Jeynes, "The Relationship Between Parental Involvement and Urban Secondary School Student Academic Achievement," *Urban Education* 42, no. 1 (2006): 82–110, https://doi.org/10.1177/0042085906293818.
16 Beng Huat See and Stephen Gorard, "The Role of Parents in Young People's Education—A Critical Review of the Causal Evidence," *Oxford Review of Education* 41, no. 3 (2015): 346–66, https://doi.org/10.1080/03054985.2015.1031648.
17 Alma Harris and Janet Goodall, "Do Parents Know They Matter? Engaging All Parents in Learning," *Educational Research* 50, no. 3 (2008): 277, https://doi.org/10.1080/00131880802309424.
18 Lant Pritchett, *The Rebirth of Education: Schooling Ain't Learning* (Washington, D.C.: Center for Global Development, 2013).
19 Pritchett, *The Rebirth of Education*, 18–19.
20 Harris and Goodall, "Do Parents Know They Matter?"
21 Lisa Boonk et al., "A Review of the Relationship Between Parental Involvement Indicators and Academic Achievement," *Educational Research Review* 24 (2018): 10–30, https://doi.org/10.1016/j.edurev.2018.02.001.
22 Ernest L. Boyer, *Ready To Learn: A Mandate for the Nation* (Princeton, New Jersey: Jossey-Bass, 1991), 84.
23 Gabrielle A. Strouse et al., "Effective Coviewing: Preschoolers' Learning From Video After a Dialogic Questioning Intervention," *Developmental Psychology* 49, no. 12 (2013): 2368–82, https://doi.org/10.1037/a0032463.
24 Roger Jon Desmond et al., "Family Mediation Patterns and Television Viewing," *Human Communication Research* 11, no. 4 (1985): 461–80, https://doi.org/10.1111/j.1468-2958.1985.tb00056.x.
25 Roger Jon Desmond et al., "Gender Differences, Mediation, and Disciplinary Styles in Children's Responses to Television," *Sex Roles* 16, no. 7–8 (1987): 375–89, https://doi.org/10.1007/bf00289549.
26 Prachi E. Shah et al., "Daily Television Exposure, Parent Conversation During Shared Television Viewing and Socioeconomic Status: Associations with Curiosity at Kindergarten," *PLoS ONE* 16, no. 10 (2021): e0258572, https://doi.org/10.1371/journal.pone.0258572.
27 Jerome L. Singer et al., "Family Mediation and Children's Cognition, Aggression, and Comprehension of Television: A Longitudinal Study," *Journal of Applied Developmental Psychology* 9, no. 3 (1988): 329–47, https://doi.org/10.1016/0193-3973(88)90034-2.
28 Gavriel Salomon, "Effects of Encouraging Israeli Mothers to Co-Observe 'Sesame Street' With Their Five-Year-Olds," *Child Development* 48, no. 3 (1977): 1146, https://doi.org/10.2307/1128378.
29 Rasmussen et al., "Explaining Parental Coviewing."
30 Chakroff and Nathanson, "Parent and School Interventions."
31 Lauren J. Myers et al., "Eyes in the Room Trump Eyes on the Screen: Effects of a Responsive Co-Viewer on Toddlers' Responses to and Learning From Video

32 Bruce Watkins et al., "Children's Recall of Television Material: Effects of Presentation Mode and Adult Labeling," *Developmental Psychology* 16, no. 6 (1980): 672–4, https://doi.org/10.1037/0012-1649.16.6.672.
33 Liebeskind, "The Exploration of U.S. Parents' Television Mediation Through Genre-Specific Scenarios."
34 Gentile et al., "Protective Effects of Parental Monitoring of Children's Media Use," 479.
35 Yuanhao Zhang et al., "How Does Parental Autonomy Support Influence Adolescents' Academic Performance? The Mediating Roles of Active Parental Internet Mediation and Parent–Child Cohesion," *Current Psychology*, 2024, https://doi.org/10.1007/s12144-024-06316-7.
36 Samuel Ball and Gerry Ann Bogatz, "A Summary of the Major Findings in "The First Year of Sesame Street: An Evaluation," Educational Testing Service, 1970.
37 Dorr et al., "Parent-Child Coviewing of Television."
38 P. S. Klein et al., "The Use of Computers in Kindergarten, With or Without Adult Mediation: Effects on Children's Cognitive Performance and Behavior," *Computers in Human Behavior* 16, no. 6 (2000): 591–608, https://doi.org/10.1016/s0747-5632(00)00027-3.
39 Klein et al., "The Use of Computers in Kindergarten, With or Without Adult Mediation," 603.
40 Angela C. Santomero, *Preschool Clues* (Touchstone, 2018).
41 Gabrielle A. Strouse et al., "Co-viewing Supports Toddlers' Word Learning from Contingent and Noncontingent Video," *Journal of Experimental Child Psychology* 166 (2017): 310–26, https://doi.org/10.1016/j.jecp.2017.09.005.
42 Singer et al., "Family Mediation and Children's Cognition, Aggression, and Comprehension of Television."
43 Ofra Korat and Daphna Shneor, "Can E-books Support Low SES Parental Mediation to Enrich Children's Vocabulary?" *First Language* 39, no. 3 (2019): 344–64, https://doi.org/10.1177/0142723718822443.
44 Ofra Korat et al., "Maternal Mediation in Book Reading, Home Literacy Environment, and Children's Emergent Literacy: A Comparison Between Two Social Groups," *Reading and Writing* 20, no. 4 (2006): 361–98, https://doi.org/10.1007/s11145-006-9034-x.
45 Melissa Morgenlander, "Adult-Child Co-Viewing of Educational Television: Enhancing Preschoolers' Understanding of Mathematics Shown on "Sesame Street" (PhD diss., Columbia University, 2010).
46 Patti M. Valkenburg et al., "The Impact of a Cultural Children's Program and Adult Mediation on Children's Knowledge of and Attitudes Towards Opera," *Journal of Broadcasting & Electronic Media* 42, no. 3 (1998): 315–26, https://doi.org/10.1080/08838159809364452.
47 Naya Choi et al., "Newspaper Reading in Families with School-Age Children: Relationship Between Parent–Child Interaction Using Newspaper, Reading Motivation, and Academic Achievement," *International Journal of Environmental Research and Public Health* 19, no. 21 (2022): 14423, https://doi.org/10.3390/ijerph192114423.

48 Mabel L. Rice et al., "Words from 'Sesame Street': Learning Vocabulary While Viewing," *Developmental Psychology* 26, no. 3 (1990): 421–8.
49 Bihui Jin and Danhui Zhang, "Linking Parental Restrictive Mediation to Adolescents' Science Achievement: A Social Cognitive Theory Perspective," *Learning and Individual Differences* 98 (2022): 102187, https://doi.org/10.1016/j.lindif.2022.102187.
50 Simin Cao et al., "Parental Beliefs and Mediation Co-Mediate the SES Effect on Chinese Preschoolers' Early Digital Literacy: A Chain-Mediation Model," *Education and Information Technologies* 29, no. 10 (2023): 12093–114, https://doi.org/10.1007/s10639-023-12300-8.
51 Jiaxue Lou et al., "The Association Between Family Socio-Demographic Factors, Parental Mediation and Adolescents' Digital Literacy: A Cross-sectional Study," *BMC Public Health* 24, no. 1 (2024), https://doi.org/10.1186/s12889-024-20284-4.
52 Erica Weintraub Austin, "Exploring the Effects of Active Parental Mediation of Television Content," *Journal of Broadcasting & Electronic Media* 37, no. 2 (1993): 147–58, https://doi.org/10.1080/08838159309364212.
53 Yueqi Shi and Shaowei Qu, "The Effect of Cognitive Ability on Academic Achievement: The Mediating Role of Self-Discipline and the Moderating Role of Planning," *Frontiers in Psychology* 13 (2022), https://doi.org/10.3389/fpsyg.2022.1014655.
54 Peng Peng and Rogier A. Kievit, "The Development of Academic Achievement and Cognitive Abilities: A Bidirectional Perspective," *Child Development Perspectives* 14, no. 1 (2020): 15–20, https://doi.org/10.1111/cdep.12352.
55 Peng and Kievit, "The Development of Academic Achievement and Cognitive Abilities."
56 An and Lee, "An Integrated Model of Parental Mediation."
57 Zhao Jinqiu and Hao Xiaoming, "Parent–Child Co-Viewing of Television and Cognitive Development of the Chinese Child," *International Journal of Early Years Education* 12, no. 1 (2004): 63–77, https://doi.org/10.1080/0966976042000182389.
58 Eun-Young Lee et al., "Television Viewing, Reading, Physical Activity and Brain Development Among Young South Korean Children," *Journal of Science and Medicine in Sport* 20, no. 7 (2017): 676, https://doi.org/10.1016/j.jsams.2016.11.014.
59 John S. Hutton et al., "Associations Between Screen-Based Media Use and Brain White Matter Integrity in Preschool-Aged Children," *JAMA Pediatrics* 174, no. 1 (2019): e193869, https://doi.org/10.1001/jamapediatrics.2019.3869.
60 John S. Hutton et al., "Associations Between Digital Media Use and Brain Surface Structural Measures in Preschool-Aged Children," *Scientific Reports* 12, no. 1 (2022), https://doi.org/10.1038/s41598-022-20922-0.
61 Tzipi Horowitz-Kraus and John S. Hutton, "Brain Connectivity in Children is Increased by the Time They Spend Reading Books and Decreased by the Length of Exposure to Screen-Based Media," *Acta Paediatrica* 107, no. 4 (2017): 685–93, https://doi.org/10.1111/apa.14176.
62 Maria T. Maza et al., "Association of Habitual Checking Behaviors on Social Media with Longitudinal Functional Brain Development," *JAMA Pediatrics* 177, no. 2 (2023): 160, https://doi.org/10.1001/jamapediatrics.2022.4924.

63 Yuan-Wei Yao et al., "Functional and Structural Neural Alterations in Internet Gaming Disorder: A Systematic Review and Meta-Analysis," *Neuroscience & Biobehavioral Reviews* 83 (2017): 313–24, https://doi.org/10.1016/j.neubiorev.2017.10.029.
64 Victor G. Carrion et al., "Stress Predicts Brain Changes in Children: A Pilot Longitudinal Study on Youth Stress, Posttraumatic Stress Disorder, and the Hippocampus," *Pediatrics* 119, no. 3 (2007): 509–16, https://doi.org/10.1542/peds.2006-2028.
65 Michael D. De Bellis et al., "Developmental Traumatology Part II: Brain Development," *Biological Psychiatry* 45, no. 10 (1999): 1271, https://doi.org/10.1016/s0006-3223(99)00045-1.
66 Sarah Whittle et al., "Observed Measures of Negative Parenting Predict Brain Development During Adolescence," *PLoS ONE* 11, no. 1 (2016): e0147774, https://doi.org/10.1371/journal.pone.0147774.
67 Sarah Whittle et al., "Positive Parenting Predicts the Development of Adolescent Brain Structure: A Longitudinal Study," *Developmental Cognitive Neuroscience* 8 (2013): 7–17, https://doi.org/10.1016/j.dcn.2013.10.006.
68 Isabella Kahhalé et al., "Positive Parenting Moderates Associations Between Childhood Stress and Corticolimbic Structure," *PNAS Nexus* 2, no. 6 (2023): 6, https://doi.org/10.1093/pnasnexus/pgad145.
69 Seulgi Lee et al., "Differential Role of Negative and Positive Parenting Styles on Resting-State Brain Networks in Middle-Aged Adolescents," *Journal of Affective Disorders* 365 (2024): 222–29, https://doi.org/10.1016/j.jad.2024.08.096.
70 Erica Weintraub Austin and Bruce E. Pinkleton, "The Role of Parental Mediation in the Political Socialization Process," *Journal of Broadcasting & Electronic Media* 45, no. 2 (2001): 221–40, https://doi.org/10.1207/s15506878jobem4502_2.
71 Jay Belsky and Michelle De Haan, "Annual Research Review: Parenting and Children's Brain Development: The End of the Beginning," *Journal of Child Psychology and Psychiatry* 52, no. 4 (2010): 409, https://doi.org/10.1111/j.1469-7610.2010.02281.x.
72 Belsky and De Haan, "Annual Research Review: Parenting and Children's Brain Development," 409–10.
73 Oakley Ray, "How the Mind Hurts and Heals the Body," *American Psychologist* 59, no. 1 (2004): 29, https://doi.org/10.1037/0003-066x.59.1.29.
74 Glenn N. Levine et al., "Psychological Health, Well-Being, and the Mind-Heart-Body Connection: A Scientific Statement from the American Heart Association," *Circulation* 143, no. 10 (2021): e764, https://doi.org/10.1161/cir.0000000000000947.
75 Levine et al., "Psychological Health, Well-Being, and the Mind-Heart-Body Connection," e764.

Chapter 11

1 Jaccard and Jacoby, *Theory Construction and Model-Building Skills*, 30.
2 Jaccard and Jacoby, *Theory Construction and Model-Building Skills*, 30.
3 Timothy R. Levine and David M. Markowitz, "The Role of Theory in Researching and Understanding Human Communication," *Human Communication Research* 50, no. 2 (2023): 157, https://doi.org/10.1093/hcr/hqad037.

4 Amy I. Nathanson, "The Effects of Mediation Content on Children's Responses to Violent Television: Comparing Cognitive and Affective Approaches" (paper presented at the annual meeting of the International Communication Association, San Diego, CA, 2003), 3.
5 Rasmussen, "Theoretical Underpinnings of Reducing the Media's Negative Effect on Children," 399.
6 Valkenburg et al., "Developing and Validating the Perceived Parental Media Mediation Scale," 461.
7 Levine and Markowitz, "The Role of Theory in Researching and Understanding Human Communication," 159.
8 Valkenburg et al., "Developing a Scale to Assess Three Styles of Television Mediation."
9 Valkenburg et al., "Developing a Scale to Assess Three Styles of Television Mediation," 53.
10 Livingstone and Helsper, "Parental Mediation of Children's Internet Use."
11 Nikken and Jansz, "Developing Scales to Measure Parental Mediation of Young Children's Internet Use."
12 Valkenburg et al., "Developing and Validating the Perceived Parental Media Mediation Scale."
13 Galit Nimrod et al., "Measuring Mediation of Children's Media Use," *International Journal of Communication* 13, 2019: 342–58, https://ijoc.org/index.php/ijoc/article/view/10237/2535.
14 Lenka Dedkova and Vojtěch Mýlek, "Parental Mediation of Online Interactions and its Relation to Adolescents' Contacts With New People Online: The Role of Risk Perception," *Information Communication & Society* 26, no. 16 (2022): 3179–96, https://doi.org/10.1080/1369118x.2022.2146985.
15 Kateřina Lukavská et al., "Measuring Parental Behavior Towards Children's Use of Media and Screen-devices: The Development and Psychometrical Properties of a Media Parenting Scale for Parents of School-aged Children," *International Journal of Environmental Research and Public Health* 18, no. 17 (2021): 9178, https://doi.org/10.3390/ijerph18179178.
16 Lukavská et al., "Measuring Parental Behavior Towards Children's Use of Media and Screen-devices," 10–11.
17 Symons et al., "A Factorial Validation of Parental Mediation Strategies With Regard to Internet Use."
18 Seffetullah Kuldas et al., "A Review and Content Validation of 10 Measurement Scales for Parental Mediation of Children's Internet Use," *International Journal of Communication* (2021): 4062, https://ijoc.org/index.php/ijoc/article/view/17265.
19 Lukavská et al., "Measuring Parental Behavior Towards Children's Use of Media and Screen-devices," 10.
20 Michael D. Slater and Laurel S. Gleason, "Contributing to Theory and Knowledge in Quantitative Communication Science," *Communication Methods and Measures* 6, no. 4 (2012): 216, https://doi.org/10.1080/19312458.2012.732626.
21 Slater and Gleason, "Contributing to Theory and Knowledge in Quantitative Communication Science," 218.
22 Slater and Gleason, "Contributing to Theory and Knowledge in Quantitative Communication Science," 219.

23 Rasmussen, "Theoretical Underpinnings of Reducing the Media's Negative Effect on Children."
24 James Price Dillard, "Persuasion," in *The Handbook of Communication Science*, 2nd ed., ed. Charles R. Berger, Michael E. Roloff, and David R. Roskos-Ewoldsen (Thousand Oaks, California: Sage, 2010), 203–18.
25 Shwadhin Sharma and Ching Yee Lee, "Parental Mediation and Preferences for Regulation Regarding Children's Digital Media Use: Role of Protection Motivation and Theory of Planned Behaviour," *Behaviour and Information Technology* 43, no. 8 (2023): 1499–517, https://doi.org/10.1080/0144929x.2023.2217275.
26 Ronald W. Rogers, "A Protection Motivation Theory of Fear Appeals and Attitude Change," *The Journal of Psychology* 91, no. 1 (1975): 93–114, https://doi.org/10.1080/00223980.1975.9915803.
27 Sharma and Lee, "Parental Mediation and Preferences for Regulation Regarding Children's Digital Media Use."
28 Sharma and Lee, "Parental Mediation and Preferences for Regulation Regarding Children's Digital Media Use," 1510.
29 Rasmussen et al., "Explaining Parental Coviewing."
30 Robert B. Zajonc, "Social Facilitation," *Science* 149, no. 3681 (1965): 269–74, https://doi.org/10.1126/science.149.3681.269.
31 Rasmussen et al., "Explaining Parental Coviewing," 380.
32 Gerlese S. Åkerlind and Carole Kayrooz, "Understanding Academic Freedom: The Views of Social Scientists," *Higher Education Research & Development* 22, no. 3 (2003): 327–44, https://doi.org/10.1080/0729436032000145176.
33 Kerlind and Kayrooz, "Understanding Academic Freedom," 336.
34 Jo Orsatti and Kai Riemer, "Identity-making: A Multimodal Approach for Researching Identity in Social Media," in *European Conference on Information Systems*, 2015, https://doi.org/10.18151/7217439.
35 Fred Rogers Center (@FredRogersCtr), "Who You Are Inside is What Helps You Make and Do Everything in Life," *Twitter (now X)*, February 5, 2019, https://twitter.com/FredRogersCtr.
36 Giovanna Colombetti, *The Feeling Body: Affective Science Meets the Enactive Mind* (Cambridge, Massachusetts: MIT Press, 2014).
37 Eric G. Zook, "Embodied Health and Constitutive Communication: Toward an Authentic Conceptualization of Health Communication, in *Communication Yearbook 17*, ed. Stanley A. Deetz (New York, NY: Routledge, 1994), 344–77.
38 Zook, "Embodied Health and Constitutive Communication," 364.
39 Zook, "Embodied Health and Constitutive Communication," 364.
40 Beauregard, "Mind Does Really Matter," 232, https://doi.org/10.1016/j.pneurobio.2007.01.005.
41 Demertzi et al., "Dualism Persists in the Science of Mind."
42 Demertzi et al., "Dualism Persists in the Science of Mind," 7.
43 J. Fahrenberg and M. Cheetham, "The Mind-Body Problem as Seen by Students of Different Disciplines," *Journal of Consciousness Studies* 7, no. 5 (2000): 47–59.
44 Pew Research Center, "Spirituality Among Americans," December 7, 2023, https://www.pewresearch.org/religion/2023/12/07/spirituality-among-americans/.
45 Barbara L. Fredrickson and Tomi-Ann Roberts, "Objectification Theory: Toward Understanding Women's Lived Experiences and Mental Health Risks," *Psychology

of *Women Quarterly* 21, no. 2 (1997): 175, https://doi.org/10.1111/j.1471-6402.1997.tb00108.x.

46 Elizabeth J. Krumrei-Mancuso et al., "Links Between Intellectual Humility and Acquiring Knowledge," *The Journal of Positive Psychology* 15, no. 2 (2019): 155–70, https://doi.org/10.1080/17439760.2019.1579359.
47 David R. Ewoldsen, "A Discussion of Falsifiability and Evaluating Research: Issues of Variance Accounted for and External Validity," *Asian Communication Research* 19, no. 2 (2022): 46, https://doi.org/10.20879/acr.2022.19.2.38.
48 Ewoldsen, "A Discussion of Falsifiability and Evaluating Research," 45.

Chapter 12

1 Elizabeth Bass, "The Importance of Bringing Science and Medicine to Lay Audiences," *Circulation* 133, no. 23 (2016): 2334, https://doi.org/10.1161/circulationaha.116.023297.
2 Bass, "The Importance of Bringing Science and Medicine to Lay Audiences," 2334.
3 Demertzi et al., "Dualism Persists in the Science of Mind."
4 Pew Research Center, "Spirituality Among Americans."
5 Larson and Witham, "Scientists Are Still Keeping the Faith."
6 Demertzi et al., "Dualism Persists in the Science of Mind," 8.
7 Suparna Choudhury et al., "Rebelling Against the Brain: Public Engagement With the 'Neurological Adolescent,'" *Social Science & Medicine* 74, no. 4 (2011): 565–73, https://doi.org/10.1016/j.socscimed.2011.10.029.
8 Martyn Pickersgill et al., "Constituting Neurologic Subjects: Neuroscience, Subjectivity and the Mundane Significance of the Brain," *Subjectivity* 4, no. 3 (2011): 346–65, https://doi.org/10.1057/sub.2011.10.
9 O'Connor and Joffe, "How Has Neuroscience Affected Lay Understandings of Personhood?"
10 O'Connor and Joffe, "How Has Neuroscience Affected Lay Understandings of Personhood?" 263.
11 Alice H. Eagly and Kathleen Telaak, "Width of the Latitude of Acceptance as a Determinant of Attitude Change," *Journal of Personality and Social Psychology* 23, no. 3 (1972): 388–97, https://doi.org/10.1037/h0033161.
12 Demertzi et al., "Dualism Persists in the Science of Mind," 8.
13 Demertzi et al., "Dualism Persists in the Science of Mind," 8.

Conclusion

1 Erik E. Noftle, "Character Across Early Emerging Adulthood: Character Traits, Character Strivings, and Moral Self-Attributes," in *Character: New Directions from Philosophy, Psychology, and Theology*, ed. Christian B. Miller, R. Michael Furr, Angela Knobel, and William Fleeson (Oxford, UK: Oxford University Press, 2015), 493.

2. Sarah Clement and Richard Bollinger, "Perspectives on Character Virtue Development," *Research in Human Development* 13, no. 2 (2016): 174–81, https://doi.org/10.1080/15427609.2016.1172445.
3. Dario Perinetti, "The Nature of Virtue," in *The Oxford Handbook of British Philosophy in the Eighteenth Century*, ed. James A. Harris (Oxford, UK: Oxford University Press, 2013), 333.
4. Taya R. Cohen and Lily Morse, "Moral Character: What It Is and What It Does," *Research in Organizational Behavior* 34 (2014): 43–61, https://doi.org/10.1016/j.riob.2014.08.003.
5. Cohen and Morse, "Moral Character."
6. Ross A. Thompson and Abby S. Lavine, "The Development of Virtuous Character: Automatic and Reflective Dispositions," in *Developing the Virtues: Integrating Perspectives*, ed. Julia Annas, Darcia Narvaez, and Nancy E. Snow (Oxford, UK: Oxford University Press, 2016).
7. Noftle, "Character Across Early Emerging Adulthood."
8. Peterson and Seligman, *Character Strengths and Virtues*.
9. Noftle, "Character Across Early Emerging Adulthood," 498.
10. VIA Institute on Character, *The VIA Classification of 24 Character Strengths*, VIACharacter.org, https://via-assets.global.ssl.fastly.net/76d1ea39-a4eb-4270-b9dc-899653415f8f/assets/VirtuesClassification-2021(R).pdf.
11. Noftle, "Character Across Early Emerging Adulthood."
12. James Aluri and Margot Kelly-Hedrick, "50 Years of Character Assessment: A Scoping Review of Psychometric Instruments Measuring Character or Virtues," *Applied Research in Quality of Life* 18, no. 4 (2023): 2107–29, https://doi.org/10.1007/s11482-023-10179-8.
13. NPR, "Read Martin Luther King Jr.'s 'I Have a Dream' Speech in its Entirety," January 16, 2023, https://www.npr.org/2010/01/18/122701268/i-have-a-dream-speech-in-its-entirety.
14. Chaim Potok, *My Name is Asher Lev* (New York, NY: Knopf, 1972).

BIBLIOGRAPHY

A˚Kerlind, Gerlese S., and Carole Kayrooz. "Understanding Academic Freedom: The Views of Social Scientists." *Higher Education Research & Development* 22, no. 3 (2003): 327–44. https://doi.org/10.1080/0729436032000145176.

Abebe, Tatek. "Reconceptualising Children's Agency as Continuum and Interdependence." *Social Sciences* 8, no. 3 (2019): 81. https://doi.org/10.3390/socsci8030081.

Achtergarde, Sandra, Christian Postert, Ida Wessing, Georg Romer, and Jörg M. Müller. "Parenting and Child Mental Health." *The Family Journal* 23, no. 2 (2014): 167–79. https://doi.org/10.1177/1066480714564316.

Ackerson, Barry J. "Coping with the Dual Demands of Severe Mental Illness and Parenting: The Parents' Perspective." *Families in Society: The Journal of Contemporary Social Services* 84, no. 1 (2003): 109–18. https://doi.org/10.1606/1044-3894.69.

Adamson, Lauren B., Roger Bakeman, and Deborah F. Deckner. "The Development of Symbol-Infused Joint Engagement." *Child Development* 75, no. 4 (2004): 1171–87. https://doi.org/10.1111/j.1467-8624.2004.00732.x.

Adigwe, Ifeanyi, Jon Mason, and Nicolas Gromik. "Investigating the Relationship Between Socio-Demographic Variables of Parents, Digital Literacy and Parental Mediation Practices in the Digital Age: Nigeria in Focus." *E-Learning and Digital Media* 22, no. 3 (2024). https://doi.org/10.1177/20427530241232495.

Ahmad, Jamilah, Ugwuoke C. Joel, Felix Olajide Talabi, et al. "Impact of Social Media-based Intervention in Reducing Youths' Propensity to Engage in Drug Abuse in Nigeria." *Evaluation and Program Planning* 94 (2022): 102122. https://doi.org/10.1016/j.evalprogplan.2022.102122.

Akcinar, Berna, and Nazli Baydar. "Parental Control is Not Unconditionally Detrimental for Externalizing Behaviors in Early Childhood." *International Journal of Behavioral Development* 38, no. 2 (2014): 118–27. https://doi.org/10.1177/0165025413513701.

Akungu, Okwach Alphonce, Sufen Chen, and Chiu-Hung Su. "Longitudinal Association of Adolescents' Perceptions of Parental Mediations and Compulsive Internet Use." *Computers in Human Behavior* 150 (2023): 107989. https://doi.org/10.1016/j.chb.2023.107989.

Aldrich, Naomi J., Jing Chen, and Louis Alfieri. "Evaluating Associations Between Parental Mind-mindedness and Children's Developmental Capacities Through Meta-Analysis." *Developmental Review* 60 (2021): 100946. https://doi.org/10.1016/j.dr.2021.100946.

Aluri, James, and Margot Kelly-Hedrick. "50 Years of Character Assessment: A Scoping Review of Psychometric Instruments Measuring Character or Virtues." *Applied Research in Quality of Life* 18, no. 4 (2023): 2107–29. https://doi.org/10.1007/s11482-023-10179-8.

American Academy of Pediatrics. *AAP-AACAP-CHA Declaration of a National Emergency in Child and Adolescent Mental Health*, 2021. https://www.aap.org/en/advocacy/child-and-adolescent-healthy-mental-development/aap-aacap-cha-declaration-of-a-national-emergency-in-child-and-adolescent-mental-health.

Amrock, Stephen M., and Michael Weitzman. "Parental Psychological Distress and Children's Mental Health: Results of a National Survey." *Academic Pediatrics* 14, no. 4 (2014): 375–81. https://doi.org/10.1016/j.acap.2014.02.005.

An, Seon-Kyoung, and Doohwang Lee. "An Integrated Model of Parental Mediation: The Effect of Family Communication on Children's Perception of Television Reality and Negative Viewing Effects." *Asian Journal of Communication* 20, no. 4 (2010): 389–403. https://doi.org/10.1080/01292986.2010.496864.

Anyaegbunam, Emenike N., Chiedu Eseadi, Chinyere Augusta Nwajiuba, et al. "Parental Mediation as a Moderator of the Relationship Between Violent Media Contents Exposure and Aggressive Behaviour of In-School Adolescents." *Global Journal of Health Science* 11, no. 14 (2019): 1. https://doi.org/10.5539/gjhs.v11n14p1.

APA Dictionary of Psychology. "Communication." April 19, 2018. https://dictionary.apa.org/folk-psychology.

APA Dictionary of Psychology. "Folk Psychology." April 19, 2018. https://dictionary.apa.org/folk-psychology.

Armstrong, Jennifer Keishin. "The Evolution of the Family Sitcom." *Peabody Finds*. Accessed April 29, 2025. https://peabodyawards.com/stories/the-evolution-of-the-family-sitcom/.

Atkin, Charles K., and Bradley S. Greenberg. "Parental Mediation of Children's Social Behavior Learning from Television." Report No. 4, U.S. Office of Child Development, 1977. https://eric.ed.gov/?id=ED151808.

Atkin, David J., Bradley S. Greenberg, and Thomas F. Baldwin. "The Home Ecology of Children's Television Viewing: Parental Mediation and the New Video Environment." *Journal of Communication* 41, no. 3 (1991): 40–52. https://doi.org/10.1111/j.1460-2466.1991.tb02322.x.

Aufderheide, Patricia. "Media Literacy: A Report of the National Leadership Conference on Media Literacy." Aspen Institute, 1993.

Austin, Erica Weintraub. "Exploring the Effects of Active Parental Mediation of Television Content." *Journal of Broadcasting & Electronic Media* 37, no. 2 (1993): 147–58. https://doi.org/10.1080/08838159309364212.

Austin, Erica Weintraub, Paul Bolls, Yuki Fujioka, and Jason Engelbertson. "How And Why Parents Take on the Tube." *Journal of Broadcasting & Electronic Media* 43, no. 2 (1999): 175–92. https://doi.org/10.1080/08838159909364483.

Austin, Erica Weintraub, and Bruce E. Pinkleton. "The Role of Parental Mediation in the Political Socialization Process." *Journal of Broadcasting & Electronic Media* 45, no. 2 (2001): 221–40. https://doi.org/10.1207/s15506878jobem4502_2.

Austin, Erica Weintraub, Bruce E. Pinkleton, and Yuki Fujioka. "The Role of Interpretation Processes and Parental Discussion in the Media's Effects on Adolescents' Use of Alcohol." *Pediatrics* 105, no. 2 (2000): 343–49. https://doi.org/10.1542/peds.105.2.343.

Austin, Erica Weintraub, Bruce E. Pinkleton, Marie Louise Radanielina-Hita, and Weina Ran. "The Role of Parents' Critical Thinking About Media in

Shaping Expectancies, Efficacy and Nutrition Behaviors for Families." *Health Communication* 30, no. 12 (2015): 1256–68. https://doi.org/10.1080/10410236.2014.930550.

Ayhan, Aynur Bütün, and Utku Beyazit. "The Associations Between Loneliness and Self-Esteem in Children and Neglectful Behaviors of Their Parents." *Child Indicators Research* 14, no. 5 (2021): 1863–79. https://doi.org/10.1007/s12187-021-09818-z.

Backholer, Kathryn, Adyya Gupta, Christina Zorbas, et al. "Differential Exposure to, and Potential Impact of, Unhealthy Advertising to Children by Socio-Economic and Ethnic Groups: A Systematic Review of the Evidence." *Obesity Reviews* 22, no. 3 (2020). https://doi.org/10.1111/obr.13144.

Badri, Masood, Ali Alnuaimi, Asma Al Rashedi, Guang Yang, and Khaled Temsah. "School Children's Use of Digital Devices, Social Media and Parental Knowledge and Involvement – The Case of Abu Dhabi." *Education and Information Technologies* 22, no. 5 (2016): 2645–64. https://doi.org/10.1007/s10639-016-9557-y.

Bagley, Sarah, Jo Salmon, and David Crawford. "Family Structure and Children's Television Viewing and Physical Activity." *Medicine & Science in Sports & Exercise* 38, no. 5 (2006): 910–18. https://doi.org/10.1249/01.mss.0000218132.68268.f4.

Bakeman, Roger, and Lauren B. Adamson. "Coordinating Attention to People and Objects in Mother-Infant and Peer-Infant Interaction." *Child Development* 55, no. 4 (1984): 1278. https://doi.org/10.2307/1129997.

Ball, Samuel, and Gerry Ann Bogatz. "A Summary of the Major Findings in 'The First Year of Sesame Street: An Evaluation.'" Educational Testing Service, 1970.

Bandura, Albert. "Human Agency in Social Cognitive Theory." *American Psychologist* 44, no. 9 (1989): 1175–84. https://doi.org/10.1037/0003-066x.44.9.1175.

Bandura, Albert. "Model of Causality in Social Learning Theory." In *Cognition and Psychotherapy*, edited by Michael J. Mahoney and Arthur Freeman. Plenum Press, 1985.

Bandura, Albert. "Social Cognitive Theory of Mass Communication." In *Media Effects: Advances in Theory and Research*, edited by Jennings Bryant and Mary Beth Oliver, 94–124. Routledge, 2009.

Bandura, Albert. *Social Learning Theory*. Prentice Hall, 1977.

Bandura, Albert. "Toward a Psychology of Human Agency." *Perspectives on Psychological Science* 1, no. 2 (2006): 164–80. https://doi.org/10.1111/j.1745-6916.2006.00011.x.

Barber, Brian K., Joseph E. Olsen, and Shobha C. Shagle. "Associations Between Parental Psychological and Behavioral Control and Youth Internalized and Externalized Behaviors." *Child Development* 65, no. 4 (1994): 1120–36. https://doi.org/10.1111/j.1467-8624.1994.tb00807.x.

Barkin, Shari, Edward Ip, Irma Richardson, Sara Klinepeter, Stacia Finch, and Marina Krcmar. "Parental Media Mediation Styles for Children Aged 2 to 11 Years." *Archives of Pediatrics and Adolescent Medicine* 160, no. 4 (2006): 395. https://doi.org/10.1001/archpedi.160.4.395.

Barr, Elissa M., Michele J. Moore, Tammie Johnson, Julie Merten, and William P. Stewart. "The Relationship Between Screen Time and Sexual Behaviors Among Middle School Students." *Health Educator* 46, no. 1 (2014): 6–13. https://eric.ed.gov/?id=EJ1046859.

Barr, Rachel, Catherine Danziger, Marisa E. Hilliard, Carolyn Andolina, and Jenifer Ruskis. "Amount, Content and Context of Infant Media Exposure: A Parental Questionnaire and Diary Analysis." *International Journal of Early Years Education* 18, no. 2 (2010): 107–22. https://doi.org/10.1080/09669760.2010.494431.

Barrett, Lisa Feldman. "The Future of Psychology: Connecting Mind to Brain." *Perspectives on Psychological Science* 4, no. 4 (2009): 326–39. https://doi.org/10.1111/j.1745-6924.2009.01134.x.

Barry, Christopher T., Chloe L. Sidoti, Shanelle M. Briggs, Shari R. Reiter, and Rebecca A. Lindsey. "Adolescent Social Media Use and Mental Health from Adolescent and Parent Perspectives." *Journal of Adolescence* 61, no. 1 (2017): 1–11. https://doi.org/10.1016/j.adolescence.2017.08.005.

Bass, Elizabeth. "The Importance of Bringing Science and Medicine to Lay Audiences." *Circulation* 133, no. 23 (2016): 2334–37. https://doi.org/10.1161/circulationaha.116.023297.

Bates, C. R., J. Buscemi, L. M. Nicholson, M. Cory, A. Jagpal, and A. M. Bohnert. "Links Between the Organization of the Family Home Environment and Child Obesity: A Systematic Review." *Obesity Reviews* 19, no. 5 (2018): 716–27. https://doi.org/10.1111/obr.12662.

Bausinger, Hermann. "Media, Technology and Daily Life." *Media, Culture and Society* 6 (1984): 349–50. https://doi.org/10.1177/016344378400600403.

Baxter, Leslie A., Carma L. Bylund, Rebecca Imes, and Tracy Routsong. "Parent-Child Perceptions of Parental Behavioral Control Through Rule-Setting for Risky Health Choices During Adolescence." *Journal of Family Communication* 9, no. 4 (2009): 251–71. https://doi.org/10.1080/15267430903255920.

Beauregard, Mario. "Mind Does Really Matter: Evidence from Neuroimaging Studies of Emotional Self-regulation, Psychotherapy, and Placebo Effect." *Progress in Neurobiology* 81, no. 4 (2007): 218–36. https://doi.org/10.1016/j.pneurobio.2007.01.005.

Behm-Morawitz, Elizabeth, Timothy Luisi, and Hillary Pennell. "Parent–Child Communication About Gender and Race Through the Films 'Black Panther' and 'Wonder Woman': The Roles of Parental Mediation and Media Literacy." *Psychology of Popular Media* 11, no. 4 (2022): 382–94. https://doi.org/10.1037/ppm0000405.

Belsky, Jay. "The Determinants of Parenting: A Process Model." *Child Development* 55, no. 1 (1984): 83. https://doi.org/10.2307/1129836.

Belsky, Jay, and Michelle De Haan. "Annual Research Review: Parenting and Children's Brain Development: The End of the Beginning." *Journal of Child Psychology and Psychiatry* 52, no. 4 (2010): 409–28. https://doi.org/10.1111/j.1469-7610.2010.02281.x.

Bennett, Amanda C., Katherine C. Brewer, and Kristin M. Rankin. "The Association of Child Mental Health Conditions and Parent Mental Health Status Among U.S. Children, 2007." *Maternal and Child Health Journal* 16, no. 6 (2011): 1266–75. https://doi.org/10.1007/s10995-011-0888-4.

Berger, Peter. "The Desecularization of the World: A Global Overview." In *The Desecularization of the World: Resurgent Religion and World Politics*, edited by Peter L. Berger. Eerdmans, 1999.

Bergfeld, Nate S., and Jan Van Den Bulck. "It's Not All About the Likes: Social Media Affordances with Nighttime, Problematic, and Adverse Use as Predictors of

Adolescent Sleep Indicators." *Sleep Health* 7, no. 5 (2021): 548–55. https://doi.org/10.1016/j.sleh.2021.05.009.

Bernard, Jonathan Y., Natarajan Padmapriya, Bozhi Chen, et al. "Predictors of Screen Viewing Time in Young Singaporean Children: The GUSTO Cohort." *International Journal of Behavioral Nutrition and Physical Activity* 14, no. 1 (2017). https://doi.org/10.1186/s12966-017-0562-3.

Bersamin, Melina, Michael Todd, Deborah A. Fisher, Douglas L. Hill, Joel W. Grube, and Samantha Walker. "Parenting Practices and Adolescent Sexual Behavior: A Longitudinal Study." *Journal of Marriage and Family* 70, no. 1 (2008): 97–112. https://doi.org/10.1111/j.1741-3737.2007.00464.x.

Beyens, Ine, and Kathleen Beullens. "Parent–Child Conflict About Children's Tablet Use: The Role of Parental Mediation." *New Media & Society* 19, no. 12 (2016): 2075–93. https://doi.org/10.1177/1461444816655099.

Beyens, Ine, Patti M. Valkenburg, and Jessica Taylor Piotrowski. "Developmental Trajectories of Parental Mediation Across Early and Middle Childhood." *Human Communication Research* 45, no. 2 (2018): 226–50. https://doi.org/10.1093/hcr/hqy016.

Bhandari, Tamara. "Mind-Body Connection is Built into Brain, Study Suggests." *WashU Medicine*, April 19, 2023. https://medicine.washu.edu/news/mind-body-connection-is-built-into-brain-study-suggests/.

Bickham, David S., Yulin Hswen, and Michael Rich. "Media Use and Depression: Exposure, Household Rules, and Symptoms Among Young Adolescents in the USA." *International Journal of Public Health* 60, no. 2 (2015): 147–55. https://doi.org/10.1007/s00038-014-0647-6.

Bleakley, Amy, Morgan Ellithorpe, and Daniel Romer. "The Role of Parents in Problematic Internet Use Among US Adolescents." *Media and Communication*, 2016. https://www.cogitatiopress.com/mediaandcommunication/article/view/523/359.

Bleakley, Amy, Amy B. Jordan, and Michael Hennessy. "The Relationship Between Parents' and Children's Television Viewing." *Pediatrics* 132, no. 2 (2013): e364–71. https://doi.org/10.1542/peds.2012-3415.

Bloom, Paul. *Descartes' Baby: How the Science of Child Development Explains What Makes Us Human*. Basic Books/Hachette Book Group, 2004.

Böcking, Saskia, and Tabea Böcking. "Parental Mediation of Television." *Journal of Children and Media* 3, no. 3 (2009): 286–302. https://doi.org/10.1080/17482790902999959.

Bögels, Susan M., Joke Hellemans, Saskia Van Deursen, Marieke Römer, and Rachel Van Der Meulen. "Mindful Parenting in Mental Health Care: Effects on Parental and Child Psychopathology, Parental Stress, Parenting, Coparenting, and Marital Functioning." *Mindfulness* 5, no. 5 (2013): 536–51. https://doi.org/10.1007/s12671-013-0209-7.

Bogl, Leonie H., Kirsten Mehlig, Wolfgang Ahrens, et al. "Like Me, Like You – Relative Importance of Peers and Siblings on Children's Fast Food Consumption and Screen Time but Not Sports Club Participation Depends on Age." *International Journal of Behavioral Nutrition and Physical Activity* 17, no. 1 (2020). https://doi.org/10.1186/s12966-020-00953-4.

Boniel-Nissim, Meyran, Yaniv Efrati, and Michal Dolev-Cohen. "Parental Mediation Regarding Children's Pornography Exposure: The Role of Parenting Style, Protection Motivation and Gender." *The Journal of Sex Research* 57, no. 1 (2019): 42–51. https://doi.org/10.1080/00224499.2019.1590795.

Boonk, Lisa, Hieronymus J. M. Gijselaers, Henk Ritzen, and Saskia Brand-Gruwel. "A Review of the Relationship Between Parental Involvement Indicators and Academic Achievement." *Educational Research Review* 24 (2018): 10–30. https://doi.org/10.1016/j.edurev.2018.02.001.

Bornstein, Marc H., Jennifer A. Kotler, and Jennifer E. Lansford. "The Future of Parenting Programs: An Introduction." *Parenting* 22, no. 3 (2022): 189–200. https://doi.org/10.1080/15295192.2022.2086808.

Borzekowski, Dina L. G., and Thomas N. Robinson. "Conversations, Control, And Couch-Time." *Journal of Children and Media* 1, no. 2 (2007): 162–76. https://doi.org/10.1080/17482790701339183.

Bouknight, Janelle, Amy Barnhill, and Noor Mobeen. "Parental Mediation and Acculturation." *Global Media Journal* 19, no. 37 (2021): 1–8.

Boyer, Ernest L. *Ready to Learn: A Mandate for the Nation*. Jossey-Bass, 1991.

Boyland, Emma, Lauren McGale, Michelle Maden, et al. "Association of Food and Nonalcoholic Beverage Marketing with Children and Adolescents' Eating Behaviors and Health." *JAMA Pediatrics* 176, no. 7 (2022): e221037. https://doi.org/10.1001/jamapediatrics.2022.1037.

Brabson, Laurel A., Carrie B. Jackson, Brittany K. Liebsack, and Amy D. Herschell. "PCIT: Summary of 40 Years of Research." In *Handbook of Parent-Child Interaction Therapy for Children on the Autism Spectrum*, edited by Cheryl Bodiford McNeil, Lauren Borduin Quetsch, and Cynthia M. Anderson. Springer, 2018.

Bradley, Robert H., and Robert F. Corwyn. "Socioeconomic Status and Child Development." *Annual Review of Psychology* 53, no. 1 (2002): 371–99. https://doi.org/10.1146/annurev.psych.53.100901.135233.

Bradt, Lowie, Eva Grosemans, Rozane De Cock, Bruno Dupont, Maarten Vansteenkiste, and Bart Soenens. "Does Parents' Perceived Style of Setting Limits to Gaming Matter? The Interplay Between Profiles of Parental Mediation and BIS/BAS Sensitivity in Problematic Gaming and Online Gambling." *Journal of Adolescence* 96, no. 3 (2023): 580–97. https://doi.org/10.1002/jad.12271.

Braghieri, Luca, Ro'ee Levy, and Alexey Makarin. "Social Media and Mental Health." *SSRN Electronic Journal*, 2021. https://doi.org/10.2139/ssrn.3919760.

Branje, Susan, Brett Laursen, and W. Andrew Collins. "Parent-Child Communication During Adolescence." In *The Routledge Handbook of Family Communication*, 2nd ed., edited by Anita L. Vangelisti. Routledge, 2012.

Brenan, Megan. "Americans' Preference for Larger Families Highest Since 1971." *Gallup*, September 25, 2023. https://news.gallup.com/poll/511238/americans-preference-larger-families-highest-1971.aspx.

Bronfenbrenner, Urie. *The Ecology of Human Development: Experiments by Nature and Design*. Harvard University Press, 1979.

Brown, Sara Catherine. "Will TV Impact if I Help You? Prosocial Media, Joint Media Engagement, and Infant Prosocial Development During the Second Year." MA thesis, Brigham Young University, 2020. ProQuest (28187302).

Brumariu, Laura E. "Parent-Child Attachment and Emotion Regulation." *New Directions for Child and Adolescent Development* 2015, no. 148 (2015): 31–45. https://doi.org/10.1002/cad.20098.

Bruner, Jerome. "Culture and Human Development: A New Look." *Human Development* 33, no. 6 (1990): 344–55. https://doi.org/10.1159/000276535.

Bryant, Jennings, and Dorina Miron. "Theory and Research in Mass Communication." *Journal of Communication* 54, no. 4 (2004): 662–704. https://doi.org/10.1111/j.1460-2466.2004.tb02650.x.

Bryant, Jennings, and Dolf Zillman. "A Retrospective and Prospective Look at Media Effects." In *The Sage Handbook of Media Processes and Effects*, edited by Robin L. Nabi and Mary Beth Oliver. Sage, 2009.

Bucci, Sandra, Matthias Schwannauer, and Natalie Berry. "The Digital Revolution and its Impact on Mental Health Care." *Psychology and Psychotherapy Theory Research and Practice* 92, no. 2 (2019): 277–97. https://doi.org/10.1111/papt.12222.

Buijzen, Moniek, and Claartje Mens. "Adult Mediation of Television Advertising Effects." *Journal of Children and Media* 1, no. 2 (2007): 177–91. https://doi.org/10.1080/17482790701339233.

Buijzen, Moniek, Juliette H. Walma Van Der Molen, and Patricia Sondij. "Parental Mediation of Children's Emotional Responses to a Violent News Event." *Communication Research* 34, no. 2 (2007): 212–30. https://doi.org/10.1177/0093650206298070.

Cabello-Hutt, Tania, Patricio Cabello, and Magdalena Claro. "Online Opportunities and Risks for Children and Adolescents: The Role of Digital Skills, Age, Gender and Parental Mediation in Brazil." *New Media & Society* 20, no. 7 (2017): 2411–31. https://doi.org/10.1177/1461444817724168.

Çalhan, Ceren, and İdris Göksu. "An Effort to Understand Parents' Media Mediation Roles and Early Childhood Children's Digital Game Addiction Tendency: A Descriptive Correlational Survey Study." *Education and Information Technologies* 29, no. 14 (2024): 17825–65. https://doi.org/10.1007/s10639-024-12544-y.

Cao, Simin, Chuanmei Dong, and Hui Li. "Parental Beliefs and Mediation Co-mediate the SES Effect on Chinese Preschoolers' Early Digital Literacy: A Chain-mediation Model." *Education and Information Technologies* 29, no. 10 (2023): 12093–114. https://doi.org/10.1007/s10639-023-12300-8.

Caprara, Gian Vittorio, Bernadette Paula Luengo Kanacri, Maria Gerbino, et al. "Positive Effects of Promoting Prosocial Behavior in Early Adolescence." *International Journal of Behavioral Development* 38, no. 4 (2014): 386–96. https://doi.org/10.1177/0165025414531464.

Carleton, David. "Old Deluder Satan Act of 1647." *Free Speech Center at Middle Tennessee State University,* January 1, 2009. https://firstamendment.mtsu.edu/article/old-deluder-satan-act-of-1647.

Carmona, Nicole E., Aleksandra Usyatynsky, Samlau Kutana, et al. "A Transdiagnostic Self-Management Web-Based App for Sleep Disturbance in Adolescents and Young Adults: Feasibility and Acceptability Study." *JMIR Formative Research* 5, no. 11 (2021): e25392. https://doi.org/10.2196/25392.

Carrion, Victor G., Carl F. Weems, and Allan L. Reiss. "Stress Predicts Brain Changes in Children: A Pilot Longitudinal Study on Youth Stress, Posttraumatic Stress Disorder, and the Hippocampus." *Pediatrics* 119, no. 3 (2007): 509–16. https://doi.org/10.1542/peds.2006-2028.

Casey Family Programs. *Strategy Brief: Strong Families,* 2022. https://www.casey.org/media/22.07-QFF-SF-Data-and-equity.pdf.

Cauberghe, Verolien, Ini Van Wesenbeeck, Steffi De Jans, Liselot Hudders, and Koen Ponnet. "How Adolescents Use Social Media to Cope with Feelings of Loneliness and Anxiety During COVID-19 Lockdown." *Cyberpsychology Behavior and Social Networking* 24, no. 4 (2020): 250–7. https://doi.org/10.1089/cyber.2020.0478.

Center for Media Literacy. *Empowerment Through Education,* 2015. http://www.medialit.org/readingroom/empowerment-through-education.

Chakroff, Jennifer L., and Amy I. Nathanson. "Parent and School Interventions: Mediation and Media Literacy." In *The Handbook of Children, Media, and Development,* edited by Sandra L. Calvert and Barbara J. Wilson. Blackwell, 2008.

Chandra, Meena, Bin Jalaludin, Susan Woolfenden, et al. "Screen Time of Infants in Sydney, Australia: A Birth Cohort Study." *BMJ Open* 6, no. 10 (2016): e012342. https://doi.org/10.1136/bmjopen-2016-012342.

Chang, Fong-Ching, Chiung-Hui Chiu, Ping-Hung Chen, et al. "Children's Use of Mobile Devices, Smartphone Addiction and Parental Mediation in Taiwan." *Computers in Human Behavior* 93 (2018): 25–32. https://doi.org/10.1016/j.chb.2018.11.048.

Chang, Fong-Ching, Chiung-Hui Chiu, Nae-Fang Miao, et al. "The Relationship Between Parental Mediation and Internet Addiction Among Adolescents, and the Association with Cyberbullying and Depression." *Comprehensive Psychiatry* 57 (2014): 21–8. https://doi.org/10.1016/j.comppsych.2014.11.013.

Chen, Liang, Xiaoming Liu, and Hongjie Tang. "The Interactive Effects of Parental Mediation Strategies in Preventing Cyberbullying on Social Media." *Psychology Research and Behavior Management* 16 (2023): 1009–22. https://doi.org/10.2147/prbm.s386968.

Chen, Liang, and Jingyuan Shi. "Reducing Harm from Media: A Meta-Analysis of Parental Mediation." *Journalism & Mass Communication Quarterly* 96, no. 1 (2018): 173–93. https://doi.org/10.1177/1077699018754908.

Chen, Vivian Hsueh Hua, and Grace S. Chng. "Active and Restrictive Parental Mediation Over Time: Effects on Youths' Self-Regulatory Competencies and Impulsivity." *Computers & Education* 98 (2016): 206–12. https://doi.org/10.1016/j.compedu.2016.03.012.

Chng, Grace S., Dongdong Li, Albert K. Liau, and Angeline Khoo. "Moderating Effects of the Family Environment for Parental Mediation and Pathological Internet Use in Youths." *Cyberpsychology Behavior and Social Networking* 18, no. 1 (2014): 30–6. https://doi.org/10.1089/cyber.2014.0368.

Choi, Naya, Jiyeon Sheo, Suji Jung, and Jisu Choi. "Newspaper Reading in Families with School-Age Children: Relationship Between Parent–Child Interaction Using Newspaper, Reading Motivation, and Academic Achievement." *International Journal of Environmental Research and Public Health* 19, no. 21 (2022): 14423. https://doi.org/10.3390/ijerph192114423.

Chou, Hui-Lien, and Chien Chou. "A Quantitative Analysis of Factors Related to Taiwan Teenagers' Smartphone Addiction Tendency Using a Random Sample of Parent-Child Dyads." *Computers in Human Behavior* 99 (2019): 335–44. https://doi.org/10.1016/j.chb.2019.05.032.

Choudhury, Suparna, Kelly A. McKinney, and Moritz Merten. "Rebelling Against the Brain: Public Engagement with the 'Neurological Adolescent.'" *Social Science & Medicine* 74, no. 4 (2011): 565–73. https://doi.org/10.1016/j.socscimed.2011.10.029.

Christakis, Dimitri A., Michelle M. Garrison, Todd Herrenkohl, et al. "Modifying Media Content for Preschool Children: A Randomized Controlled Trial." *Pediatrics* 131, no. 3 (2013): 431–8. https://doi.org/10.1542/peds.2012-1493.

Christodoulou, Georgia, Anuja Majmundar, Chih-Ping Chou, and Mary Ann Pentz. "Anhedonia, Screen Time, and Substance Use in Early Adolescents: A Longitudinal Mediation Analysis." *Journal of Adolescence* 78, no. 1 (2019): 24–32. https://doi.org/10.1016/j.adolescence.2019.11.007.

Chung, Chung Joo, George A. Barnett, Kitae Kim, and Derek Lackaff. "An Analysis on Communication Theory and Discipline." *Scientometrics* 95, no. 3 (2012): 985–1002. https://doi.org/10.1007/s11192-012-0869-4.

Ciarrochi, Joseph, Philip Parker, Baljinder Sahdra, et al. "The Development of Compulsive Internet Use and Mental Health: A Four-Year Study of Adolescence." *Developmental Psychology* 52, no. 2 (2015): 272–83. https://doi.org/10.1037/dev0000070.

Cillero, Itziar Hoyos, and Russell Jago. "Systematic Review of Correlates of Screen-Viewing Among Young Children." *Preventive Medicine* 51, no. 1 (2010): 3–10. https://doi.org/10.1016/j.ypmed.2010.04.012.

Cingel, Drew P., and Marina Krcmar. "Predicting Media Use in Very Young Children: The Role of Demographics and Parent Attitudes." *Communication Studies* 64, no. 4 (2013): 374–94. https://doi.org/10.1080/10510974.2013.770408.

Clark, Lynn Schofield. "Parental Mediation Theory for the Digital Age." *Communication Theory* 21, no. 4 (2011): 323–43. https://doi.org/10.1111/j.1468-2885.2011.01391.x.

Clement, Sarah, and Richard Bollinger. "Perspectives on Character Virtue Development." *Research in Human Development* 13, no. 2 (2016): 174–81. https://doi.org/10.1080/15427609.2016.1172445.

Cohen, Taya R., and Lily Morse. "Moral Character: What It Is and What It Does." *Research in Organizational Behavior* 34 (2014): 43–61. https://doi.org/10.1016/j.riob.2014.08.003.

Collier, Kevin M., Sarah M. Coyne, Eric E. Rasmussen, et al. "Does Parental Mediation of Media Influence Child Outcomes? A Meta-Analysis on Media Time, Aggression, Substance Use, and Sexual Behavior." *Developmental Psychology* 52, no. 5 (2016): 798–812.

Collins, Rebecca L., Victor C. Strasburger, Jane D. Brown, Edward Donnerstein, Amanda Lenhart, and L. Monique Ward. "Sexual Media and Childhood Well-Being and Health." *Pediatrics* 140, no. Supplement_2 (2017): S162–6. https://doi.org/10.1542/peds.2016-1758x.

Colombetti, Giovanna. *The Feeling Body: Affective Science Meets the Enactive Mind*. MIT Press, 2017.

Connell, Sabrina L., Alexis R. Lauricella, and Ellen Wartella. "Parental Co-Use of Media Technology with Their Young Children in the USA." *Journal of Children and Media* 9, no. 1 (2015): 5–21. https://doi.org/10.1080/17482798.2015.997440.

Conway, L. J., P. A. Levickis, F. Mensah, J. A. Smith, M. Wake, and S. Reilly. "The Role of Joint Engagement in the Development of Language in a Community-Derived

Sample of Slow-to-Talk Children." *Journal of Child Language* 45, no. 6 (2018): 1275–93. https://doi.org/10.1017/s030500091800017x.

Corcoran, Erin, Jennifer Doty, Pamela Wisniewski, and Joy Gabrielli. "Youth Sexting and Associations with Parental Media Mediation." *Computers in Human Behavior* 132 (2022): 107263. https://doi.org/10.1016/j.chb.2022.107263.

Coto, Jennifer, Elizabeth R. Pulgaron, Paulo A. Graziano, et al. "Parents as Role Models: Associations Between Parent and Young Children's Weight, Dietary Intake, and Physical Activity in a Minority Sample." *Maternal and Child Health Journal* 23, no. 7 (2019): 943–50. https://doi.org/10.1007/s10995-018-02722-z.

Cox, Melissa J., Tim Janssen, Joy Gabrielli, and Kristina M. Jackson. "Profiles of Parenting in the Digital Age: Associations with Adolescent Alcohol and Marijuana Use." *Journal of Studies on Alcohol and Drugs* 82, no. 4 (2021): 460–9. https://doi.org/10.15288/jsad.2021.82.460.

Coyne, Sarah M., Jennifer Ruh Linder, Eric E. Rasmussen, David A. Nelson, and Victoria Birkbeck. "Pretty as a Princess: Longitudinal Effects of Engagement with Disney Princesses on Gender Stereotypes, Body Esteem, and Prosocial Behavior in Children." *Child Development* 87, no. 6 (2016): 1909–25. https://doi.org/10.1111/cdev.12569.

Coyne, Sarah M., Laura M. Padilla-Walker, Hailey G. Holmgren, et al. "A Meta-Analysis of Prosocial Media on Prosocial Behavior, Aggression, and Empathic Concern: A Multidimensional Approach." *Developmental Psychology* 54, no. 2 (2017): 331–47. https://doi.org/10.1037/dev0000412.

Coyne, Sarah M., Laura M. Padilla-Walker, Laura Stockdale, and Randal D. Day. "Game on… Girls: Associations Between Co-Playing Video Games and Adolescent Behavioral and Family Outcomes." *Journal of Adolescent Health* 49, no. 2 (2011): 160–5. https://doi.org/10.1016/j.jadohealth.2010.11.249.

Coyne, Sarah M., Adam Rogers, Hailey G. Holmgren, et al. "Masters of Media: A Longitudinal Study of Parental Media Efficacy, Media Monitoring, and Child Problematic Media Use Across Early Childhood in the United States." *Journal of Children and Media* 17, no. 3 (2023): 318–35. https://doi.org/10.1080/17482798.2023.2200958.

Crone, Eveline A., and Michelle Achterberg. "Prosocial Development in Adolescence." *Current Opinion in Psychology* 44 (2021): 220–5. https://doi.org/10.1016/j.copsyc.2021.09.020.

Cubberley, Ellwood P. *Readings in the History of Education*. Houghton Mifflin Company, 1920.

Cullen, Julie, Alex Muntz, Samantha Marsh, et al. "Impact of Digital Screen Use on Health and Wellbeing of Children and Adolescents: A Narrative Review." *New Zealand Journal of Physiotherapy* 52, no. 1 (2024): 62–77. https://doi.org/10.15619/nzjp.v52i1.364.

D'Amico, Elizabeth J., Jeremy N. V. Miles, and Joan S. Tucker. "Gateway to Curiosity: Medical Marijuana Ads and Intention and Use During Middle School." *Psychology of Addictive Behaviors* 29, no. 3 (2015): 613–19. https://doi.org/10.1037/adb0000094.

Dalton, Madeline A., Anna M. Adachi-Mejia, Meghan R. Longacre, et al. "Parental Rules and Monitoring of Children's Movie Viewing Associated with Children's Risk for Smoking and Drinking." *Pediatrics* 118, no. 5 (2006): 1932–42. https://doi.org/10.1542/peds.2005-3082.

Danet, Marie. "Parental Concerns About Their School-aged Children's Use of Digital Devices." *Journal of Child and Family Studies* 29, no. 10 (2020): 2890–904. https://doi.org/10.1007/s10826-020-01760-y.

Davies, John J., and Douglas A. Gentile. "Responses to Children's Media Use in Families With and Without Siblings: A Family Development Perspective." *Family Relations* 61, no. 3 (2012): 410–25. https://doi.org/10.1111/j.1741-3729.2012.00703.x.

Davison, Kirsten Krahnstoever, Lori A. Francis, and Leann L. Birch. "Links Between Parents' and Girls' Television Viewing Behaviors: A Longitudinal Examination." *The Journal of Pediatrics* 147, no. 4 (2005): 436–42. https://doi.org/10.1016/j.jpeds.2005.05.002.

De Bellis, Michael D., Matcheri S. Keshavan, Duncan B. Clark, et al. "Developmental Traumatology Part II: Brain Development." *Biological Psychiatry* 45, no. 10 (1999): 1271–84. https://doi.org/10.1016/s0006-3223(99)00045-1.

De Cock, Rozane. "Mediating Flemish Children's Reactions of Fear and Sadness to Television News and its Limitations." *Journal of Children and Media* 6, no. 4 (2012): 485–501. https://doi.org/10.1080/17482798.2012.740414.

De Coen, Jolien, Sandra Verbeken, and Lien Goossens. "Media Influence Components as Predictors of Children's Body Image and Eating Problems: A Longitudinal Study of Boys and Girls During Middle Childhood." *Body Image* 37 (2021): 204–13. https://doi.org/10.1016/j.bodyim.2021.03.001.

De Leeuw, Rebecca N. H., and Christa A. Van Der Laan. "Helping Behavior in Disney Animated Movies and Children's Helping Behavior in the Netherlands." *Journal of Children and Media* 12, no. 2 (2017): 159–74. https://doi.org/10.1080/17482798.2017.1409245.

Dedkova, Lenka, and Vojtěch Mýlek. "Parental Mediation of Online Interactions and its Relation to Adolescents' Contacts with New People Online: The Role of Risk Perception." *Information Communication & Society* 26, no. 16 (2022): 3179–96. https://doi.org/10.1080/1369118x.2022.2146985.

Dedkova, Lenka, and David Smahel. "Online Parental Mediation: Associations of Family Members' Characteristics to Individual Engagement in Active Mediation and Monitoring." *Journal of Family Issues* 41, no. 8 (2019): 1112–36. https://doi.org/10.1177/0192513x19888255.

Demertzi, Athena, Charlene Liew, Didier Ledoux, et al. "Dualism Persists in the Science of Mind." *Annals of the New York Academy of Sciences* 1157, no. 1 (2009): 1–9. https://doi.org/10.1111/j.1749-6632.2008.04117.x.

Densley, Rebecca L., Willow S. Sauermilch, Jes Fyall Cardenas, Shannon L. Bichard, and Maya Neufeld-Wall. "Media Parenting in a Pandemic: Understanding U.S. Parents' Motivations for Parental Mediation During the COVID-19 Lockdown." *Journal of Children and Media* 19 (2024): 1–20. https://doi.org/10.1080/17482798.2024.2409669.

Desmond, Roger Jon, Bennett Hirsch, Dorothy Singer, and Jerome Singer. "Gender Differences, Mediation, and Disciplinary Styles in Children's Responses to Television." *Sex Roles* 16, no. 7-8 (1987): 375–89. https://doi.org/10.1007/bf00289549.

Desmond, Roger Jon, Jerome L. Singer, Dorothy G. Singer, Rachel Calam, and Karen Colimore. "Family Mediation Patterns and Television Viewing." *Human*

Communication Research 11, no. 4 (1985): 461–80. https://doi.org/10.1111/j.1468-2958.1985.tb00056.x.

Dey, M., R. Paz Castro, S. Haug, and M. P. Schaub. "Quality of Life of Parents of Mentally-Ill Children: A Systematic Review and Meta-Analysis." *Epidemiology and Psychiatric Sciences* 28, no. 5 (2018): 563–77. https://doi.org/10.1017/s2045796018000409.

Dillard, James Price. "Persuasion." In *The Handbook of Communication Science*, 2nd ed., edited by Charles R. Berger, Michael E. Roloff, and David R. Roskos-Ewoldsen. Sage, 2010.

Dishion, Thomas J., and Robert J. McMahon. "Parental Monitoring and the Prevention of Child and Adolescent Problem Behavior: A Conceptual and Empirical Formulation." *Clinical Child and Family Psychology Review* 1, no. 1 (1998): 61–75. https://doi.org/10.1023/a:1021800432380.

Dittus, Patricia J., Shannon L. Michael, Jeffrey S. Becasen, Kari M. Gloppen, Katharine McCarthy, and Vincent Guilamo-Ramos. "Parental Monitoring and its Associations with Adolescent Sexual Risk Behavior: A Meta-Analysis." *Pediatrics* 136, no. 6 (2015): e1587–99. https://doi.org/10.1542/peds.2015-0305.

Donaldson, Scott I., Allison Dormanesh, Cindy Perez, Anuja Majmundar, and Jon-Patrick Allem. "Association Between Exposure to Tobacco Content on Social Media and Tobacco Use." *JAMA Pediatrics* 176, no. 9 (2022): 878. https://doi.org/10.1001/jamapediatrics.2022.2223.

Dorr, Aimee, Peter Kovaric, and Catherine Doubleday. "Parent-Child Coviewing of Television." *Journal of Broadcasting & Electronic Media* 33, no. 1 (1989): 35–51. https://doi.org/10.1080/08838158909364060.

Douglas, Kimberly D., Kandy K. Smith, Mary W. Stewart, Jean Walker, Leandro Mena, and Lei Zhang. "Exploring Parents' Intentions to Monitor and Mediate Adolescent Social Media Use and Implications for School Nurses." *The Journal of School Nursing* 39, no. 3 (2020): 248–61. https://doi.org/10.1177/1059840520983286.

Dredge, Rebecca, and Lara Schreurs. "Social Media Use and Offline Interpersonal Outcomes During Youth: A Systematic Literature Review." *Mass Communication & Society* 23, no. 6 (2020): 885–911. https://doi.org/10.1080/15205436.2020.1810277.

Durkheim, Émile. "The Dualism of Human Nature and its Social Conditions." *Durkheimian Studies* 11, no. 1 (2005). https://doi.org/10.3167/175223005783472211.

Dutta, Sarmistha, Jennifer Ma, and Munmun De Choudhury. "Measuring the Impact of Anxiety on Online Social Interactions." *Proceedings of the International AAAI Conference on Web and Social Media* 12, no. 1 (2018). https://doi.org/10.1609/icwsm.v12i1.15081.

Eagly, Alice H., and Kathleen Telaak. "Width of the Latitude of Acceptance as a Determinant of Attitude Change." *Journal of Personality and Social Psychology* 23, no. 3 (1972): 388–97. https://doi.org/10.1037/h0033161.

East, Patricia, Erin Delker, Estela Blanco, Raquel Burrows, Betsy Lozoff, and Sheila Gahagan. "Home and Family Environment Related to Development of Obesity: A 21-Year Longitudinal Study." *Childhood Obesity* 15, no. 3 (2019): 156–66. https://doi.org/10.1089/chi.2018.0222.

Edgerly, Stephanie, Kjerstin Thorson, Esther Thorson, Emily K. Vraga, and Leticia Bode. "Do Parents Still Model News Consumption? Socializing News Use Among

Adolescents in a Multi-Device World." *New Media & Society* 20, no. 4 (2017): 1263–81. https://doi.org/10.1177/1461444816688451.

Eirich, Rachel, Brae Anne McArthur, Ciana Anhorn, Claire McGuinness, Dimitri A. Christakis, and Sheri Madigan. "Association of Screen Time with Internalizing and Externalizing Behavior Problems in Children 12 Years or Younger." *JAMA Psychiatry* 79, no. 5 (2022): 393–405. https://doi.org/10.1001/jamapsychiatry.2022.0155.

Eisenberg, Nancy. *Altruistic Emotion, Cognition, and Behavior*. Lawrence Erlbaum, 1986.

Eisenberg, Nancy, Natalie D. Eggum, and Laura Di Giunta. "Empathy-Related Responding: Associations with Prosocial Behavior, Aggression, and Intergroup Relations." *Social Issues and Policy Review* 4, no. 1 (2010): 143–80. https://doi.org/10.1111/j.1751-2409.2010.01020.x.

Eisenberg, Nancy, Richard A. Fabes, Mariss Karbon, et al. "The Relations of Children's Dispositional Prosocial Behavior to Emotionality, Regulation, and Social Functioning." *Child Development* 67, no. 3 (1996): 974–92. https://doi.org/10.1111/j.1467-8624.1996.tb01777.x.

Elias, Nelly, Dafna Lemish, and Galit Nimrod. "From Experiencing Parental Mediation as a Child to Practicing It as a Parent: An Exploratory Study with Israeli Mothers." *Journal of Children and Media* 18, no. 1 (2024): 50–9. https://doi.org/10.1080/17482798.2023.2265513.

Ewin, Carrie A., Andrea E. Reupert, Louise A. McLean, and Christopher J. Ewin. "The Impact of Joint Media Engagement on Parent–Child Interactions: A Systematic Review." *Human Behavior and Emerging Technologies* 3, no. 2 (2020): 230–54. https://doi.org/10.1002/hbe2.203.

Ewoldsen, David R. "A Discussion of Falsifiability and Evaluating Research: Issues of Variance Accounted for and External Validity." *Asian Communication Research* 19, no. 2 (2022): 38–47. https://doi.org/10.20879/acr.2022.19.2.38.

Fahrenberg, J., and M. Cheetham. "The Mind-Body Problem as Seen by Students of Different Disciplines." *Journal of Consciousness Studies* 7, no. 5 (2000): 47–59.

Faltýnková, Anna, Lukas Blinka, Anna Ševčíková, and Daniela Husarova. "The Associations Between Family-Related Factors and Excessive Internet Use in Adolescents." *International Journal of Environmental Research and Public Health* 17, no. 5 (2020): 1754. https://doi.org/10.3390/ijerph17051754.

Fan, Xitao, and Michael Chen. "Parental Involvement and Students' Academic Achievement: A Meta-Analysis." *Educational Psychology Review* 13 (2001): 1–22. https://doi.org/10.1023/A:1009048817385.

Fardouly, Jasmine, Natasha R. Magson, Carly J. Johnco, Ella L. Oar, and Ronald M. Rapee. "Parental Control of the Time Preadolescents Spend on Social Media: Links with Preadolescents' Social Media Appearance Comparisons and Mental Health." *Journal of Youth and Adolescence* 47, no. 7 (2018): 1456–68. https://doi.org/10.1007/s10964-018-0870-1.

Fardouly, Jasmine, Natasha R. Magson, Ronald M. Rapee, et al. "Investigating Longitudinal and Bidirectional Relationships Between Parental Factors and Time Spent on Social Media During Early Adolescence." *New Media & Society* 26, no. 3 (2022): 1610–26. https://doi.org/10.1177/14614448221076155.

Farmer, Elizabeth M. Z., Barbara J. Burns, Adrian Angold, and Elizabeth J. Costello. "Impact of Children's Mental Health Problems on Families." *Journal of Emotional and Behavioral Disorders* 5, no. 4 (1997): 230–8. https://doi.org/10.1177/106342669700500406.

Federal Interagency Forum on Child and Family Statistics. *America's Children: Key National Indicators of Well-Being, 2023*, 2023. https://www.childstats.gov/americaschildren23/demo.asp.

Feudtner, Chris, Jennifer K. Walter, Jennifer A. Faerber, et al. "Good-Parent Beliefs of Parents of Seriously Ill Children." *JAMA Pediatrics* 169, no. 1 (2014): 39. https://doi.org/10.1001/jamapediatrics.2014.2341.

Fiellin, Lynn E., Kimberly D. Hieftje, Tyra M. Pendergrass, et al. "Video Game Intervention for Sexual Risk Reduction in Minority Adolescents: Randomized Controlled Trial." *Journal of Medical Internet Research* 19, no. 9 (2017): e314. https://doi.org/10.2196/jmir.8148.

Fikkers, Karin M., Jessica Taylor Piotrowski, and Patti M. Valkenburg. "A Matter of Style? Exploring the Effects of Parental Mediation Styles on Early Adolescents' Media Violence Exposure and Aggression." *Computers in Human Behavior* 70 (2017): 407–15. https://doi.org/10.1016/j.chb.2017.01.029.

Fisher, Deborah A., Douglas L. Hill, Joel W. Grube, Melina M. Bersamin, Samantha Walker, and Enid L. Gruber. "Televised Sexual Content and Parental Mediation: Influences on Adolescent Sexuality." *Media Psychology* 12, no. 2 (2009): 121–47. https://doi.org/10.1080/15213260902849901.

Fitzpatrick, Caroline, Alexa Johnson, Angélique Laurent, Mathieu Bégin, and Elizabeth Harvey. "Do Parent Media Habits Contribute to Child Global Development?" *Frontiers in Psychology* 14 (2024). https://doi.org/10.3389/fpsyg.2023.1279893.

Foulds, Kim. "Co-Viewing Mass Media to Support Children and Parents' Emotional ABCs: An Evaluation of Ahlan Simsim." *Early Childhood Education Journal* 51, no. 8 (2022): 1479–88. https://doi.org/10.1007/s10643-022-01408-0.

Fred Rogers Center. "Who You Are Inside is What Helps You Make and Do Everything in Life." *Twitter (now X)*, February 5, 2019. https://twitter.com/FredRogersCtr.

Fred Rogers Productions. "Our Story." Accessed April 18, 2025. https://www.fredrogers.org/our-story/.

Fredrickson, Barbara L., and Tomi-Ann Roberts. "Objectification Theory: Toward Understanding Women's Lived Experiences and Mental Health Risks." *Psychology of Women Quarterly* 21, no. 2 (1997): 173–206. https://doi.org/10.1111/j.1471-6402.1997.tb00108.x.

Fu, Xinyuan, Laura M. Padilla-Walker, and Michael N. Brown. "Longitudinal Relations Between Adolescents' Self-Esteem and Prosocial Behavior Toward Strangers, Friends and Family." *Journal of Adolescence* 57, no. 1 (2017): 90–8. https://doi.org/10.1016/j.adolescence.2017.04.002.

Fujioka, Yuki, and Erica Weintraub Austin. "The Relationship of Family Communication Patterns to Parental Mediation Styles." *Communication Research* 29, no. 6 (2002): 642–65. https://doi.org/10.1177/009365002237830.

Garcia-Conde, Miguel Giménez, Longinos Marin, Salvador Ruiz De Maya, and Pedro J. Cuestas. "Parental Attitudes to Childhood Overweight: The Multiple Paths Through Healthy Eating, Screen Use, and Sleeping Time." *International Journal of*

Environmental Research and Public Health 17, no. 21 (2020): 7885. https://doi.org /10.3390/ijerph17217885.

Gardner, Frances, Sarah Ward, Jennifer Burton, and Charlotte Wilson. "The Role of Mother-Child Joint Play in the Early Development of Children's Conduct Problems: A Longitudinal Observational Study." *Social Development* 12, no. 3 (2003): 361–78. https://doi.org/10.1111/1467-9507.00238.

Gazendam, Naomi, Kathryn Cleverley, Nathan King, William Pickett, and Susan P. Phillips. "Individual and Social Determinants of Early Sexual Activity: A Study of Gender-based Differences Using the 2018 Canadian Health Behaviour in School-aged Children Study (HBSC)." *PLoS ONE* 15, no. 9 (2020): e0238515. https://doi .org/10.1371/journal.pone.0238515.

Gebremariam, M. K., T. M. Altenburg, J. Lakerveld, et al. "Associations Between Socioeconomic Position and Correlates of Sedentary Behaviour Among Youth: A Systematic Review." *Obesity Reviews* 16, no. 11 (2015): 988–1000. https://doi.org/10 .1111/obr.12314.

Genner, S., and D. Süss. "Socialization as Media Effect." In *The International Encyclopedia of Media Effects*, edited by P. Rössler, C. A. Hoffner, and L. Zoonen. Wiley-Blackwell, 2017.

Gentile, Douglas A., Amy I. Nathanson, Eric E. Rasmussen, Rachel A. Reimer, and David A. Walsh. "Do You See What I See? Parent and Child Reports of Parental Monitoring of Media." *Family Relations* 61, no. 3 (2012): 470–87. https://doi.org/10 .1111/j.1741-3729.2012.00709.x.

Gentile, Douglas A., Rachel A. Reimer, Amy I. Nathanson, David A. Walsh, and Joey C. Eisenmann. "Protective Effects of Parental Monitoring of Children's Media Use." *JAMA Pediatrics* 168, no. 5 (2014): 479. https://doi.org/10.1001/jamapediatrics.2014 .146.

Gerards, S. M. P. L., and S. P. J. Kremers. "The Role of Food Parenting Skills and the Home Food Environment in Children's Weight Gain and Obesity." *Current Obesity Reports* 4, no. 1 (2015): 30–6. https://doi.org/10.1007/s13679-015-0139-x.

Gerull, Friederike C., and Ronald M. Rapee. "Mother Knows Best: Effects of Maternal Modelling on the Acquisition of Fear and Avoidance Behaviour in Toddlers." *Behaviour Research and Therapy* 40, no. 3 (2002): 279–87. https://doi.org/10.1016/ s0005-7967(01)00013-4.

Geržičáková, Michaela, Lenka Dedkova, and Vojtěch Mýlek. "What Do Parents Know About Children's Risky Online Experiences? The Role of Parental Mediation Strategies." *Computers in Human Behavior* 141 (2022): 107626. https://doi.org/10 .1016/j.chb.2022.107626.

Geurts, Suzanne M., Ina M. Koning, Helen G. M. Vossen, and Regina J. J. M. Van Den Eijnden. "Rules, Role Models or Overall Climate at Home? Relative Associations of Different Family Aspects with Adolescents' Problematic Social Media Use." *Comprehensive Psychiatry* 116 (2022): 152318. https://doi.org/10.1016/j.comppsych .2022.152318.

Gladstone, Brenda M., Katherine M. Boydell, Mary V. Seeman, and Patricia D. McKeever. "Children's Experiences of Parental Mental Illness: A Literature Review." *Early Intervention in Psychiatry* 5, no. 4 (2011): 271–89. https://doi.org/10.1111/j .1751-7893.2011.00287.x.

Glatz, Terese, Elizabeth Crowe, and Christy M. Buchanan. "Internet-Specific Parental Self-Efficacy: Developmental Differences and Links to Internet-Specific Mediation." *Computers in Human Behavior* 84 (2018): 8–17. https://doi.org/10.1016/j.chb.2018.02.014.

Glynn, Laura M., Elysia Poggi Davis, Joan L. Luby, Tallie Z. Baram, and Curt A. Sandman. "A Predictable Home Environment May Protect Child Mental Health During the COVID-19 Pandemic." *Neurobiology of Stress* 14 (2021): 100291. https://doi.org/10.1016/j.ynstr.2020.100291.

Goodwin, Huw, Emma Haycraft, and Caroline Meyer. "Sociocultural Correlates of Compulsive Exercise: Is the Environment Important in Fostering a Compulsivity Towards Exercise Among Adolescents?" *Body Image* 8, no. 4 (2011): 390–5. https://doi.org/10.1016/j.bodyim.2011.05.006.

Gordon, Evan M., Roselyne J. Chauvin, Andrew N. Van, et al. "A Somato-Cognitive Action Network Alternates with Effector Regions in Motor Cortex." *Nature* 617, no. 7960 (2023): 351–9. https://doi.org/10.1038/s41586-023-05964-2.

Granich, J., M. Rosenberg, M. Knuiman, and A. Timperio. "Understanding Children's Sedentary Behaviour: A Qualitative Study of the Family Home Environment." *Health Education Research* 25, no. 2 (2008): 199–210. https://doi.org/10.1093/her/cyn025.

Greene, Kathryn. "An Integrated Model of Health Disclosure Decision-making." In *Uncertainty, Information Management, and Disclosure Decisions*, edited by Tamara D. Afifi and Walid A. Afifi. Routledge, 2009.

Greene, Sheila, and Elizabeth Nixon. *Children as Agents in Their Worlds: A Psychological-Relational Perspective*. Routledge, 2020.

Griffith, Shayl F. "Parent Beliefs and Child Media Use: Stress and Digital Skills as Moderators." *Journal of Applied Developmental Psychology* 86 (2023): 101535. https://doi.org/10.1016/j.appdev.2023.101535.

Grusec, Joan E., and Davidov, Maayan. "Analyzing Socialization from a Domain-Specific Perspective." In *Handbook of Socialization: Theory and Research*, 2nd ed., edited by Joan E. Grusec and Paul D. Hastings. Guilford Press, 2015.

Guo, Wenxiu, and Amy I. Nathanson. "The Effects of Parental Mediation of Sexual Content on the Sexual Knowledge, Attitudes, and Behaviors of Adolescents in the US." *Journal of Children and Media* 5, no. 4 (2011): 358–78. https://doi.org/10.1080/17482798.2011.587141.

Haghjoo, Purya, Goli Siri, Ensiye Soleimani, Mahdieh Abbasalizad Farhangi, and Samira Alesaeidi. "Screen Time Increases Overweight and Obesity Risk Among Adolescents: A Systematic Review and Dose-Response Meta-Analysis." *BMC Primary Care* 23, no. 1 (2022). https://doi.org/10.1186/s12875-022-01761-4.

Hallden, Gunilla. "The Child as Project and the Child as Being: Parents' Ideas as Frames of Reference." *Children & Society* 5, no. 4 (1991): 334–46. https://doi.org/10.1111/j.1099-0860.1991.tb00499.x.

Hammer, Molly, Katharina Scheiter, and Kathleen Stürmer. "New Technology, New Role of Parents: How Parents' Beliefs and Behavior Affect Students' Digital Media Self-efficacy." *Computers in Human Behavior* 116 (2020): 106642. https://doi.org/10.1016/j.chb.2020.106642.

Hanewinkel, Reiner, Matthis Morgenstern, Susanne E. Tanski, and James D. Sargent. "Longitudinal Study of Parental Movie Restriction on Teen Smoking and Drinking in Germany." *Addiction* 103, no. 10 (2008): 1722–30. https://doi.org/10.1111/j.1360-0443.2008.02308.x.

Hanna, Robert, and Michelle Maiese. *Embodied Minds in Action*. Oxford University Press, 2009.

Hardy, Louise L., Louise A. Baur, Sarah P. Garnett, et al. "Family and Home Correlates of Television Viewing in 12–13 Year Old Adolescents: The Nepean Study." *International Journal of Behavioral Nutrition and Physical Activity* 3, no. 1 (2006): 24. https://doi.org/10.1186/1479-5868-3-24.

Harries, C. I., D. M. Smith, L. Gregg, and A. Wittkowski. "Parenting and Serious Mental Illness (SMI): A Systematic Review and Metasynthesis." *Clinical Child and Family Psychology Review* 26, no. 2 (2023): 303–42. https://doi.org/10.1007/s10567-023-00427-6.

Harris, Alma, and Janet Goodall. "Do Parents Know They Matter? Engaging All Parents in Learning." *Educational Research* 50, no. 3 (2008): 277–89. https://doi.org/10.1080/00131880802309424.

Harris, Jennifer L., and John A. Bargh. "Television Viewing and Unhealthy Diet: Implications for Children and Media Interventions." *Health Communication* 24, no. 7 (2009): 660–73. https://doi.org/10.1080/10410230903242267.

Harris, Russ. *The Happiness Trap*. Shambhala Publications, Inc., 2022.

Harrison, Kristen, and Janet M. Liechty. "US Preschoolers' Media Exposure and Dietary Habits: The Primacy of Television and the Limits of Parental Mediation." *Journal of Children and Media* 6, no. 1 (2011): 18–36. https://doi.org/10.1080/17482798.2011.633402.

He, Zihao, Hua Wu, Fengyu Yu, et al. "Effects of Smartphone-Based Interventions on Physical Activity in Children and Adolescents: Systematic Review and Meta-Analysis." *JMIR Mhealth and Uhealth* 9, no. 2 (2021): e22601. https://doi.org/10.2196/22601.

Hefner, Dorothée, Karin Knop, Stefanie Schmitt, and Peter Vorderer. "Rules? Role Model? Relationship? The Impact of Parents on Their Children's Problematic Mobile Phone Involvement." *Media Psychology* 22, no. 1 (2018): 82–108. https://doi.org/10.1080/15213269.2018.1433544.

Helsper, Ellen J., Veronika Kalmus, Uwe Hasebrink, Bence Sagvari, and Jos de Haan. *Country Classification: Opportunities, Risks, Harm, and Parental Mediation*. EU Kids Online, 2013.

Herget, Sabine, Sandra Reichardt, Andrea Grimm, et al. "High-Intensity Interval Training for Overweight Adolescents: Program Acceptance of a Media Supported Intervention and Changes in Body Composition." *International Journal of Environmental Research and Public Health* 13, no. 11 (2016): 1099. https://doi.org/10.3390/ijerph13111099.

Hernandez, Maria Y., and Kurt C. Organista. "Entertainment–Education? A Fotonovela? A New Strategy to Improve Depression Literacy and Help-Seeking Behaviors in At-Risk Immigrant Latinas." *American Journal of Community Psychology* 52, no. 3–4 (2013): 224–35. https://doi.org/10.1007/s10464-013-9587-1.

Herrera, Aubrey V., Corina Benjet, Enrique Méndez, Leticia Casanova, and Maria Elena Medina-Mora. "How Mental Health Interviews Conducted Alone, in the Presence of an Adult, a Child or Both Affects Adolescents' Reporting of

Psychological Symptoms and Risky Behaviors." *Journal of Youth and Adolescence* 46, no. 2 (2016): 417–28. https://doi.org/10.1007/s10964-016-0418-1.

Hill, Nancy E., and Diana F. Tyson. "Parental Involvement in Middle School: A Meta-Analytic Assessment of the Strategies That Promote Achievement." *Developmental Psychology* 45, no. 3 (2009): 740–63. https://doi.org/10.1037/a0015362.

Hisler, Garrett, Jean M. Twenge, and Zlatan Krizan. "Associations Between Screen Time and Short Sleep Duration Among Adolescents Varies by Media Type: Evidence from a Cohort Study." *Sleep Medicine* 66 (2019): 92–102. https://doi.org/10.1016/j.sleep.2019.08.007.

Ho, Shirley, May O. Lwin, Liang Chen, and Minyi Chen. "Development and Validation of a Parental Social Media Mediation Scale Across Child and Parent Samples." *Internet Research* 30, no. 2 (2019): 677–94. https://doi.org/10.1108/intr-02-2018-0061.

Hogan, Marjorie J. "Parents and Other Adults: Models and Monitors of Healthy Media Habits." In *Handbook of Children and the Media*, edited by Dorothy G. Singer and Jerome L. Singer. Sage Publications, 2001.

Hoge, Elizabeth, David Bickham, and Joanne Cantor. "Digital Media, Anxiety, and Depression in Children." *Pediatrics* 140, no. Supplement_2 (2017): S76–80. https://doi.org/10.1542/peds.2016-1758g.

Holiday, Steven, Bradley J. Bond, and Eric E. Rasmussen. "Coming Attractions: Parental Mediation Responses to Transgender and Cisgender Film Trailer Content Targeting Adolescents." *Sexuality & Culture* 22, no. 4 (2018): 1154–70. https://doi.org/10.1007/s12119-018-9517-3.

Holmgren, Hailey G., McCall A. Booth, Sarah Ashby, Sarah M. Coyne, Brandon N. Clifford, and Emilie Davis. "Patterns of Parent Media Use: The Influence of Parent Media Use Profiles on Parental Mediation, Technoference, and Problematic Media Use." *Computers in Human Behavior* 161 (2024): 108410. https://doi.org/10.1016/j.chb.2024.108410.

Holmgren, Hailey G., Laura M. Padilla-Walker, Laura A. Stockdale, and Sarah M. Coyne. "Parental Media Monitoring, Prosocial Violent Media Exposure, and Adolescents' Prosocial and Aggressive Behaviors." *Aggressive Behavior* 45, no. 6 (2019): 671–81. https://doi.org/10.1002/ab.21861.

Holvoet, Sanne, Ini Vanwesenbeeck, Liselot Hudders, and Laura Herrewijn. "Predicting Parental Mediation of Personalized Advertising and Online Data Collection Practices Targeting Teenagers." *Journal of Broadcasting & Electronic Media* 66, no. 2 (2022): 213–34. https://doi.org/10.1080/08838151.2022.2051511.

Horowitz-Kraus, Tzipi, and John S. Hutton. "Brain Connectivity in Children Is Increased by the Time They Spend Reading Books and Decreased by the Length of Exposure to Screen-Based Media." *Acta Paediatrica* 107, no. 4 (2017): 685–93. https://doi.org/10.1111/apa.14176.

Hosman, Clemens M. H., Karin T. M. Van Doesum, and Floor Van Santvoort. "Prevention of Emotional Problems and Psychiatric Risks in Children of Parents with a Mental Illness in the Netherlands: I. The Scientific Basis to a Comprehensive Approach." *Australian E-Journal for the Advancement of Mental Health* 8, no. 3 (2009): 250–63. https://doi.org/10.5172/jamh.8.3.250.

Howie, Erin K., John Joosten, Courtenay J. Harris, and Leon M. Straker. "Associations Between Meeting Sleep, Physical Activity or Screen Time Behaviour Guidelines and

Academic Performance in Australian School Children." *BMC Public Health* 20, no. 1 (2020). https://doi.org/10.1186/s12889-020-08620-w.

Hsu, Michelle S. H., Anika Rouf, and Margaret Allman-Farinelli. "Effectiveness and Behavioral Mechanisms of Social Media Interventions for Positive Nutrition Behaviors in Adolescents: A Systematic Review." *Journal of Adolescent Health* 63, no. 5 (2018): 531–45. https://doi.org/10.1016/j.jadohealth.2018.06.009.

Hu, Bi Ying, Gregory Kirk Johnson, Timothy Teo, and Zhongling Wu. "Relationship Between Screen Time and Chinese Children's Cognitive and Social Development." *Journal of Research in Childhood Education* 34, no. 2 (2020): 183–207. https://doi.org/10.1080/02568543.2019.1702600.

Huang, Shunsen, Xiaoxiong Lai, Yajun Li, et al. "Does Parental Media Mediation Make a Difference for Adolescents? Evidence from an Empirical Cohort Study of Parent-Adolescent Dyads." *Heliyon* 9, no. 4 (2023): e14897. https://doi.org/10.1016/j.heliyon.2023.e14897.

Huang, Shunsen, Xiaoxiong Lai, Xinmei Zhao, et al. "Beyond Screen Time: Exploring the Associations Between Types of Smartphone Use Content and Adolescents' Social Relationships." *International Journal of Environmental Research and Public Health* 19, no. 15 (2022): 8940. https://doi.org/10.3390/ijerph19158940.

Hutchings-Tryon, Mallory. "Yes, School Should Teach Morality. But Whose Morals?" *Time*, January 9, 2024. https://time.com/6451192/history-civic-morality-schools/.

Hutton, Alison, Ivanka Prichard, Dean Whitehead, et al. "mHealth Interventions to Reduce Alcohol Use in Young People: A Systematic Review of the Literature." *Comprehensive Child and Adolescent Nursing* 43, no. 3 (2019): 171–202. https://doi.org/10.1080/24694193.2019.1616008.

Hutton, John S., Jonathan Dudley, Thomas DeWitt, and Tzipi Horowitz-Kraus. "Associations Between Digital Media Use and Brain Surface Structural Measures in Preschool-Aged Children." *Scientific Reports* 12, no. 1 (2022). https://doi.org/10.1038/s41598-022-20922-0.

Hutton, John S., Jonathan Dudley, Tzipi Horowitz-Kraus, Tom DeWitt, and Scott K. Holland. "Associations Between Screen-Based Media Use and Brain White Matter Integrity in Preschool-Aged Children." *JAMA Pediatrics* 174, no. 1 (2019): e193869. https://doi.org/10.1001/jamapediatrics.2019.3869.

Illingworth, Gaby. "Maternal Mind-Mindedness: A Cognitive-Behavioural Trait or a Relational Construct?" PhD thesis, Oxford Brookes University, 2014.

Ingold, Tim. "Why We Disagree About Human Nature." Review of *Why We Disagree About Human Nature*, by Elizabeth Hannon and Tim Lewens. *Notre Dame Philosophical Reviews*, May 3, 2019.

Inguglia, Cristiano, Sebastiano Costa, Sonia Ingoglia, Francesca Cuzzocrea, and Francesca Liga. "The Role of Parental Control and Coping Strategies on Adolescents' Problem Behaviors." *Current Psychology* 41, no. 3 (2020): 1287–300. https://doi.org/10.1007/s12144-020-00648-w.

Inkeles, Alex. "Social Change and Social Character: The Role of Parental Mediation." *Journal of Social Issues* 11, no. 2 (1955): 12–23. https://doi.org/10.1111/j.1540-4560.1955.tb00311.x.

Iqbal, Sarosh, Rubeena Zakar, and Florian Fischer. "Predictors of Parental Mediation in Teenagers' Internet Use: A Cross-Sectional Study of Female Caregivers in Lahore,

Pakistan." *BMC Public Health* 21, no. 1 (2021). https://doi.org/10.1186/s12889-021-10349-z.

Irzalinda, Vivi, and Melly Latifah. "Screen Time and Early Childhood Well-Being: A Systematic Literature Review Approach." *Journal of Family Sciences* 31 (2023): 18–34. https://doi.org/10.29244/jfs.vi.49792.

Izrael, Pavel. "Religiousness, Values, and Parental Mediation of Children's Television Viewing in Slovakia." *Journal of Children and Media* 7, no. 4 (2013): 507–24. https://doi.org/10.1080/17482798.2013.827129.

Jaccard, James, and Jacob Jacoby. *Theory Construction and Model-Building Skills: A Practical Guide for Social Scientists*. Guilford Press, 2010.

Jack, Gordon. "Ecological Perspectives in Assessing Children and Families." In *The Child's World: Assessing Children in Need*, edited by Jan Horwatch. Jessica Kingsley Publishers, 2001.

Jackson, Kristina M., Tim Janssen, Melissa J. Cox, Suzanne M. Colby, Nancy P. Barnett, and James Sargent. "Mechanisms Underlying Associations Between Media Alcohol Exposure, Parenting, and Early Adolescent Drinking: A Moderated Sequential Mediation Model." *Journal of Youth and Adolescence* 50, no. 9 (2021): 1896–910. https://doi.org/10.1007/s10964-020-01373-0.

Jacobson, Kristen C., and Lisa J. Crockett. "Parental Monitoring and Adolescent Adjustment: An Ecological Perspective." *Journal of Research on Adolescence* 10, no. 1 (2000): 65–97. https://doi.org/10.1207/sjra1001_4.

Jago, Russell, Emmanuel Stamatakis, Augusta Gama, et al. "Parent and Child Screen-Viewing Time and Home Media Environment." *American Journal of Preventive Medicine* 43, no. 2 (2012): 150–8. https://doi.org/10.1016/j.amepre.2012.04.012.

Janssen, Xanne, Anne Martin, Adrienne R. Hughes, Catherine M. Hill, Grigorios Kotronoulas, and Kathryn R. Hesketh. "Associations of Screen Time, Sedentary Time and Physical Activity with Sleep in Under 5s: A Systematic Review and Meta-Analysis." *Sleep Medicine Reviews* 49 (2019): 101226. https://doi.org/10.1016/j.smrv.2019.101226.

Jarman, Hannah K., Mathew D. Marques, Siân A. McLean, Amy Slater, and Susan J. Paxton. "Social Media, Body Satisfaction and Well-Being Among Adolescents: A Mediation Model of Appearance-Ideal Internalization and Comparison." *Body Image* 36 (2020): 139–48. https://doi.org/10.1016/j.bodyim.2020.11.005.

Jernigan, David, Jonathan Noel, Jane Landon, Nicole Thornton, and Tim Lobstein. "Alcohol Marketing and Youth Alcohol Consumption: A Systematic Review of Longitudinal Studies Published Since 2008." *Addiction* 112, no. S1 (2016): 7–20. https://doi.org/10.1111/add.13591.

Jeynes, William H. "The Relationship Between Parental Involvement and Urban Secondary School Student Academic Achievement." *Urban Education* 42, no. 1 (2006): 82–110. https://doi.org/10.1177/0042085906293818.

Ji, Xiaoqing, Ningning Feng, and Lijuan Cui. "The Serial Mediation Role of Parent-Child Attachment and Empathy in the Relationship Between Parental Technoference and Social Anxiety." *Current Psychology* 43, no. 29 (2024): 24418–28. https://doi.org/10.1007/s12144-024-06109-y.

Jin, Bihui, and Danhui Zhang. "Linking Parental Restrictive Mediation to Adolescents' Science Achievement: A Social Cognitive Theory Perspective." *Learning and*

Individual Differences 98 (2022): 102187. https://doi.org/10.1016/j.lindif.2022.102187.

Jing, Mengguo, Ting Ye, Heather L. Kirkorian, and Marie-Louise Mares. "Screen Media Exposure and Young Children's Vocabulary Learning and Development: A Meta-Analysis." *Child Development* 94, no. 5 (2023): 1398–418. https://doi.org/10.1111/cdev.13927.

Jinqiu, Zhao, and Hao Xiaoming. "Parent-Child Co-viewing of Television and Cognitive Development of the Chinese Child." *International Journal of Early Years Education* 12, no. 1 (2004): 63–77. https://doi.org/10.1080/0966976042000182389.

Jordan, Amy. "The Role of Media in Children's Development: An Ecological Perspective." *Developmental and Behavioral Pediatrics* 25, no. 3 (2004): 196–206.

Kahhalé, Isabella, Kelly R. Barry, and Jamie L. Hanson. "Positive Parenting Moderates Associations Between Childhood Stress and Corticolimbic Structure." *PNAS Nexus* 2, no. 6 (2023). https://doi.org/10.1093/pnasnexus/pgad145.

Kahn, Robert S., Dominique Brandt, and Robert C. Whitaker. "Combined Effect of Mothers' and Fathers' Mental Health Symptoms on Children's Behavioral and Emotional Well-being." *Archives of Pediatrics and Adolescent Medicine* 158, no. 8 (2004): 721. https://doi.org/10.1001/archpedi.158.8.721.

Kakihara, Fumiko, and Lauree Tilton-Weaver. "Adolescents' Interpretations of Parental Control: Differentiated by Domain and Types of Control." *Child Development* 80, no. 6 (2009): 1722–38. https://doi.org/10.1111/j.1467-8624.2009.01364.x.

Kakihara, Fumiko, Lauree Tilton-Weaver, Margaret Kerr, and Håkan Stattin. "The Relationship of Parental Control to Youth Adjustment: Do Youths' Feelings About Their Parents Play a Role?" *Journal of Youth and Adolescence* 39, no. 12 (2009): 1442–56. https://doi.org/10.1007/s10964-009-9479-8.

Kalmus, Veronika, Lukas Blinka, and Kjartan Ólafsson. "Does it Matter What Mama Says: Evaluating the Role of Parental Mediation in European Adolescents' Excessive Internet Use." *Children & Society* 29, no. 2 (2013): 122–33. https://doi.org/10.1111/chso.12020.

Kalmus, Veronika, Marit Sukk, and Kadri Soo. "Towards More Active Parenting: Trends in Parental Mediation of Children's Internet Use in European Countries." *Children & Society* 36, no. 5 (2022): 1026–42. https://doi.org/10.1111/chso.12553.

Kamhawi, Rasha, and David Weaver. "Mass Communication Research Trends From 1980 to 1999." *Journalism & Mass Communication Quarterly* 80, no. 1 (2003): 7–27. https://doi.org/10.1177/107769900308000102.

Kanter, Maggie, Tamara Afifi, and Stephanie Robbins. "The Impact of Parents 'Friending' Their Young Adult Child on Facebook on Perceptions of Parental Privacy Invasions and Parent-Child Relationship Quality." *Journal of Communication* 62, no. 5 (2012): 900–17. https://doi.org/10.1111/j.1460-2466.2012.01669.x.

Karpov, Yuriy. "Vygotsky's Concept of Mediation." *Journal of Cognitive Education and Psychology* 3, no. 1 (2003): 46–53.

Karreman, Annemiek, Cathy Van Tuijl, Marcel A. G. Van Aken, and Maja Deković. "Parenting and Self-Regulation in Preschoolers: A Meta-Analysis." *Infant and Child Development* 15, no. 6 (2006): 561–79. https://doi.org/10.1002/icd.478.

Karsay, Kathrin, Desirée Schmuck, Anja Stevic, and Jörg Matthes. "Sleeping With the Smartphone: A Panel Study Investigating Parental Mediation, Adolescents'

Tiredness, and Physical Well-Being." *Behaviour and Information Technology* 42, no. 11 (2022): 1833–44. https://doi.org/10.1080/0144929x.2022.2100277.

Karsay, Kathrin, Jolien Trekels, Steven Eggermont, and Laura Vandenbosch. "'I (Don't) Respect My Body': Investigating the Role of Mass Media Use and Self-Objectification on Adolescents' Positive Body Image in a Cross-National Study." *Mass Communication & Society* 24, no. 1 (2020): 57–84. https://doi.org/10.1080/15205436.2020.1827432.

Katz, Vikki S., Meghan B. Moran, and Carmen Gonzalez. "Connecting with Technology in Lower-Income US Families." *New Media & Society* 20, no. 7 (2017): 2509–33. https://doi.org/10.1177/1461444817726319.

Keles, Betul, Niall McCrae, and Annmarie Grealish. "A Systematic Review: The Influence of Social Media on Depression, Anxiety and Psychological Distress in Adolescents." *International Journal of Adolescence and Youth* 25, no. 1 (2019): 79–93. https://doi.org/10.1080/02673843.2019.1590851.

Kerai, Salima, Alisa Almas, Martin Guhn, Barry Forer, and Eva Oberle. "Screen Time and Developmental Health: Results from an Early Childhood Study in Canada." *BMC Public Health* 22, no. 1 (2022). https://doi.org/10.1186/s12889-022-12701-3.

Kerr, Margaret, Håkan Stattin, and William J. Burk. "A Reinterpretation of Parental Monitoring in Longitudinal Perspective." *Journal of Research on Adolescence* 20, no. 1 (2010): 39–64. https://doi.org/10.1111/j.1532-7795.2009.00623.x.

King, Jr., Martin Luther. "The Purpose of Education." *Maroon Tiger*, January 1, 1947. https://kinginstitute.stanford.edu/king-papers/documents/purpose-education#fn1.

Kirwil, Lucyna. "Parental Mediation of Children's Internet Use in Different European Countries." *Journal of Children and Media* 3, no. 4 (2009): 394–409. https://doi.org/10.1080/17482790903233440.

Klahr, A. M., S. A. Burt, and M. Nikolas. "Developmental Psychopathology." In *Elsevier eBooks*, 697–701, 2012. https://doi.org/10.1016/b978-0-12-375000-6.00132-4.

Klein, P. S., O. Nir-Gal, and E. Darom. "The Use of Computers in Kindergarten, With or Without Adult Mediation: Effects on Children's Cognitive Performance and Behavior." *Computers in Human Behavior* 16, no. 6 (2000): 591–608. https://doi.org/10.1016/s0747-5632(00)00027-3.

Klin, Anat, and Dafna Lemish. "Mental Disorders Stigma in the Media: Review of Studies on Production, Content, and Influences." *Journal of Health Communication* 13, no. 5 (2008): 434–49. https://doi.org/10.1080/10810730802198813.

Koch, Teresa, Franziska Laaber, and Arnd Florack. "Socioeconomic Status and Young People's Digital Maturity: The Role of Parental Mediation." *Computers in Human Behavior* 154 (2024): 108157. https://doi.org/10.1016/j.chb.2024.108157.

Koning, Ina M., Margot Peeters, Catrin Finkenauer, and Regina J. J. M. Van Den Eijnden. "Bidirectional Effects of Internet-Specific Parenting Practices and Compulsive Social Media and Internet Game Use." *Journal of Behavioral Addictions* 7, no. 3 (2018): 624–32. https://doi.org/10.1556/2006.7.2018.68.

Korat, Ofra, Pnina Klein, and Ora Segal-Drori. "Maternal Mediation in Book Reading, Home Literacy Environment, and Children's Emergent Literacy: A Comparison Between Two Social Groups." *Reading and Writing* 20, no. 4 (2006): 361–98. https://doi.org/10.1007/s11145-006-9034-x.

Korat, Ofra, and Daphna Shneor. "Can E-books Support Low SES Parental Mediation to Enrich Children's Vocabulary?" *First Language* 39, no. 3 (2019): 344–64. https://doi.org/10.1177/0142723718822443.

Krauss, Samantha, Ulrich Orth, and Richard W. Robins. "Family Environment and Self-Esteem Development: A Longitudinal Study from Age 10 to 16." *Journal of Personality and Social Psychology* 119, no. 2 (2019): 457–78. https://doi.org/10.1037/pspp0000263.

Krcmar, Marina, and Drew P. Cingel. "Examining Two Theoretical Models Predicting American and Dutch Parents' Mediation of Adolescent Social Media Use." *Journal of Family Communication* 16, no. 3 (2016): 247–62. https://doi.org/10.1080/15267431.2016.1181632.

Kroll, Brynna. "Living with an Elephant: Growing up with Parental Substance Misuse." *Child & Family Social Work* 9, no. 2 (2004): 129–40. https://doi.org/10.1111/j.1365-2206.2004.00325.x.

Krumrei-Mancuso, Elizabeth J., Megan C. Haggard, Jordan P. LaBouff, and Wade C. Rowatt. "Links Between Intellectual Humility and Acquiring Knowledge." *The Journal of Positive Psychology* 15, no. 2 (2019): 155–70. https://doi.org/10.1080/17439760.2019.1579359.

Kuhn, Thomas, S. *The Structure of Scientific Revolutions*. The University of Chicago Press, 1996.

Kuldas, Seffetullah, Aikaterini Sargioti, Tijana Milosevic, and James O'Higgins Norman. "A Review and Content Validation of 10 Measurement Scales for Parental Mediation of Children's Internet Use." *International Journal of Communication*, 2021. https://ijoc.org/index.php/ijoc/article/view/17265.

Kullberg, Marie-Louise J., Renate S. M. Buisman, Charlotte C. Van Schie, et al. "Linking Internalizing and Externalizing Problems to Warmth and Negativity in Observed Dyadic Parent–Offspring Communication." *Family Relations* 72, no. 5 (2023): 2777–99. https://doi.org/10.1111/fare.12847.

Laird, Robert D., Matthew D. Marrero, and Miranda Sentse. "Revisiting Parental Monitoring: Evidence that Parental Solicitation Can Be Effective When Needed Most." *Journal of Youth and Adolescence* 39, no. 12 (2009): 1431–41. https://doi.org/10.1007/s10964-009-9453-5.

Lan, Qiu-Ye, Kate C. Chan, Kwan N. Yu, et al. "Sleep Duration in Preschool Children and Impact of Screen Time." *Sleep Medicine* 76 (2020): 48–54. https://doi.org/10.1016/j.sleep.2020.09.024.

Landry, Megan, Monique Turner, Amita Vyas, and Susan Wood. "Social Media and Sexual Behavior Among Adolescents: Is There a Link?" *JMIR Public Health and Surveillance* 3, no. 2 (2017): e28. https://doi.org/10.2196/publichealth.7149.

Lang, Annie. "Discipline in Crisis? The Shifting Paradigm of Mass Communication Research." *Communication Theory* 23, no. 1 (2013): 10–24. https://doi.org/10.1111/comt.12000.

Lang, Annie, and Rachel L. Bailey. "Understanding Information Selection and Encoding from a Dynamic, Energy Saving, Evolved, Embodied, Embedded Perspective." *Human Communication Research* 41, no. 1 (2014): 1-20. https://doi.org/10.1111/hcre.12040.

Lang, Annie, and David Ewoldsen. "Beyond Effects: Conceptualizing Communication as Dynamic, Complex, Nonlinear, and Fundamental." In *Rethinking Communication*, edited by S. Allan. Hampton Press, 2010.

Lang, Annie, Robert F. Potter, and Paul Bolls. "Where Psychophysiology Meets the Media: Taking the Effects Out of Mass Media Research." In *Media Effects: Advances in Theory and Research*, edited by Jennings Bryant and Mary Beth Oliver. Routledge, 2009.

Langøy, Amund, Otto R. F. Smith, Bente Wold, Oddrun Samdal, and Ellen M. Haug. "Associations Between Family Structure and Young People's Physical Activity and Screen Time Behaviors." *BMC Public Health* 19, no. 1 (2019). https://doi.org/10.1186/s12889-019-6740-2.

Lanjekar, Purva D., Shiv H. Joshi, Puja D. Lanjekar, and Vasant Wagh. "The Effect of Parenting and the Parent-Child Relationship on a Child's Cognitive Development: A Literature Review." *Cureus*, 2022. https://doi.org/10.7759/cureus.30574.

Lansford, Jennifer E. "Annual Research Review: Cross-Cultural Similarities and Differences in Parenting." *Journal of Child Psychology and Psychiatry* 63, no. 4 (2021): 466–79. https://doi.org/10.1111/jcpp.13539.

Larson, Edward J., and Larry Witham. "Scientists Are Still Keeping the Faith." *Nature* 386, no. 6624 (1997): 435–36. https://doi.org/10.1038/386435a0.

Latomme, Julie, Vicky Van Stappen, Greet Cardon, et al. "The Association Between Children's and Parents' Co-TV Viewing and Their Total Screen Time in Six European Countries: Cross-Sectional Data from the Feel4diabetes-Study." *International Journal of Environmental Research and Public Health* 15, no. 11 (2018): 2599. https://doi.org/10.3390/ijerph15112599.

Latzer, Yael, Zohar Spivak-Lavi, and Ruth Katz. "Disordered Eating and Media Exposure Among Adolescent Girls: The Role of Parental Involvement and Sense of Empowerment." *International Journal of Adolescence and Youth* 20, no. 3 (2015): 375–91. https://doi.org/10.1080/02673843.2015.1014925.

Lauricella, Alexis R., and Drew P. Cingel. "Parental Influence on Youth Media Use." *Journal of Child and Family Studies* 29, no. 7 (2020): 1927–37. https://doi.org/10.1007/s10826-020-01724-2.

Lauricella, Alexis R., Drew P. Cingel, Leanne Beaudoin-Ryan, Michael B. Robb, Melissa Saphir, and Ellen Wartella. "The Common Sense Census: Plugged-in Parents of Tweens and Teens." Common Sense Media, 2016.

Lauricella, Alexis R., Ellen Wartella, and Victoria J. Rideout. "Young Children's Screen Time: The Complex Role of Parent and Child Factors." *Journal of Applied Developmental Psychology* 36 (2015): 11–17. https://doi.org/10.1016/j.appdev.2014.12.001.

Layton, Christopher, and David Hansen. "Religion and Gender in the Impact of Parental Mediation on Self-Censorship and Attitudes Toward Mediation." *Journal of Undergraduate Research* 2013, no. 1 (2013). https://scholarsarchive.byu.edu/jur/vol2013/iss1/170/.

Lee, Eun-Young, Yoon-Kyung Song, Stephen Hunter, et al. "Levels and Correlates of Physical Activity and Screen Time Among Early Years Children (2–5 Years): Cross-Cultural Comparisons Between Canadian and South Korean Data." *Child: Care, Health and Development* 47, no. 3 (2021): 377–86. https://doi.org/10.1111/cch.12850.

Lee, Eun-Young, John C. Spence, and Valerie Carson. "Television Viewing, Reading, Physical Activity and Brain Development Among Young South Korean Children." *Journal of Science and Medicine in Sport* 20, no. 7 (2017): 672–7. https://doi.org/10.1016/j.jsams.2016.11.014.

Lee, Hye Eun, Ji Young Kim, and Changsook Kim. "The Influence of Parent Media Use, Parent Attitude on Media, and Parenting Style on Children's Media Use." *Children* 9, no. 1 (2022): 37. https://doi.org/10.3390/children9010037.

Lee, Jungup, and Karen A. Randolph. "Effects of Parental Monitoring on Aggressive Behavior Among Youth in the United States and South Korea: A Cross-National Study." *Children and Youth Services Review* 55 (2015): 1–9. https://doi.org/10.1016/j.childyouth.2015.05.008.

Lee, Seulgi, Haemi Choi, Min-Hyeon Park, and Bumhee Park. "Differential Role of Negative and Positive Parenting Styles on Resting-State Brain Networks in Middle-Aged Adolescents." *Journal of Affective Disorders* 365 (2024): 222–9. https://doi.org/10.1016/j.jad.2024.08.096.

Lee, Sook-Jung. "Parental Restrictive Mediation of Children's Internet Use: Effective for What and for Whom?" *New Media & Society* 15, no. 4 (2012): 466–81. https://doi.org/10.1177/1461444812452412.

Lee, Sook-Jung, Silvia Bartolic, and Elizabeth A. Vandewater. "Predicting Children's Media Use in the USA: Differences in Cross-Sectional and Longitudinal Analysis." *British Journal of Developmental Psychology* 27, no. 1 (2009): 123–43. https://doi.org/10.1348/026151008x401336.

Leigh, Eleanor, and David M. Clark. "Understanding Social Anxiety Disorder in Adolescents and Improving Treatment Outcomes: Applying the Cognitive Model of Clark and Wells (1995)." *Clinical Child and Family Psychology Review* 21, no. 3 (2018): 388–414. https://doi.org/10.1007/s10567-018-0258-5.

Lemish, Dafna. *Children and Media: A Global Perspective*. John Wiley & Sons, 2015.

Len-Ríos, María E., Hilary E. Hughes, Laura G. McKee, and Henry N. Young. "Early Adolescents as Publics: A National Survey of Teens with Social Media Accounts, Their Media Use Preferences, Parental Mediation, and Perceived Internet Literacy." *Public Relations Review* 42, no. 1 (2015): 101–8. https://doi.org/10.1016/j.pubrev.2015.10.003.

Leonard, Heather, and Atika Khurana. "Parenting Behaviors and Family Conflict as Predictors of Adolescent Sleep and Bedtime Media Use." *Journal of Youth and Adolescence* 51, no. 8 (2022): 1611–21. https://doi.org/10.1007/s10964-022-01614-4.

Levine, Glenn N., Beth E. Cohen, Yvonne Commodore-Mensah, et al. "Psychological Health, Well-Being, and the Mind-Heart-Body Connection: A Scientific Statement from the American Heart Association." *Circulation* 143, no. 10 (2021): e763–83. https://doi.org/10.1161/cir.0000000000000947.

Levine, Timothy R., and David M. Markowitz. "The Role of Theory in Researching and Understanding Human Communication." *Human Communication Research* 50, no. 2 (2023): 154–61. https://doi.org/10.1093/hcr/hqad037.

Li, Chao, Gang Cheng, Tingting Sha, Wenwei Cheng, and Yan Yan. "The Relationships Between Screen Use and Health Indicators Among Infants, Toddlers, and Preschoolers: A Meta-Analysis and Systematic Review." *International Journal of Environmental Research and Public Health* 17, no. 19 (2020): 7324. https://doi.org/10.3390/ijerph17197324.

Li, Juan, Jingyao Wang, Bowen Xiao, Yan Li, and Hui Li. "Translation and Validation of the Chinese Version of the Problematic Media Use Measure." *Early Education and Development* 35, no. 1 (2023): 26–41. https://doi.org/10.1080/10409289.2023.2193856.

Li, Juan, Bowen Xiao, Yanan Zhao, Bingda Zhang, and Yan Li. "Chinese Parental Mediation, Predictors, and Associations with Children's Problematic Media Use: A Latent Profile Analysis." *Early Education and Development* 36 (2024): 1–18. https://doi.org/10.1080/10409289.2024.2360867.

Li, Xiaojing, Ying Ding, Xianchun Bai, and Lisha Liu. "Associations Between Parental Mediation and Adolescents' Internet Addiction: The Role of Parent–Child Relationship and Adolescents' Grades." *Frontiers in Psychology* 13 (2022). https://doi.org/10.3389/fpsyg.2022.1061631.

Li, Xiaoyun, Yuke Fu, Wanjuan Weng, Mowei Liu, and Yan Li. "Maternal Phubbing and Problematic Media Use in Preschoolers: The Independent and Interactive Moderating Role of Children's Negative Affectivity and Effortful Control." *Psychology Research and Behavior Management* 17 (2024): 3083–100. https://doi.org/10.2147/prbm.s471208.

Liau, Albert Kienfie, Angeline Khoo, and Peng Hwa Ang. "Parental Awareness and Monitoring of Adolescent Internet Use." *Current Psychology* 27, no. 4 (2008): 217–33. https://doi.org/10.1007/s12144-008-9038-6.

Liebeskind, Kara M. "The Exploration of U.S. Parents' Television Mediation Through Genre-Specific Scenarios." *Journal of Children and Media* 9, no. 1 (2015): 113–32. https://doi.org/10.1080/17482798.2015.997100.

Lin, Carolyn A., and David J. Atkin. "Parental Mediation and Rulemaking for Adolescent Use of Television and VCRs." *Journal of Broadcasting & Electronic Media* 33, no. 1 (1989): 53–67. https://doi.org/10.1080/08838158909364061.

Lin, Wen-Hsu, Chia-Hua Liu, and Chin-Chun Yi. "Exposure to Sexually Explicit Media in Early Adolescence is Related to Risky Sexual Behavior in Emerging Adulthood." *PLoS ONE* 15, no. 4 (2020): e0230242. https://doi.org/10.1371/journal.pone.0230242.

Lin, W.-Y. "From Human Nature Belief to Parenting Behavior: Mediation Process Hypothesis." *Chinese Journal of Psychology* 47, no. 3 (2005): 229–48.

Lin, Yi-Ching, Meng-Che Tsai, Carol Strong, Yi-Ping Hsieh, Chung-Ying Lin, and Clara S. C. Lee. "Exploring Mediation Roles of Child Screen-Viewing Between Parental Factors and Child Overweight in Taiwan." *International Journal of Environmental Research and Public Health* 17, no. 6 (2020): 1878. https://doi.org/10.3390/ijerph17061878.

Lindsey, Eric W., and Jacquelyn Mize. "Parent-Child Physical and Pretense Play: Links to Children's Social Competence." *Merrill-Palmer Quarterly* 46, no. 4 (2000): 565–91. https://www.jstor.org/stable/23092565.

Ling, Crystal, and Hon Kai Yee. "Parental Mediation: Its Impact on Contexts of Emotional Behavioral Adjustment Among Children in Kota Kinabalu District." *Cogent Social Sciences* 7, no. 1 (2021). https://doi.org/10.1080/23311886.2020.1870070.

Lionetti, Francesca, Benedetta Emanuela Palladino, Christina Moses Passini et al. "The Development of Parental Monitoring During Adolescence: A Meta-Analysis."

European Journal of Developmental Psychology 16, no. 5 (2018): 552–80. https://doi.org/10.1080/17405629.2018.1476233.

Liu, Lisha, Qian Wang, and Yanfang Li. "Developing Children's Humanity: The Unique and Interactive Role of Parents' and Peers' Humanity." *Educational Psychology* 43, no. 8 (2023): 967–88. https://doi.org/10.1080/01443410.2023.2272068.

Liu, Qinxue, and Jiayin Wu. "What Children Learn in a Digital Home: The Complex Influence of Parental Mediation and Smartphone Interference." *Education and Information Technologies* 29, no. 5 (2023): 6273–91. https://doi.org/10.1007/s10639-023-12071-2.

Livingstone, Sonia, and Ellen J. Helsper. "Parental Mediation of Children's Internet Use." *Journal of Broadcasting & Electronic Media* 52, no. 4 (2008): 581–99. https://doi.org/10.1080/08838150802437396.

Livingstone, Sonia, Giovanna Mascheroni, Michael Dreier, Stéphane Chaudron, and Kaat Lagae. "How Parents of Young Children Manage Digital Devices at Home: The Role of Income, Education and Parental Style." EU Kids Online, 2015.

Livingstone, Sonia, Kjartan Ólafsson, Ellen J. Helsper, Francisco Lupiáñez-Villanueva, Giuseppe A. Veltri, and Frans Folkvord. "Maximizing Opportunities and Minimizing Risks for Children Online: The Role of Digital Skills in Emerging Strategies of Parental Mediation." *Journal of Communication* 67, no. 1 (2017): 82–105. https://doi.org/10.1111/jcom.12277.

López-de-Ayala-López, María Cruz, and Leslie Haddon. "The Parental Mediation Strategies of Parents with Young Children." *Media@LSE Working Paper Series* 50 (2018): 1–26.

Lou, Jiaxue, Menmen Wang, Xiaoliang Xie, et al. "The Association Between Family Socio-Demographic Factors, Parental Mediation and Adolescents' Digital Literacy: A Cross-Sectional Study." *BMC Public Health* 24, no. 1 (2024). https://doi.org/10.1186/s12889-024-20284-4.

Louka, Konstantina, and Stamatios Papadakis. "Enhancing Computational Thinking in Early Childhood Education Through ScratchJr Integration." *Heliyon* 10, no. 10 (2024): e30482. https://doi.org/10.1016/j.heliyon.2024.e30482.

Lukavská, Kateřina, Jaroslav Vacek, Ondřej Hrabec, et al. "Measuring Parental Behavior Towards Children's Use of Media and Screen-Devices: The Development and Psychometrical Properties of a Media Parenting Scale for Parents of School-Aged Children." *International Journal of Environmental Research and Public Health* 18, no. 17 (2021): 9178. https://doi.org/10.3390/ijerph18179178.

Lund, Lisbeth, Ida Nielsen Sølvhøj, Dina Danielsen, and Susan Andersen. "Electronic Media Use and Sleep in Children and Adolescents in Western Countries: A Systematic Review." *BMC Public Health* 21, no. 1 (2021). https://doi.org/10.1186/s12889-021-11640-9.

Luo, Ting, M. S. Li, D. Williams, et al. "Using Social Media for Smoking Cessation Interventions: A Systematic Review." *Perspectives in Public Health* 141, no. 1 (2020): 50–63. https://doi.org/10.1177/1757913920906845.

Luther, Martin. "A Sermon or Discourse of Martin Luther: That Children Be Kept at School." *The Open Court*, 423–32. https://opensiuc.lib.siu.edu/cgi/viewcontent.cgi?article=1067&context=ocj.

Lwin, May O., Shelly Malik, Hardinsyah Ridwan, and Cyndy Sook Sum Au. "Media Exposure and Parental Mediation on Fast-Food Consumption Among Children in

Metropolitan and Suburban Indonesia." *PubMed* 26, no. 5 (2017): 899–905. https://doi.org/10.6133/apjcn.122016.04.

Mabaso, Wakithi Siza, Sascha Hein, Gabriela Pavarini, and Mina Fazel. "Exploring the Relationship Between Public Social Media Accounts, Adolescent Mental Health, and Parental Guidance in England: Large Cross-Sectional School Survey Study." *Journal of Medical Internet Research* 26 (2024): e57154. https://doi.org/10.2196/57154.

Macrynikola, Natalia, Emelyn Auad, Jose Menjivar, and Regina Miranda. "Does Social Media Use Confer Suicide Risk? A Systematic Review of the Evidence." *Computers in Human Behavior Reports* 3 (2021): 100094. https://doi.org/10.1016/j.chbr.2021.100094.

Madigan, Sheri, Brae Anne McArthur, Ciana Anhorn, Rachel Eirich, and Dimitri A. Christakis. "Associations Between Screen Use and Child Language Skills." *JAMA Pediatrics* 174, no. 7 (2020): 665–75. https://doi.org/10.1001/jamapediatrics.2020.0327.

Maes, Chelly, Lara Schreurs, Johanna M. F. Van Oosten, and Laura Vandenbosch. "#(Me)Too Much? The Role of Sexualizing Online Media in Adolescents' Resistance Towards the Metoo-movement and Acceptance of Rape Myths." *Journal of Adolescence* 77, no. 1 (2019): 59–69. https://doi.org/10.1016/j.adolescence.2019.10.005.

Magar, Emily C. E., Louise H. Phillips, and Judith A. Hosie. "Self-Regulation and Risk-Taking." *Personality and Individual Differences* 45, no. 2 (2008): 153–9. https://doi.org/10.1016/j.paid.2008.03.014.

Mageau, Geneviève A., Mireille Joussemet, Chantal Paquin, and Fanny Grenier. "How-to-Parenting-Program: Change in Parenting and Child Mental Health Over One Year." *Journal of Child and Family Studies* 31, no. 12 (2022): 3498–513. https://doi.org/10.1007/s10826-022-02442-7.

Mancone, Stefania, Stefano Corrado, Beatrice Tosti, Giuseppe Spica, and Pierluigi Diotaiuti. "Integrating Digital and Interactive Approaches in Adolescent Health Literacy: A Comprehensive Review." *Frontiers in Public Health* 12 (2024). https://doi.org/10.3389/fpubh.2024.1387874.

Männikkö, Niko, Heidi Ruotsalainen, Jouko Miettunen, Kaisa Marttila-Tornio, and Maria Kääriäinen. "Parental Socioeconomic Status, Adolescents' Screen Time and Sports Participation Through Externalizing and Internalizing Characteristics." *Heliyon* 6, no. 2 (2020): e03415. https://doi.org/10.1016/j.heliyon.2020.e03415.

Manohar, Uttara. "The Role of Culture in Parental Mediation." MA thesis, The Ohio State University, 2011.

Marciano, Laura, Michelle Ostroumova, Peter Johannes Schulz, and Anne-Linda Camerini. "Digital Media Use and Adolescents' Mental Health During the Covid-19 Pandemic: A Systematic Review and Meta-Analysis." *Frontiers in Public Health* 9 (2022). https://doi.org/10.3389/fpubh.2021.793868.

Mares, Marie-Louise, and Zhongdang Pan. "Effects of Sesame Street: A Meta-Analysis of Children's Learning in 15 Countries." *Journal of Applied Developmental Psychology* 34, no. 3 (2013): 140–51. https://doi.org/10.1016/j.appdev.2013.01.001.

Marsh, Samantha, Rosie Dobson, and Ralph Maddison. "The Relationship Between Household Chaos and Child, Parent, and Family Outcomes: A Systematic Scoping

Review." *BMC Public Health* 20, no. 1 (2020). https://doi.org/10.1186/s12889-020-08587-8.

Martellozzo, Elena, Andy Monaghan, Joanna R. Adler, Julia Davidson, Rodolfo Leyva, and Miranda A. H. Horvath. "'I Wasn't Sure it was Normal to Watch it...': A Quantitative and Qualitative Examination of the Impact of Online Pornography on the Values, Attitudes, Beliefs and Behaviours of Children and Young People." Middlesex University, 2017. https://doi.org/10.6084/m9.figshare.3382393.

Martínez-González, Miguel Angel, Pilar Gual, Francisca Lahortiga, Yolanda Alonso, Jokin De Irala-EsteVez, and Salvador Cervera. "Parental Factors, Mass Media Influences, and the Onset of Eating Disorders in a Prospective Population-Based Cohort." *Pediatrics* 111, no. 2 (2003): 315–20. https://doi.org/10.1542/peds.111.2.315.

Martins, Nicole, Marie-Louise Mares, and Amy I. Nathanson. "Mixed Messages: Inconsistent Parental Mediation Indirectly Predicts Teens' Online Relational Aggression." *Journal of Family Communication* 19, no. 4 (2019): 311–28. https://doi.org/10.1080/15267431.2019.1649264.

Martins, Nicole, Nicholas L. Matthews, and Rabindra A. Ratan. "Playing by the Rules: Parental Mediation of Video Game Play." *Journal of Family Issues* 38, no. 9 (2015): 1215–38. https://doi.org/10.1177/0192513x15613822.

Mauriello, Leanne M., Mary Margaret H. Ciavatta, Andrea L. Paiva, et al. "Results of a Multi-Media Multiple Behavior Obesity Prevention Program for Adolescents." *Preventive Medicine* 51, no. 6 (2010): 451–6. https://doi.org/10.1016/j.ypmed.2010.08.004.

Maza, Maria T., Kara A. Fox, Seh-Joo Kwon, et al. "Association of Habitual Checking Behaviors on Social Media with Longitudinal Functional Brain Development." *JAMA Pediatrics* 177, no. 2 (2023): 160. https://doi.org/10.1001/jamapediatrics.2022.4924.

McArthur, Brae Anne, Dillon Browne, Suzanne Tough, and Sheri Madigan. "Trajectories of Screen Use During Early Childhood: Predictors and Associated Behavior and Learning Outcomes." *Computers in Human Behavior* 113 (2020): 106501. https://doi.org/10.1016/j.chb.2020.106501.

McCabe, Kristen M., Argero Zerr, Mariah Cook, Lindsey Ringlee, and May Yeh. "The Relation Between Parent Mental Health and Child Internalizing Symptoms in Parent–Child Interaction Therapy." *Journal of Child and Family Studies* 31, no. 8 (2022): 2065–76. https://doi.org/10.1007/s10826-022-02254-9.

McCarthy, Elizabeth, Michelle Tiu, and Linlin Li. "Learning Math with Curious George and the Odd Squad: Transmedia in the Classroom." *Technology Knowledge and Learning* 23, no. 2 (2018): 223–46. https://doi.org/10.1007/s10758-018-9361-4.

McCool, Judith, Linda D. Cameron, and Elizabeth Robinson. "Do Parents Have Any Influence Over How Young People Appraise Tobacco Images in the Media?" *Journal of Adolescent Health* 48, no. 2 (2010): 170–5. https://doi.org/10.1016/j.jadohealth.2010.06.012.

McCown, Nance. "Recognizing the Imago Dei in Employee Publics: A Challenge for Christian Public Relations Scholars, Faculty, and Practitioners." *Journal of Communication & Religion* 43, no. 1 (2020): 75–88. https://doi.org/10.5840/jcr20204315.

McMillan, Rachel, Michael McIsaac, and Ian Janssen. "Family Structure as a Predictor of Screen Time Among Youth." *PeerJ* 3 (2015): e1048. https://doi.org/10.7717/peerj.1048.

Meeus, Anneleen, Ine Beyens, Femke Geusens, An Katrien Sodermans, and Kathleen Beullens. "Managing Positive and Negative Media Effects Among Adolescents: Parental Mediation Matters—But Not Always." *Journal of Family Communication* 18, no. 4 (2018): 270–85. https://doi.org/10.1080/15267431.2018.1487443.

Mejia, Raul, Adriana Pérez, Lorena Peña, et al. "Parental Restriction of Mature-Rated Media and its Association with Substance Use Among Argentinean Adolescents." *Academic Pediatrics* 16, no. 3 (2015): 282–9. https://doi.org/10.1016/j.acap.2015.11.004.

Melching, Jessica. "Exploring Parent-Adolescent Conflict: An Examination of Correlates and Longitudinal Predictors in Early Adolescence." MS thesis, The University of New Orleans, 2011.

Merriam-Webster Dictionary. "Child." Accessed April 1, 2025. https://www.merriam-webster.com/dictionary/child.

Mertens, Stefan, and Leen D'Haenens. "Parental Mediation of Internet Use and Cultural Values Across Europe: Investigating the Predictive Power of the Hofstedian Paradigm." *Communications* 39, no. 4 (2014). https://doi.org/10.1515/commun-2014-0018.

Miller, Ann Neville, Charles Gabolya, Richard Mulwanya, et al. "The Relationship Between Parental Mediation of Adolescent Media Use and Ugandan Adolescents' Sexual Attitudes and Behavior." *Howard Journal of Communications* 29, no. 2 (2017): 165–78. https://doi.org/10.1080/10646175.2017.1354788.

Miller, Scott A. "Parents' Beliefs About Children." *Psychology* (2023). https://doi.org/10.1093/obo/9780199828340-0317.

Minkin, Rachel, and Juliana Menasce Horowitz. "Parenting in America Today: Mental Health Concerns Top the List of Worries for Parents; Most Say Being a Parent Is Harder Than They Expected." *Pew Research Social & Demographic Trends*, January 24, 2023. https://www.pewresearch.org/social-trends/2023/01/24/parenting-in-america-today/.

"Mister Fred Rogers: Senate Statement on PBS Funding." American Rhetoric. Last modified April 26, 2024. https://www.americanrhetoric.com/speeches/fredrogerssenatetestimonypbs.htm.

Morelli, Mara, Federica Graziano, Antonio Chirumbolo, et al. "Parental Mediation of COVID-19 News and Children's Emotion Regulation During Lockdown." *Journal of Child and Family Studies* 31, no. 6 (2022): 1522–34. https://doi.org/10.1007/s10826-022-02266-5.

Morgenlander, Melissa. "Adult-Child Co-Viewing of Educational Television: Enhancing Preschoolers' Understanding of Mathematics Shown on "Sesame Street." PhD diss., Columbia University, 2010.

Mullan, Killian, and Sandra L. Hofferth. "A Comparative Time-Diary Analysis of UK and US Children's Screen Time and Device Use." *Child Indicators Research* 15, no. 3 (2021): 795–818. https://doi.org/10.1007/s12187-021-09884-3.

Mun, Il Bong, and Seyoung Lee. "How Does Parental Smartphone Addiction Affect Adolescent Smartphone Addiction?: Testing the Mediating Roles of Parental

Rejection and Adolescent Depression." *Cyberpsychology Behavior and Social Networking* 24, no. 6 (2020): 399–406. https://doi.org/10.1089/cyber.2020.0096.

Myers, Lauren J., Emily Crawford, Claire Murphy, Edoukou Aka-Ezoua, and Christopher Felix. "Eyes in the Room Trump Eyes on the Screen: Effects of a Responsive Co-Viewer on Toddlers' Responses to and Learning From Video Chat." *Journal of Children and Media* 12, no. 3 (2018): 275–94. https://doi.org/10.1080/17482798.2018.1425889.

Naderer, Brigitte, Jörg Matthes, Alice Binder, et al. "Shaping Children's Healthy Eating Habits with Food Placements? Food Placements of High and Low Nutritional Value in Cartoons, Children's BMI, Food-Related Parental Mediation Strategies, and Food Choice." *Appetite* 120 (2017): 644–53. https://doi.org/10.1016/j.appet.2017.10.023.

Nagata, Jason M., Puja Iyer, Jonathan Chu, et al. "Contemporary Screen Time Modalities Among Children 9–10 Years Old and Binge-Eating Disorder at One-Year Follow-up: A Prospective Cohort Study." *International Journal of Eating Disorders* 54, no. 5 (2021): 887–92. https://doi.org/10.1002/eat.23489.

Nagata, Jason M., Gurbinder Singh, Omar M. Sajjad, et al. "Social Epidemiology of Early Adolescent Problematic Screen Use in the United States." *Pediatric Research* 92, no. 5 (2022): 1443–9. https://doi.org/10.1038/s41390-022-02176-8.

Nagy, Beáta, Kitti Kutrovátz, Gábor Király, and Márton Rakovics. "Parental Mediation in the Age of Mobile Technology." *Children & Society* 37, no. 2 (2022): 424–51. https://doi.org/10.1111/chso.12599.

Nathanson, Amy I. "Identifying and Explaining the Relationship Between Parental Mediation and Children's Aggression." *Communication Research* 26, no. 2 (1999): 124–43. https://doi.org/10.1177/009365099026002002.

Nathanson, Amy I. "Mediation of Children's Television Viewing: Working Toward Conceptual Clarity and Common Understanding." In *Communication Yearbook 25*, edited by William B. Gudykunst. Lawrence Erlbaum Associates, 2001.

Nathanson, Amy I. "The Effects of Mediation Content on Children's Responses to Violent Television: Comparing Cognitive and Affective Approaches." Paper presented at the annual meeting of the International Communication Association, San Diego, CA, May 2003.

Nathanson, Amy I. "The Unintended Effects of Parental Mediation of Television on Adolescents." *Media Psychology* 4, no. 3 (2002): 207–30. https://doi.org/10.1207/s1532785xmep0403_01.

Nathanson, Amy I., and Renée A. Botta. "Shaping the Effects of Television on Adolescents' Body Image Disturbance." *Communication Research* 30, no. 3 (2003): 304–31. https://doi.org/10.1177/0093650203030003003.

Nathanson, Amy I., and William P. Eveland. "Parental Mediation During the U.S. 2016 Presidential Election Campaign: How Parents Criticized, Restricted, and Co-Viewed News Coverage." *Communication Monographs* 86, no. 2 (2018): 184–204. https://doi.org/10.1080/03637751.2018.1527035.

National Center for Health Statistics. *National Health Interview Survey-Teen,* 2024. https://www.cdc.gov/nchs/nhis/teen/index.html.

National Institute of Mental Health. *Mental Illness,* 2024. https://www.nimh.nih.gov/health/statistics/mental-illness.

Nesi, Jacqueline, and Mitchell J. Prinstein. "Using Social Media for Social Comparison and Feedback-Seeking: Gender and Popularity Moderate Associations with

Depressive Symptoms." *Journal of Abnormal Child Psychology* 43, no. 8 (2015): 1427–38. https://doi.org/10.1007/s10802-015-0020-0.

Nesi, Jacqueline, Jennifer C. Wolff, and Jeffrey Hunt. "Patterns of Social Media Use Among Adolescents Who Are Psychiatrically Hospitalized." *Journal of the American Academy of Child & Adolescent Psychiatry* 58, no. 6 (2019): 635–9.e1. https://doi.org/10.1016/j.jaac.2019.03.009.

Nikkelen, Sanne, Helen Vossen, Jessica Piotrowski, and Patti Valkenburg. "Media Violence and Adolescents' ADHD-Related Behaviors: The Role of Parental Mediation." *Journal of Broadcasting & Electronic Media* 60, no. 4 (2016): 657–75. https://doi.org/10.1080/08838151.2016.1234476.

Nikken, Peter, and Hanneke De Graaf. "Reciprocal Relationships Between Friends' and Parental Mediation of Adolescents' Media Use and Their Sexual Attitudes and Behavior." *Journal of Youth and Adolescence* 42, no. 11 (2012): 1696–707. https://doi.org/10.1007/s10964-012-9873-5.

Nikken, Peter, and Jeroen Jansz. "Developing Scales to Measure Parental Mediation of Young Children's Internet Use." *Learning Media and Technology* 39, no. 2 (2013): 250–66. https://doi.org/10.1080/17439884.2013.782038.

Nikken, Peter, and Jeroen Jansz. "Parental Mediation of Children's Videogame Playing: A Comparison of the Reports by Parents and Children." *Learning Media and Technology* 31, no. 2 (2006): 181–202. https://doi.org/10.1080/17439880600756803.

Nikken, Peter, and Suzanna J. Opree. "Guiding Young Children's Digital Media Use: SES-Differences in Mediation Concerns and Competence." *Journal of Child and Family Studies* 27, no. 6 (2018): 1844–57. https://doi.org/10.1007/s10826-018-1018-3.

Nikken, Peter, and Marjon Schols. "How and Why Parents Guide the Media Use of Young Children." *Journal of Child and Family Studies* 24, no. 11 (2015): 3423–35. https://doi.org/10.1007/s10826-015-0144-4.

Nimrod, Galit, Nelly Elias, and Dafna Lemish. "Measuring Mediation of Children's Media Use." *International Journal of Communication* 13, 2019: 342–58. https://ijoc.org/index.php/ijoc/article/view/10237/2535.

Noftle, Erik E. "Character Across Early Emerging Adulthood: Character Traits, Character Strivings, and Moral Self-Attributes." In *Character: New Directions from Philosophy, Psychology, and Theology*, edited by Christian B. Miller, R. Michael Furr, Angela Knobel, and William Fleeson. Oxford University Press, 2015.

Nosich, Gerald. "What is Ignorance?" The University of Arizona: Q-Cubed. Accessed April 2, 2025. https://ignorance.medicine.arizona.edu/about-us/what-ignorance.

Notten, Natascha, Gerbert Kraaykamp, and Jochem Tolsma. "Parents, Television and Children's Weight Status." *Journal of Children and Media* 7, no. 2 (2012): 235–52. https://doi.org/10.1080/17482798.2012.712917.

NPR. "Read Martin Luther King Jr.'s 'I Have a Dream' Speech in its Entirety." January 16, 2023. https://www.npr.org/2010/01/18/122701268/i-have-a-dream-speech-in-its-entirety.

O'Connor, Cliodhna, and Helene Joffe. "How Has Neuroscience Affected Lay Understandings of Personhood? A Review of the Evidence." *Public Understanding of Science* 22, no. 3 (2013): 254–68. https://doi.org/10.1177/0963662513476812.

O'Reilly, Michelle, Nisha Dogra, Jason Hughes, Paul Reilly, Riya George, and Natasha Whiteman. "Potential of Social Media in Promoting Mental Health in Adolescents."

Health Promotion International 34, no. 5 (2018): 981–91. https://doi.org/10.1093/heapro/day056.

Ofcom. *Children and Parents: Media Use and Attitudes Report*, March 20, 2023, 1–48. https://www.ofcom.org.uk/siteassets/resources/documents/research-and-data/media-literacy-research/children/childrens-media-use-and-attitudes-2023/childrens-media-use-and-attitudes-report-2023.pdf?v=329412.

Ólafsson, Kjartan, Lelia Green, and Elisabeth Staksrud. "Is Big Brother More at Risk Than Little Sister? The Sibling Factor in Online Risk and Opportunity." *New Media & Society* 20, no. 4 (2017): 1360–79. https://doi.org/10.1177/1461444817691531.

Olfson, Mark, Steven C. Marcus, Benjamin Druss, Harold Alan Pincus, and Myrna M. Weissman. "Parental Depression, Child Mental Health Problems, and Health Care Utilization." *Medical Care* 41, no. 6 (2003): 716–21. https://doi.org/10.1097/01.mlr.0000064642.41278.48.

Orsatti, Jo, and Kai Riemer. "Identity-Making: A Multimodal Approach for Researching Identity in Social Media." Paper, 23rd European Conference on Information Systems, Munster, 2015.

Overbeek, Geertjan, Daphne Van De Bongardt, and Laura Baams. "Buffer or Brake? The Role of Sexuality-Specific Parenting in Adolescents' Sexualized Media Consumption and Sexual Development." *Journal of Youth and Adolescence* 47, no. 7 (2018): 1427–39. https://doi.org/10.1007/s10964-018-0828-3.

Paakkari, Leena, Jorma Tynjälä, Henri Lahti, Kristiina Ojala, and Nelli Lyyra. "Problematic Social Media Use and Health Among Adolescents." *International Journal of Environmental Research and Public Health* 18, no. 4 (2021): 1885. https://doi.org/10.3390/ijerph18041885.

Paavonen, E. J., M. Roine, M. Pennonen, and A. R. Lahikainen. "Do Parental Co-Viewing and Discussions Mitigate TV-induced Fears in Young Children?" *Child: Care, Health and Development* 35, no. 6 (2009): 773–80. https://doi.org/10.1111/j.1365-2214.2009.01009.x.

Padilla-Walker, Laura M., and Katherine J. Christensen. "Empathy and Self-Regulation as Mediators Between Parenting and Adolescents' Prosocial Behavior Toward Strangers, Friends, and Family." *Journal of Research on Adolescence* 21, no. 3 (2010): 545–51. https://doi.org/10.1111/j.1532-7795.2010.00695.x.

Padilla-Walker, Laura M., and Sarah M. Coyne. "'Turn That Thing off!' Parent and Adolescent Predictors of Proactive Media Monitoring." *Journal of Adolescence* 34, no. 4 (2010): 705–15. https://doi.org/10.1016/j.adolescence.2010.09.002.

Padilla-Walker, Laura M., Sarah M. Coyne, and Kevin M. Collier. "Longitudinal Relations Between Parental Media Monitoring and Adolescent Aggression, Prosocial Behavior, and Externalizing Problems." *Journal of Adolescence* 46, no. 1 (2015): 86–97. https://doi.org/10.1016/j.adolescence.2015.11.002.

Padilla-Walker, Laura M., Sarah M. Coyne, and Ashley M. Fraser. "Getting a High-Speed Family Connection: Associations Between Family Media Use and Family Connection." *Family Relations* 61, no. 3 (2012): 426–40. https://doi.org/10.1111/j.1741-3729.2012.00710.x.

Padilla-Walker, Laura M., Sarah M. Coyne, Ashley M. Fraser, W. Justin Dyer, and Jeremy B. Yorgason. "Parents and Adolescents Growing up in the Digital Age: Latent Growth Curve Analysis of Proactive Media Monitoring." *Journal of Adolescence* 35, no. 5 (2012): 1153–65. https://doi.org/10.1016/j.adolescence.2012.03.005.

Padilla-Walker, Laura M., Sarah M. Coyne, Savannah L. Kroff, and Madison K. Memmott-Elison. "The Protective Role of Parental Media Monitoring Style from Early to Late Adolescence." *Journal of Youth and Adolescence* 47, no. 2 (2017): 445–59. https://doi.org/10.1007/s10964-017-0722-4.

Padilla-Walker, Laura M., Laura A. Stockdale, and Ryan D. McLean. "Associations Between Parental Media Monitoring, Media Use, and Internalizing Symptoms During Adolescence." *Psychology of Popular Media* 9, no. 4 (2019): 481–92. https://doi.org/10.1037/ppm0000256.

Padilla-Walker, Laura M., Laura A. Stockdale, Daye Son, Sarah M. Coyne, and Sara C. Stinnett. "Associations Between Parental Media Monitoring Style, Information Management, and Prosocial and Aggressive Behaviors." *Journal of Social and Personal Relationships* 37, no. 1 (2019): 180–200. https://doi.org/10.1177/0265407519859653.

Padilla-Walker, Laura M., and Ross A. Thompson. "Combating Conflicting Messages of Values: A Closer Look at Parental Strategies." *Social Development* 14, no. 2 (2005): 305–23. https://doi.org/10.1111/j.1467-9507.2005.00303.x.

Padilla-Walker, Laura M., Katey Workman, Anna Calley, et al. "Longitudinal Associations Between Parents' Prosocial Behavior and Media Use and Young Children's Prosocial Development: The Mediating Role of Children's Media Use." *Infancy* 29, no. 2 (2023): 95–112. https://doi.org/10.1111/infa.12576.

Pantic, Igor, Aleksandar Damjanovic, Jovana Todorovic, et al. "Association Between Online Social Networking and Depression in High School Students: Behavioral Physiology Viewpoint." *Psychiatria Danubina* 24, no. 1 (2012): 90–3.

Parfitt, Ylva, Alison Pike, and Susan Ayers. "The Impact of Parents' Mental Health on Parent–Baby Interaction: A Prospective Study." *Infant Behavior and Development* 36, no. 4 (2013): 599–608. https://doi.org/10.1016/j.infbeh.2013.06.003.

Parkes, Alison, Daniel Wight, Kate Hunt, Marion Henderson, and James Sargent. "Are Sexual Media Exposure, Parental Restrictions on Media Use and Co-viewing TV and DVDs with Parents and Friends Associated with Teenagers' Early Sexual Behaviour?" *Journal of Adolescence* 36, no. 6 (2013): 1121–33. https://doi.org/10.1016/j.adolescence.2013.08.019.

Patti Valkenburg. "Patti Valkenburg Gives Seminar at Stanford Policy Center." May 3, 2024. https://www.pattivalkenburg.nl/news/patti-valkenburg-gives-seminar-at-stanford-policy-center.

Pawellek, Sabine, Alexandra Ziegeldorf, and Hagen Wulff. "Strategien Und Effekte Digitaler Interventionen Bei Der Übergewichts- Und Adipositastherapie Von Kindern Und Jugendlichen – Ein Systematischer Review." *Bundesgesundheitsblatt - Gesundheitsforschung - Gesundheitsschutz* 65, no. 5 (2022): 624–34. https://doi.org/10.1007/s00103-022-03512-3.

Pedersen, Jesper, Martin Gillies Rasmussen, Line Grønholt Olesen, Heidi Klakk, Peter Lund Kristensen, and Anders Grøntved. "Recreational Screen Media Use in Danish School-Aged Children and the Role of Parental Education, Family Structures, and Household Screen Media Rules." *Preventive Medicine* 155 (2021): 106908. https://doi.org/10.1016/j.ypmed.2021.106908.

Peebles, Alanna, and Y. Anthony Chen. "Parental Internet Practices in the Family System: Restrictive Mediation, Problematic Internet Use, and Adolescents' Age-Related Variations in Perceptions of Parent-Child Relationship Quality." *Journal of*

Social and Personal Relationships 41, no. 6 (2023): 1347–69. https://doi.org/10.1177/02654075231221581.

Pelham, William E., Sarah J. Racz, Isabella S. Davis, et al. "What Is Parental Monitoring?" *Clinical Child and Family Psychology Review* 27, no. 2 (2024): 576–601. https://doi.org/10.1007/s10567-024-00490-7.

Pempek, Tiffany A., Lindsay B. Demers, Katherine G. Hanson, Heather L. Kirkorian, and Daniel R. Anderson. "The Impact of Infant-Directed Videos on Parent–Child Interaction." *Journal of Applied Developmental Psychology* 32, no. 1 (2010): 10–19. https://doi.org/10.1016/j.appdev.2010.10.001.

Peng, Peng, and Rogier A. Kievit. "The Development of Academic Achievement and Cognitive Abilities: A Bidirectional Perspective." *Child Development Perspectives* 14, no. 1 (2020): 15–20. https://doi.org/10.1111/cdep.12352.

Perez-Felkner, Lara. "Socialization in Childhood and Adolescence." In *Handbook of Social Psychology*, 2nd ed., edited by John DeLamater and Amanda Ward. Springer, 2013.

Perinetti, Dario. "The Nature of Virtue." In *The Oxford Handbook of British Philosophy in the Eighteenth Century*, edited by James A. Harris. Oxford University Press, 2013.

Perner, Josef. *Understanding the Representational Mind*. MIT Press, 1993.

Peters, M. S. "Television and Families: Parental Coviewing and Young Children's Language Development, Social Behaviour, and Television Processing." *Resources in Education* 25, no. 3 (1990). http://files.eric.ed.gov/fulltext/ED312040.pdf.

Peterson, Christopher, and Martin E. P. Seligman. *Character Strengths and Virtues: A Handbook and Classification*. Oxford University Press, 2004.

Pew Research Center. "Spirituality Among Americans." December 7, 2023. https://www.pewresearch.org/religion/2023/12/07/spirituality-among-americans/.

Pew Research Center. "Teens, Social Media and Technology 2023." December 11, 2023. https://www.pewresearch.org/internet/2023/12/11/teens-social-media-and-technology-2023/.

Piaget, Jean. "Piaget's Theory." In *Handbook of Child Psychology: Vol. I History, Theory, and Methods*, edited by Paul H. Mussen and William Kessen. John Wiley, 1983.

Pickersgill, Martyn, Sarah Cunningham-Burley, and Paul Martin. "Constituting Neurologic Subjects: Neuroscience, Subjectivity and the Mundane Significance of the Brain." *Subjectivity* 4, no. 3 (2011): 346–65. https://doi.org/10.1057/sub.2011.10.

Pila, Sarah, Alexis R. Lauricella, Anne Marie Piper, and Ellen Wartella. "The Power of Parent Attitudes: Examination of Parent Attitudes Toward Traditional and Emerging Technology." *Human Behavior and Emerging Technologies* 3, no. 4 (2021): 540–51. https://doi.org/10.1002/hbe2.279.

Pinquart, Martin. "Do the Parent–Child Relationship and Parenting Behaviors Differ Between Families with a Child With and Without Chronic Illness? A Meta-Analysis." *Journal of Pediatric Psychology* 38, no. 7 (2013): 708–21. https://doi.org/10.1093/jpepsy/jst020.

Piotrowski, Jessica Taylor, and Patti M. Valkenburg. "Finding Orchids in a Field of Dandelions." *American Behavioral Scientist* 59, no. 14 (2015): 1776–89. https://doi.org/10.1177/0002764215596552.

Pirkis, Jane, R. Warwick Blood, Catherine Francis, and Kerry McCallum. "On-Screen Portrayals of Mental Illness: Extent, Nature, and Impacts." *Journal of Health Communication* 11, no. 5 (2006): 523–41. https://doi.org/10.1080/10810730600755889.

Porter, Chris L., Laura A. Stockdale, Peter Reschke, McCall Booth, Madison K. Memmott-Elison, and Sarah M. Coyne. "'Katerina Gets Mad': Infants' Physiological and Behavioral Responses to Co-Viewing Educational, Self-Regulatory Media." *Developmental Psychobiology* 64, no. 8 (2022). https://doi.org/10.1002/dev.22337.

Potok, Chaim. *My Name is Asher Lev*. Knopf, 1972.

Potter, James W. *Media Effects*. Sage Publications, 2012.

Poulain, Tanja, Mandy Vogel, Madlen Neef, et al. "Reciprocal Associations Between Electronic Media Use and Behavioral Difficulties in Preschoolers." *International Journal of Environmental Research and Public Health* 15, no. 4 (2018). https://doi.org/10.3390/ijerph15040814.

Pouliou, Theodora, Francesco Sera, Lucy Griffiths, et al. "Environmental Influences on Children's Physical Activity." *Journal of Epidemiology & Community Health* 69, no. 1 (2014): 77–85. https://doi.org/10.1136/jech-2014-204287.

Prasad, Sakshi, Sara Ait Souabni, Gibson Anugwom, et al. "Anxiety and Depression Amongst Youth as Adverse Effects of Using Social Media: A Review." *Annals of Medicine and Surgery* 85, no. 8 (2023): 3974–81. https://doi.org/10.1097/ms9.0000000000001066.

Pritchett, Lant. *The Rebirth of Education: Schooling Ain't Learning*. Center for Global Development, 2013.

Priya, Nandhini, and P. Uma Maheswari. "Influence of Different Parental Mediation Strategies on Adolescents' Hedonistic Smartphone Use: Parent–Adolescent Reports." *Mobile Media & Communication*, 2024. https://doi.org/10.1177/20501579241260649.

Prot, Sara, Douglas A. Gentile, Craig A. Anderson, et al. "Long-Term Relations Among Prosocial-Media Use, Empathy, and Prosocial Behavior." *Psychological Science* 25, no. 2 (2013): 358–68. https://doi.org/10.1177/0956797613503854.

Psalti, Anastasia, and Kostas Zafiropoulos. "The Role of Parents in Digital Media Use by Preschool-Age Children in Greece." *Zenodo (CERN European Organization for Nuclear Research)*, 2023. https://doi.org/10.5281/zenodo.7812927.

Racine, Nicole, Brae Anne McArthur, Jessica E. Cooke, Rachel Eirich, Jenney Zhu, and Sheri Madigan. "Global Prevalence of Depressive and Anxiety Symptoms in Children and Adolescents During COVID-19." *JAMA Pediatrics* 175, no. 11 (2021): 1142–50. https://doi.org/10.1001/jamapediatrics.2021.2482.

Radanielina-Hita, Marie Louise. "Parental Mediation of Media Messages Does Matter: More Interaction About Objectionable Content Is Associated with Emerging Adults' Sexual Attitudes and Behaviors." *Health Communication* 30, no. 8 (2014): 784–98. https://doi.org/10.1080/10410236.2014.900527.

Radanielina-Hita, Marie Louise, Ioannis Kareklas, and Bruce Pinkleton. "Parental Mediation in the Digital Era: Increasing Children's Critical Thinking May Help Decrease Positive Attitudes Toward Alcohol." *Journal of Health Communication* 23, no. 1 (2017): 98–108. https://doi.org/10.1080/10810730.2017.1411997.

Radesky, Jenny S., Heidi M. Weeks, Rosa Ball, et al. "Young Children's Use of Smartphones and Tablets." *Pediatrics* 146, no. 1 (2020). https://doi.org/10.1542/peds.2019-3518.

Radesky, Jenny S., Heidi M. Weeks, Alexandria Schaller, Michael B. Robb, Supreet Mann, and Amanda Lenhart. "Constant Companion: A Week in the Life of a Young Person's Smartphone Use." *Common Sense Media*, 2023.

Rai, Jasmine, Nicholas Kuzik, and Valerie Carson. "Demographic, Parental and Home Environment Correlates of Traditional and Mobile Screen Time in Preschool-Aged Children." *Child: Care, Health and Development* 48, no. 4 (2022): 544–51. https://doi.org/10.1111/cch.12958.

Rasmussen, Eric E. "Proactive Vs. Retroactive Mediation: Effects of Mediation's Timing on Children's Reactions to Popular Cartoon Violence." *Human Communication Research* 40, no. 3 (2014): 396–413. https://doi.org/10.1111/hcre.12030.

Rasmussen, Eric E., Sarah M. Coyne, Nicole Martins, and Rebecca L. Densley. "Parental Mediation of US Youths' Exposure to Televised Relational Aggression." *Journal of Children and Media* 12, no. 2 (2017): 192–210. https://doi.org/10.1080/17482798.2017.1405829.

Rasmussen, Eric E. "Theoretical Underpinnings of Reducing the Media's Negative Effect on Children: Person-Centered, Negative-Evaluative Mediation within a Persuasion Framework." In *Communication Yearbook 37*, edited by Elisia L. Cohen. Routledge, 2013.

Rasmussen, Eric E., Justin Robert Keene, Collin K. Berke, Rebecca L. Densley, and Travis Loof. "Explaining Parental Coviewing: The Role of Social Facilitation and Arousal." *Communication Monographs* 84, no. 3 (2016): 365–84. https://doi.org/10.1080/03637751.2016.1259532.

Rasmussen, Eric E., Rebecca R. Ortiz, and Shawna R. White. "Emerging Adults' Responses to Active Mediation of Pornography During Adolescence." *Journal of Children and Media* 9, no. 2 (2015): 160–76. https://doi.org/10.1080/17482798.2014.997769.

Rasmussen, Eric E., Narissra Punyanunt-Carter, Jenna R. LaFreniere, Mary S. Norman, and Thomas G. Kimball. "The Serially Mediated Relationship Between Emerging Adults' Social Media Use and Mental Well-Being." *Computers in Human Behavior* 102 (2020): 206–13. https://doi.org/10.1016/j.chb.2019.08.019.

Rasmussen, Eric E., Nancy Rhodes, Rebecca R. Ortiz, and Shawna R. White. "The Relation Between Norm Accessibility, Pornography Use, and Parental Mediation Among Emerging Adults." *Media Psychology* 19, no. 3 (2016): 431–54. https://doi.org/10.1080/15213269.2015.1054944.

Rasmussen, Eric E., Autumn Shafer, Malinda J. Colwell, et al. "Relation Between Active Mediation, Exposure to Daniel Tiger's Neighborhood, and US Preschoolers' Social and Emotional Development." *Journal of Children and Media* 10, no. 4 (2016): 443–61. https://doi.org/10.1080/17482798.2016.1203806.

Rasmussen, Eric E., Kay Leigh Shannon, and Bethany Pitchford. "Adolescents' Disclosure of Mental Illness to Parents: Preferences and Barriers." *Health Communication* 37, no. 3 (2020): 346–55. https://doi.org/10.1080/10410236.2020.1839201.

Rasmussen, Eric E., Gabrielle A. Strouse, Malinda J. Colwell, et al. "Promoting Preschoolers' Emotional Competence Through Prosocial TV and Mobile App Use." *Media Psychology* 22, no. 1 (2018): 1–22. https://doi.org/10.1080/15213269.2018.1476890.

Rasmussen, Eric E., Shawna White, Andy King, Steven Holiday, and Rebecca Densley. "Predicting Parental Mediation Behaviors: The Direct and Indirect Influence of Parents' Critical Thinking About Media and Attitudes About Parent-Child Interactions." *Journal of Media Literacy Education* 8, no. 2 (2017): 1–22. https://doi.org/10.23860/jmle-2016-08-02-01.

Ray, Oakley. "How the Mind Hurts and Heals the Body." *American Psychologist* 59, no. 1 (2004): 29–40. https://doi.org/10.1037/0003-066x.59.1.29.

Rees, Gwyther. "Children's Activities and Time Use: Variations Between and Within 16 Countries." *Children and Youth Services Review* 80 (2017): 78–87. https://doi.org/10.1016/j.childyouth.2017.06.057.

Rega, Valeria, Francesca Gioia, and Valentina Boursier. "Parental Mediation and Cyberbullying: A Narrative Literature Review." *Marriage & Family Review* 58, no. 6 (2022): 495–530. https://doi.org/10.1080/01494929.2022.2069199.

Rega, Valeria, Francesca Gioia, and Valentina Boursier. "Problematic Media Use Among Children up to the Age of 10: A Systematic Literature Review." *International Journal of Environmental Research and Public Health* 20, no. 10 (2023): 5854. https://doi.org/10.3390/ijerph20105854.

Ren, Wei, and Xiaowen Zhu. "Parental Mediation and Adolescents' Internet Use: The Moderating Role of Parenting Style." *Journal of Youth and Adolescence* 51, no. 8 (2022): 1483–96. https://doi.org/10.1007/s10964-022-01600-w.

Reupert, Andrea, and Darryl Maybery. "What Do We Know About Families Where Parents Have a Mental Illness? A Systematic Review." *Child & Youth Services* 37, no. 2 (2015): 98–111. https://doi.org/10.1080/0145935x.2016.1104037.

Rice, Mabel L., Aletha C. Huston, Rosemarie Truglio, and John Wright. "Words from 'Sesame Street': Learning Vocabulary While Viewing." *Developmental Psychology* 26, no. 3 (1990): 421–8.

Richardson, C., N. Magson, J. Fardouly, E. Oar, C. Johnco, and R. Rapee. "A Longitudinal Investigation of Sleep and Technology Use in Early Adolescence: Does Parental Control of Technology Use Protect Adolescent Sleep?" *Sleep Medicine* 84 (2021): 368–79. https://doi.org/10.1016/j.sleep.2021.06.003.

Richert, Rebekah, and Paul Harris. "The Ghost in My Body: Children's Developing Concept of the Soul." *Journal of Cognition and Culture* 6, no. 3–4 (2006): 409–27. https://doi.org/10.1163/156853706778554913.

Rideout, Victoria J., Ulla G. Foehr, and Donald F. Roberts. "Generation M^2: Media in the Lives of 8- to 18-Year-Olds." Henry J. Kaiser Family Foundation, 2010.

Rideout, Victoria J., Alanna Peebles, Supreet Mann, and Michael B. Robb. "The Common Sense Census: Media Use by Tweens and Teens, 2021." Common Sense, 2021.

Rideout, Victoria J., and Michael B. Robb. "Social Media, Social Life: Teens Reveal Their Experiences." Common Sense Media, 2018.

Rideout, Victoria J., and Michael B. Robb. "The Common Sense Census: Media Use by Kids Age Zero to Eight." Common Sense, 2022.

Riggs, Rachel E., and Eric E. Rasmussen. "The Influence of Video-Modeled Sexual Assault Disclosure and Self-Efficacy Messages on Sexual Assault Disclosure Efficacy of Adolescent Girls." *Journal of Health Communication* 26 (2021): 1–10. https://doi.org/10.1080/10810730.2021.1943729.

Roberts, Donald F., Ulla G. Foehr, and Victoria Rideout. *Generation M: Media in the Lives of 8–18-Year-Olds*. Kaiser Family Foundation, 2005.

Robson, Elsbeth, Stephen Bell, and Natascha Klocker. "Conceptualising Agency in the Lives of Rural Young People." In *Global Perspectives on Rural Childhood and Youth: Young Rural Lives*, edited by Ruth Panelli, Samantha Punch, and Elsbeth Robson. Routledge, 2007.

Rogers, Ronald W. "A Protection Motivation Theory of Fear Appeals and Attitude Change." *The Journal of Psychology* 91, no. 1 (1975): 93–114. https://doi.org/10.1080/00223980.1975.9915803.

Romo, Dina L., Chelsea Garnett, Alayna P. Younger, et al. "Social Media Use and its Association with Sexual Risk and Parental Monitoring Among a Primarily Hispanic Adolescent Population." *Journal of Pediatric and Adolescent Gynecology* 30, no. 4 (2017): 466–73. https://doi.org/10.1016/j.jpag.2017.02.004.

Roper, Mona. "Positive Parenting." *Article 19* 2, no. 3 (2006): 2.

Rose, Taylor, Mary Barker, Chandni Maria Jacob, et al. "A Systematic Review of Digital Interventions for Improving the Diet and Physical Activity Behaviors of Adolescents." *Journal of Adolescent Health* 61, no. 6 (2017): 669–77. https://doi.org/10.1016/j.jadohealth.2017.05.024.

Rote, Wendy M., and Judith G. Smetana. "Within-Family Dyadic Patterns of Parental Monitoring and Adolescent Information Management." *Developmental Psychology* 54, no. 12 (2018): 2302–15. https://doi.org/10.1037/dev0000615.

Rothwell, Jonathan. "How Parenting and Self-Control Mediate the Link Between Social Media Use and Youth Mental Health." Institute for Family Studies, 2023, 3.

Rudi, Jessie, and Jodi Dworkin. "Is Technology-Mediated Parental Monitoring Related to Adolescent Substance Use?" *Substance Use & Misuse* 53, no. 8 (2018): 1331–41. https://doi.org/10.1080/10826084.2017.1408653.

Rudnova, Natalia, Dmitry Kornienko, Yuri Semenov, and Vladimir Egorov. "Characteristics of Parental Digital Mediation: Predictors, Strategies, and Differences Among Children Experiencing Various Parental Mediation Strategies." *Education Sciences* 13, no. 1 (2023): 57. https://doi.org/10.3390/educsci13010057.

Rutherford, Leonie, Judith E. Brown, Helen Skouteris, Matthew Fuller-Tyszkiewicz, and Michael Bittman. "Screen Media, Parenting Practices, and the Family Environment in Australia: A Longitudinal Study of Young Children's Media Use, Lifestyles, and Outcomes for Healthy Weight." *Journal of Children and Media* 9, no. 1 (2015): 22–39. https://doi.org/10.1080/17482798.2015.997101.

Ryan, Jill, Nicolette Roman V., and Auma Okwany. "The Effects of Parental Monitoring and Communication on Adolescent Substance Use and Risky Sexual Activity: A Systematic Review." *The Open Family Studies Journal* 7, no. suppl 1_m3 (2015): 12–27. http://hdl.handle.net/10566/2422.

Sacks, Jonathan. *Not in God's Name: Confronting Religious Violence*. Schocken Books, 2015.

Sadza, Anne, Esther Rozendaal, Serena Daalmans, and Moniek Buijzen. "Let's Talk About Risks. Parental and Peer Mediation and Their Relation to Adolescents' Perceptions of On- and Off-screen Risk Behavior." *Communications* 49, no. 2 (2022): 175–98. https://doi.org/10.1515/commun-2021-0143.

Sala, Arianna, Lorenzo Porcaro, and Emilia Gómez. "Social Media Use and Adolescents' Mental Health and Well-Being: An Umbrella Review." *Computers in*

Human Behavior Reports 14 (2024): 100404. https://doi.org/10.1016/j.chbr.2024 .100404.

Salomon, Gavriel. "Effects of Encouraging Israeli Mothers to Co-Observe 'Sesame Street' With Their Five-Year-Olds." *Child Development* 48, no. 3 (1977): 1146. https://doi.org/10.2307/1128378.

Sampasa-Kanyinga, Hugues, Ian Colman, Gary S. Goldfield, Hayley A. Hamilton, and Jean-Philippe Chaput. "Sex Differences in the Relationship Between Social Media Use, Short Sleep Duration, and Body Mass Index Among Adolescents." *Sleep Health* 6, no. 5 (2020): 601–8. https://doi.org/10.1016/j.sleh.2020.01.017.

Sampasa-Kanyinga, Hugues, Gary S. Goldfield, Mila Kingsbury, Zahra Clayborne, and Ian Colman. "Social Media Use and Parent–Child Relationship: A Cross-Sectional Study of Adolescents." *Journal of Community Psychology* 48, no. 3 (2019): 793–803. https://doi.org/10.1002/jcop.22293.

Santomero, Angela C. *Preschool Clues*. Touchstone, 2018.

Santos, Amanda, Sandra Silva-Santos, Alynne Andaki, Edmar Lacerda Mendes, Susana Vale, and Jorge Mota. "Screen Time Between Portuguese and Brazilian Children: A Cross-Cultural Study." *Motriz: Revista de Educação Fisica* 23, no. 2 (2017): e101636. http://dx.doi.org/10.1590/S1980-6574201700020006.

Sarsour, Khaled, Margaret Sheridan, Douglas Jutte, Amani Nuru-Jeter, Stephen Hinshaw, and W. Thomas Boyce. "Family Socioeconomic Status and Child Executive Functions: The Roles of Language, Home Environment, and Single Parenthood." *Journal of the International Neuropsychological Society* 17, no. 1 (2011): 120–32.

Sasson, Hagit, and Gustavo Mesch. "Parental Mediation, Peer Norms and Risky Online Behavior Among Adolescents." *Computers in Human Behavior* 33 (2014): 32–8. https://doi.org/10.1016/j.chb.2013.12.025.

Satir, Virginia. *The New Peoplemaking*. Science & Behavior Books, 1988.

Schooler, Deborah, Janna L. Kim, and Lynn Sorsoli. "Setting Rules or Sitting Down: Parental Mediation of Television Consumption and Adolescent Self-Esteem, Body Image, and Sexuality." *Sexuality Research and Social Policy* 3, no. 4 (2006): 49–62. https://doi.org/10.1525/srsp.2006.3.4.49.

Schwartz, Jeffrey M., Henry P. Stapp, and Mario Beauregard. "Quantum Physics in Neuroscience and Psychology: A Neurophysical Model of Mind–Brain Interaction." *Philosophical Transactions of the Royal Society B* 360, no. 1458 (2005): 1309–27. https://doi.org/10.1098/rstb.2004.1598.

Sciacca, Beatrice, Derek A. Laffan, James O'Higgins Norman, and Tijana Milosevic. "Parental Mediation in Pandemic: Predictors and Relationship with Children's Digital Skills and Time Spent Online in Ireland." *Computers in Human Behavior* 127 (2021): 107081. https://doi.org/10.1016/j.chb.2021.107081.

Scull, Tracy M., Christina V. Dodson, Jacob G. Geller, Liz C. Reeder, and Kathryn N. Stump. "A Media Literacy Education Approach to High School Sexual Health Education: Immediate Effects of 'Media Aware' on Adolescents' Media, Sexual Health, and Communication Outcomes." *Journal of Youth and Adolescence* 51, no. 4 (2022): 708–23. https://doi.org/10.1007/s10964-021-01567-0.

See, Beng Huat, and Stephen Gorard. "The Role of Parents in Young People's Education—A Critical Review of the Causal Evidence." *Oxford Review of Education* 41, no. 3 (2015): 346–66. https://doi.org/10.1080/03054985.2015.1031648.

Seh, Tassi Yunga Celine. "Children's Excessive Internet Use and its Relationship to the Family Bond: The Case of Helsinki, Finland." Master's thesis, Catholic University and University Institute of Lisbon, 2023.

Sela, Yaron, Merav Zach, Yair Amichay-Hamburger, Moshe Mishali, and Haim Omer. "Family Environment and Problematic Internet Use Among Adolescents: The Mediating Roles of Depression and Fear of Missing Out." *Computers in Human Behavior* 106 (2019): 106226. https://doi.org/10.1016/j.chb.2019.106226.

Sell, Marlit, Anne Daubmann, Holger Zapf, et al. "Family Functioning in Families Affected by Parental Mental Illness: Parent, Child, and Clinician Ratings." *International Journal of Environmental Research and Public Health* 18, no. 15 (2021): 7985. https://doi.org/10.3390/ijerph18157985.

Serbin, Lisa A., Danielle Kingdon, Paula L. Ruttle, and Dale M. Stack. "The Impact of Children's Internalizing and Externalizing Problems on Parenting: Transactional Processes and Reciprocal Change Over Time." *Development and Psychopathology* 27, no. 4_1 (2015): 969–86. https://doi.org/10.1017/s0954579415000632.

Shah, Prachi E., Kathy Hirsh-Pasek, Todd B. Kashdan, et al. "Daily Television Exposure, Parent Conversation During Shared Television Viewing and Socioeconomic Status: Associations with Curiosity at Kindergarten." *PLoS ONE* 16, no. 10 (2021): e0258572. https://doi.org/10.1371/journal.pone.0258572.

Shalani, Bita, Parviz Azadfallah, and Hojjatollah Farahani. "Correlates of Screen Time in Children and Adolescents: A Systematic Review Study." *Journal of Modern Rehabilitation*, 2021. https://doi.org/10.18502/jmr.v15i4.7740.

Sharma, Shwadhin, and Ching Yee Lee. "Parental Mediation and Preferences for Regulation Regarding Children's Digital Media Use: Role of Protection Motivation and Theory of Planned Behaviour." *Behaviour and Information Technology* 43, no. 8 (2023): 1499–1517. https://doi.org/10.1080/0144929x.2023.2217275.

Shavazi, Mohammad Taghi Abbasi, Leila Zadebagheri, Habib Ahmadi, and Aliyar Ahmadi. "Family, Mediation & Internet Risks: The Study of the Relation between Parental Mediation Strategies and Adolescents' Exposure to Internet Risks." *Cultural Studies & Communication*, 2022. https://www.jcsc.ir/article_702031.html?lang=en.

Shawcroft, Jane, Hallie Blake, Alexi Gonzalez, and Sarah M. Coyne. "Structures for Screens: Longitudinal Associations Between Parental Media Rules and Problematic Media Use in Early Childhood." *Technology Mind and Behavior* 3, no. 2 (2023). https://doi.org/10.1037/tmb0000104.

Shegog, Ross, Melissa F. Peskin, Christine Markham, et al. "It's Your Game-Tech: Toward Sexual Health in the Digital Age." *Creative Education* 05, no. 15 (2014): 1428–47. https://doi.org/10.4236/ce.2014.515161.

Sheldrick, Michael P., Clover Maitland, Kelly A. Mackintosh, et al. "Associations Between the Home Physical Environment and Children's Home-Based Physical Activity and Sitting." *International Journal of Environmental Research and Public Health* 16, no. 21 (2019): 4178. https://doi.org/10.3390/ijerph16214178.

Shi, Dasheng, Yongqi Xu, and Lin Chu. "The Association Between Parents Phubbing and Prosocial Behavior Among Chinese Preschool Children: A Moderated Mediation Model." *Frontiers in Psychology* 15 (2024). https://doi.org/10.3389/fpsyg.2024.1338055.

Shi, Yueqi, and Shaowei Qu. "The Effect of Cognitive Ability on Academic Achievement: The Mediating Role of Self-Discipline and the Moderating Role of Planning." *Frontiers in Psychology* 13 (2022). https://doi.org/10.3389/fpsyg.2022.1014655.

Shin, Wonsun. "Empowered Parents: The Role of Self-Efficacy in Parental Mediation of Children's Smartphone Use in the United States." *Journal of Children and Media*, 2018, 1–13. https://doi.org/10.1080/17482798.2018.1486331.

Shin, Wonsun, and May O. Lwin. "Parental Mediation of Children's Digital Media Use in High Digital Penetration Countries: Perspectives from Singapore and Australia." *Asian Journal of Communication* 32, no. 4 (2022): 309–26. https://doi.org/10.1080/01292986.2022.2026992.

Shutzman, Bar, and Naama Gershy. "Children's Excessive Digital Media Use, Mental Health Problems and the Protective Role of Parenting During COVID-19." *Computers in Human Behavior* 139 (2022): 107559. https://doi.org/10.1016/j.chb.2022.107559.

Silva, Raquel Nogueira Avelar e, Anne Wijtzes, Daphne Van De Bongardt, Petra Van De Looij-Jansen, Rienke Bannink, and Hein Raat. "Early Sexual Intercourse: Prospective Associations with Adolescents Physical Activity and Screen Time." *PLoS ONE* 11, no. 8 (2016): e0158648. https://doi.org/10.1371/journal.pone.0158648.

Silverstone, Roger, David Morley, Andrea Dahlberg, and Sonia Livingstone. "Families, Technologies and Consumption: The Household and Information and Communication Technologies." Discussion paper, Centre for Research into Innovation, Culture & Technology, Uxbridge, 1989.

Singer, Jerome L., Dorothy G. Singer, Roger Desmond, Bennett Hirsch, and Anne Nicol. "Family Mediation and Children's Cognition, Aggression, and Comprehension of Television: A Longitudinal Study." *Journal of Applied Developmental Psychology* 9, no. 3 (1988): 329–47. https://doi.org/10.1016/0193-3973(88)90034-2.

Sjolie, Hege, Cecilie Fromholt Olsen, and Marte Fjelnseth Hempel. "Attachments or Affiliations? The Impact of Social Media on the Quality of Peer Relationships—A Qualitative Study Among Norwegian High School Students." *Youth & Society* 56, no. 4 (2023): 673–92. https://doi.org/10.1177/0044118x231171180.

Slater, Michael D., and Laurel S. Gleason. "Contributing to Theory and Knowledge in Quantitative Communication Science." *Communication Methods and Measures* 6, no. 4 (2012): 215–36. https://doi.org/10.1080/19312458.2012.732626.

Smetana, Judith G., and Christopher Daddis. "Domain-Specific Antecedents of Parental Psychological Control and Monitoring: The Role of Parenting Beliefs and Practices." *Child Development* 73, no. 2 (2002): 563–80. https://doi.org/10.1111/1467-8624.00424.

Smit, Crystal R., Laura Buijs, Thabo J. Van Woudenberg, Kirsten E. Bevelander, and Moniek Buijzen. "The Impact of Social Media Influencers on Children's Dietary Behaviors." *Frontiers in Psychology* 10 (2020). https://doi.org/10.3389/fpsyg.2019.02975.

Smith, Connie B., Lauren B. Adamson, and Roger Bakeman. "Interactional Predictors of Early Language." *First Language* 8, no. 23 (1988): 143–56. https://doi.org/10.1177/014272378800802304.

Smith, Frederick James. "The Evolution of the Motion Picture." *The New York Dramatic Mirror*, July 9, 1913.

Smith, Lisa J., Michael Gradisar, and Daniel L. King. "Parental Influences on Adolescent Video Game Play: A Study of Accessibility, Rules, Limit Setting, Monitoring, and Cybersafety." *Cyberpsychology, Behavior, and Social Networking* 18, no. 5 (2015): 273–9. https://doi.org/10.1089/cyber.2014.0611.

Smith, Lisa J., Michael Gradisar, Daniel L. King, and Michelle Short. "Intrinsic and Extrinsic Predictors of Video-Gaming Behaviour and Adolescent Bedtimes: The Relationship Between Flow States, Self-Perceived Risk-Taking, Device Accessibility, Parental Regulation of Media and Bedtime." *Sleep Medicine* 30 (2016): 64–70. https://doi.org/10.1016/j.sleep.2016.01.009.

Sonck, Nathalie, Peter Nikken, and Jos De Haan. "Determinants of Internet Mediation: A Comparison of the Reports by Dutch Parents and Children." *Journal of Children and Media* 7, no. 1 (2012): 96–113. https://doi.org/10.1080/17482798.2012.739806.

Sorbring, Emma, Jonas Hallberg, Margareta Bohlin, and Therése Skoog. "Parental Attitudes and Young People's Online Sexual Activities." *Sex Education* 15, no. 2 (2014): 129–43. https://doi.org/10.1080/14681811.2014.981332.

Sørensen, Sarah Overgaard, Anne Kær Gejl, Jesper Pedersen, et al. "Recreational Screen Media Use Among Danish Children Aged 6–11 Years: Influence of Parental Screen Media Habits and Attitudes." *Scandinavian Journal of Public Health* 51, no. 8 (2022): 1173–81. https://doi.org/10.1177/14034948221103463.

Spigel, Lynn. *TV Snapshots: An Archive of Everyday Life*. Duke University Press, 2022.

St-Amand-Guitard, Catherine. "Emotion Recognition and Emotional Self-Regulation in Students with LDs." *LD@school*, April 14, 2023. https://www.ldatschool.ca/ate-emotion-recognition-regulation/#:~:text=Emotion%20recognition%20is%20a%20fundamental,Feldman%20&%20Matjasko%2C%202005).

St Peters, Michelle, Marguerite Fitch, Aletha C. Huston, John C. Wright, and Darwin J. Eakins. "Television and Families: What Do Young Children Watch with Their Parents?" *Child Development* 62, no. 6 (1991): 1409–23. https://doi.org/10.2307/1130815.

Steinfeld, Nili. "Parental Mediation of Adolescent Internet Use: Combining Strategies to Promote Awareness, Autonomy and Self-Regulation in Preparing Youth for Life on the Web." *Education and Information Technologies* 26, no. 2 (2020): 1897–920. https://doi.org/10.1007/s10639-020-10342-w.

Steinsbekk, Silje, Oda Bjørklund, Patti Valkenburg, Jacqueline Nesi, and Lars Wichstrøm. "The New Social Landscape: Relationships Among Social Media Use, Social Skills, and Offline Friendships from Age 10–18 Years." *Computers in Human Behavior* 156 (2024): 108235. https://doi.org/10.1016/j.chb.2024.108235.

Stiglic, Neza, and Russell M. Viner. "Effects of Screentime on the Health and Well-Being of Children and Adolescents: A Systematic Review of Reviews." *BMJ Open* 9, no. 1 (2019): e023191. https://doi.org/10.1136/bmjopen-2018-023191.

Stockdale, Laura A., Chris L. Porter, Peter J. Reschke, et al. "Infants' Physiological Responses to Emotionally Salient Media with Links to Parent and Child, Empathy, Prosocial Behaviors and Media Use." *Computers in Human Behavior* 139 (2022): 107497. https://doi.org/10.1016/j.chb.2022.107497.

Stone, Joseph, and Joseph Church. *Childhood and Adolescence: A Psychology of the Growing Person*. Random House, 1973.

Strouse, Gabrielle A., Katherine O'Doherty, and Georgene L. Troseth. "Effective Coviewing: Preschoolers' Learning from Video After a Dialogic Questioning Intervention." *Developmental Psychology* 49, no. 12 (2013): 2368–82. https://doi.org/10.1037/a0032463.

Strouse, Gabrielle A., Georgene L. Troseth, Katherine D. O'Doherty, and Megan M. Saylor. "Co-Viewing Supports Toddlers' Word Learning from Contingent and Noncontingent Video." *Journal of Experimental Child Psychology* 166 (2017): 310–26. https://doi.org/10.1016/j.jecp.2017.09.005.

Sukk, Marit, and Andra Siibak. "Caring Dataveillance and the Construction of 'Good Parenting': Estonian Parents' and Pre-teens' Reflections on the Use of Tracking Technologies." *Communications* 46, no. 3 (2021): 446–67. https://doi.org/10.1515/commun-2021-0045.

Sun, Tao. "Parental Mediation of Children's TV Viewing in China: An Urban-Rural Comparison." *Young Consumers Insight and Ideas for Responsible Marketers* 10, no. 3 (2009): 188–98. https://doi.org/10.1108/17473610910986008.

Symons, Katrien, Koen Ponnet, Kathleen Emmery, Michel Walrave, and Wannes Heirman. "A Factorial Validation of Parental Mediation Strategies with Regard to Internet Use." *Psychologica Belgica* 57, no. 2 (2017): 93–111. https://doi.org/10.5334/pb.372.

Symons, Katrien, Koen Ponnet, Kathleen Emmery, Michel Walrave, and Wannes Heirman. "Parental Knowledge of Adolescents' Online Content and Contact Risks." *Journal of Youth and Adolescence* 46, no. 2 (2016): 401–16. https://doi.org/10.1007/s10964-016-0599-7.

Takeuchi, Lori, Reed Stevens, Brigid Barron, et al. *The New Co-Ciewing: Designing for Learning through Joint Media Engagement*. The Joan Ganz Cooney Center at Sesame Workshop and LIFE Center, 2011.

Taraban, Lindsay, and Daniel S. Shaw. "Parenting in Context: Revisiting Belsky's Classic Process of Parenting Model in Early Childhood." *Developmental Review* 48 (2018): 55–81. https://doi.org/10.1016/j.dr.2018.03.006.

The Charters and General Laws of the Colony and Province of Massachusetts Bay. T.B. Waite & Co, 1814.

The Laws and Liberties of Massachusetts: Old Deluder Satan Law of 1647. Harvard University Press, 1929.

Thompson, Ellen M., and Albert C. Gunther. "Cigarettes and Cinema: Does Parental Restriction of R-Rated Movie Viewing Reduce Adolescent Smoking Susceptibility?" *Journal of Adolescent Health* 40, no. 2 (2006): 181.e1–e6. https://doi.org/10.1016/j.jadohealth.2006.09.017.

Thompson, Ross A. and Abby S. Lavine. "The Development of Virtuous Character: Automatic and Reflective Dispositions." In *Developing the Virtues: Integrating Perspectives*, edited by Julia Annas, Darcia Narvaez, and Nancy E. Snow. Oxford University Press, 2016.

Thygesen, Hilde, Tore Bonsaksen, Mariyana Schoultz, et al. "Social Media Use and its Associations with Mental Health 9 Months After the COVID-19 Outbreak: A Cross-National Study." *Frontiers in Public Health* 9 (2022). https://doi.org/10.3389/fpubh.2021.752004.

Tiberio, Stacey S., David C. R. Kerr, Deborah M. Capaldi, Katherine C. Pears, Hyoun K. Kim, and Paulina Nowicka. "Parental Monitoring of Children's Media Consumption." *JAMA Pediatrics* 168, no. 5 (2014): 414. https://doi.org/10.1001/jamapediatrics.2013.5483.

Tolson, Jay. "Is There Room for the Soul?" *CBS News*, October 16, 2006. https://www.cbsnews.com/news/is-there-room-for-the-soul/.

Totland, Torunn H., Mona Bjelland, Nanna Lien, et al. "Adolescents' Prospective Screen Time by Gender and Parental Education, the Mediation of Parental Influences." *International Journal of Behavioral Nutrition and Physical Activity* 10, no. 1 (2013): 89. https://doi.org/10.1186/1479-5868-10-89.

Trinh, Mai-Han, Rajeshwari Sundaram, Sonia L. Robinson, et al. "Association of Trajectory and Covariates of Children's Screen Media Time." *JAMA Pediatrics* 174, no. 1 (2019): 71. https://doi.org/10.1001/jamapediatrics.2019.4488.

Tripathi, Madhvi, and Shailendra Kumar Mishra. "Screen Time and Adiposity Among Children and Adolescents: A Systematic Review." *Journal of Public Health* 28, no. 3 (2019): 227–44. https://doi.org/10.1007/s10389-019-01043-x.

Twenge, Jean M., Jonathan Haidt, Andrew B. Blake, Cooper McAllister, Hannah Lemon, and Astrid Le Roy. "Worldwide Increases in Adolescent Loneliness." *Journal of Adolescence* 93, no. 1 (2021): 257–69. https://doi.org/10.1016/j.adolescence.2021.06.006.

Uddin, Md Jamal, Claus Thorn Ekstrøm, Nicoline Hemager, et al. "Is the Association Between Parents' Mental Illness and Child Psychopathology Mediated via Home Environment and Caregiver's Psychosocial Functioning? A Mediation Analysis of the Danish High Risk and Resilience Study—VIA7, a Population-Based Cohort Study." *Schizophrenia Bulletin Open* 2, no. 1 (2021). https://doi.org/10.1093/schizbullopen/sgab024.

Ulvi, Osman, Ajlina Karamehic-Muratovic, Mahdi Baghbanzadeh, Ateka Bashir, Jacob Smith, and Ubydul Haque. "Social Media Use and Mental Health: A Global Analysis." *Epidemiologia* 3, no. 1 (2022): 11–25. https://doi.org/10.3390/epidemiologia3010002.

UNICEF, *How Many Children Are There in the World?* 2023. https://data.unicef.org/how-many/how-many-children-under-18-are-in-the-world/.

United Nations Department of Economic and Social Affairs. Population Division. *World Population Prospects 2022: Summary of Results*. 2022. https://www.un.org/development/desa/pd/sites/www.un.org.development.desa.pd/files/wpp2022_summary_of_results.pdf.

United Nations Human Rights, Office of the High Commissioner. *Convention on the Rights of the Child*, 1989. https://www.Ohchr.Org/En/Instruments-Mechanisms/Instruments/Convention-Rights-Child.

United States Census Bureau. *Global Population Estimates Vary but Trends Are Clear: Population Growth is Slowing*, 2023. https://www.census.gov/library/stories/2023/11/world-population-estimated-eight-billion.html.

U.S. Department of Health and Human Services. *Key Substance Use and Mental Health Indicators in the United States: Results from the 2016 National Survey on Drug Use and Health*, 2017. (HHS Publication No. SMA 17-5044, NSDUH Series H-52). Rockville, MD: Center for Behavioral Health Statistics and Quality, Substance Abuse, and Mental Health Services Administration. Retrieved from https://www.samhsa.gov/data/.

U.S. Department of Health and Human Services. Our Epidemic of Loneliness and Isolation: The U.S. Surgeon General's Advisory on the Healing Effects of Social Connection and Community, 2023, 9. https://surgeongeneral.gov.

U.S. Department of Health and Human Services. *Social Media and Youth Mental Health: The U.S. Surgeon General's Advisory*, 2023. https://www.hhs.gov/sites/default/files/sg-youth-mental-health-social-media-advisory.pdf.

Vaala, Sarah E., and Amy Bleakley. "Monitoring, Mediating, and Modeling: Parental Influence on Adolescent Computer and Internet Use in the United States." *Journal of Children and Media* 9, no. 1 (2015): 40–57. https://doi.org/10.1080/17482798.2015.997103.

Vaala, Sarah E., Amy Bleakley, and Amy B. Jordan. "The Media Environments and Television-Viewing Diets of Infants and Toddlers: Findings from a National Survey of Parents." *Zero to Three* 33, no. 4 (2013): 18–24. https://eric.ed.gov/?id=EJ1125720.

Valkenburg, Patti M., Marina Krcmar, and Sandy De Roos. "The Impact of a Cultural Children's Program and Adult Mediation on Children's Knowledge of and Attitudes Towards Opera." *Journal of Broadcasting & Electronic Media* 42, no. 3 (1998): 315–26. https://doi.org/10.1080/08838159809364452.

Valkenburg, Patti M., Marina Krcmar, Allerd L. Peeters, and Nies M. Marseille. "Developing a Scale to Assess Three Styles of Television Mediation: 'Instructive Mediation,' 'Restrictive Mediation,' and 'Social Coviewing.'" *Journal of Broadcasting & Electronic Media* 43, no. 1 (1999): 52–66. https://doi.org/10.1080/08838159909364474.

Valkenburg, Patti M., and Jochen Peter. "The Differential Susceptibility to Media Effects Model." *Journal of Communication* 63, no. 2 (2013): 221–43. https://doi.org/10.1111/jcom.12024.

Valkenburg, Patti M., Jessica Taylor Piotrowski, Jo Hermanns, and Rebecca De Leeuw. "Developing and Validating the Perceived Parental Media Mediation Scale: A Self-Determination Perspective." *Human Communication Research* 39, no. 4 (2013): 445–69. https://doi.org/10.1111/hcre.12010.

Van Den Berg, Patricia, Dianne Neumark-Sztainer, Peter J. Hannan, and Jess Haines. "Is Dieting Advice from Magazines Helpful or Harmful? Five-Year Associations with Weight-Control Behaviors and Psychological Outcomes in Adolescents." *Pediatrics* 119, no. 1 (2007): e30–7. https://doi.org/10.1542/peds.2006-0978.

Van Den Eijnden, Regina J. J. M., Suzanne M. Geurts, Tom F. M. Ter Bogt, Vincent G. Van Der Rijst, and Ina M. Koning. "Social Media Use and Adolescents' Sleep: A Longitudinal Study on the Protective Role of Parental Rules Regarding Internet Use Before Sleep." *International Journal of Environmental Research and Public Health* 18, no. 3 (2021): 1346. https://doi.org/10.3390/ijerph18031346.

Van Kruistum, Claudia, and Roel Van Steensel. "The Tacit Dimension of Parental Mediation." *Cyberpsychology Journal of Psychosocial Research on Cyberspace* 11, no. 3 (2017). https://doi.org/10.5817/cp2017-3-3.

Van Loon, Linda M. A., Monique O. M. Van De Ven, Karin T. M. Van Doesum, Cilia L. M. Witteman, and Clemens M. H. Hosman. "The Relation Between Parental Mental Illness and Adolescent Mental Health: The Role of Family Factors." *Journal of Child and Family Studies* 23, no. 7 (2013): 1201–14. https://doi.org/10.1007/s10826-013-9781-7.

Van Petegem, Stijn, Evelien De Ferrerre, Bart Soenens, Antonius J. Van Rooij, and Jan Van Looy. "Parents' Degree and Style of Restrictive Mediation of Young Children's Digital Gaming: Associations with Parental Attitudes and Perceived Child

Adjustment." *Journal of Child and Family Studies* 28, no. 5 (2019): 1379–91. https://doi.org/10.1007/s10826-019-01368-x.

Vanbecelaere, Stefanie, Katrien Van Den Berghe, Frederik Cornillie, Delphine Sasanguie, Bert Reynvoet, and Fien Depaepe. "The Effects of Two Digital Educational Games on Cognitive and Non-Cognitive Math and Reading Outcomes." *Computers & Education* 143 (2019): 103680. https://doi.org/10.1016/j.compedu.2019.103680.

Vandebosch, Heidi, and Katrien Van Cleemput. "Television Viewing and Obesity Among Pre-School Children: The Role of Parents." *Communications* 32, no. 4 (2007): 417–46. https://doi.org/10.1515/commun.2007.031.

Vannucci, Anna, Emily G. Simpson, Sonja Gagnon, and Christine McCauley Ohannessian. "Social Media Use and Risky Behaviors in Adolescents: A Meta-Analysis." *Journal of Adolescence* 79, no. 1 (2020): 258–74. https://doi.org/10.1016/j.adolescence.2020.01.014.

VIA Institute on Character. *The VIA Classification of 24 Character Strengths*. VIACharacter.org. https://via-assets.global.ssl.fastly.net/76d1ea39-a4eb-4270-b9dc-899653415f8f/assets/VirtuesClassification-2021(R).pdf

Vogels, Emily A., and Risa Gelles-Watnick. "Teens and Social Media: Key Findings from Pew Research Center Surveys." *Pew Research Center*, April 24, 2023. https://www.pewresearch.org/short-reads/2023/04/24/teens-and-social-media-key-findings-from-pew-research-center-surveys/.

Vossen, Helen G. M., Regina J. J. M. Van Den Eijnden, Ilse Visser, and Ina M. Koning. "Parenting and Problematic Social Media Use: A Systematic Review." *Current Addiction Reports* 11, no. 3 (2024): 511–27. https://doi.org/10.1007/s40429-024-00559-x.

Vygotsky, Lev S. *Mind in Society: The Development of Higher Psychological Processes*. Harvard University Press, 1978.

Vygotsky, Lev. S. *Thought and Language: Translation Newly Revised and Edited by Alex Kozulin*. MIT Press, 1986.

Wallace, Lacey N. "Associations Between Parental Monitoring and Parents' Social Media Use and Social Media Perceptions." *Social Sciences & Humanities Open* 6, no. 1 (2022): 100294. https://doi.org/10.1016/j.ssaho.2022.100294.

Wallace, Sandi D., and Jake Harwood. "Associations Between Shared Musical Engagement and Parent–Child Relational Quality: The Mediating Roles of Interpersonal Coordination and Empathy." *Journal of Family Communication* 18, no. 3 (2018): 202–16. https://doi.org/10.1080/15267431.2018.1466783.

Walsh, Dylan. "Study: Social Media Use Linked to Decline in Mental Health." *MIT Management Sloan School*, September 14, 2022. https://mitsloan.mit.edu/ideas-made-to-matter/study-social-media-use-linked-to-decline-mental-health.

Walter, Nathan, Michael J. Cody, and Sandra J. Ball-Rokeach. "The Ebb and Flow of Communication Research: Seven Decades of Publication Trends and Research Priorities." *Journal of Communication* 68, no. 2 (2018): 424–40. https://doi.org/10.1093/joc/jqx015.

Wang, Jia, Ru-De Liu, Yi Ding, Wei Hong, and Jiabin Liu. "How Parental Mediation and Parental Phubbing Affect Preschool Children's Screen Media Use: A Response Surface Analysis." *Cyberpsychology Behavior and Social Networking* 27, no. 9 (2024): 651–7. https://doi.org/10.1089/cyber.2023.0638.

Warren, Ron. "Parental Mediation of Children's Television Viewing in Low-Income Families." *Journal of Communication* 55, no. 4 (2005): 847–63. https://doi.org/10.1111/j.1460-2466.2005.tb03026.x.

Warren, Ron. "Parental Mediation of Preschool Children's Television Viewing." *Journal of Broadcasting & Electronic Media* 47, no. 3 (2003): 394–417. https://doi.org/10.1207/s15506878jobem4703_5.

Watkins, Bruce, Sandra Calvert, Aletha Huston-Stein, and John C. Wright. "Children's Recall of Television Material: Effects of Presentation Mode and Adult Labeling." *Developmental Psychology* 16, no. 6 (1980): 672–74. https://doi.org/10.1037/0012-1649.16.6.672.

Weaver, Warren. "Recent Contributions to the Mathematical Theory of Communication." In *The Mathematical Theory of Communication*, edited by Claude E. Shannon and Warren Weaver. University of Illinois Press, 1964.

Weisman, Kara, Cristine H. Legare, Rachel E. Smith et al. "Similarities and Differences in Concepts of Mental Life Among Adults and Children in Five Cultures." *Nature Human Behaviour* 5, no. 10 (2021): 1358–68. https://doi.org/10.1038/s41562-021-01184-8.

Wells, Karen. *Childhood in a Global Perspective*. Polity Press, 2009.

Werner-Seidler, Aliza, Quincy Wong, Lara Johnston, Bridianne O'Dea, Michelle Torok, and Helen Christensen. "Pilot Evaluation of the Sleep Ninja: A Smartphone Application for Adolescent Insomnia Symptoms." *BMJ Open* 9, no. 5 (2019): e026502. https://doi.org/10.1136/bmjopen-2018-026502.

White, Shawna R., Eric E. Rasmussen, and Andy J. King. "Restrictive Mediation and Unintended Effects: Serial Multiple Mediation Analysis Explaining the Role of Reactance in US Adolescents." *Journal of Children and Media* 9, no. 4 (2015): 510–27. https://doi.org/10.1080/17482798.2015.1088873.

Whiting, Stephen, Marta Buoncristiano, Peter Gelius, et al. "Physical Activity, Screen Time, and Sleep Duration of Children Aged 6–9 Years in 25 Countries: An Analysis Within the WHO European Childhood Obesity Surveillance Initiative (COSI) 2015–2017." *Obesity Facts* 14, no. 1 (2020): 32–44. https://doi.org/10.1159/000511263.

Whitney, Daniel G., and Mark D. Peterson. "US National and State-Level Prevalence of Mental Health Disorders and Disparities of Mental Health Care Use in Children." *JAMA Pediatrics* 173, no. 4 (2019): 389. https://doi.org/10.1001/jamapediatrics.2018.5399.

Whittle, Sarah, Julian G. Simmons, Meg Dennison, et al. "Positive Parenting Predicts the Development of Adolescent Brain Structure: A Longitudinal Study." *Developmental Cognitive Neuroscience* 8 (2013): 7–17. https://doi.org/10.1016/j.dcn.2013.10.006.

Whittle, Sarah, Nandita Vijayakumar, Meg Dennison, et al. "Observed Measures of Negative Parenting Predict Brain Development During Adolescence." *PLoS ONE* 11, no. 1 (2016): e0147774. https://doi.org/10.1371/journal.pone.0147774.

Wiecha, Jean L., Arthur M. Sobol, Karen E. Peterson, and Steven L. Gortmaker. "Household Television Access: Associations with Screen Time, Reading, and Homework Among Youth." *Ambulatory Pediatrics* 1, no. 5 (2001): 244–51. https://doi.org/10.1367/1539-4409(2001)001<0244:HTAAWS>2.0.CO;2.

Williams, Alyssa R., and Cliff McKinney. "Indirect Effects of Parental Psychological Control on Emerging Adult Psychological Problems." *Journal of Child and Family Studies* 33, no. 4 (2023): 1058–69. https://doi.org/10.1007/s10826-023-02623-y.

Williams, Kate E., and Donna Berthelsen. "The Development of Prosocial Behaviour in Early Childhood: Contributions of Early Parenting and Self-Regulation." *International Journal of Early Childhood* 49, no. 1 (2017): 73–94. https://doi.org/10.1007/s13158-017-0185-5.

Wilson, Sylia, and Nathalie M. Dumornay. "Rising Rates of Adolescent Depression in the United States: Challenges and Opportunities in the 2020s." *Journal of Adolescent Health* 70, no. 3 (2022): 354–5. https://doi.org/10.1016/j.jadohealth.2021.12.003.

Wisniewski, Pamela, Heng Xu, Mary Beth Rosson, and John M. Carroll. "Parents Just Don't Understand: Why Teens Don't Talk to Parents About Their Online Risk Experiences." In *CSCQ '17: Proceedings of the 2017 ACM Conference on Computer Supported Cooperative Work and Social Computing*, 2017, 523–40.

Wong, Daniel Fu Keung, Xiao Yu Zhuang, and Ting Kin Ng. "Is Parental Control Beneficial or Harmful to the Development of Young Children in Hong Kong?" *Journal of Child and Family Studies* 28, no. 3 (2018): 831–8. https://doi.org/10.1007/s10826-018-1301-3.

Wood, Lara A., Rachel L. Kendal, and Emma G. Flynn. "Whom Do Children Copy? Model-Based Biases in Social Learning." *Developmental Review* 33, no. 4 (2013): 341–56. https://doi.org/10.1016/j.dr.2013.08.002.

Woolf, Kimberly Duyck. "Children, Parents and Prosocial Television for Children: Accounting for Viewing and Looking for Effects." PhD diss., University of Pennsylvania, 2019.

World Health Organization. *Adolescent Mental Health*, 2019. https://www.who.int/news-room/fact-sheets/detail/adolescent-mental-health.

World Health Organization. *Mental Disorders*, 2022. https://www.who.int/news-room/fact-sheets/detail/mental-disorders.

World Health Organization. *Mental Health of Adolescents*, 2024. https://www.who.int/news-room/fact-sheets/detail/adolescent-mental-health.

Wright, Michelle F. "Cyberbullying Victimization Through Social Networking Sites and Adjustment Difficulties: The Role of Parental Mediation." *Journal of the Association for Information Systems* 19, no. 2 (2018). https://aisel.aisnet.org/jais/vol19/iss2/1/.

Wright, Michelle F. "Cyber Victimization and Depression Among Adolescents with Autism Spectrum Disorder: The Buffering Effects of Parental Mediation and Social Support." *Journal of Child & Adolescent Trauma* 11, no. 1 (2017): 17–25. https://doi.org/10.1007/s40653-017-0169-5.

Wright, Michelle F., and Sebastian Wachs. "Does Parental Mediation of Technology Use Moderate the Associations Between Cyber Aggression Involvement and Substance Use? A Three-Year Longitudinal Study." *International Journal of Environmental Research and Public Health* 16, no. 13 (2019): 2425. https://doi.org/10.3390/ijerph16132425.

Wu, Yiling, Azita Amirfakhraei, Farnoosh Ebrahimzadeh, Leila Jahangiry, and Mahdieh Abbasalizad-Farhangi. "Screen Time and Body Mass Index Among Children and Adolescents: A Systematic Review and Meta-Analysis." *Frontiers in Pediatrics* 10 (2022). https://doi.org/10.3389/fped.2022.822108.

Xiao, Xiaofang, and Xifu Zheng. "The Effect of Parental Phubbing on Depression in Chinese Junior High School Students: The Mediating Roles of Basic Psychological Needs Satisfaction and Self-Esteem." *Frontiers in Psychology* 13 (2022). https://doi.org/10.3389/fpsyg.2022.868354.

Yan, Fuyun, Qi Zhang, Guangming Ran, Song Li, and Xiang Niu. "Relationship Between Parental Psychological Control and Problem Behaviours in Youths: A Three-Level Meta-Analysis." *Children and Youth Services Review* 112 (2020): 104900. https://doi.org/10.1016/j.childyouth.2020.104900.

Yan, Ni, Arya Ansari, and Peng Peng. "Reconsidering the Relation Between Parental Functioning and Child Externalizing Behaviors: A Meta-Analysis on Child-Driven Effects." *Journal of Family Psychology* 35, no. 2 (2020): 225–35. https://doi.org/10.1037/fam0000805.

Yang, Hwajin, Wee Qin Ng, Yingjia Yang, and Sujin Yang. "Inconsistent Media Mediation and Problematic Smartphone Use in Preschoolers: Maternal Conflict Resolution Styles as Moderators." *Children* 9, no. 6 (2022): 816. https://doi.org/10.3390/children9060816.

Yang, Xiaohui, Zhe Chen, Zhenhong Wang, and Liqi Zhu. "The Relations Between Television Exposure and Executive Function in Chinese Preschoolers: The Moderated Role of Parental Mediation Behaviors." *Frontiers in Psychology* 8 (2017). https://doi.org/10.3389/fpsyg.2017.01833.

Yang, Yi, Ru-De Liu, Jingxuan Liu, Yi Ding, Wei Hong, and Shuyang Jiang. "The Relations Between Parental Active Mediation, Parent-Child Relationships and Children's Problematic Mobile Phone Use: A Longitudinal Study." *Media Psychology* 25, no. 4 (2021): 513–30. https://doi.org/10.1080/15213269.2021.1981945.

Yao, Liang-Shuang, Xiao-Jun Sun, Geng-Feng Niu, Yue-Li Zheng, and Tinashe Chinyani. "Parental Mediation Moderates the Association Between Social Media Exposure and Tobacco and Alcohol Use: Differences Between Elementary and Middle School Students." *Journal of Studies on Alcohol and Drugs* 83, no. 2 (2022): 267–75. https://doi.org/10.15288/jsad.2022.83.267.

Yao, Yuan-Wei, Lu Liu, Shan-Shan Ma, et al. "Functional and Structural Neural Alterations in Internet Gaming Disorder: A Systematic Review and Meta-Analysis." *Neuroscience & Biobehavioral Reviews* 83 (2017): 313–24. https://doi.org/10.1016/j.neubiorev.2017.10.029.

York, Chance, and Rosanne M. Scholl. "Youth Antecedents to News Media Consumption." *Journalism & Mass Communication Quarterly* 92, no. 3 (2015): 681–99. https://doi.org/10.1177/1077699015588191.

Yoshizaki, Arika, Emi Murata, Tomoka Yamamoto, et al. "Improving Children's Sleep Habits Using an Interactive Smartphone App: Community-Based Intervention Study." *JMIR mHealth and uHealth* 11 (2023): e40836. https://doi.org/10.2196/40836.

Young, Rachel, Melissa Tully, Leandra Parris, Marizen Ramirez, Mallory Bolenbaugh, and Ashley Hernandez. "Barriers to Mediation Among U.S. Parents of Adolescents: A Mixed-Methods Study of Why Parents Do Not Monitor or Restrict Digital Media Use." *Computers in Human Behavior* 153 (2023): 108093. https://doi.org/10.1016/j.chb.2023.108093.

Yu, Lu, and Xiaohua Zhou. "Social Media Addiction Among Hong Kong Adolescents Before and After the Pandemic: The Effects of Parenting Behaviors." *Computers in Human Behavior* 156 (2024): 108233. https://doi.org/10.1016/j.chb.2024.108233.

Zajonc, Robert B. "Social Facilitation." *Science* 149, no. 3681 (1965): 269–74. https://doi.org/10.1126/science.149.3681.269.

Zapf, Holger, Johannes Boettcher, Yngvild Haukeland, Stian Orm, Sarah Coslar, and Krister Fjermestad. "A Systematic Review of the Association Between Parent-Child Communication and Adolescent Mental Health." *JCPP Advances* 4, no. 2 (2023). https://doi.org/10.1002/jcv2.12205.

Zarra-Nezhad, Maryam, Jaana Viljaranta, Nina Sajaniemi, Kaisa Aunola, and Marja-Kristiina Lerkkanen. "The Impact of Children's Socioemotional Development on Parenting Styles: The Moderating Effect of Social Withdrawal." *Early Child Development and Care* 192, no. 7 (2020): 1032–44. https://doi.org/10.1080/03004430.2020.1835879.

Zhang, Youjie, Shun Tian, Dan Zou, Hengyan Zhang, and Chen-Wei Pan. "Screen Time and Health Issues in Chinese School-Aged Children and Adolescents: A Systematic Review and Meta-Analysis." *BMC Public Health* 22, no. 1 (2022). https://doi.org/10.1186/s12889-022-13155-3.

Zhang, Yuanhao, Gengfeng Niu, Min Cao, Jianzhong Hong, and Zongkui Zhou. "How Does Parental Autonomy Support Influence Adolescents' Academic Performance? The Mediating Roles of Active Parental Internet Mediation and Parent–Child Cohesion." *Current Psychology*, 2024. https://doi.org/10.1007/s12144-024-06316-7.

Zhao, Pengfei, Natalie N. Bazarova, and Natercia Valle. "Digital Parenting Divides: The Role of Parental Capital and Digital Parenting Readiness in Parental Digital Mediation." *Journal of Computer-Mediated Communication* 28, no. 5 (2023). https://doi.org/10.1093/jcmc/zmad032.

Zhu, Xiaoqin, Diya Dou, and Thanos Karatzias. "Editorial: Parental Influence on Child Social and Emotional Functioning." *Frontiers in Psychology* 15 (2024). https://doi.org/10.3389/fpsyg.2024.1392772.

Zook, Eric G. "Embodied Health and Constitutive Communication: Toward an Authentic Conceptualization of Health Communication." In *Communication Yearbook 17*, edited by Stanley A. Deetz. Routledge, 1994.

INDEX

Abebe, Tatek 56
academic responsibility 146
Achtergarde, Sandra 117
Ackerson, Barry J 121
active mediation 48, 53, 59, 69, 84, 108, 140, 143, 145
adolescents
    adults' pornography 96
    aggressive behavior 107
    in cyberbullying 78
    depression 37
    initiation of oral sex 97
    loneliness 38
    media choice autonomy 159
    media use 68
    mental illness 122, 124
    online sexual activity 97
    parental media control 52
    psychological reactance 81
    sexual health 33–4
    social anxiety 112
    on social media 19
    social media addiction 79, 87
    substance use 34
adult mediation 132
Afifi, Tamara 112
age, children 21, 66–7
American Psychological Association 10, 103
antisocial behavior 51, 105
    physical aggression 107–9
    relational aggression 109
anxiety and depression 38, 119, 120, 124
Armstrong, Jennifer Keishin 15
Australia 19, 23, 33, 38, 39, 59, 64, 79

Ball, Samuel 132
Bandura, Albert 2, 6
Barry, Christopher T. 118
Bass, Elizabeth 153
Beauregard, Mario 7, 148
Belsky, Jay 57, 136
Bogatz, Gerry Ann 132
Boonk, Lisa 130
Bradt, Lowie 69
brain development 135–6
Bronfenbrenner, Urie 16
    child's microsystem 18, 26
    ecological systems theory 43
Bryant, Jennings 5

Caprara, Gian Vittorio 104
Carnegie Report 130
child-centered media parenting 49, 55–6
child development 15, 18, 44, 48, 51, 117, 124, 134, 137, 165
children's well-being 1, 16, 17, 29, 30, 83, 147, 148
civic morality 129
cognitions 6, 7, 33, 34, 40, 51–4, 58, 60, 84, 95, 101, 102, 144, 145, 159
cognitive abilities 134
cognitive approach 166
cognitive development 134–5, 156, 158, 160
cognitive processes 3, 7
Colombetti, Giovanna 147
communicate knowledge 8, 163
communication research 2–8, 40, 115, 146, 148, 150, 166
cultural norms 63–4

Demertzi, Athena   163, 164
demographic data   2
Denmark   19, 24
Densley, Rebecca L.   73
descriptive research   139
developmental vulnerability, of children   30
Differential Susceptibility to Media Effects Model (DSMM)   39, 68
Dillard, James Price   144

Edison, Thomas   127–8
educational content   20, 35, 39, 128
educational development   18
embodied mind   89
  defined   3
  human condition and human communication   4
  vs. "mind embodied"   5
  motivation and emotions   4
  psychophysiological data   3
emotional well-being   29, 68, 118
emotion recognition   106, 110
Ernest L. Boyer   130
Ewoldsen, David   43

family structure   63–5
Farmer, Elizabeth M. Z.   123
folk psychology   7, 10
formal schooling   130

gender   1, 15, 21–2, 61, 67
Gleason, Laurel S.   144
Google Scholar   142

Haan, Michelle De   136
Hallden, Gunilla   12
Harris, Russ   75
home environment, of child
  ages   21
  Bronfenbrenner's ecological systems theory   16
  characteristics of   15
  childhood well-being   16
  context   25–7
  digital devices   20
  effects   17–18

family connection, bonding, and communication   25
family income   22–3
gender   21–2
geography   24–5
media, availability of   65–6
parent education   23
parents' attitudes   20
parents' marital status   24
parents' media use   19–20
race/ethnicity   22
relationship with media   18–19
siblings   23–4
human communication   4, 6, 8, 147, 148

Ingold, Tim   4
intellectual humility   150–1
interpersonal communication   37, 40, 103–4, 124
intuitive dualism   11

Jansz, Jeroen   142
Ji, Xiaoqing   112
Joffe, Helene   163
joint media engagement   49, 54–5, 85–8, 97, 107, 131
Jordan, Amy   18

Kanter, Maggie   112
Karpov, Yuriy   44
Kuhn, Thomas, S.   3

Lang, Annie   3, 43
Levine, Glenn N.   138
Levine, Timothy R.   140
Lin, W.-Y.   10
Lin, Yi-Ching   144
Luther, Martin   128–9

macro-oriented organizations   2
Makarin, Alexey   124
maternal aggression   135
media parenting
  brain development   135–6
  child-centered media parenting   49, 55–6

child characteristics 66–8
child development and child
  psychology 48
cognitive development 134–5
comprehend media content 131
cultural norms 63–4
family structure 64–5
home media environment 65–6
joint media engagement 49, 54–5
language/literacy/math/
  science 133–4
media parenting model
  (MPM) 68–9
media parenting profiles 69–73
and mental health (*see* mental health)
parental control 49, 52–3
parental media monitoring 49–51
parental phubbing 47
parent characteristics 58–63
parent–child media
  conversations 49, 53–4
parenting scholarship 46
parenting strategies and
  characteristics 48
parenting styles and family
  interaction styles 65
and physical health (*see* physical
  health and media parenting)
profiles 69–73
school performance/academic
  achievement 131–2
of sexual content 97
socio-emotional well-being and (*see*
  socio-emotional well-being)
supportive and responsive role 47
Media Parenting Model (MPM) 48,
  68–9, 75, 140, 143, 160
Media Parenting Typology 165
mediation 44–7, 91, 140, 143
media use, of children 67–8
  cognitive development/academic
    performance 38–9
  home environment (*see* home
    environment, of child)
  mental health 36–8
  physical health effects 30–5
  processes 40–1

socio-emotional well-being 35–6
susceptibility to media effects 39–40
media violence 81
mental health 36–8, 158, 160, 165
  media and parent–child
    communication 125–6
  and media parenting 118–20
  and media use 124–5
  parent and child mental
    health 120–4
Michael D. Slater 144
Miller, Scott A. 9
mind–brain dichotomy 7
mind embodied 4, 5, 89, 146–50
  elitism and secular objectivity 9
  human communication and
    behavior 8, 147
  philosophy 3
  transposition of 5
Murthy, Vivek 36
My Name is Asher Lev (Potok,
  Chaim) 168

Nathanson, Amy I 140
neuroimaging 6, 7
Nikken, Peter 142
Nimrod, Galit 143
Noftle, Erik E. 166, 167
non-intrusive inspection 76, 78

objectification 149, 150
observational research 144
O'Connor, Cliodhna 163

Padilla-Walker, Laura M. 86
parental media control 49, 52–3
parental media modeling 75–6, 106
parental media monitoring 49–51,
  76–9
parental mediation 44
  children's experiences with television
    content 44–5
  conflict resolution 46
  defined 43
  theoretical and statistical
    mediation 46
  Vygotsky's conceptualization of 45

parental mind-mindedness 11
parental phubbing 47
parental responsiveness 87
parent characteristics
  attitudes toward media 58
  education and income 61–2
  media literacy 58–9
  parent gender 61
  parenting efficacy 59–60
  political orientation 63
  race/ethnicity 62
  religion/religiosity 62–3
  values 60
parent-child interactions 19, 80, 82–4, 99, 101, 118, 133
parent cognitions 58
parenting behaviors 10–12
parenting customs 121
parenting styles
  behavioral control 123
  children's overweight and obesity 17
  cultures 64
  and family interaction styles 65
parents' actions 16
parents' attitudes 20
parents' beliefs 9, 10
Perceived Parental Media Mediation Scale (PPMMS) 143
Peter, Jochen 68
Peters, M. S. 39
physical aggression 107–9
physical assault 80
physical health, of children 155, 157, 159, 165
  disordered eating and body image 35–6
  sleep 32–3
  substance use 34
  weight/diet/fitness 31–2
physical health and media parenting
  body mass index (BMI) 91–2
  children's TV viewing and eating habits 82
  fast food consumption 82
  intervention conditions 89
  parental media control 93

self-esteem 93
sexual health 95–8
sleep 93–5
substance use 98–100
TV violence 90
Piaget's theory of human development 40
Piotrowski, Jessica Taylor 39
policymaking organizations 1
Potok, Chaim 168
prescriptive models, of media parenting
  adolescents (ages 13–17) 158–60
  early childhood/toddlers (ages 0–2) 154–5
  media parenting science communication 161, 163–4
  media parenting typology 161–2
  pre/early adolescents (ages 7–12) 156–8
  preschoolers/young children (ages 3–6) 155–6
prosocial behavior 104–7
protection motivation theory 144
psychological aggression 80
Psychoneural Translation Hypothesis (PTH) 7
public education 128–30

quantitative methods 146
quantitative surveys 141
quasi-scientific content analysis 153

Ray, Oakley 137–8
reactive restrictive mediation 79
relational aggression 36, 58, 107, 109, 160
respiratory sinus arrhythmia (RSA) 106
restrictive mediation 51, 52, 69, 80, 81, 108, 113
Robbins, Stephanie 112
Rogers, Fred 126–7
Roper, Mona 82
Russia 24, 120

Sacks, Rabbi Jonathan 7
Santomero, Angela 133
Sciacca, Beatrice 67
science communication 164

secularism 8
self-actualization 2
self-esteem 18, 82, 93, 96, 97, 120
self-generated influences 6
self-regulation 110–12
Serbin, Lisa A. 123
sexual assault disclosure 126
sexual media content 33, 95, 97, 98
Sharma, Shwadhin 144
Smith, Frederick James 128–9
social consequences 103
social facilitation 145
social influences 147
socialization agents 43
social programs 1
social psychology 40, 41, 141
socio-emotional well-being 35–6, 155–7, 159–60
  antisocial behavior 107–9
  emotion/self-regulation 110–12
  parent–child relationship quality and conflict 112–13
  prosocial behavior 104–7

Stockdale, Laura A. 106
substance use
  adolescents 34
  physical health 34, 98–100

technical mediation 77, 78
theoretical research 139

Uganda, parental media control in 98
U.S. Federal Interagency Forum on Child and Family Statistics 1

Valkenburg, Patti M. 39, 68, 112, 140, 142
Values in Action Inventory of Strengths 167
Vygotsky, Lev S 44, 46

White, Shawna R. 81
Woolf, Kimberly Duyck 86–7

Zillmann, Dolf 5

ABOUT THE AUTHOR

Eric E. Rasmussen is professor of public relations and strategic communication management at Texas Tech University, USA. He has authored and co-authored articles that have appeared in some of the top academic journals in the fields of communication and child development, such as *Journal of Communication, Human Communication Research, Journal of Children and Media, Media Psychology, Child Development,* and *Developmental Psychology,* among others. His research has also been presented at conferences for the Society for Research in Child Development, Association for Education in Journalism and Mass Communication, International Communication Association, and International Public Relations Research Conference.